STUDENT CONDUCT PRACTICE

STUDENT CONDUCT PRACTICE

The Complete Guide for Student Affairs Professionals

Edited by

Diane M. Waryold and James M. Lancaster

Foreword by William L. Kibler

SECOND EDITION

STERLING, VIRGINIA

Published by Stylus Publishing, LLC.
22883 Quicksilver Drive
Sterling, Virginia 20166-2019

Library of Congress Cataloging-in-Publication Data

Names: Waryold, Diane M., 1959- editor. | Lancaster, James M., editor.
Title: Student conduct practice : the complete guide for student affairs
    professionals / Edited by Diane M. Waryold and James M. Lancaster :
    Foreword by William L. Kibler.
Description: Second edition. | Sterling, Virginia : Stylus Publishing,
    [2020] | Includes bibliographical references and index.
Identifiers: LCCN 2020007708 | ISBN 9781642671049 (hardcover) |
    ISBN 9781642671056 (paperback) | ISBN 9781642671063 (pdf) |
    ISBN 9781642671070 (ebook)
Subjects: LCSH: College discipline--United States. | College students--
    United States--Discipline.
Classification: LCC LB2344 .S78 2020 | DDC 378.1/95--dc23
LC record available at https://lccn.loc.gov/2020007708

13-digit ISBN: 978-1-64267-104-9 (cloth)
13-digit ISBN: 978-1-64267-105-6 (paperback)
13-digit ISBN: 978-1-64267-106-3 (library networkable e-edition)
13-digit ISBN: 978-1-64267-107-0 (consumer e-edition)

Printed in the United States of America

All first editions printed on acid-free paper
that meets the American National Standards Institute
Z39-48 Standard.

Bulk Purchases

Quantity discounts are available for use in workshops and for staff development.

Call 1-800-232-0223

First Edition, 2020

CONTENTS

FOREWORD   ix
William L. Kibler

ACKNOWLEDGMENTS   xiii

INTRODUCTION   1
Diane M. Waryold and James M. Lancaster

1 EVOLUTION OF THE STUDENT CONDUCT PROFESSION   5
Brian M. Glick and Christopher T. Haug

2 THE PHILOSOPHY OF STUDENT CONDUCT AND THE STUDENT
CONDUCT PROFESSIONAL   23
Fran'Cee L. Brown-McClure and Catherine L. Cocks

3 CRAFTING AND REVISING YOUR STUDENT CONDUCT CODE   36
Seann S. Kalagher and Regina D. Curran

4 LAWS, POLICIES, AND MANDATES   58
John Wesley Lowery

5 TYPES AND FORUMS FOR RESOLUTION   84
Eugene L. Zdziarski II and Patience L. Bartunek

6 BREAKING THE CYCLE
Embedding Social Justice Into Student Conduct Practice   101
Ryan C. Holmes and Reyna M. Anaya

7 ETHICS AND DECISION-MAKING   126
James A. Lorello and Jeffrey A. Bates

8 ASSESSMENT AND STUDENT CONDUCT   138
Matthew T. Stimpson and Brent E. Ericson

9 BIAS INCIDENTS ON CAMPUS   153
Patience D. Bryant and Derrick D. Dixon

10 SEXUAL MISCONDUCT   169
    Kristen A. Harrell and Michael R. Gillilan

11 THE FIRST AMENDMENT ON CAMPUS   191
    Lee E. Bird, Mackenzie E. Wilfong, and Saundra K. Schuster

12 THREAT ASSESSMENT AND BEHAVIORAL INTERVENTIONS   215
    Jonathan M. Adams

13 STUDENT ORGANIZATIONS THROUGH THE STUDENT
    CONDUCT LENS   223
    Kathleen A. Shupenko and Jane A. Tuttle

14 ACADEMIC INTEGRITY   243
    Kara E. Latopolski and Tricia L. Bertram Gallant

15 THOUGHTS ON THE FUTURE   258
    John D. Zacker

    CONCLUSION
    Challenges and Changes   269
    James M. Lancaster and Diane M. Waryold

    CONTRIBUTORS   273

    INDEX   291

FOREWORD

Over 30 years ago a small group of professionals gathered at the Stetson University Law and Higher Education Conference. They were drawn together by common commitments and purposes. Although holding different titles and backgrounds and hailing from a diversity of higher education institutions, they shared a common responsibility of how to effectively address student conduct and behavioral issues from educational and developmental perspectives while also ensuring compliance with legal requirements. Their common desire was to find a more productive means of sharing and learning from each other in order to improve their understanding and confidence in fulfilling this often-burdensome responsibility.

I was very fortunate to be a part of this gathering of committed and passionate professionals who decided that forming a professional association was the answer to their yearning. There was a yearning to spend time with and learn from others that shared our burden. There was a yearning to fully understand the ever-growing federal and state legal decisions and expectations that impacted our work every day. There was a desire to remain true to our commitment to assure that education and development was always a part of what we did. We understood that the students who were confronted with student conduct processes due to their behavior were motivated and attentive, thus providing unique opportunities to make a difference in their development and their perspectives. These students had rights that had to be honored, but they also needed to be held accountable for behavior that had somehow put them in conflict with the standards and expectations of their educational community. Ultimately it was the preservation of the civility of our campus communities that was our collective "call to arms."

The challenge of dealing with noncompliant behavior on the part of college students was certainly not a new issue in the 1980s when this group of professionals came together. President Thomas Jefferson, who founded the University of Virginia, wrote to a colleague in 1822, "The article of [student] discipline is the most difficult in American education" (Stoner, 2008, p. 46). The result of these conversations and collective interests was the formation of the Association for Student Judicial Affairs (ASJA) in 1988. This organization, which later became the Association for Student Conduct Administration (ASCA), soon grew and matured and became known and respected as the preeminent professional organization for those professionals on virtually every campus in our country and beyond who were expected to address the challenges presented every day by individual and organizational misbehavior. Predictably, our daily work involves knowledge, expertise, and competence in such areas as free speech and the First Amendment, sexual misconduct/Title IX, behavioral manifestations of mental health, academic dishonesty/integrity, individual and organizational misbehavior, bias-motivated misbehavior, threat assessments and intervention, and many other aspects of this complicated and challenging work. It was not surprising that at an early ASJA strategic planning session the term *besieged clan* was adopted as an appropriate descriptor of those in the student conduct profession.

The professionals who made up ASJA and ASCA continued to reflect on the roles and purposes of the association. As those dedicated professionals continued their work at the intersection of student development and legal issues it became important that the student conduct profession find its voice in the academy. Research and publication of the concepts, principles, and best practices of the profession became essential. Most in the student conduct profession had benefited from the groundbreaking written work of pioneers in our profession. *The College Student and the Courts*, published and edited in 1977 by D. Parker Young and Donald D. Gehring and followed by monthly supplements, became a "must-have" source to help us understand the legal implications of our work. Gehring and numerous associates produced important manuscripts on a variety of topics in the 1980s and 1990s that helped us all understand the administrative and legal implications of our work through the *Higher Education Administration Series* published by College Administrative Publications. Gary Pavela enlightened us all with his early written work in the fields of ethics, academic dishonesty, and mental health implications of misbehavior and continues to contribute law and policy analysis to higher education professionals. In 2004 Ed Stoner and John Wesley Lowery introduced the most comprehensive and legally grounded model student code of conduct at an ASJA annual conference (Stoner & Lowery, 2004). As the student conduct profession continued to grow and mature, more written contributions were developed that enabled us all to keep pace with the ever-changing and evolving nature of our work. Speakers and presentations at the annual ASJA/ASCA conferences and the written word helped keep us informed on everything from the Family Education Rights and Privacy Act of 1974 to the ever-present implications that Title IX has on our daily work.

In 2008 *Student Conduct Practice: The Complete Guide for Student Affairs Professionals* (Lancaster & Waryold, 2008) was published. This book made a significant contribution to the scholarship in the field. The comprehensive descriptions of best practices in the field as well as an insightful focus on present and emerging issues made this book a valued resource to all in the field of student conduct. In the 12 years since the book was published much has transpired in the field of student conduct, the larger field of student affairs administration, and our society as a whole. New legal decisions have emerged; revised guidance from federal and state agencies is ongoing; the impact of technology continues to grow and change rapidly; the demographics, characteristics, and needs of students have changed; and our current highly charged sociopolitical environment impacts the discussions, teaching, debates, and life on our campuses. All these emerging trends and forces require constant vigilance and called for an update to this valuable guidebook. This second edition of *Student Conduct Practice: The Complete Guide for Student Affairs Professionals* provides up-to-date guidance and insight into all these issues and others. Given my many years in the student affairs and the student conduct professions, I have the pleasure of knowing well the editors and many of the authors of this exceptional resource book.

As my career progressed from my early years in student conduct, I had the privilege of serving as a vice president for student affairs for many years. That gave me a much broader perspective on the importance of staying on the cutting edge of all these issues. Five years ago I had the honor of beginning my service as a university president. Serving as a president has allowed me to understand, appreciate, and benefit from "lessons learned" in my many years in the student affairs profession. I learned well the importance of staying informed and up to date on the issues that direct the lives of our students every day. I can assure you that presidents and the institutions they lead are impacted regularly by the conduct of students and the effectiveness of their institution's response. I learned and continue to promote the importance of professional development for staff and faculty. Attending conferences and seminars; reading the latest books, manuscripts, and journal articles; and presenting and writing in one's profession helps ensure that a president is surrounded by professionals who will ensure that the advice and counsel they receive is current and sound.

Our colleges and universities are compelled to respond to issues on a regular basis that are best understood in the practice, the research, and the writing in the student affairs and student conduct profession. All too often institutions of higher education are publicly measured by the effectiveness of their response to student-driven issues such as free speech and resulting protests and demonstrations; drugs and the constantly shifting realities of their possession, sale, misuse, and behavioral outcomes; guns and violence and the societal and political responses; sexual misconduct and compliance with Title IX and other applicable laws and the often life-changing results;

the destructive and sometimes fatal outcomes of hazing and other forms of organizational misconduct; and our ability to assess threats on our campuses and the effectiveness of our interventions. I can assure that these issues impact the work and the life on my campus and that we are not unique. In the few years I have led my institution I have relied on my background in student affairs and student conduct regularly. We developed a behavioral intervention team to assess real and perceived threats; we developed a well-trained team and state-of-the-art response protocols for sexual assault, sexual misconduct, and other Title IX violations; we are revising our student code of conduct; and we are engaging the campus community in developing a code of honor that will promote academic integrity and address the corrosive implications of academic dishonesty.

This newly revised edition of *Student Conduct Practice: The Complete Guide for Student Affairs Practice* addresses all these issues and will assure that new professionals and experienced veterans have the very latest in terms of best practices that are shaped by current law and professional standards. The editors and authors also present current and emerging issues and trends that will continue to impact our work in the years ahead. I highly recommend this book as a resource that you not only need to read but also keep handy as a reference that will inform your daily work. I salute each of you as members of the "besieged clan" who dedicate your work and your lives to the education and the development of our students.

William L. Kibler, PhD
President
Sul Ross State University
Alpine, Texas

References

Lancaster, J.M. & Waryold, D.M. (Eds.). (2008). *Student conduct practice: The complete guide for student affairs professionals.* Sterling, VA: Stylus.

Stoner, E.N., II. (2008). Revising you student conduct code. In Lancaster, J.M. & Waryold, D.M. (Eds.). *Student conduct practice: The complete guide for student affairs professionals.* Sterling, VA: Stylus, p. 46

Stoner, E.N., II, & Lowery, J.W. (2004). Navigating past the "spirit of insubordination": A twenty-first century model student conduct code with a model hearing script. *The Journal of College and University Law*, 31 (1).

Young, D.P. & Gehring, D.M., (1977). *The college student and the courts.* Asheville, NC: College Administration Publications.

ACKNOWLEDGMENTS

As we noted in the first edition of this book, those who choose to work in student affairs, especially those working with student conduct issues, face considerable challenges. As editors, we continue to be inspired by those who are called to this work. Helping students to mature and to reach their academic goals is no small task in a climate in which personal, institutional, and societal concerns threaten the very purpose of this important work. We acknowledge and are grateful to colleagues across the United States who persevere in demanding times. The late Dr. Melvene Hardee, a professor at Florida State University, was always quick to remind graduate students enrolled in the program that "dreams are what students are made of." Thus, we are grateful for the dedication that student conduct administrators have toward helping students realize their dreams.

We are thankful for the contributions of the authors within this text. We have been strategic in gathering the voices of professionals from different types of institutions (public, private, community colleges, colleges, and universities) as well as authors with varying identities. We are grateful that these authors were willing to commit countless hours toward crafting their chapters and to have their voices heard.

We are grateful to the professional colleagues who serve the Association for Student Conduct Administration (ASCA) and other professional associations as they help to shape, and reshape, the student conduct profession. We are indebted to the founding members of the Association for Student Judicial Affairs (ASJA), now ASCA, for their vision in establishing professional communities for like-minded student conduct administrators to gather and to find support. And we would like to recognize our founder, Dr. Don Gehring, for his passion and foresight in recognizing that student conduct administration has a special place within the academy and within student affairs. Dr. Gehring was asked to contribute to this text but, instead, like all good leaders, yielded to those who are younger and more contemporary; he stated, "I really appreciate the invitation, but I have stopped doing any writing or speaking. I think the younger people need to take over now" (Don Gehring, personal communication, February, 17, 2019).

INTRODUCTION

Diane M. Waryold and James M. Lancaster

Colleges and universities continue to grapple with issues brought on by contemporary society. Campuses are microcosms of the larger society and must act according to what is happening during a specific period of time. The social, political, and cultural context cannot be ignored and has a pervasive impact on student conduct practice. As the demographics of the U.S. population have changed, so has the composition of the student body on campuses across the nation. As a larger segment of the population has come to campus, student behaviors have reflected many of the challenges found in our larger society: a marked increase in student mental health challenges and changing social and political dynamics and governments at all levels that perceive the need for heightened involvement in the addressing of such concerns. Thus, it is no surprise that the current edition of this text has lengthened as the profession has become more specialized and complex in nature.

The original *Student Conduct Practice* book was published in 2008. Much has transpired in the field of student affairs in the last 10-plus years, especially in the area of student conduct. The 2008 book was focused on providing a description of best practices as well as a highlight of the key issues in student conduct work. The student conduct profession was in search of its "voice" in the academy when the inaugural book was authored. Since this time, the landscape of student conduct has matured and has shifted dramatically. Institutions of higher learning have a greater awareness of the importance of preparing students to function competently in a diverse society. Student affairs professionals have embraced the need to employ social justice as a lens by which we perform our work (Adams, Bell, & Griffin, 2016; Lee & LaDousa, 2015). This text suggests that student conduct as a functional unit within student affairs is well positioned to recognize the interface of multiple identities as we engage in a productive learning experience for all. This text invites student conduct administrators to examine current programs and policies to ensure that the spaces that they create during interactions with students are spaces in which all students feel welcome and heard. It is within this intentionality of practice that maximum growth can occur. Thus, a revision of the previous work, which reflects changes in the profession as well as the demographics (and the needs) of the current generation of diverse students, was in order.

In 1978, Appleton, Briggs and Rhatigan spoke of the importance of looking to the past to affect the future. They astutely contend that "both genius and knowledge, with an unlimited source of wisdom thrown in, will be needed in abundance in the years ahead" (p. 159). Their wisdom has rung true as the field of student conduct administration has experienced tremendous change since the founding of the Association for Student Judicial Affairs (the then ASJA) in 1988. However, the educational purpose of student conduct has remained the same. As we look back to the past, the purpose of student conduct as first authored by Gary Pavela in the *ASJA Preamble* is the "development and enforcement of standards of conduct and resolution of conflict for students as an educational endeavor that fosters students' personal and social development" (Kibler, 2013, p. 8). Appleton, Briggs, and Rhatigan (1978) warned that society will expect more of higher education as the "university must try to educate for life [citizenry] at least in the same proportion as it educates for livelihood" (p. 160). Preparing students not only to be productive members of today's workforce, but more importantly to be good people and upright citizens, is of primary importance in a time in which our country is divided along sociopolitical and ideological lines. Such divisions in our society suggest that students will continue to test mores, rules, and policies in their time at institutions of higher education. This text accentuates the delicate balance between responding to regulatory mandates and meeting the educational aims of student conduct. Thus, we hope that those with an interest in student conduct and those professionals who are new or seasoned student conduct administrators will find the compendium of chapters on best practices and vexing issues beneficial and thought provoking.

The editors have collaborated with the leadership of the Association for Student Conduct Administration (ASCA) to depict the most pressing conduct issues on our campuses and to identify a variety of practitioners and faculty who offer varied voices and expert opinions on such issues in student conduct work.

In chapter 1, Brian Glick and Christopher Haug outline the history of student discipline and the development of student conduct administration as a profession. They pay homage to the formation of ASJA/ASCA as the premier association formed to support professionals charged with administering student conduct work. They conclude with some cautionary notes as they identify emerging threats to the profession that include rapidly changing governmental compliance and oversight and compassion fatigue and moral distress that threaten the well-being and retention of student conduct professionals. Fran'Cee Brown-McClure and Catherine Cocks, in chapter 2, consider the personal and professional philosophy that must ground the practice of student conduct. They urge continuing attention to the educational mission of this work and suggest that, rather than simply punishing violations of policies, we must assist students in their personal and cognitive development.

In chapter 3, Seann Kalagher and Regina Curran describe the elements of a student code of conduct as a tool to guide student conduct practice. They offer practical tips for revising and crafting a student code of conduct. John Lowery follows with chapter 4, discussing the complexity and evolving challenges of staying abreast of latest laws, policies, and government mandates that affect practice. Eugene Zdziarski and Patience Bartunek, in chapter 5, offer perspectives on the various forums for resolution of student conduct on U.S. campuses. They provide a detailed description of the administrative hearing process, student conduct board, and alternative methods of dispute resolution and the advantages and disadvantages of each forum. In chapter 6, Ryan Holmes and Reyna Anaya challenge readers to embed social justice into student conduct practice in order for systems to be fair, just, and educational. James Lorello and Jeffrey Bates focus on the critical role of the sense of self in applying chapter 7's discussion of ethics and decision-making in our work. They suggest the importance of balancing "head and heart" concerns in the work of student conduct administration.

Chapter 8 speaks to the importance of accountability and assessment as a means of validating student conduct as important work. Matthew Stimpson and Brent Ericson implore administrators to think of themselves as educators and to show how student conduct professionals assess the efficacy and outcomes of student conduct interventions. Patience Bryant and Derrick Dixon address the complexity of addressing bias issues that occur on campus. They provide an overview of these concerns as well as suggested philosophic and practical approaches for attending to this growing issue on campuses in chapter 9. The complexities of addressing and adjudicating sexual misconduct on a college or university campus are addressed by Kristen Harrell and Michael Gillilan in chapter 10. These authors astutely request readers to reframe the ways in which they view sexual misconduct cases and to view the increased attention to campus sexual misconduct as a welcomed progression. Contributors Lee Bird, Mackenzie Wilfong, and Saundra Schuster revisit First Amendment issues on campus in chapter 11. Of critical assistance is their careful defining of what constitutes protected as well as unprotected speech, and they suggest methodologies for addressing the concerns these divisive issues create. Jonathan Adams, in chapter 12, explores threat assessment and behavioral intervention and the need for intervention teams suitable for responding to such crises. In chapter 13, Kathleen Shupenko and Jane Tuttle explore the similarities and the differences in student organizational misconduct. They carefully examine the potential differences in approaches to individuals as members of organizations versus the treatment of the organization as an entity. Academic integrity issues are sometimes administered under academic administration offices while at other places they may be in part or totally embedded as part of the student conduct office. In chapter 14, Kara Latopolski and Tricia Bertram Gallant explain the concerns academic honesty presents, regardless of administrative reporting, and focus on how student conduct administrators can apply their particular expertise in the prevention and resolution of such misconduct.

In chapter 15, John Zacker looks into the future and offers a commentary of what lies ahead, including some bewildering challenges for current practitioners. In conclusion, James Lancaster and Diane Waryold offer considerations about the application of this book and the meaning of conduct practice in an evolving academic and social environment. In all, as with the previous edition of this text, we hope that those who are interested in student conduct practice will find this book a useful resource and addition to their professional library. It is difficult to know what the social, political, and cultural climate will look like in the next 10 years. Our hope is that the genius and knowledge acquired by looking to the past and to the perspectives offered by years of work with students in a disciplinary setting will contribute to the collective wisdom of this noble profession.

References

Adams, M., Bell, L. A., & Griffin, P. (2016). *Teaching for diversity and social justice* (3rd ed.). New York, NY: Routledge.

Appleton, J. R., Briggs, C. M., & Rhatigan, J. J. (1978). *Pieces of eight: The rites, roles and styles of the dean by eight who have been there.* Portland, OR: NASPA.

Kibler, W. (2013). Reflections upon the crafting of the Preamble and the relevance it has today. In D. M. Waryold & J. M. Lancaster (Eds.), *The state of student conduct: Current forces and future challenges: Revisited.* College Station, TX: ASCA.

Lee, E. M., & LaDousa, C. (2015). *College students' experiences of power and marginality: Sharing spaces and negotiating differences.* New York, NY: Routledge.

I

EVOLUTION OF THE STUDENT CONDUCT PROFESSION

Brian M. Glick and Christopher T. Haug

Introduction

Current practice indicates that the administrative function of student conduct administration in the context of U.S. higher education is complex. Today, the work of student conduct is steeped in institutional risk, governmental compliance, and rapidly changing student demographics. The earliest days of student conduct administration are in stark contrast to the practice we see today on the modern college or university campus. This evolution reflects the growing complexity of higher education, along with an emerging and deepening understanding of society, culture, and student development.

This chapter outlines the history of student discipline and the student conduct administration profession, the formation of professional associations serving student affairs personnel, and foundational research establishing student conduct administration as a profession. The chapter concludes by highlighting documented emerging threats to the profession that include rapidly changing governmental compliance and oversight along with factors such as compassion fatigue and moral distress that threaten the well-being and retention of student conduct professionals.

History of Student Discipline and the Student Conduct Administration Profession

In order to make sound decisions for the future of the student conduct profession, it is imperative to know from where the profession originated. The practice of disciplining students for misconduct has existed since the earliest days of higher education (Dannells, 1997). Earliest documented sanctions for student misconduct in the United States included "public confessions and ridicule, floggings, fines and expulsion" (Paterson & Kibler, 1998, p. xi). Although this practice has dramatically changed throughout the evolution of higher education, at its core colleges have a long history of established rules to guide student behavior, and institutions have adapted over time to respond to cultural and societal changes. When students violated the rules, it was up to the administration and faculty to hold the student accountable for the violation. Responsibility for student conduct functions has shifted throughout history.

A thorough search of the literature does not yield much information on the profession of student conduct from the colonial period through about the 1930s. Throughout the history of the college and university, the exercise of student discipline was less formal, and as a result, not many records were kept. Much of the growth of the student conduct profession occurred because of the evolution of the American institution of higher education. The progress made during the student personnel movement subsequently increased the scholarly literature available about the growth of the student conduct profession.

Colonial America

The first institutions of higher education in the United States date back to the American colonial period, with the founding of Harvard College in 1636, and additional institutions opening through the 1700s and 1800s (Rudolph, 1962). The American colonists adopted the tradition of higher education from Europe, through primarily British influence, by the founding and chartering of these first institutions. During the pre-Revolutionary and early Federalist Era (1630s–1800s), the primary purpose of higher education in the American colonies was to train clergy (Lancaster & Waryold, 2008; Rudolph, 1962).

Higher education during the pre–Revolutionary War period did not closely resemble today's higher education institutions. The subjects taught and the grade level at which the material was presented was more closely related to current secondary school (high school) standards for teaching (Rudolph, 1962). College life was a highly structured environment with significant oversight from the college faculty (Rudolph, 1962) and had a general expectation of being *in loco parentis* or "in place of parents" (Hoekema, 1994). With that oversight, "the president of the college, and later faculty tutors, were responsible for advising students about such things as their moral life and intellectual habits" (Lancaster & Waryold, 2008, p. 9). The types of issues that the president and faculty had to respond to were rather limited in nature compared to the types of issues that student conduct administrators would respond to in future years.

Early Federalist Era

Colleges and universities experienced relatively minimal operational changes after the American Revolution. During the early Federalist Era in higher education, institutions still continued to mostly restrict enrollment to White males, although Oberlin College started to admit women as early as 1814 (Rudolph, 1962). In addition to gender segregation, racial and ethnic segregation was prevalent in institutions of higher education. There were no significant changes or innovations for the profession of student conduct during this period in history.

Reconstruction (Post-Civil War)

The American Civil War and the Reconstruction Era had a significant impact on the field of higher education. It was during this time that the rationale for why a student sought higher education began to shift. Changes in the academic program offerings within institutions reflected a movement in the curriculum from a predominant focus on theology to a distinct shift toward the sciences, especially on the industrial output of the country and economy (Rudolph, 1962).

With its passage in Congress, the Morrill Act (1862) required the states to establish or expand college teaching of science subject matters. The states began to recognize that while its agricultural roots were important, the country and its economic output was shifting in a new direction based on science and mechanical production of items (Rudolph, 1962). These new processes and technology required training and education.

During this period in history, the responsibilities for student conduct transitioned from the faculty and rested with new positions that became known as dean of men and dean of women (Rudolph, 1962). American culture during this period continued to expect that colleges and universities operate *in loco parentis* (Rudolph, 1962) and the institutions created operational and administrative structures that supported that expectation.

The Student Personnel Movement

During the 1930s, while the United States of America was mired by the Great Depression, citizens turned to higher education in an attempt to raise their quality of life (Rudolph, 1962). As a result, a movement among U.S. colleges and universities began to incorporate research as part of their fundamental mission. During this time, the American Council on Education (ACE) called for a report on what institutions were doing to assist their students to become more well- rounded individuals outside of the classroom (American Council on Education, 1937).

In 1937, a subcommittee from ACE delivered the *Student Personnel Point of View* (American College Personnel Association, 1937). While this report may not be completely responsible for the shift in how modern-day student conduct systems function, the report had a significant impact on how institutions changed their operations related to handling student misconduct. American families sending their children to college continued to expect and embrace the philosophy of *in loco parentis* during this period, and court cases supported this notion, as evidenced by the U.S. Supreme Court decision *Gott v. Berea College* (1913). Institutions were on the precipice of a major shift in how colleges and universities delivered the higher education experience.

Post-World War II

After World War II and the start of the Baby Boomer generation, institutions of higher education saw an exponential increase in the number of students attending college, due in large part to the Servicemen's Readjustment Act of 1944 (also known as the GI Bill) (Komives & Woodward, 2003). It was during this time that the community college model and branch campuses of four-year institutions expanded to serve a wider and more diverse pool of students (Komives & Woodward, 2003). The changes to the landscape of higher education had a trickle-down effect on the profession of student conduct. With an increase in enrolled students, there were more potential rule violations. Additionally, returning soldiers who experienced difficulty in readjusting to civilian life sometimes disrupted the education environment (Rudolph, 1962).

Institutions still maintained rules for the students. In addition to the traditional-aged students on campus, now institutions also included returning service members, who were older and had different needs and expectations of their college experience (Komives & Woodward, 2003; Rudolph, 1962). The returning service members, who were used to the rules of the military, now had to readjust to civilian life and institutional rules of higher education (Komives & Woodward, 2003; Rudolph, 1962).

The Civil Rights Era and Student Conduct

As society evolved, and the landscape of higher education changed, so did the tenets of student conduct (Lancaster & Waryold, 2008). In 1961, with the advent of the Civil Rights Era, the Fifth Circuit Court of Appeals ruled in the case of *Dixon v. Alabama State Board of Education* (1961). In this ruling, the court began to define the rights that college students had in terms of the concept of "due process." Chapter 4 provides more detail about the concept of due process. The court outlined differences between the administrative process of the institution and the criminal justice system. The court ruled that "due process" in the institutional setting involved notice and an opportunity to be heard. As a result, this point in history is generally accepted as the cultural and institutional shift away from the philosophy of *in loco parentis* within U.S. higher education (Hoekema, 1994).

The courts further enumerated student rights in 1968 when the court in the Western District of Missouri included, as part of its decision, the "General Order on Judicial Standards of Procedure and Substance Review of Student Discipline in Tax-Supported Institutions of Higher Education." Within this document, the court laid out additional specific differences between the court system and the institutional administrative process (Code of Federal Regulations, 1968). Specifically, the court called the student conduct process an educational endeavor, which was different from a criminal process. The court specifically stated that the safeguards built into the criminal process did not and should not apply to institutional process. The court went on to state that if institutions attempted to treat the student conduct process in the manner of a criminal proceeding, additional safeguards must be imposed (Code of Federal Regulations, 1968). The *Dixon* case (1961) and the subsequent "General Order" (1968) apply only to public institutions. Private institutions have always enjoyed, and continue to enjoy, a contractual relationship with their students. Students are granted only those rights that are enumerated by the institution. It should be noted, however, that depending on how Congress controls money, such as research grants and federal student aid, private institutions that receive federal money are sometimes mandated to incorporate certain similar rights for students.

It was during this period that institutions started to include students on hearing panels. The University of Georgia (n.d.) started one of the first student conduct boards, called the university judiciary, in 1968, and began operating in 1969. Shortly after that, other institutions started to incorporate hearing panels, involving students in their conduct process. It was over the course of several years that the evolution of the modern student conduct system arose.

Present-Day Student Conduct

The modern student conduct approach bears little resemblance to its historical roots. Today's conduct system incorporates legalistic requirements while aiming to create an educational and developmental conversation between the conduct administrator and the student. Student affairs professionals recognize that just as much learning takes place outside the classroom as it does inside (Komives & Woodward, 2003; Lancaster & Waryold, 2008).

The conversations that student conduct professionals have with students are intended to be informative, educational, developmental, and thought provoking. It is generally accepted practice today that the process is designed to be one whereby students, through guided reflection, come to understand why institutional rules exist and what happens when these rules are not followed. Students are provided an opportunity to learn from the situation that brought the student to the attention of the conduct office. There is emphasis on personal growth and community restoration. On many campuses, the tenets of restorative justice are incorporated into the student conduct process (Schrage & Giacomini, 2009). Restorative justice practices can include shuttle diplomacy, facilitated dialogue, and mediation (Schrage & Giacomini, 2009). These integrated processes allow for students to learn from encountered situations without the need for the formal conduct process. Chapter 5 offers a thorough narrative on additional forums of adjudication.

In the current political environment, state and federal legislators have resorted to passing new legislation and legal requirements that institutions must meet in order to maintain their federal funding and institutional aid distributions. These additional mandates and requirements illustrate the enduring friction between the educational nature of the student conduct process and the need to meet procedural mandates. Several concerns emerge with these additional legal requirements. For instance, not all of the regulations apply to all institutions uniformly. As a result, there may be a disparate impact whereby students at one institution receive the safeguards, while students at another institution do not receive these safeguards. An example is the protection of a fair and equitable process for the investigation and resolution of incidents that fall under the protection of Title IX of the Education Amendments of 1972. For schools that do not receive any form of federal funding, they are not required to provide these protections to their students. Another challenge with the legal requirements is that with each additional requirement, the line separating the criminal process from the educational process becomes unclear. Institutions have never tried to act like courts of law, but institutions are being forced to act in this way as a result of said regulations. Criminal proceedings generally are more punitive in nature, and if institutions are forced to function more like a court system, the student conduct process may depart further from its intended educational aim. Student conduct administrators strive to promote the educational goals of their work but struggle to incorporate regulatory requirements.

The Future of Student Conduct

In an increasingly complex world, student conduct professionals must respond to both individual and student organization issues. The fundamentals of student conduct, whereby an institution holds individuals and organizations accountable for their actions, are essential and must remain at the forefront of the student conduct process.

Where does the profession of student conduct go from here? There are some things that remain constant for the student conduct profession, and there are some things that will continue to change. Student conduct will continue to adapt in response to seminal global and local events. Institutions change over time, and student conduct must change with the institution while remaining true to core principles established by the profession. Although it is very difficult to predict the future direction of our work and the profession, student conduct administrators must continue to work to understand why our students are coming to our institutions, what their needs are, and how they want to grow while in college. When student conduct professionals know and understand this information, we can help our students to be successful and contributing members of our institutions and our society.

Formation of Professional Associations

As higher education in the United States progressed, the professional landscape was challenged to adapt and fulfill the needs of an ever-transforming professional structure. As the professional structure of student personnel administrators grew over the decades, so did the organizations that supported those professionals. In response to the student personnel movement and the affirmation that citizenship should be taught in the academy (Dublon, 2008), two primary professional organizations emerged: the American College Personnel Association (ACPA) and the National Association of Student Personnel Administrators (NASPA). These two organizations emerged as the primary sources of career development opportunities for student affairs professionals.

Student conduct administrators found professional development opportunities through both ACPA and NASPA over the years. These organizations still provide information, materials, and offerings for student conduct professionals. However, in response to an ever-changing student conduct landscape and national conversation, there was an unmet need to provide a "professional home" for student conduct professionals where they could engage in content-specific dialogue annually about the issues that impacted their work most.

Many student conduct professionals met annually at the Stetson University Law in Higher Education conference. It was out of that gathering that, in 1987, Dr. Don Gehring assembled a group of student conduct administrators who would eventually form the Association for Student Judicial Affairs (ASJA) (Gehring, 2013). The association started small, with 40 members (Gehring, 2013). Today, the membership of the association is over 2,800 members. The association developed over the following years by drafting a constitution, gaining nonprofit status, and hosting an annual conference each winter along with a summer training institute. In 1993, a committee of ASJA membership drafted a "Statement of Ethical Principles and Standards of Conduct" (Gehring, 2013). These were all significant accomplishments and milestones as they set the stage for how ASJA would serve its members and how its members would come to identify themselves as a professional body.

Student conduct work continues to evolve and respond to societal changes and the changing landscape within higher education. In 2012, ASJA modified its name to reflect a more contemporary description of student conduct work by adopting the use of the term *conduct administration* in place of *judicial affairs*. The now Association for Student Conduct Administration (ASCA) has expanded services and offerings to meet the professional development needs of its members. As Gehring (2013) stated when recalling the impetus for the name change, it was with the urging of a fellow member's advice, Ed Stoner, who pointed out that it would be "difficult to go before a judge and argue that discipline on a campus was an educational function not akin to judicial procedures when the name of the organization was the Association for Student Judicial Affairs" (p. 5). A move away from the use of the term *judicial* in student conduct work was in line with industry standards and best practices at the time. The change in name for the organization reflected the national landscape in how student conduct professionals framed their work.

The work of student conduct professionals continues to respond to changes in higher education. ASCA has situated itself as a key professional resource for colleagues across the country who are responsible for leading changes on their campuses related to the practice of student conduct administration. As a professional association, ASCA has a responsibility to continue to adapt and support the professionals who carry out this important work on a daily basis.

Establishing Student Conduct as a Profession

What makes a profession? A profession does not just occur because people perform a job or a task. Research has established criteria for what is considered a profession. Specifically, in the student affairs environment, Horton (as cited in Wrenn & Darley, 1950) and Wrenn and Darley (1950) provide the seminal research and criteria for establishing and determining a profession. What follows are the 10 criteria for a profession in the field of student affairs:

1. A profession must satisfy an indispensable social need and be based upon well-established and socially accepted scientific principles.
2. It must demand adequate pre-professional and cultural training.
3. It must demand the possession of a body of specialized and systematized knowledge.
4. It must give evidence of needed skills the general public does not possess.
5. It must have developed a scientific technique that is the result of tested experience.
6. It must require the exercise of discretion and judgment as to the time and manner of the performance of duty.
7. It must be a type of beneficial work, the result of which is not subject to standardization in terms of unit performance or time element.
8. It must have a group consciousness designed to extend scientific knowledge in a technical language.
9. It must have sufficient self-impelling power to retain its members throughout life (i.e., it must not be used as a mere stepping-stone to other occupations).
10. It must recognize its obligations to society by insisting that its members live up to an established and accepted code of ethics (as cited in Wrenn & Darley, 1950).

Horton (as cited in Wrenn & Darley, 1950) postulated that if one's work met each of the 10 criteria, the work was considered a profession. Horton did not test whether the more general field of student affairs administration met the criteria. However, Wrenn and Darley (1950) considered whether the field of student personnel work, as it was called at the time, constituted a profession as defined by Horton's 1944 criteria (as cited in Wrenn & Darley, 1950). Wrenn and Darley (1950) argued that student personnel work, as a whole, was not a profession under the 10 Horton criteria. However, Wrenn and Darley (1950) evaluated some segments of student personnel work as coming closer to being considered a profession at that time than others, such as student activities and university housing (Glick, 2016).

It has taken a considerable period of time, but the practice of student conduct can now be considered a profession. The following section includes empirical evidence that the work of student conduct professionals meets each of the criteria.

Indispensable Social Need and Socially Accepted Scientific Principles (Criterion #1)

Institutions of higher education exist for the betterment of society. Institutions have rules, and someone at the institution must enforce the rules. A main responsibility of a student conduct professional is to hold students accountable under the student code of conduct, while another responsibility is to be an educator (ASCA, 2012; Glick, 2016; Waller, 2013). "Many student conduct offices operate according to best practices. The Council for the Advancement of Standards in effect expanded on Horton's criteria and identified further benchmarks that a profession must utilize to operate at best practices level. These benchmarks are set by research and accepted scientific principles" (Glick, 2016, p. 20, internal citations omitted).

Adequate Pre-Professional and Cultural Training (Criterion #2)

The majority of student conduct positions require a master's degree in a student affairs–related field. The student affairs degree provides a baseline of information, which the student conduct professional needs to perform the position functions adequately. Additional training and experience will allow the conduct professional to become more adept at completing position responsibilities (Glick, 2016).

Specialized and Systematized Knowledge (Criterion #3)

Student conduct professionals perform a unique function at an institution. A skilled conduct professional has knowledge from a variety of fields and combines the knowledge precisely to appropriately and effectively perform the job function (Gehring, 2006; Glick, 2016; Waller, 2013). Incorporation of the knowledge from these fields, often in precise amounts, creates a specialized and systematized knowledge base, which allows for the success of the student in student conduct matters (Glick, 2016).

Needed Skills the General Public Does Not Possess (Criterion #4)

Student conduct professionals perform many roles (Gehring, 2006; Glick, 2016; Stoner & Lowery, 2004; Waller, 2013). An effective conduct professional investigates, adjudicates, and, on occasion, functions as a counselor (Glick, 2016; Waller, 2013). To be an effective conduct professional, it is necessary to possess and articulate knowledge, self-confidence, and tact (Waller, 2013; Wannamaker, 2005). "Incorporating education with discipline is not a skill that most of the general public has" (Glick, 2016, p. 21).

Scientific Technique That Is the Result of Tested Experience (Criterion #5)

As the student population on campus becomes more diverse, the "technique" or method utilized to address individual student developmental needs varies by the professional style and stance of the professional administrator. One approach does not meet the needs of all. The process operates the same way, but the path to get to the outcome is different among institutions and even intrainstitutionally between student conduct staff. Competent student conduct professionals adhere to best-practice guidelines. Best practice is developed by scientific method and is backed up by empirical data (Glick, 2016).

Discretion and Judgment as to the Time and Manner of the Performance of Duty (Criterion #6)

Federal and state privacy laws exist to protect individuals involved in student conduct matters (Family Educational Rights and Privacy Act, 1974). It is a violation of law for student conduct professionals to disclose information outside of specific parameters, as well as a violation of the ASCA Code of Ethics (ASCA, 1993). Further discretionary authority rests with the student conduct professional who selects appropriate sanctions for a student found responsible for violating institutional policy. Students learn differently, and a standard set of sanctions is not always the most appropriate educational tool (Glick, 2016; Komives & Woodward, 2003; Waller, 2013).

Beneficial Work, the Result of Which Is Not Subject to Standardization in Terms of Unit Performance or Time Element (Criterion #7)

The standards of student conduct practice provide for an educational experience for the student, while balancing the safety of the campus community and the cultural needs of individuals involved in the process (ASCA, 1993; Glick, 2016). Some elements of safety are universal, yet the definition of *campus safety* may vary by institution. Professionals must view each interaction with students as a multicultural interface of identities (Sue & Sue, 2016). It is appropriate for student conduct professionals to treat each student as an individual when making a decision about appropriate sanctions. The end result of the individual treatment generates beneficial work in which the campus is safe, cultural needs are met to ensure an equitable process, and the standardization of education for the student is subject only to the individual student (Glick, 2016).

16

Group Consciousness (Criterion #8)

In general, professionals within the field have not advocated for themselves or the profession as a whole until relatively recently (Glick, 2016; Jutenin, 2014). The professional association (ASCA) and scholars (Bernstein Chernoff, Dowd, Glick, Haug, Waller, and Wannamaker) have all called for further research on various aspects of the field of student conduct. ASCA, as an association, and individual ASCA members, continue to publish scholarly documents and articles for the benefit of the profession and the general public. As a profession, additional research is required to illustrate and assess the effectiveness of the practice of student conduct administration within higher education institutions.

Self-Impelling Power to Retain Its Members Throughout Life (Criterion #9)

ASJA was founded in 1987 (ASCA, 2016a). The association has consistently increased its membership base since its founding. Student conduct professionals recognize the need for a "professional home," and membership in ASCA provides student conduct administrators with just that. One aspect that sets ASCA apart from other student conduct organizations and supports the requirement to retain its members is the establishment of the Raymond H. Goldstone Foundation. The continued support of the Goldstone Foundation makes it possible for the association to retain its members and recruit new members (Glick, 2016). The function and practice of student conduct work is not well understood outside of those who choose to perform these challenging and demanding functions. ASCA provides multiple platforms for these professionals to come together to learn and support each other, thus retaining members.

Recognition of Its Obligations to Society by Insisting That Its Members Live Up to an Established and Accepted Code of Ethics (Criterion #10)

ASCA has a published code of ethics (ASCA, 2017a). Core values demand that professionals act in an ethical manner. It would be inappropriate to attempt to hold a student responsible for a violation if the conduct professional was not held accountable for unprofessional or unethical acts. It is a requirement for membership that all members abide by the code of ethics to maintain membership within the association. This requirement is codified in the ASCA bylaws (ASCA, 2017b).

Our Emerging Understanding of Student Conduct as a Profession

Student conduct professionals are often considered experts in knowledge of the college's or university's student code of conduct, along with the student conduct process for the institution. Internal and external colleagues routinely ask for assistance and guidance from conduct professionals. Research was published by multiple scholars beginning in 2005 and include Dowd (2012), Hyde (2014), Justice (2008), Mikus (2014), Waller (2013), and Wannamaker (2005), each helping to provide evidence that the practice of student conduct constituted a profession. However, it was not until Glick (2016) published a dissertation, which provided enough evidence, that the practice of student conduct work met all of the criteria to establish a profession. Practitioners would discuss the concept of a profession anecdotally. With the establishment of the student conduct administration field as a profession, student conduct professionals are now able to build on that finding with future research and scholarship that reflects an evolving and responsive profession.

Advocacy on the Campus Level

In recent years, student conduct professionals have participated in a greater level of advocacy for their profession. This advocacy has taken several forms, including communicating with internal and external stakeholders on how the work of student conduct administration is vital to the health and functioning of the institution. It is necessary that colleagues across the academy understand the service and expertise student conduct administrators provide to students and the institutional community. Student conduct administrators should reach out to faculty and share information about responding to disruptive students in the classroom or share ideas for how faculty can partner with their student conduct colleagues to prevent or respond to academic misconduct matters.

Advocacy in the Political Arena

Recently, ASCA representatives have been invited to speak before state legislatures on pending legislation (Laura Bennett, personal communication, February 12, 2016). ASJA in its earliest years did provide numerous Amicus briefs and responded to challenges from FIRE, Clery, and letters from the U.S. Department of Education as they surfaced. The difference lies in the fact that the academy is under "attack" with increased legal mandates that warrant a much more assertive approach from ASCA (Diane Waryold, personal communication, July 8, 2019). Representatives from the ASCA leadership have participated in meetings with policy makers and congressional staffers in Washington DC, as well as submitted comments and feedback regarding proposed federal legislation and regulations (Jill Creighton, personal communication, April 15, 2016). As governmental oversight and regulation continue to dictate how student conduct work is performed, professionals must remain informed and prepared to respond to our government mandates. ASCA representatives must take a proactive approach in lobbying at state and federal levels to raise awareness of the issues that impact this important work and to ensure that our work is taking an intentional direction.

Differing From the Courts

The work of the student conduct process is separate and distinct from criminal and civil court processes. This is long established in court rulings, such as *Dixon* (1961) and the "General Order on Judicial Standards of Procedure and Substance in Review of Student Discipline in Tax-Supported Institutions of Higher Education" (1968). The distinction between the work of student conduct administration and the criminal justice system has never been more important than now. Today, student conduct professionals find themselves in a time of increasing governmental and court intervention. Legislators, judges, and legal counsel who do not understand the educational goals of the student conduct process exert pressure and dictate policies, which force campus student conduct systems to function as miniature versions of courts of law. Clearly, the student conduct profession is threatened by these pressures and this changes the work of student conduct administration and detracts from the educational outcomes established by the student conduct process.

Continued Research

As noted in the Horton (as cited in Wrenn & Darley, 1950) criteria and by the Council for the Advancement of Standards in Higher Education (2015), it is imperative to continue to research and publish on best practices of the student conduct profession. Future research will help to define and legitimize the field and will provide insight into the effectiveness of our work. It is no longer acceptable to speculate on learning outcomes. Standardized and recurring assessment practices must be put into place to measure individual and organizational outcomes. As noted in the first edition of this text (Lancaster & Waryold, 2008), "How can one possibly look to the future without first assessing current effectiveness?" (p. 292).

Threats to Our Professional Staff

The work of a student conduct professional is significant and laden in procedure and compliance. While student conduct administrators work to ensure student learning and development are underpinning the student conduct processes, the nature of the work can produce more stress than other areas of student affairs work. Rapidly changing governmental compliance and oversight, increased litigation, compressed budgets, and personnel resource challenges all add to the stress that student conduct administrators take on each day in their role (Lake, 2013).

Recent studies have revealed risks to the professional well-being of conduct administrators in the form of compassion fatigue and burnout (Bernstein Chernoff, 2016), as well as moral distress (Haug, 2018). Compassion fatigue and burnout is the emotional and physical exhaustion impacting student conduct professionals when they exhibit symptoms of depression, exhaustion, and frustration through their work as student conduct administrators (Bernstein Chernoff, 2016). Moral distress is when a student conduct administrator knows the ethically correct action to take but is otherwise constrained from taking it due to internal or external factors (Haug, 2018). The research suggests that fear of retaliation or job loss, perceived lack of control or power, lack of support from supervisor or senior-level leadership, or unprofessional or manipulative colleagues increase experiences of moral distress among student conduct administrators (Haug, 2018). The modern higher education workplace is not without power imbalances, structural issues, and competition for resources, all of which may contribute to workplace stress to varying degrees. With emerging research specifically documenting compassion fatigue (Bernstein Chernoff, 2016) and moral distress (Haug, 2018) among student conduct professionals, we can begin to understand the unfortunate consequences of this demanding work and the threat of attrition present in offices of student conduct on college and university campuses.

Conclusion

As this chapter outlined, the practice of student conduct administration is demanding and complex. The work of the student conduct administrator is essential as it complements the educational mission of the academy. Highly trained professionals meet with students who often feel vulnerable as they answer to possible infractions of institutional rules and regulations. Student conduct professionals work to deliver a fair and equitable process that protects the community and promotes learning and growth for the student. As described throughout this chapter, this work is both challenging and reward-ing. It challenges practitioners to stay abreast with the cultural needs of students and the "student experience" while simultaneously affording the institution the ability to mitigate risk and keep the community and students safe. As the work of student conduct administration has changed in the evolving land-scape of U.S. higher education, the need for professionals to be well prepared is fundamental. Despite the challenges, there has never been a more exciting and rewarding time to be a student conduct professional. The field of student conduct administration is a direct result of the leadership of dedicated and committed student conduct professionals over the years who saw the need for a nationwide network of professionals who exchange and share ideas of best practice and creatively solve problems. Student conduct professionals can rest assured that through their graduate professional preparation, active member-ship in a professional association, and regular professional development they are well positioned to address the changing needs of students and institutions in the future.

References

American Council on Education. (1937). *The student personnel point of view: A report of a conference on the philosophy and development of student personnel work in college and university*. Washington DC: Author. Retrieved from http://www.myacpa.org/sites/default/files/student-personnel-point-of-view-1937.pdf

Association for Student Conduct Administration. (1993). *Ethical principles*. College Station, TX: Author. Retrieved from https://www.theasca.org/files/Governing%20Documents/ASCA%20Principles%20and%20Practices%20-%20Feb%202017.pdf

Association for Student Conduct Administration. (2012). *Bylaws, governing documents*. Retrieved from https://www.theasca.org/files/ASCA%20Bylaws%20FINAL%20-%20Member%20Approved%20July-31-2019.pdf

Association for Student Conduct Administration. (2017a). *Ethical principles and practices in student conduct administration*. Retrieved from https://www.theasca.org/files/Governing%20Documents/ASCA%20Principles%20and%20Practices%20-%20Feb%202017.pdf

Bernstein Chernoff, C. R. (2016). *The crisis of caring: Compassion satisfaction and compassion fatigue among student conduct and behavior intervention professionals* (Doctoral dissertation). Retrieved from ProQuest Dissertations & Theses Global (1789879166).

Code of Federal Regulations (1968). *General order on judicial standards of procedure and substance review of student discipline in tax-supported institutions of higher education*, 45 F.R.D. 133 C.F.R. Washington DC: Office of the Attorney General.

Council for the Advancement of Standards in Higher Education. (2015). *CAS professional standards for higher education* (9th ed.). Washington DC: Author.

Dannells, M. (1997). *From discipline to development: Rethinking student conduct in higher education.* ASHE-ERIC Higher Education Report *25*(2). Washington DC: George Washington University, Graduate School of Education and Human Development.

Dixon v. Alabama State Board of Education, 294 F. 2d 150 (5th Cir. 1961).

Dowd, M. C. (2012). *A national study of the ethical dilemmas faced by student conduct administrators* (Doctoral dissertation). Retrieved from Proquest Dissertations and Theses. (915575060)

Dublon, F. (2008). Demystifying governance. In J. M. Lancaster & D. M. Waryold (Eds.), *Student conduct practice: The complete guide for student affairs professionals* (pp. 38–39). Sterling, VA: Stylus.

Family Educational Rights and Privacy Act (1974), 20 U.S.C. § 1232g; 34 C.F.R. 99.

Gehring, D. D. (2006). Revisiting the history of modern conduct practice. In J. M. Lancaster (Ed.), *Exercising power with wisdom: Bridging legal and ethical practice with intention* (pp. 9–18). Asheville, NC: College Administration Publications.

Gehring, D. (2013). The history and founding of the association. In D. M. Waryold & J. M. Lancaster (Eds.), *The state of student conduct: Current forces and future challenges: Revisited.* College Station, TX: Association for Student Conduct Administration.

Glick, B. M. (2016). *The professional identity of student conduct administrators* (Doctoral dissertation). Retrieved from Proquest Dissertations and Theses. (10239174)

Gott v. Berea College, 161 S.W. 204 (KY, 1913).

Haug, C. (2018). *Identifying moral distress within student affairs administration in higher education: Its sources and lived experiences among student conduct administrators* (Doctoral dissertation). Retrieved from Proquest Dissertations and Theses. (10931242)

Hoekema, D. (1994). *Campus rules and moral community: In place of in loco parentis.* Lanham, MD: Rowman & Littlefield.

Hyde, M. (2014). *The effect of student conduct practices on student development in Christian higher education.* (Doctoral dissertation). Retrieved from Proquest Dissertations and Theses Database. (1536400719)

Justice. R. (2008). *Due process in student judicial affairs at the University of Illinois at Urbana-Champaign: Planning for the year 2000 and beyond.* (Doctoral dissertation). Accessible from Proquest Dissertations and Theses database. (304438849)

Jutenin, D. (2014, February). Opening remarks presented at the annual conference of the Association for Student Conduct Administration, St. Petersburg Beach, FL.

Komives, S. R., & Woodward, D. B., Jr. (2003). *Student services: A handbook for the profession* (4th ed.). San Francisco, CA: Jossey-Bass.

Lake, P. (2013). *The rights and responsibilities of the modern university: The rise of the facilitator university* (2nd ed.). Durham, NC: Carolina Academic Press.

Lancaster, J. M., & Waryold, D. M. (2008). *Student conduct practice: The complete guide for student affairs professionals.* Sterling, VA: Stylus.

Mikus, R. L. (2014). *Restorative practices in the collegiate student conduct process: A qualitative analysis of student conduct administrators* (Doctoral dissertation). Retrieved from Proquest Dissertations and Theses Database. (151324773)

National Center for Higher Education Risk Management (NCHERM). (2014). *The model code.* Retrieved from https://tngconsulting.com/resources/model-code-project/

Paterson, B. G., & Kibler, W. L. (1998). *The administration of campus discipline: Student, organizational and community issues.* Asheville, NC: College Administration Publications.

Rudolph, F. (1962). *A history of the American college and university.* Athens, GA: University of Georgia Press.

Schrage J. M., & Giacomini N. G. (2009). *Reframing campus conflict: Student conduct practice through a social justice lens.* Sterling, VA: Stylus.

Stoner, E. N., II, & Lowery, J. W. (2004). Navigating past the "spirit of insubordination": A twenty-first century model student conduct code with a model hearing script. *Journal of College and University Law, 31*(1), 1–78.

Sue, D. W., & Sue, D. (2016). *Counseling the culturally diverse: Theory and practice.* Hoboken, NJ: Wiley.

Sullivan, M. (2016, February). Opening remarks presented at the annual conference of the Association for Student Conduct Administration, St. Petersburg Beach, FL.

University of Georgia. (n.d.). *University judiciary history.* Retrieved from https://conduct.uga.edu/content_page/university-judiciary-history-content-page

Wannamaker, C. M. (2005). *A study of the need for emotional intelligence in university judicial officers* (Doctoral dissertation). Retrieved from Proquest Dissertations and Theses. (305326261)

Waller, J. L. (2013). *Intersecting philosophies: A qualitative study of student conduct administrators and their decision making utilizing the concepts of justice and care* (Doctoral dissertation). Retrieved from Proquest Dissertations and Theses. (149727586)

Wrenn, C. G., & Darley, J. G. (1950). An appraisal of the professional status of personnel work. In E. G. Williamson (Ed.), *Trends in student personnel work (Parts I and II)* (pp. 264–287). Minneapolis: University of Minnesota Press.

2

THE PHILOSOPHY OF STUDENT CONDUCT AND THE STUDENT CONDUCT PROFESSIONAL

Fran'Cee L. Brown-McClure and Catherine L. Cocks

In 1968, the Western District of Missouri court declared,

> The discipline of students in the educational community, is in all but the case of irrevocable expulsion, a part of the teaching process. In the case of irrevocable expulsion for misconduct, the process is not punitive or deterrent in the criminal law sense, but the process is rather the determination that the student is unqualified to continue as a member of the educational community. . . . The attempted analogy of student discipline to criminal proceedings against adults and juveniles is not sound.

Though conduct processes have evolved over the years and compliance requirements have increased, the philosophy, or fundamental belief, that student conduct is an educational process must remain the main tenet of student conduct work. Student conduct processes exist to address behavior that is inconsistent with an institution's mission, values, and policies while providing the student with opportunities to learn, grow, and succeed. As one colleague recently suggested, we diminish these goals and especially our educational impact if our focus becomes teaching students *what to think* rather than *how to think*.

Conduct Processes: Driving in Multiple Lanes

The senior student conduct practitioner at an institution is the ultimate keeper of the student code. It is their responsibility to nurture the code and its process to reflect the institution's values and expectations. They must ensure the process is fundamentally fair. They must also be able to articulate and demonstrate the philosophy of the work. The "why" behind the work is just as important as the "how." Chapter 3, on crafting a code of conduct, discusses the code in greater detail.

Role of Student Conduct Within an Institution

As discussed in chapter 1, the student conduct practitioner has evolved considerably over the years. One must keep in focus that the field emerged from the legal interpretation and subsequent professional belief that students have a right to be heard and treated fairly. Institutions have a right to have expectations and to hold students accountable under these expectations. The student conduct practitioner is an advocate for the *rights* of both students and the institution. They do not assume an advocacy position for one party to prevail over another but to ensure that both the student's and institution's rights are maintained throughout the process. Edward Stoner and John Lowery (2004) wrote,

> Generations of higher education administrators have tried both to give educational leadership to those wishing to develop into good citizens and, at the same time, to respond appropriately to aberrant behavior that damages the living/learning environment on campus, even if the unwanted behavior is prompted by the "spirit of insubordination." (p. 3)

Though at times challenging, the responsibility owed to both student and institution speaks to the heart of the work. Student conduct practitioners are educators first and foremost.

Navigating an academic community, either as a recent high school graduate or as someone with other life experiences, is challenging. Students are faced with decisions each day that speak to their character, values, and goals. The practitioner often sees students during their worst moments. Being kind and respectful is not behaving in a biased manner but in an educational and humane manner. For many students, this is an opportunity to connect with a practitioner and redefine their college experience. Rather than having a behavior define students, helping students to define how the behavior impacted them and others is embracing one's role as a community member. Student conduct practitioners often live in the "intent versus impact" world as they work with individuals and groups to recognize that one's intent may be quite different from the impact that occurred. Ultimately, the practitioner strives to teach students how to assess the potential impact prior to the behavior.

The importance of having strong, clear, and fair processes enables the student conduct practitioner to focus on the learning process. Retired Vice President of Student Affairs John Saddlemire often explained that "our student code is tough enough so that we don't have to be" (personal communication, January, 2005). Dr. Saddlemire understood that conduct processes should not be adversarial processes. They are a means to resolve issues within the academic community that encourage growth and development. Many of the most difficult students are the ones who need a student conduct practitioner's help the most.

As stated, a student conduct practitioner is not an advocate in the sense of arguing on behalf of someone or representing them. Student conduct practitioners do not "choose" their students as some other higher education practitioners do due to the nature of their work (e.g., a faculty member in a specific field of study, honors program staff, athletics). Student conduct practitioners work with all students either directly or indirectly. They work with students regardless of GPA, major, identity group, and so on. All students are valued members of the community and should be treated as such.

A student conduct practitioner serves the student and the institution in providing an environment that is respectful, and students, regardless of their role within the process, are heard. (A student may be a respondent, complainant, witness, support person, or board member.) They have a responsibility to ensure that the student's institutional rights are protected and to work with the student to restore whatever harm has been caused. They also serve as an institutional advocate, protecting the integrity of the academic mission of the institution, ensuring policies and procedures are followed, addressing issues, and working toward developing safe and healthy learning environments. The mission of the institution is always part of the work. Student conduct practitioners have the opportunity to provide a unique and distinct viewpoint of what a community is actually like versus the aspirational learning community.

The Punitive (Learning) Compliance Continuum

As the student conduct field moves on the continuum from punitive to educational, there is an increasing concern about a move toward what Peter F. Lake describes as "Compliance U" (Kattner, 2015). Regulatory guidance along with court decisions provides a critical framework to ensure students' rights are met. They also run the risk of turning conduct processes into merely compliance programs rather than educational processes. Conduct processes can be both with the appropriate diligence.

Regulatory guidance serves to provide a blueprint for institutions in protecting students. Some guidance can stray from the educational mission of the institution or disadvantage a student based on an identity (e.g., socioeconomic status). There is a great deal at stake when a student is facing suspension or expulsion. Realistically, not all sanctions equally impact a student in the same way. Maintaining the philosophy of student conduct processes as educational processes requires an understanding of compliance issues and how students and the institution are impacted and a commitment to having a process that serves both educational and compliance interests.

Part of staying true to the student conduct philosophy includes building strong relationships with colleagues throughout the institution. If the community (students, administration, staff, faculty, families, etc.) sees the conduct process as purely compliance and therefore equates it to processes like the criminal court process, then the educational value is lost. Student conduct practitioners who are well versed in compliance issues and student development theory can position themselves to advocate for strong, fundamentally fair educational processes that meet regulatory expectations.

The Philosophical Side of Fundamental Fairness

There is a philosophical element of being fundamentally fair. Being committed as an educator working in student conduct, it helps to remember that compliance is the floor and not the ceiling. In addition, most student conduct cases do not fall under regulations such as Title IX, yet the concept of fundamental fairness remains.

Ethics and fundamental fairness are intertwined. Ethical decision-making on both the student's and institution's part is at the core of the work. Rushworth Kidder (2003) wrote, "Ethics is not a blind impartiality, doling out right and wrong according to some stone cold canon of ancient and immutable law. It's a warm and supremely human activity that cares enough for others to want right to prevail" (p. 50).

The student conduct process needs to be supremely human just as much as it needs to be fundamentally fair. The individuals involved are not checkboxes; they are not pieces of paper. To be fundamentally fair recognizes that those impacted by the behavioral situation have been personally impacted. Therefore, the approach and mind-set of the student conduct practitioner can enhance or diminish the legal side of fundamental fairness.

Consistency

A common mistake of practitioners new to student conduct is to believe that consistency is making the same decision for similar circumstances. For example, Student A and Student B were both found to be driving under the influence of alcohol in separate incidents. One may believe that their sanctions should be exactly the same. That is not being consistent and it becomes fundamentally unjust. Circumstances can be similar, but they are rarely the same. Aggravating and mitigating factors must be considered. What it means to be consistent is to use the same decision-making process. If the process of determining violations or sanctions changes arbitrarily or if the decision is always the same regardless of the factors, then the process loses its educational value.

Explicit Versus Implicit Messaging

Student conduct practitioners must remember that there are messages that are being transmitted throughout the student conduct process. These messages are coming from the students, parents, administrative staff, and ultimately the institution. The messages that we send, and, more importantly, the messages that students receive throughout their conduct process, can shape their experience moving forward.

Students come to campus with a wide variety of experiences and ways of being. They learn to respond appropriately according to criteria that can be explicitly stated (Gasparini, 2004). The concept of what is *implicit* has been defined as "suggested but not communicated directly," versus what is *explicit*, which is defined as "fully revealed or expressed without vagueness, implication, or ambiguity; leaving no question as to meaning or intent" (Cambridge English Dictionary, n.d.). The difference is clear and can have a very different and often detrimental impact on students in a conduct process. It is important for conduct practitioners to be aware of when messages need to be explicit. Making the assumption that a student will clearly understand what is being implied in verbal and written communication is detrimental to student learning and development. Different messages can be implied differently; for example, someone may say, "My stomach is growling." It could be inferred that the person is hungry; it could also be inferred that the person has a stomach sickness. Both of those assumptions could be correct, and they also could be incorrect. It is vital to our work to ensure that our messaging is clear.

One final note regarding implicit and explicit messaging centers around our implicit biases. Stallman (2015) found that implicit biases of student conduct professionals exist at similar levels to those found in the general public. Furthermore, at times this bias was expressed in the decisions they made in sample conduct cases. Conduct practitioners will engage in a number of conversations with students and at times their families. The implicit and explicit messages that are sent during these encounters can impact the perspective that students take toward the case or their impression of the way that they are viewed in the situation. Referring back to the stomach example, if the response to that individual is "You should get something to eat," there is an assumption that the person is hungry and they have the means to procure food. This could be an incorrect assumption as there may be other reasons for the growling or the person may not have the means to pay for or obtain food. Such a response could inhibit the person with the growling stomach from continuing to engage in the conversation. Regardless of the intention of the message sender, the impact that it can have on the receiver can have long-lasting effects. Conduct professionals should strive to ensure that their intentions are aligning with the impact on the community base. Chapter 6, on social justice, examines this area in great detail.

"What Does Due Process Look Like When Due Process Doesn't Look Like You?"

At the 2019 Association for Student Conduct Administration (ASCA) annual conference, Melissa Harris-Perry, keynote speaker, challenged the participants to reflect on this question.

Managing the Perception Versus the Reality of the Profession

Many come into this profession because of a commitment to helping other people. They may see value in higher education as a means to accomplishing that goal. Good intentions and positive attitudes show up with the practitioner who is new to the conduct world. While practitioners may believe that their role is to educate and to help, that is not always the belief of the students who may come in contact with the office. For some students, their only interaction with a conduct office of any form has been their high school counselor or principal's office or, for some, the court system. None of those scenarios for most students engenders the warm and welcoming educational environment that we are seeking to create for students. That does not mean that it cannot happen; however, practitioners must be aware of possible perceptions, as well as being intentional with their efforts to create open and welcoming spaces.

Practitioners should focus on the environment provided. When was the last time an assessment was conducted of office space and the experience of students who have to enter the space? What messages are being conveyed by the pamphlets and brochures in the office? What is the physical setup of the office? What feeling does the office elicit in terms of furniture, wall art, and paint color? Consider the experience of students who have to visit. It could be helpful to ask a randomly selected group of students to do an office walk-through. These same students could also be a test group for the review of letters and processes. At times, practitioners can be so close to the work that they cannot see the way that something can be interpreted by others.

Managing the perception with the reality of the students' experience can be challenging. It is, however, essential to creating an environment where students feel supported in the midst of a crisis. The goal of the work will continue to be to support students during their academic journey while honoring the choices that they have made, be they good or bad. This means being aware of the needs and experiences of all students who interact with student conduct practitioners and come into the space. Practitioners must continue to educate themselves on the ever-changing society that we live in while being sensitive and aware to the experiences of individuals who are different from themselves.

Culture

With the diversity of most modern universities growing at an increasing rate, higher education institutions are microcosms of society. Each institution has its own unique culture and way of existing and being. At times these cultures can mirror larger society or provide what some may view as an inaccurate reflection of the larger societal culture. Regardless of institution type, as a conduct practitioner, one should be aware of the current societal and campus culture. Many practitioners who have been in practice for some time may have overlooked the ideas inherent and defined in the notions of privilege. Colby, Ehrlich, Beaumont, and Stephens (2004) note the following:

> Understanding the influence of the campus climate is never a simple matter, because culture, even within a single institution, is heterogeneous and dynamic. Students experience many cultural currents, some of which may conflict with each other. To add to the complexity, people pay attention to different things in their environment and may understand the same experiences differently. For that reason, many aspects of campus culture will have different meanings and salience for different people.
>
> Another central value for higher education institutions is respect for people whose backgrounds, cultures, or beliefs differ from one's own. The campus culture can play an important role in supporting growth in students' understanding of unfamiliar cultural traditions and in promoting respectful engagement across difference, thus preparing graduates to function well in a diverse society and a globally interdependent world.

A campus climate in which these values are salient can help students become more reflective about their own cultural backgrounds as well as developing better understanding of and respect for others.

Understanding the role of campus as well as societal culture and their impact on students' orientation and behavior is helpful to deciding the way that we will develop our office practices and the way in which we engage with helping our students.

We bring ourselves to our work and campuses in the same way that students do. Experiences can shape our work in both negative and positive ways. What pieces of our own personal culture and experiences impact the way that we view ourselves and our students? It can also be helpful to examine our relationship with the institution where we work. For example, if you are an alumnus of the institution, your relationship with and view of the institution could be influenced by the experiences that you had as a student. That can shape the lens through which you view students and the work. We must ensure that we are consistently checking the campus and societal cultural temperature and are being aware of how our own experiences can influence our work with students.

Managing Codes That Were Modeled After Courts

Lancaster (2012) discusses how the early case law *Gott v. Berea College* (1913) established that colleges stood *in loco parentis* concerning the physical and moral training of their students (Kaplin & Lee, 1997). Lancaster (2012) discusses that this embedded the concept of moral training in college. *Dixon v. Alabama* (1961) brought the idea of due process into the higher education conduct landscape. Dixon heralded a turn toward due process in conduct proceedings and, while not clearly required by this or subsequent cases, toward the beginning of a more structured and legalistic practice of student conduct (Lancaster, 2012).

This model has shifted over time in practice and in policy. However, the current social climate has the potential to shift student conduct practice back to a more legalistic way of being. Parents and attorneys are far more involved in the current conduct process than they have been in the past. This involvement can turn an environment designed to be educational into one that becomes a highly contested legal battle. In these situations, conduct practitioners need to be aware of what messages are being sent to students who might not be able to afford an attorney or whose family situation does not allow them the support that other families may be able to provide. An unfair advantage whether real or perceived can show up in these situations. It is important to take time to review the code to ensure that there are not procedures that may disadvantage or advantage one party over the other.

The influence of legal parties and concerned parents can have the potential to influence conduct practitioners to respond or act in a certain way. Practitioners must be grounded in their policies, ethics, and values in the face of such influences. They must seek ways to ensure that all students understand and have access to a process that supports them as members of the college community.

Opportunities for Engagement With Campus Communities

While student conduct work is often managed by a specific individual at the institution, that individual conduct professional works with and for the entire campus community. With that comes an opportunity for engagement and outreach. Does the entire campus community understand the work of the conduct office? This is not just the volume or type of work, but the philosophy behind it, as well as the outcomes both intended and unintended. Often, the answer would be no. How can that be changed? Changing campuses' understanding and perception of offices can contribute to culture change and the overall effectiveness of the student experience.

The first opportunity for change is with faculty. Faculty are the primary individuals on campus who will refer academic conduct concerns. It is necessary for them to have a thorough understanding of the code and the process. It is also critical for them to trust the office and the process as well as the practitioners. They should see themselves as partners in the conduct process. ASCA (n.d.) notes that "the ultimate goals of student conduct processes are student growth and development and the preservation of the educational environment." Consider an effective way to engage faculty in this process and help them understand the critical role that they play in it and in the subsequent success of the students.

The second opportunity is with the student body. A good question to ask is "Does the office reflect the demographics of the campus?" If the answer is no, staff need to be mindful of the way that may be interpreted by the student body. It can be helpful to be aware of the concerns and/or assumptions that students from certain identities may hold about the conduct office, process, and those who work in it. There is an opportunity to work with student leaders who represent these and other identities to assist with outreach and education to the campus. Some of the best advocates on behalf of student conduct processes are students who have been through that process. Students also hear and respond differently to their peers than they do to administrators.

Students can also be involved in engaging with faculty and staff regarding the conduct process. This engagement may not be direct because of the sensitive nature of the topic. Students should feel comfortable expressing themselves and being able to ask questions without fear of repercussion from faculty or staff. Students as well as faculty and staff should be involved in a way that does not put either in a compromising or uncomfortable position. For example, the students could create an informational video on their experiences of participating in an academic integrity matter, which would give faculty and staff members an opportunity to learn about those experiences in a nonconfrontational and reflective manner.

The final opportunity to foster change is through parent engagement. Are families engaged with student conduct professionals during new student orientation? Does the student conduct staff participate in any family calls or updates throughout the year? There is an opportunity to proactively engage and educate parents on the ethos and processes of the department. This could engender a new partnership for the student conduct office. It also creates an open door for proactive questions from families regarding potential situations. For families that are distrustful of administrative processes and may liken them to criminal proceedings, this engagement can significantly impact their understanding and experience for the better. This creates an environment that encourages families to become allies in our mission to educate and develop more successful students.

Conduct concerns are campus concerns. When the campus has a healthy understanding of the process and the work of the office as well as the ways in which they can partner, the institution benefits. Engagement from all stakeholders is vital; however, it is the responsibility of the conduct office to initiate this engagement, education, and outreach.

Case Studies

We provide two case studies for your consideration as you put philosophy into practice.

Case Study #1

Stephanie is a Latinx student at your institution. She identifies as a first-generation, low-income, first-year student. She comes to your office to share her experience with sorority recruitment. As she begins to talk about her experience, she is visibly upset. She has disclosed what on the surface sounds like it could be hazing. She shares that the sorority is one of the largest and most prestigious organizations on campus. The two main people whom she describes being involved in this incident are the student body president and the daughter of a very well-known, generous donor of the college. She is terrified about what will happen to her socially on campus and is fearful that she may lose her scholarship because of her poor academic performance as a result of her experiences.

1. How do you engage with this student?
2. What are some possible implicit and explicit messages that can be conveyed to this student, the other students involved, and the larger student body in the situation?
3. Who has power and privilege in this situation? What role does that play?
4. Are there any biases that you have that may show up for you in this situation? If yes, how do you handle them?

Case Study #2

You work at an institution with a strong religious culture, not affiliation. The LGBTQIA organization decides to have a drag show for their PRIDE week. During the event, a group of students who are opposed to the show attend and a verbal altercation turns into a physical altercation. The entire incident is caught on camera, but it is unclear who started the physical altercation. The students who were opposed to the show feel like they had a right to protest the show because it offended their religious and moral beliefs. The students hosting the drag show feel that their safety has been compromised and do not feel like they are welcomed and supported on the campus.

1. Are there any campus partners you should work with?
2. What are the issues at play for your office in this situation?
3. What are some of the possible implicit and explicit messages that can be conveyed to each group of students and to the larger campus community?
4. What role does campus culture have in this situation?
5. Are there biases that may show up for you in this situation? If yes, how do you handle them?

Challenge to the Reader

Our hope is that as you have read this chapter, you have begun to examine your own professional philosophy asking questions such as the following:

1. What is my professional philosophy?
2. How do I live this in my daily practice?

3. How does this philosophy affect the image I portray, especially related to fairness and student advocacy?
4. How do I demonstrate my professional philosophy?
5. What does it mean to me to be fundamentally fair?

If you are uncertain about these questions, do not be alarmed; that is okay. Have realistic self-evaluations on a consistent basis. The field is changing every day and the way in which we do our work will change along with it. As the field evolves, so should our practice and understanding. We need to take time to reflect and discuss our professional identity and commitment to the work that we have an opportunity to do and that impacts the lives of students.

As you move forward with the rest of this text, we challenge you to continually ask yourself the following questions:

1. Am I an advocate for students and the institution?
2. Through what lens am I viewing this work?
3. How does my privilege show up in my work?
4. How does the privilege of others impact my ability to do impactful work?

References

Association for Student Conduct Administration. (n.d). *About ASCA*. Retrieved from https://www.theasca.org/content.asp?contentid=23

Cambridge English Dictionary. (n.d.). *Explicit.* Retrieved from https://dictionary cambridge.org/us/dictionary/english/explicit?q=Explicit

Code of Federal Regulations (1968). *General order on judicial standards of procedure and substance review of student discipline in tax-supported institutions of higher education,* 45 F.R.D. 133 C.F.R. Washington DC: Office of the Attorney General.

Colby, A., Ehrlich, T., Beaumont, E., & Stephens, J. (2004). Educating citizens. *New York Times.* Retrieved from https://archive.nytimes.com/www.nytimes.com/ref/college/collegespecial2/coll_aascu_ecintro.html

Dixon v. Alabama, 294 F. 2d 150 (5th Cir. 1961)

Gasparini, S. (2004). Implicit versus explicit learning: Some implications for L2 teaching. *European Journal of Psychology of Education,19*(2), 203–219. doi:10.1007/bf03173232

Gott v. Berea College, et al., 156 Ky. 376; 161 S.W. 204; 1913 Ky. LEXIS 441 (1913)

Kattner, T. (2015, May 11). Balancing federal regulatory compliance with educational missions. *Campus Law Considered*. Retrieved from http://www.campuslaw-considered.com/articles/campus-safety/balancing-federal-regulatory-compliance-with-educational-missions/

Kidder, R. (2003). *How good people make tough choices*. New York, NY: Morrow.

Lancaster, J. M. (2012). Conduct systems designed to promote moral learning. *New Directions for Student Services, 2012*(139), 51–61. doi:10.1002/ss.20022

Stallman, S. (2015). *Implicit bias in college student conduct systems* (Unpublished doctoral dissertation). Illinois State University, Normal, IL.

Stoner II, E., & Lowery, J. (2004). Navigating past the "spirit of insubordination": A twenty-first century model student conduct code with a model hearing script. *Journal of College and University Law 31*(1), 1–78.

3

CRAFTING AND REVISING YOUR STUDENT CONDUCT CODE

Seann S. Kalagher and Regina D. Curran

Introduction

Through their ubiquity, codes of conduct serve as one of the most important elements of student conduct practice. They are common in that each institution of higher education has one in some form, but their ubiquitous nature sometimes causes professionals to ignore that they are all very different, and while codes may share similarities, very few are the same. It is this juxtaposition between commonality and uniqueness that makes crafting and revising a student code of conduct one of the hardest tasks to accomplish in student affairs. This is easy to understand when realizing that student conduct is, perhaps more than any other area of student affairs, indelibly tied to the history, values, and mission of an institution, and that the code of conduct is a reflection of that relationship.

The student code of conduct is, in the abstract, a form of institutional history. For example, some "honor codes" at institutions in the United States date back to the first half of the eighteeenth century, and with that comes a connection to broader institutional expectations (College of William & Mary, 2019). At other institutions, codes of conduct can change quite frequently, reflecting the needs and demands of the current institution, unencumbered by decades of history and precedent. Student codes of conduct can provide a window into what an institution has experienced in its past, and how the expectations placed on students reflect what those past leaders and administrators valued; viewed as risks; and, in some cases, feared. There is often a story behind the code, as policy, and student conduct administrators are often involved on both ends of those stories: as a person who experienced a situation that necessitated a change in policy and as a professional attempting to determine why a policy is written the way it is, or even exists in the first place. It is a process that is, ideally, continuous. The demands and challenges of the modern university also require a consistent and continuous cycle of review and revision of codes of conduct. Legal and compliance mandates have a considerable impact on code development and revision, even more so in recent years. Courts and government authorities, at the federal and state levels, enact legislation, promulgate regulations, and make decisions that impact the student conduct process in profound ways.

Beyond the legal consideration, the composition of student bodies at U.S. institutions of higher learning is in a constant state of change. Nowadays, defining a "typical" student is even more difficult. Thus, student codes of conduct must adapt to serve a more diverse student body populated by larger percentages of first-generation students and students attending more professional and career-focused programs. Student populations are increasingly older, are as likely to be part-time students as full-time students, are more likely to have documented disabilities, are more racially diverse, and so on (New America, 2019). The diversifying of the student body, coupled with differing institutional types, necessitates an individualized approach to the delivery of student support. As Manning (2013) notes, the "one-size-fits-all" approach to practice provides little attention to the diversity across institutions of higher learning. In addition to these changes, a new wave of student activism and awareness puts institutional processes related to student discipline, institutional response to incidents and activism, and the sometimes conflicting expectations of institutional stakeholders as matters of constant concern for conduct administrators. In the center of those conversations are the foundation provided by codes of conduct and their related processes.

With all of this in mind, what is the best way to revise a code? What does a student conduct administrator need to know? Like many questions posed in this chapter, the answer will be "It depends." Codes of conduct are unique to their institutions, and the methods and means of revision vary similarly. Before delving into the mechanics of the revision process, the first question a conduct administrator should answer is "What kind of review is this?" Is the institution conducting a regular, perhaps annual, review or has there been a conscious decision to engage in a broader overhaul of the student code of conduct? Is the review limited to a particular area of the code of conduct? Answering these questions provides an early lens on the scope and goals of the revision process in which the institution will engage. Revisions are also not a singular process (no matter how some professionals wish it could be). The administrators who are often most invested in the code of conduct and their processes are usually not the same administrators with final approval authority. Therefore, a successful revision process often involves relationship building; engaging in campus politics; persuasion; constituent relations; and, most importantly, time and patience.

Another necessary element prior to engaging in a revision process is information. At a base level, conduct administrators should have accessible to them statistics about their system, including the number of reports the conduct office (or equivalent office) receives, the demographics of the students involved in university infractions, how many proceed through the institutional student conduct process, how far those cases move throughout the system (if there are multiple steps), information on disciplinary findings and sanctions, appeals information, and an analysis on how staff members are utilized within the conduct process. Along with these internal numbers, state- and federal-mandated statistical disclosures, like the federal Jeanne Clery Disclosure of Campus Security Policy and Campus Crime Statistics Act (1998) and state legislation (e.g., New York's Enough Is Enough disclosures), can provide useful information to those involved in a review process, especially if that process includes campus partners not intimately familiar with the student conduct process. Beyond the statistical information, information collected through qualitative assessments of students (ideally of those who have and have not gone through the conduct process) and staff involved in the process can provide an essential window into how the campus community experiences the conduct process in a way that mere statistics cannot. Conduct systems that incorporate academic integrity will likely have a different set of information that speaks directly to those matters. Chapter 14 speaks to the intricate nature of academic integrity cases. All of this information provides necessary guidance and context for any recommended changes.

With that information collected, a conduct administrator can move forward with the revision process. As discussed earlier, there is no typical code of conduct. Model codes exist as a guide and can provide general requirements (Stoner, 2000; Stoner & Lowery, 2004), but codes tend to reflect the values and needs of their institution. With that in mind, while this chapter will not dictate what the code of conduct has to be, it will endeavor to inform conduct administrators of what options are available and what questions need to be asked throughout the code revision process.

Institutional Knowledge

Any code revision should start from knowing your institution. If you are new to an institution and are charged with the undertaking of a major revision, be sure you take the time to get to know your campus. Questions to explore include "Is the institution public or private, two-year or four-year, religiously affiliated or not? Is the student population single gender?" Additionally, you will want to think about your student body, who are they, what their precollege experiences may have been like, and where they came from. What is the predominant academic emphasis (e.g., liberal arts, law, medicine and health professions)? Throughout this chapter we will discuss some important factors in institutional knowledge and why they matter to a code revision.

Institution Type

Understanding the type of institution where you work is important in understanding various influences on your code. The following are some items to address as you assess your institution:

- *What is your institution type?* Is the institution public or private, religious or nonsectarian, two-year or four-year? Are there particular academic emphases? At the process level public and private colleges and universities have essential differences in which laws and court decisions apply to them. A religiously affiliated institution, for example, would necessitate an inquiry of prescribed conduct prohibitions or values statements. Other institutional differences can inform sanction options: Is expulsion an option? Is removal from campus housing a relevant sanction? Do any sanctions impact ability to study abroad or hold a campus job or student leadership position?
- *Who are your students?* Do students rein from local or global locations? Do you have a strong ROTC/military affiliation? Should your code address student organizations in addition to individual students? (See chapter 13 for more information on organizations and misconduct.) Does your institution have an honor code? (If your students are committed to this code, you may want to use shared language in your student conduct code.) Do students actively participate in campus policy creation? Understanding who your students are will inform the language that resonates with them, the level of involvement they may want in your process, whether your code speaks to shared values, and how many terms you may need to define. If your students are, or desire to be, heavily involved in policy development, getting them involved early can help with everything from understanding institutional type to considering what terms to define.
- *Is there benchmarking with peer institutions?* Understanding whom your institution compares itself to (both peers and aspirants) is essential when benchmarking policies or trying to make persuasive arguments for change. You may seek this information within your division, from an institutional research office, or other campus

partners, like admissions, who regularly benchmark other schools. While we are not suggesting that what is right for a peer institution is necessarily right for your institution, having this information may assist you in proposing policies similar to those of your peers or explaining why your institution should differentiate itself on an issue. The benchmarking process also provides an opportunity to get students and other constituents involved, and they may appreciate the opportunity to find policies or procedures that speak to them while engaging in the code review process.

- *What type of campus safety/security or law enforcement entity do you have?* A public safety or private security unit is likely to engage differently with the conduct process than a state-certified campus police unit. For example, the granting of arrest powers and carrying firearms is typical for larger public universities in which campus police perform much like local, county, and state counterparts. In addition to understanding who your campus security or law enforcement is, you will want to know if they have any memorandum of understanding (MOU) or mutual aid agreement with local law enforcement, as this may have implications for knowledge sharing among other conduct process considerations. Some colleges and universities have moved in the direction of creating MOUs within the institution, between conduct and campus security or campus police, for example. Having a better understanding of how involved, or not, your campus security or law enforcement will be with your process might indicate how useful an MOU will be for your work. At a minimum, involving campus safety/security or law enforcement personnel in conversations about their involvement with code revision processes will account for their role in the process and will help to build a vital partnership.
- *Is there a reporting structure?* If your division falls under the purview of the provost versus a vice president of student affairs, there may be different expectations for the code. Making sure you are aware of any divisional policy expectations and also who the relevant roles are in the chain of command will make it easier to create a policy that fits your institution. As you consider who in the chain of command will have responsibility for things like interim measures or appeals, be sure to keep in mind what type of training they will receive, who will provide it, and how often.
- *How is student conduct situated within the division?* This not only relates to chains of command, but also to who may be most important in getting code changes approved. If the code will pass through several

layers of the upper administration, and perhaps a general statewide authority before being accepted, it may be prudent to gather input early in the process from stakeholders in order to ensure support. Other implications include how many administrators exist above the office to serve as appellate bodies and how much influence donors or board members may have on the office.

We have provided some thoughts on each of these considerations, but as you gain institutional knowledge, asking these questions may lead you down other paths that have potential to directly impact your code. While it may seem obvious, especially if you have been on the campus for a while, taking the time to truly understand your institution can impact both the substance of the code and the ease with which it is approved through campus processes. When done well, institutional knowledge building can also be a tool for creating partnerships and finding champions for the work.

Process and Code Development

Having taken the time to understand your institution, the process of creating or revising a student code of conduct should be relatively straight forward from here. To begin, it is imperative to check institutional policies for any institution-specific requirements. For example, you might have a "policy on policies" or information on the "formulation and issuance of university policies" (e.g., American University, 2019; Carnegie Mellon University, 2015; Indiana University, 2013; Northeastern University, 2017; Pennsylvania State University, 2013). If your institution has such a policy it may be necessary for your student conduct code to be in compliance with this.

Whether you have such a policy directive, knowing your campus and how your code relates to campus will provide you with information on how to proceed.

Process Constituents

It is important to carefully consider what stakeholders need to be involved in the code revision process. You may be required to involve certain groups (e.g., student government, general counsel, advisory boards, or standing committees), and you may also choose to involve certain people to lend credibility to the process (e.g., students, fraternity and sorority life leadership, campus security or police, faculty). As you begin, have a plan for whom to involve when. Some constituents are best involved in the benchmarking and drafting stages, while others are necessary in the editing and review phase. Still others are vital in ratifying the final product.

Process Timeline

Now that you have a sense of who will be involved and the necessary steps, it is helpful to have an understanding of how long it will take. Are you undertaking an annual review and update or a complete code overhaul? This will surely inform your timeline even if you have a clear direction of where you are headed. The timeline for a review can and should be standardized. For example, an institution may devise a timeline in which every spring a defined group meets to review, make suggestions, or consider proposals for code revisions. However, if the code requires a more extensive revision, it may take an academic year or more to complete. Being realistic about this up front will help with participant engagement and your own project management expectations.

Now that your road map is in place and you have a good sense of the scope of the project, who is involved, and your timeline for completion, the next piece of this chapter will focus on the substance of the code itself.

Essential Elements and Code Construction

While each code of conduct is different, all codes should share similar foundational elements. In the previous edition of this text, Stoner (2008) thoroughly described elements to consider. As such, we have delineated the following elements as the most important elements. The first is parameters and definitions. This section should clearly define terms. It is always useful to craft a code with an audience in mind. Thus, using language and terms that are age appropriate and gender neutral may resonate well with student populations.

- *Authority:* Defines the boundaries, foundations, and participants within the institutional student conduct system. As noted in chapter 5, on the forums of resolution, there are many ways to resolve an allegation.
- *Workflow and process:* What is the specific process used? How many levels are included in the student conduct system? What are student rights and expectations as part of that process?
- *Conduct and behavior:* What are the behaviors that the institution wishes to address, or in some cases has to address, within the code of conduct? How are those decisions tied to institutional values and mission?

Parameters and Definitions

In defining the scope and boundaries of a student conduct process, conduct administrators and those with the authority to approve and amend codes of conduct must answer several questions. Those questions may seem basic, but the answers have far-reaching implications on how, and to whom, the code applies.

The first question is in two parts: Who is a student and when does the code of conduct apply? Asking who a student is may seem like a basic question to answer, but that answer is an important one. Does the code apply to students when they apply for admission, when their first semester at the institution officially starts, or some time in between? If students attend a summer orientation session, are they accountable to the code of conduct? The answer to this question impacts whether behavior that occurs before a student officially matriculates but has some sort of relationship with the institution can be addressed through the institutional conduct process. On the other end of the student experience is the question of when students cease to be students. Is it upon graduation? When does "graduation" happen? A student who walks at commencement may still have unresolved matters. For example, the student could have participated in commencement but has a course or two remaining to be completed at the institution. Many institutions use "conferring of a degree" as the end date of a student's relationship, but when specifically does that occur? The policies and language that accompany the code of conduct must address this. Also, will the institution entertain or investigate complaints if the alleged infraction occurs after the degree is confirmed? If so, under what circumstances? Did the incident related to the complaint happen while the student was enrolled and subject to the code? To what lengths will an institution honor those complaints? Institutions have different answers to these questions, but each institution must have an answer.

Another way in which students sever their relationship with an institution is by withdrawing. If a withdrawal means that the code of conduct no longer applies to that student (former student), how does the institution address other periods of absence, like suspensions and official leave of absences? Can behavior that occurs while a student is suspended or on leave be addressed by the code of conduct? Given that a period of absence like a suspension or approved leave of absence indicates a continued relationship with the institution, the answer may likely be yes, but it should be delineated within a code. Graduate and professional programs are another matter to address when defining students and the code of conduct process. In many graduate programs, particularly in professional programs like medical and law schools, academic units may have their own student affairs units that administer their own codes of conduct. These distinct codes and adjudicating authority, if they exist, should clearly differentiate the student populations to which they serve and apply.

Along with who the code of conduct applies to, another vitally important question is "Where does the code apply?" The question of physical jurisdiction is one colleges and universities have struggled with in recent years and has been conversation in courthouses as well (*Farmer v. Kansas State University*, 2019). Jurisdiction issues have also been a topic that federal regulators seek to address in proposed Title IX guidance (Kreighbaum, 2018). While some institutions seek to limit the reach of the code of conduct to the physical boundaries of a campus or institutional property, the realities of student interaction and legal expectations can make that difficult. Limiting the reach of the code of conduct can leave students in a position where student-to-student behavior, which takes place off campus but impacts their on-campus and in-class experience, is left unaddressed by the college or university. While some institutions take this route, it is important to note that codes of conduct are setting behavioral expectations that institutions want their students to reflect and model. Thus, behavioral expectations do not disappear when the student leaves the physical boundaries of a campus. The same principle applies to students who participate in distance or online programs. Students, even if they do not matriculate on the main or physical campus, maintain the same behavioral expectations. Another element to consider is institutional programming and organizations with off-campus activities or locations. College-affiliated events related to athletics, student clubs and organizations, and other institutional events are areas that should be affirmatively addressed in the code of conduct. Chapter 13, on student organizations, addresses this in greater detail. Another area that needs to be considered is international study abroad programs. The variety and diversity of these programs, and who controls them, can pose difficult questions for conduct administrators. Generally speaking, an institution that exercises off-campus jurisdiction would also have jurisdiction over incidents that happen abroad. How information is communicated by various programs may need to be determined on an individual basis or with the assistance of an institution's international education and study abroad office.

These activities, regardless of location, are ones that a reasonable person looking in from the outside would associate with the institution, and institutions are well served to address this when defining the physical jurisdiction of the code of conduct.

One last question that needs to be addressed in each individual code of conduct is the categories of behavior that a particular process will address.

As mentioned, academic integrity is an area sometimes incorporated into a larger student code of conduct, or academic integrity may be under a separate policy and administered by separate staff members or faculty. With the renewed federal and state focus on Title IX and sexual violence over the past decade, many institutions developed separate, stand-alone policies and processes to address those complaints. While Title IX directives do not mandate a stand-alone policy, institutions have often separated them out, especially when a common sexual violence policy addresses all community members, including faculty and staff.

One of the most important parameters that needs to be addressed is who is involved in the student conduct process. All who may be involved in the process should be addressed in some way, even if their involvement does not occur in each case. Participants in the process often fall in the following categories:

- *Parties:* Obviously, the responding party (the student or students charged with a violation) is a primary participant in the conduct process. The code should also address the role that a complainant, if there is one, may have in the conduct process.
- *Conduct administrator:* In systems that use one-on-one meetings as the main mechanism for hearing student conduct cases, this will be the person who meets with the responding student and likely makes a decision as to the responding student's responsibility for the alleged violation as well as possible sanctions. This may also be a staff member who serves as a prehearing meeting administrator or another role whereby a student meets with a conduct administrator prior to proceeding to a formal hearing.
- *Hearing panel members:* For institutions that utilize hearing boards, the code should spell out the size of hearing panels as well as their composition (faculty, staff, students, etc.). Again, chapter 5 in this text addresses potential forums in great detail.
- *Advisers:* This topic will be discussed further later in the chapter, but most processes allow for an adviser to assist the responding students. Who they are and in what manner they serve is a matter that will be discussed further.
- *Appeal administrators:* Who serves in an appellate role, assuming the institution provided an appeal process, should be disclosed, as well as how many people are involved in appellate decisions. This may include a single administrator r a hearing panel.
- *Institutional counsel:* Institutions may reserve the right to have their own counsel in hearings. This can be for reasons such as pending or

ongoing litigation, the presence of an attorney as a student adviser, or other concerns identified by an institutional general counsel's office.

- *Observers:* Observers at a hearing are not often discussed, but there are several reasons why an institution may want an observer in a conduct hearing. The most important reason is for training or supervision purposes. One of the best ways for a new conduct administrator or a panelist to learn about the process is to watch more experienced colleagues perform in their respective roles. Also, supervisors may want to sit in on a conduct meeting conducted by a staff member for evaluation purposes. Another instance where an observer may be helpful is in the case of an institution that does not use hearing boards. In this instance, to have another staff member sit in on sensitive or serious conduct hearings provides another set of "eyes and ears" in the room as a precautionary strategy. If, for any of these or other reasons, an institution may have an observer inside a conduct meeting or hearing, that should be disclosed in the code.

The topic of advisers in student conduct meetings and what role they are afforded must be carefully described in the code of conduct and is one of the most important issues currently facing the student conduct profession. Historically, the adviser role in the conduct process was established by the policies of institutions themselves. Over the past decade, as public and legal scrutiny of student conduct processes has increased, the adviser role has become one of the most scrutinized. There are several facets and questions that an institution must answer regarding the role of advisers in campus conduct processes:

- *Does the process permit advisers?* As discussed, this has historically been left to institutional choice. However, as denoted in chapter 5 in greater detail, nowadays it is expected and recommended that institutions allow the option of an adviser for both the complainant and the respondent. Also, from the perception of fairness, students typically desire the opportunity to have a person in a support role to assist them in navigating the student conduct system—a system that is often an intimidating and unfamiliar experience.
- *Who can serve as an adviser?* The code of conduct should answer the question of who can serve as adviser and if attorneys can serve as advisers. Again, this is an answer that largely falls to the institution. While institutions can, and have, limited advisers to people who are members of their own campus communities, it is important to remember that there are laws at the state and federal level that

do mandate institutional compliance in this area. The federal Campus SaVE Act requires that parties have access to the adviser of their choice (regardless of institutional affiliation and including attorneys). Also, several states have passed legislation that requires public institutions to permit attorneys' active representation as advisers in campus conduct hearings. This leads to the next question.

• *What role can advisers play in the conduct process?* Institutions, understandably, have a desire to ensure that their processes do not become de facto court proceedings. Active participation by an adviser acting in a protective stance (e.g., an attorney) can be disruptive to proceedings and may detract from the educational goals of the process. However, as mentioned, some states do mandate the active representation by attorneys in certain types of cases. Allowing active representation means an attorney or adviser may speak and advocate for a responding student and may ask questions of witness or complaining parties, if they are actively part of an institutional process. (At the time of this writing, states that permit active attorney participation in some level of the student conduct process include Arkansas, North Carolina, North Dakota, and Tennessee.) The role of the attorney in proceedings may also include that of adviser in which this person acts as a support person for the responding student. In this role, advisers can speak and provide advice directly to the student they are working with but cannot address the conduct administrator or hearing panel (or other parties or witnesses) directly. The benefits of this approach provide for fewer disruptions in the proceedings and responding students must speak and advocate for themselves, which is seen as adding to the educational value of the conduct process.

As institutions look to develop their policy on advisers, they would be well served to ask if there is a proposal to place stringent limitations on advisers why this decision was made. Are decisions being made for the sake of administrative convenience or is it to enhance the educational experience of the student? That is a question that needs a substantive answer, as internal and external forces within higher education are expecting, more and more, that a respondent's access to assistance, advocacy, and moral support be broad and easily achieved.

A final and crucially important definition that must be included within each code of conduct is the standard of information by which a student will be found responsible. Phrased differently, "What is the threshold that needs to be met in order for a conduct administrator or a hearing panel to find a student responsible for a violation?" There are three main standards of information:

1. *Beyond a reasonable doubt:* This well-known standard is used in the American criminal justice system. This standard requires the fact finder to be "fully satisfied or entirely convince[d]" that the person accused is responsible (State of North Carolina, 2019). It is the highest standard of information and requires near certainty of responsibility.

2. *Clear and convincing evidence:* This intermediate standard requires that the information show that it is much more probable than not and establish for the trier of fact a "firm belief" that a respondent is responsible for the alleged violations (Ripy, 1999). Some institutions have and still do use this standard for some student conduct cases.

3. *Preponderance of the evidence:* This is the standard used in the American civil system and the most common standard of information used in student conduct systems. Preponderance of the information is often phrased as whether it is "more likely than not" that a responding student is responsible for an alleged violation. Another way of addressing the preponderance standard is any level of certainty over 50%. While this standard has historically been the most common standard utilized in campus conduct systems prior to the past decade, the 2011 "Dear Colleague" letter on Title IX issues mandates the preponderance standard for cases involving sexual violence, and several states also have enacted legislation mandating the use of the preponderance standard for sexual violence matters (Ali, 2011).

Stages of the Student Conduct Process

While each code of conduct is different, a code, regardless of institution type or other variables, should have certain foundational elements that describe the workflow of the conduct process as well as a thorough explanation of what students can expect as they progress through the process. These expectations include options and choices students may have through the conduct process as well as minimum expectations that the institution must meet in order to meet its stated obligations and ensure a fair process for all involved parties. A thorough revision process will ensure that all of these matters are addressed within the code and the policies that support it in a way that reinforces the institution's educational philosophy and mission.

These essential items can be broken down into 10 elements. Importantly, not every process will use or progress through all 10, but all 10 are areas that an institution's code needs to address in writing in some way. Here are those elements, presented in chronological order:

1. *Report submission:* It is important to address how allegations are first entered into the student conduct process. Most institutions have a system by which reports are received. Are there other methods by which a person can submit a report or concern? The code should address whether campus community members can submit reports in person to an office of student conduct. This section should also address law enforcement reports and how they interrelate with the campus conduct system. Are reports from local and national media outlets, or even social media, sufficient to qualify as a report received by the institution? Can the institution use a public source of information as a means of generating a report for a student conduct matter? If multiple sources are permissible, the language used in the code of conduct needs to be broad enough to encompass those options.

2. *Report review:* Each report that comes into an office of student conduct must be reviewed in some way. Some institutions may use a single person (or designee) to review the report, while others may refer cases to other offices depending on the content and location of the alleged violation (e.g., residential cases being referred to a residence life office). The initial review should be based on specific criteria that determine if the matter will be pursued and whether the allegation warrants further investigation. If more information is needed, the case should be referred appropriately (see number 3). It should be noted that a staff member conducting a review may discover that what occurred did indeed happen; however, the allegations do not constitute a violation, or there simply is not enough information to move forward. If the decision is made not to move forward, this action should be documented in the appropriate file or database. Since student conduct processes are intended to be educational, in cases whereby allegations do not warrant formal disciplinary action, it is possible that a student could benefit from an informal follow-up (conversation with a staff member). Discretion is one of the most important functions of the conduct administrator. The ability to evaluate a case and to decide whether it merits further examination, or a referral to the student conduct system itself, is one that can have a major impact on students. It also entails a high level of trust that an institution is placing in a conduct administrator to make those decisions fairly and appropriately.

When staff members at an institution decide whether to bring a case forward, what factors are involved in that decision? It is imperative that those decisions are made with integrity and are devoid of bias, discrimination, and conflicts of interest.

3. *Investigations:* The investigation stage of the student conduct process is of utmost importance to successful outcomes. Thus, it is crucial for the code of conduct to define who has the authority to conduct an investigation. Institutional investigators often include campus police; nonsworn public safety, conduct, or other student affairs staff; or stand-alone investigators. The code of conduct should address how findings from the investigation are referred to the process, who reviews the report (which may be a repeat of the previous step), and how long investigations typically take (which may differ for different types of cases).

4. *Interim action:* In certain circumstances, an incident, after review, requires measures be put into place to ensure the safety of those allegedly involved in the incident as well as the safety of the campus community. In addition, interim action can serve as a preventive measure by lessening the likelihood of compounding the situation with further misconduct. Common measures included within interim action are no contact orders between students; housing relocation; and interim suspensions from housing, classes, or other campus activities. As noted, the code of conduct should spell out the criteria used to determine the need for interim measures, including a threat to the health and safety of a person or community and perhaps the overall severity of the alleged violation. Interim measures should be resolved through the regular student conduct process.

5. *Forum of resolution:* As the case moves forward, a decision must be made as to where and how the case is heard. As discussed in chapter 5, an institution may have multiple avenues available to a student going through the student conduct process. This may include a hearing panel, a meeting with a single conduct administrator, an informal process, or a form of restorative justice or alternative dispute resolution. Whatever those options are, they must be spelled out thoroughly within the code of conduct.

6. *Notice:* Notice is a fundamental element of a conduct process. Students should be provided with some type of written notice to inform them of what institutional policies are in question as well as the date, time, and location for the meeting with the person(s) who will decide whether the student violated the said policies. Beyond this, notice should also provide the accused student with basic information about the date, time, and location of the alleged violation(s) (when available); who else may

have been involved in the incident; as well as substantive information about the conduct process, including information about advisers and student rights in the process. Notice, properly given, makes a process truly accessible to a student. Given how many steps some processes have, in particular before an actual hearing is scheduled, a student may need multiple notices of different types, such as before and during an investigation process. Given the variety seen across conduct processes, methods and appropriate timing of notice will vary by institution.

7. *Hearing:* Earlier in this chapter and elsewhere in this book, issues such as who can attend hearings and the methods used for resolving the student conduct case are discussed. As the word implies, this is an opportunity for the person(s) deciding the case to hear the responding student's response to the alleged violations. It also provides a forum for the conduct administrator or hearing panel to ask questions of the responding student about the alleged incident. This process can be as simple as a conversation between a conduct administrator and a student. It can also be a multiperson hearing panel, with witnesses appearing in person, and with more formalized questions from parties and hearing panelists. The amount of process that is required within a hearing is something that is subject to significant debate and is currently in flux as a result of significant legal decisions. Generally speaking, however, it is prudent to provide more extensive examination of the allegations when the alleged behaviors are of a serious nature and the sanctions that are likely to be imposed will materially impact the status of the respondent. In some cases, such as those that involve sexual violence or may result in a removal from the institution, process elements like cross-examination of parties and witnesses and requirements that parties or witnesses be present for questioning have been required in certain circumstances (*Doe v. Baum*, 2018). The code of conduct should stipulate the guidelines for the hearing process including who is present, the order in which the hearing typically transpires, the typical length of a hearing, and whether the hearing can be extended to subsequent days if necessary.

8. *Decision and sanctions:* The code of conduct should disclose how and when decisions are issued. For some cases, particularly those that are of a lower level of seriousness, decisions may be issued the same day. For many others, decisions will necessitate a further communication or meeting. The code should disclose the time frame that the institution has to issue that decision in writing. Along with that decision, students should have

the opportunity to know the rationale behind a decision (especially in situations where the student contests the alleged violation). Decisions are often delivered along with the assigned sanctions. Sanctions vary widely by institution, including warnings, probationary statuses, educational and restorative sanctions, and suspensions and expulsions. Sanctions are an expression of the institution's conduct philosophy and should relate to the underlying conduct while also reinforcing academic values and goals as they relate to the educational purpose of the conduct process. Whatever sanctions an institution may use should be disclosed in the code of conduct, with a notation as to whether the list is exhaustive. An additional sanctioning factor that should be spelled out in the language of the code of conduct is what discretion conduct administrators have in addressing aggravating and mitigating factors in sanctioning. A common aggravating factor might include misbehavior that is a repeated offense and if the behavior occurs within a short period of time. Other factors can include issues related to bias, provocation, or the impact on the campus community, whereas mitigating factors might include lack of intent to do harm, provocation, and a student's attitude and willingness to accept responsibility during the conduct process.

9. *Appeal:* The appeal, if an institution provides one (as in most circumstances, but note that institutions are not required to provide an appeal) (Ali, 2011), is an area of the process where institutions have great latitude. It is important to emphasize that the appeal is not a rehearing of the original conduct case. Instead, an appeal is intended to provide an opportunity for a student to bring forward specific concerns that may have impacted the result of the original hearing. Accordingly, codes of conduct should include certain conditions that serve as "grounds" for appeal, and these grounds must be met in order for the case to be considered under the appeal process. Common grounds for appeal often include the following:

   a. *Procedural error:* Obviously, if a staff member made a material or substantial error that impacted the result of the conduct process, students should have the opportunity to have that error corrected. However, in order to justify an appeal, the error should materially affect the outcome of the conduct process. Minor errors, while the institution should address and acknowledge them, do not necessarily justify an appeal.

   b. *New information:* If new information that was not available during the original process becomes available for review on appeal, that is an appropriate item for review. Note that information that was known but that a student made a conscious choice not to disclose during the original conduct process does not fall under the grounds of "new information."

   c. *Sanctioning guidelines:* Some institutions provide specific guidance for sanctions, and a decision that deviates from that guidance may be an appropriate ground for appeal.

   d. *Severity of sanction:* Students may appeal if they believe the sanction they received was more severe than their behavior warranted. The difficulty with this ground is that it opens up almost any case to an appeal, as long as a student feels that the sanction is too severe. Establishing clear grounds for appeal makes the process transparent and thus more accessible for students. Clear guidelines also provide a benefit to the institution by creating and defining an appeals structure that is administratively manageable.

10. *Records retention:* Conduct administrators are charged with the responsibility of managing sensitive, complex, and private disciplinary records on a campus. An electronic record management system is often utilized to maintain disciplinary records. Beyond storage and management of the records, the code of conduct should address specific questions regarding records. Most importantly, how long are they kept? Due to the Clery Act requirements, many institutions use seven years as a guideline for conduct record retention (U.S. Department of Education, 2016). However, if an institution notates certain student conduct outcomes on an academic transcript, exceptions should be made for those specific files. The Association for Student Conduct Administration (ASCA) has been a consistent advocate for transcript notation in order to mitigate risk and assist in providing safe campuses (ASCA, 2014). An academic transcript is a permanent record, and any notation on that permanent record needs to retain the records that support the notation. Student access to student conduct records should be governed by an institutional records policy, and, if so, that can be referenced in the code of conduct.

Language and Construction

To assist conduct administrators in this task, several model codes of conduct exist that can provide guidance on language and behaviors that institutions would like to address in their codes. Two significant model codes of conduct are as follows:

1. "A Twenty-First Century Model Student Conduct Code" by Ed Stoner and John W. Lowery (included in the first edition of this book) (Stoner & Lowery, 2004)
2. Model Code Project from the NCHERM Group, which includes guidance for different institution types (Sokolow et al., 2013)

The behaviors that an institution identifies and addresses within the code of conduct can vary depending on the type of institution (public or private); the functional areas of the student conduct system (e.g., the inclusion of academic integrity); and the vision, mission, and values of the institution and conduct system. For example, faith-based institutions may address certain conduct that is not discussed in a code of conduct at a public institution. For institutions that receive federal or state funding, certain behaviors must be addressed in the code of conduct in order to adhere to those federal and state mandates. Harassment, campus disturbances, alcohol and drug use, theft, and property concerns are common behaviors addressed in institutional codes.

The most common demonstration of this principle is the substitution of *responsible* for *guilt* and *guilty*. Conduct administrators are educating students on the responsibility they have for their behaviors, not finding guilt beyond a reasonable doubt. The rise of the term *student conduct* to replace the previously common term *judicial affairs* is another example. While this may look like semantics, language sends a powerful message to those inside and outside campus communities. Utilizing terminology that espouses the trappings of legal proceedings sends a message to students that the conduct process may be adversarial and not conducive to their educational interests. Of equal importance are the messages sent to the outside campus community, particularly the courts themselves. Using language commonly found in the criminal or legal system may subject institutions to the same legal definitions, even if that is not the institution's desire. For example, defining *harassment* or *possession* (in relation to illegal substances) in a novel and unfamiliar way will not only confuse students, but may be rejected by outside authorities. It is well established that when determining the definition of a contested term, those "words will be interpreted as taking their ordinary, contemporary, common meaning" (*Perrin v. United States*, 1979). Using language in institutional codes that differs from established criminal and legal terminology will help institutions alleviate those concerns.

Inclusive Language

Focusing on inclusive language ensures that all members of your community are integrated within the community guidelines promulgated in the code. It means that the institution values statements and policies that reflect the identities of every member of the community. Chapter 6 provides a detailed description of the importance of embedding social justice into conduct work. Simply put, you should avoid gendered and exclusive terms, as well as everyday phrases with racist origins. Since codes typically do not include colloquial phrases, your primary focus may be ensuring language that refers to individuals or groups that is not exclusive, unless you intended to exclude. For example, using the pronouns *he* or *she* to refer to groups of students should be replaced with *student(s)* or *person(s)*. You may also consider using the singular they, which is both grammatically correct and has a long history of use (Baron, 2018). It is also helpful to focus on people-first language, language that emphasizes the person not the diagnosis or characteristic. For example, if your code has occasion to discuss accommodations or students with disabilities, use language that focuses on the person first: *students with disabilities* versus *disabled students*. A similar approach should be taken if you refer to the citizenship status of students; *undocumented students* is a term that focuses on their relationship to us first as students without going into unnecessary conclusions about findings of law or "illegality." As you do this work on your code, do not forget about the other materials distributed by your office; handouts, online materials, and other content should reflect the same care you have taken in crafting an inclusive code. If we keep our focus on serving our students and ensuring they all feel both protected and called to action by our policies, inclusive language fits naturally within these goals.

Flexible Language

In addition to inclusive language, you also want to keep your language flexible, where necessary, to ensure processes can run correctly regardless of staffing or other administrative changes. When assigning responsibility to a role, for example, it may be prudent to consider if this person will always be available to fulfill this role. Circumstances may arise (vacation, leave of absence, job changes, conflict of interest) and flexible language allows for a more adaptable system. Simply noting, for example, a title with a notation of "or designee" anytime you assign a responsibility to a specific person or role provides for a more agile system.

Keeping other language broad or flexible can also help manage unexpected circumstances. Where appropriate, saying what you "typically" do or what you "strive" to do may allow for flexible timelines or leeway if a specific circumstance warrants. When there are factors outside your control, such as availability of witnesses, having a code that is flexible enough to ensure a fair process is important. When bringing this idea forward, be prepared with examples from your institution's history regarding when flexible language was or would have been helpful in avoiding unnecessary procedural modifications.

The process for crafting and revising a student code of conduct can be as individual as the institution itself. The frameworks and principles outlined will provide any conduct administrator at any institution the knowledge to ask the necessary questions to make the revision process that is right for their institution.

References

Ali, R. (2011). *Dear Colleague Letter.* Washington DC: U.S. Department of Education. Retrieved from https://www2.ed.gov/about/offices/list/ocr/letters/colleague-201104.pdf

American University. (2019, April 1). *University policy: Formulation and issuance of university policies.* Retrieved from https://www.american.edu/policies/upload/formulation-and-issuance-of-university-policies.pdf

Association for Student Conduct Administration. (2014). *Transcript notation.* College Station, TX: Author. Retrieved from https://www.theasca.org/files/Publications/Transcript%20Notation%20-%201%20page.pdf

Baron, D. (2018, September 4). A brief history of the singular "they." *Oxford English Dictionary.* Retrieved from https://public.oed.com/blog/a-brief-history-of-singular-they/

Carnegie Mellon University. (2015, April 1). *University policy on policy development.* Retrieved from https://www.cmu.edu/policies/university-policy-development/index.html

College of William & Mary. (2019, June 15). *The honor code and honor councils.* Retrieved from https://www.wm.edu/offices/deanofstudents/services/communityvalues/honorcodeandcouncils/honorcode/index.php

Doe v. Baum, 903 F.3d 575 (United States Court of Appeals for the Sixth Circuit 2018)

Farmer v. Kansas State University, 2:16-CV-02255-JAR-GEB (United State Court of Appeals for the Tenth Circuit March 18, 2019)

Indiana University. (2013, April 14). *Establishing university policies.* (2013, April 14). Retrieved from https://policies.iu.edu/policies/ua-08-establishing-university-policies/index.html

Kreighbaum, A. (2018, November 27). What the DeVos Title IX rule means for misconduct off campus. *Inside Higher Ed.* Retrieved from https://www.insidehighered.com/news/2018/11/27/what-title-ix-plan-would-mean-misconduct-campus

Manning, K. (2013). *One size does not fit all.* New York, NY: Routledge.

New America. (2019, June 15). *Varying degrees of perception versus reality.* Retrieved from http://na-production.s3.amazonaws.com/documents/VaryingDegrees-PvR.pdf

Northeastern University. (2017, January 23). *Policy on policies.* Retrieved from https://www.northeastern.edu/policies/pdfs/Policy_on_Policies.pdf

Pennsylvania State University. (2013, April 24). *AD00 policy on policies.* Retrieved from https://policy.psu.edu/policies/ad00

Perrin v. United States, 444 U.S. 37 (Supreme Court of the United States November 27, 1979). Retrieved from https://scholar.google.com/scholar_case?case=701735113951820806&q=ordinary+meaning+of+the+term&hl=en&as_sdt=6,33

Ripy, T. B. (1999). *Standard of proof in Senate impeachment proceedings.* Washington DC: Congressional Research Service. Retrieved from http://congressionalresearch.com/98-990/document.php

Sokolow, B. A., Lewis, W. S., Schuster, S. K., Fischer, W., Swinton, D. C., & Lowery, J. W. (2013). *Model code project.* The NCHERM Group. Retrieved from https://tngconsulting.com/resources/model-code-project/

State of North Carolina. (2019). Burden of proof and reasonable doubt. *North Carolina Pattern Jury Instructions, General Criminal Volume.* Retrieved from https://www.sog.unc.edu/sites/www.sog.unc.edu/files/pji-master/criminal/101.10.pdf

Stoner, E. (2000). *Reviewing your student discipline policy: A project worth the investment* (Report No. CG-030-188). Chevy Chase, MD: United Educators Insurance Risk Retention Group Retrieved from ERIC Database. (ED444074)

Stoner, E., & Lowery, J. W. (2004). Navigating past the "spirit of insubordination": A twenty-first century model student code of conduct with a model hearing script. *Journal of College and University Law, 31*(1), 1–78.

U.S. Department of Education. (2016). *The handbook for campus safety and security reporting.* Washington DC: Author. Retrieved from https://ifap.ed.gov/eannouncements/attachments/HandbookforCampusSafetyandSecurityReporting.pdf

4

LAWS, POLICIES, AND MANDATES

John Wesley Lowery

Governmental Regulation of Student Conduct

While few college students recognize this, the basic rights that they are afforded through the campus conduct system are largely a result of court decisions handed down before they were even born. The courts first meaningfully addressed the rights enjoyed by public college students under the U.S. Constitution in *Dixon v. Alabama State Board of Education* (1961). The students in *Dixon* were expelled from Alabama State College for Negroes (now Alabama State University) in Montgomery as a result of their participation in civil rights demonstrations in February and March 1960. However, the students only officially learned that they were facing disciplinary action upon being notified that they had been suspended or expelled. Represented by Fred Gray of Birmingham, who was supported by the NAACP Legal Defense and Education Fund, a group of the expelled students brought suit in federal court against the Alabama State Board of Education claiming that their constitutional rights had been violated. After the district court sided with the Board of Education, the students appealed the decision to the U.S. Court of Appeals for the Fifth Circuit. That court ruled that "due process requires notice and some opportunity for [a] hearing before students at a tax-supported college are expelled for misconduct" (*Dixon*, 1961, p. 151). The court concluded,

> In the disciplining of college students there are no considerations of immediate danger to the public, or of peril to the national security, which should prevent the Board from exercising at least the fundamental principles of fairness by giving the accused students notice of the charges and an opportunity to be heard in their own defense. (*Dixon*, 1961, p. 157)

This decision stood in stark contrast to earlier cases in which courts considered challenges to the student conduct process and consistently sided with the institution (e.g., *Anthony v. Syracuse University,* 1928; *Gott v. Berea College*, 1913). While the Supreme Court declined to hear the case when the Alabama State Board of Education appealed the decision, the Supreme Court would later refer to this ruling as a "landmark decision" (*Goss v. Lopez*, 1975, p. 576).

Elements of Due Process at Public Universities

As the court in *Dixon v. Alabama State Board of Education* (1961) noted, the U.S. Constitution serves to define the legal relationship between a public institution and its students. Under the Fifth Amendment, which applies to public institutions through the Fourteenth Amendment, students at public colleges and universities may not "be deprived of life, liberty, or property, without due process of law." In suspension or expulsion cases, both liberty and property interests are at stake for the student. However, the courts have not precisely delineated the exact standards of due process that must be met (Kaplin & Lee, 2014; Silverglate & Gewolb, 2003; Wood, 2004). Considering the general question of due process, the Supreme Court noted, "Due process is an elusive concept. Its exact boundaries are undefinable, and its content varies according to specific factual contexts" (*Hannah v. Larche,* 1960, p. 442). The Supreme Court built on this ruling in *Goss v. Lopez* (1975), requiring only that students "be given *some* kind of notice and afforded *some* kind of hearing" (p. 579). While the *Goss* case involved K–12 students, the principles apply in higher education as well.

While procedural due process is focused on the process, substantive due process is focused on the nature of the institution's rules and the need to avoid the problems of vagueness and overbreadth. Kaplin and Lee (2014) noted that many of these cases have involved claims related to violations of students' rights under the First Amendment. The relationship between the campus conduct system and the First Amendment is discussed in a later chapter of this book.

In *Connally v. General Construction Co.* (1926), the Supreme Court addressed the standards applied to avoid the problem of unconstitutionally vague rules:

> [The rule] must be sufficiently explicit to inform those who are subject to it what conduct on their part will render them liable to its penalties, is a well-recognized requirement, consonant alike with ordinary notions of fair play and the settled rules of law. And a statute [or rule] which either forbids or requires the doing of an act in terms so vague that men of common intel-

ligence must necessarily guess at its meaning and differ as to its application, violates the first essential of due process of law. (p. 391)

However, Kaplin and Lee (2014) noted that seldom have the courts invalidated college rules for vagueness, citing *Soglin v. Kauffman* (1969) as one of the few cases to reach this result. In *Soglin*, the University of Wisconsin's rules simply prohibited "misconduct" (p. 167) without further elaboration. The U.S. Court of Appeals for the Seventh Circuit concluded,

> The inadequacy of the rule is apparent on its face. It contains no clues which could assist a student, an administrator or a reviewing judge in determining whether conduct not transgressing statutes is susceptible to punishment by the University as "misconduct." We do not require university codes of conduct to satisfy the same rigorous standards as criminal statutes. We only hold that expulsion and prolonged suspension may not be imposed on students by a university simply on the basis of allegations of "misconduct" without reference to any preexisting rule which supplies an adequate guide. The possibility of the sweeping application of the standard of "misconduct" to protected activities does not comport with the guarantees of the First and Fourteenth Amendments. The desired end must be more narrowly achieved. (*Soglin*, 1969, pp. 167–168)

The U.S. Court of Appeals for the Eight Circuit in *Esteban v. Central Missouri State College* (1968/1969) reached a similar conclusion even while upholding an institutional rule and warned, "We do not hold that any college regulation, however loosely framed, is necessarily valid" (p. 1089). Silverglate and Gewolb (2003), citing *Woodis v. Westark Community College* (1998) as illustrative, noted that the more obvious it would be to the average person that a behavior was prohibited, the less likely the court would be to void a rule for vagueness. Beyond the issues of the First Amendment discussed in a later chapter, the issues of vagueness and overbreadth are most likely to arise in the context of rules that are unique to the college campus.

After ensuring that the institution's rules are drafted with an appropriate degree of specificity, public colleges and universities must also provide for a campus conduct system that affords students procedural due process. In seeking to determine the content of the due process required in a particular case, the courts seek to balance the rights of the individual and the legitimate interests of the state (Wood, 2004). In *Osteen v. Henley* (1993), the U.S. Court of Appeals for the Seventh Circuit cited the Supreme Court's "canonical test" (p. 226) from *Mathews v. Eldridge* (1976) for determining the process due that requires consideration of the following:

1. The cost of the additional procedure sought
2. The risk of error if it is withheld
3. The consequences of error to the person seeking the procedure

The courts have largely addressed the process required in cases in which students face suspension or expulsion. However, the courts have not carefully outlined the process required in less serious cases. In fact, the courts have even suggested that some cases are so minor as to require "very little or no process" (Silverglate & Gewolb, 2003, p. 22).

Due Process Before the Hearing

Since *Dixon v. Alabama Sate Board of Education* (1961), the courts have expected that students be provided notice of their alleged conduct and which institutional rules or policies they are alleged to have violated. The courts have left institutions considerable leeway in determining how specific the notice must be. The U.S. Court of Appeals for the Fifth Circuit built on its *Dixon* ruling regarding the notice required but did not require the same degree of specificity required in the criminal court system. The court required that the notice be "in sufficient detail to fairly enable them [the accused students] to present a defense" (*Jenkins v. Louisiana State Board of Education*, 1975, p. 1000).

The notice provided to students should also include information regarding the evidence to be presented against them. However, the information provided need only be general. The Supreme Court in *Goss v. Lopez* (1975) was more specific regarding the notice, stating that: "The student first be told what he is accused of doing and what the basis of the accusation is" (p. 582). Silverglate and Gewolb (2003) warned students, "While committed to appropriate notice in theory, the courts, in practice, unfortunately find almost all notice appropriate" (p. 55). However, in at least some cases, the courts have required new hearings when the notice was insufficient, including when students were found responsible for violations not included in the notice (*Fellheimer v. Middlebury College*, 1994) or when evidence was presented of which they were not made aware (*Weidemann v. SUNY College at Cortland*, 1992).

The courts have not consistently held that the Constitution requires a specific number of days prior to the hearing that notice must be provided—only that the notice be provided in advance (Kaplin & Lee, 2014; Stoner & Cerminara, 1990; Stoner & Lowery, 2004). The notice requirement has varied from as few as 2 days (*Jones v. State Board of Education*, 1968/1969; *Nash v. Auburn University*, 1987) to as long as 10 days (*Esteban v. Central Missouri State College*, 1968/1969). Kaplin and Lee (2014) noted that most courts have identified some period of time between these outer limits, but also required institutions to comply with their policies regarding the timing of this notice. In *Goss v. Lopez* (1975), the Supreme Court held that in K–12 cases "there need be no delay between the time 'notice' is given and the time of the hearing. In the great majority of cases the disciplinarian may informally discuss the alleged misconduct with the student minutes after it has occurred" (p. 582). This approach is most likely to be defensible in higher education for less serious offenses in which suspension or expulsion is not a possible consequence. Silverglate and Gewolb (2003) noted regarding higher education, "In the case of less serious misconduct, notice may be oral and may be given immediately before the informal give and take between the student and administrator that fulfills the minimal constitutional requirement for a hearing" (p. 54).

Due Process During the Hearing

The fundamental right that public colleges and universities must provide for during the hearing is

> that the hearing provide students with an opportunity to speak in their own defense and explain their side of the story. . . . But courts usually will accord students the right to hear the evidence against them and to present oral testimony or, at minimum, written statements from witnesses. Formal rules of evidence need not be followed. Cross-examination, the right to counsel, the right to a transcript, and an appellate procedure have generally not been constitutional essentials, but where institutions have voluntarily provided these procedures, courts have often cited them approvingly as enhancers of the hearing's fairness. (Kaplin & Lee, 2014, p. 594)

Beyond the opportunity to be heard, students have also raised other legal concerns and courts have reached varying conclusions regarding specific aspects of the hearing, including allegations of bias by board members, a right to consult counsel, and a right to cross-examine witnesses and complainants.

Students have also claimed that their due process rights were violated by public institutions of higher education when members of the hearing body were allegedly biased against them. However, the courts have been generally unreceptive to these claims. In *Gorman v. University of Rhode Island* (1988), the U.S. Court of Appeals for the First Circuit noted, "Generally, in examining administrative proceedings, the presumption [regarding bias] favors the administrators, and the burden is upon the party [the student] challenging the action to produce evidence sufficient to rebut this presumption" (p. 15). The court noted that merely having prior knowledge of a case or working in a particular office did not give rise to bias, observing, "In the intimate setting of a college or university, prior contact between the participants is likely, and does not *per se* indicate bias or partiality" (*Gorman v. University of Rhode Island*, 1988, p. 15). A related claim often raised by students relates to the multiple roles played by university administrators. Courts have repeatedly rejected this claim (*Gorman v. University of Rhode Island*, 1988; *Nash v. Auburn University*, 1987; *Osteen v. Henley*, 1993). In *Nash v. Auburn* (1987), a student board member had specific knowledge of the case in question, but absent specific evidence of bias, the court did not find the board member's participation in the hearing violated the accused student's rights. In either case, the burden rests with the student to demonstrate the existence of bias, as "the disciplinary committee, which included a student representative, is entitled to a presumption of honesty and integrity, absent a showing of actual bias, such as animosity, prejudice, or a personal or financial stake in the outcome" (*Holert v. University of Chicago*, 1990, p. 1301; see also *Hill v. Board of Trustees of Michigan State University*, 2001).

A more complicated question is the circumstances under which a student could have a right to consult with an attorney during the hearing and what role the attorney may play. The courts have "never recognized any absolute right to counsel in school disciplinary proceedings" (*Donohue v. Baker*, 1997, p. 146). However, the courts have recognized limited circumstances in which students might have a right to consult an attorney. In *Gabrilowitz v. Newman* (1978), the U.S. Court of Appeals for the First Circuit recognized the right to consult counsel when the student was facing criminal charges resulting from the same set of facts. However, the accused student was entitled to receive advice, but not the active representation, of counsel regarding his pending criminal case during the disciplinary hearing. In *Osteen v. Henley* (1993), the U.S. Court of Appeals for the Seventh Circuit concluded upon reviewing these issues that

> [t]he most interesting question is whether there is a right to counsel, somehow derived from the due process clause of the Fourteenth Amendment, in student disciplinary proceedings. An oldish case (by the standards of constitutional law at any rate) says yes, but the newer cases say no, at most the student has a right to get the advice of a lawyer; the lawyer need not be allowed to participate in the proceeding in the usual way of trial counsel, as by examining and cross-examining witnesses and addressing the tribunal. Especially when the student faces potential criminal charges (Osteen was charged with two counts of aggravated battery; the record is silent on the disposition of the charges), it is at least arguable that the due process clause entitles him to consult a lawyer, who might for example advise him to take the Fifth Amendment. (p. 225, internal citations omitted)

The court in *Osteen* concluded that a requirement that the student's attorney be allowed to play an active role in the disciplinary hearing could be detrimental. Most recently, in *Holmes v. Poskanzer* (2007), the court concluded, "Due process does not require that Plaintiffs be represented by counsel to perform the traditional function of a trial lawyer and convert the proceedings into the mold of adversary litigation" (p. 22) (see also *Nguyen v. University of Louisville*, 2006). The other two situations in which any court found an affirmative right for a student to be accompanied by his attorney was when the university was represented by an attorney or a senior law student only months before graduating from law school, as in the case of *French v. Bashful* (1969), or "the hearing [was] subject to complex rules of evidence or procedure" (*Jaska v. University of Michigan*, 1984, p. 1252). As noted later in this chapter, under the Clery Act (as amended by VAWA), the institution cannot limit the choice of advisers in cases involving allegations of sexual assault, domestic violence, dating violence, and stalking. However, the institution can limit the role of adviser as long as those restrictions are applied equally to both parties. Over the course of the past decade, several states have also passed legislation that requires the opportunity for accused students to be actively represented by attorneys in at least some student conduct hearings, a trend that began in North Carolina in 2013.

The last major issue regarding due process during the hearing relates to the cross-examination of witnesses, especially those witnesses presenting information that is adverse to the accused student's case. Kaplin and Lee (2014) have noted that the right of cross-examination is not generally acknowledged as a constitutional requirement (see also *Dixon v. Alabama State Board of Education*, 1961; *Winnick v. Manning*, 1972). In *Donohue v. Baker* (1997), the court noted that while generally "the right to cross-examine witnesses has not been considered an essential requirement of due process in school disciplinary proceedings . . . [i]f a case is essentially one of credibility, the cross-examination of witnesses might [be] essential to a fair hearing" (p. 147). The U.S. Court of Appeals for the Eleventh Circuit concluded, "There was no denial of appellants' constitutional rights to due process by their inability to question the adverse witnesses in the usual, adversarial manner" (*Nash v. Auburn University*, 1987, p. 664; see also *Jaksa v. University of Michigan*, 1984/1986). In systems that allow for some limited form of cross-examination, some commentators (Stoner & Cerminara, 1990; Stoner & Lowery, 2004) have recommended an indirect form of questioning during which questions by the accused student are directed through the judicial board. In *Donohue v. Baker* (1997), the court specifically accepted this limited form of cross-examination, concluding,

At the very least, in light of the disputed nature of the facts and the importance of witness credibility in this case, due process required that the panel permit the plaintiff to hear all evidence against him and to direct questions to his accuser through the panel. (p. 147)

Related to the issue of cross-examination of witnesses is the use of a visual barrier between the accused student and a witness. These barriers are most commonly used in sexual assault cases and are for the purpose of preventing direct visual contact, rather than shielding the identity of the witness (Stoner & Lowery, 2004). The court in *Cloud v. Boston University* (1983) specifically approved the use of visual barriers as adequately providing for a student's due process rights, and the court in *Gomes v. University of Maine System* (2004) seemed generally accepting of some use of screens in sexual assault cases.

In the wake of the 2011 "Dear Colleague" letter, a number of college students who had been expelled under disciplinary procedures revised in the response to the Obama administration's guidance have sued their institutions. Many of these students have claimed that the disciplinary process discriminated against male students, violating Title IX, but were unsuccessful in those efforts. However, when institutions have failed to follow their own policies, the courts have been quite willing to step (e.g., *Doe v. Brown University*, 2016; *Prasad v. Cornell University*, 2016). In a number of cases, students' constitutional due process and fundamental fairness claims were well received by the courts (e.g., *Doe v. Alger*, 2016; *Doe v. Rector and Visitors of George Mason University*, 2016; *Doe v. University of Southern California*, 2016). With a clear-enough fact pattern, the courts have also ruled that specific administrators or the system itself was biased against accused students (*Doe v. Brown University*, 2016; *Doe v. Ohio State University*, 2017; *Sterrett v. Cowan*, 2015). Among the most significant cases are several from the U.S. Court of Appeals for the Sixth Circuit addressing the role of cross-examination in some form (*Doe v. Baum*, 2018; *Doe v. University of Cincinnati*, 2017). Often the disciplinary process employed in these cases bore little resemblance to those typically used in suspension- or expulsion-level cases. It remains to be seen whether the courts will be as willing to apply these standards to the more traditional models.

Due Process After the Hearing

After the conduct of the hearing itself, there remain due process considerations that must also be considered. In determining whether the student violated the code of student conduct, the decision must be based on the information presented during the hearing and rise to the level of the standard of proof established by the institution. The courts have not imposed any specific standard of proof that colleges and universities must employ in the student conduct systems. The most commonly used standard of proof in campus student conduct systems is a preponderance of the evidence or a more-likely-than-not standard. The courts do not generally rehear cases when students bring lawsuits challenging the outcome of the campus judicial system. The courts instead require that the decision be supported by substantial evidence, which is an even lower standard (*Papachristou v. University of Tennessee*, 2000; Silverglate & Gewolb, 2003; Stoner & Cerminara, 1990; Stoner & Lowery, 2004).

Once a decision has been reached in the case, the courts will require that the institution notify the student in writing, at least in serious cases, of its decision. The courts have not generally required a specific content beyond some brief explanation of the reasons for its decision (*Jaksa v. Regents of University of Michigan*, 1984/1986). Although in *Jaksa* (1984/1986), the court noted that the written decision did not require the degree of detail required under the federal code of civil procedure (see also *Herman v. University of South Carolina, 1971/1972*). In *Jaksa* (1984/1986), the student also claimed the failure to create a transcript of the hearing had violated his due process rights, an argument that was soundly rejected by that court and many others (see also *Due v. Florida A&M University*, 1961; *Gorman v. University of Rhode Island*, 1988; *Schaer v. Brandeis University*, 2000; *Trahms v. Columbia University*, 1997). In *Jaksa* (1984), the court noted, "While this case illustrates the wisdom of recording such hearings, it is clear that the Constitution does not impose such a requirement" (p. 1252). A final posthearing consideration is the question of the right to appeal. Most commentators (Kaplin & Lee, 2014; Silverglate & Gewolb, 2003; Stoner & Cerminara, 1990; Stoner & Lowery, 2004; Wood, 2004) agree that students have no constitutional right to an appeal, but an institution may create such a right (see also *Nash v. Auburn*, 1975; *Winnick v. Manning*, 1972). Stoner and Lowery (2014) further encouraged institutions to establish an appeal process to promote "an image of fairness" (p. 60).

Institutional Promises

Beyond those minimal due process requirements established by the courts, public institutions will also be expected to meet those contractual promises made through their student handbooks for other documents. In fact, many institutions have gone far beyond these minimal procedural due process requirements and created systems that more closely mirrored the criminal courts (Dannells, 1977, 1990, 1991, 1997; Dannells & Lowery, 2004).

Writing in 1987, Travelstead described the impact of *Dixon v. Alabama State Board of Education* (1961) and the cases that followed on the practice of student conduct:

> The courts have intervened when the constitutional rights of students have been abridged or ignored. This is only to be expected. Much of the complaining about excessive proceduralism and legalism is hollow. The excessive proceduralism, where it exists, has largely been caused by the institutions themselves. (p. 15)

Gehring (2001) argued that many institutions have "unnecessarily formalized their procedures" (p. 477). These institutions seemed to have forgotten the important advice offered by Justice Blackmun in *Esteban v. Central Missouri State University* (1969) who wrote, "It is not sound to draw an analogy between student discipline and criminal procedure" (p. 1088). Stoner (2000) advised, "This unfortunate situation is often compounded by misunderstandings about criminal law and why criminal principles are the wrong perspective from which to understand a college's efforts to deal with student misconduct" (p. 7). Regarding the impact of this trend, Dannells (1997) concluded, "This trend—often called 'creeping legalism' or proceduralism—undermined the informal and uniquely educational element of college student discipline" (p. 69). This is not to suggest that all provisions for student rights not required by the courts are inappropriate or ill-advised, but to rather to caution institutions to bear in mind the fundamental educational purpose of the student conduct system. Pavela and Pavela (2012) spoke what they frame as "the ethical and educational imperative of due process" (p. 626).

The Process Due at Private Institutions

Private institutions are not legally required to provide students the rights required at public colleges and universities by the Constitution unless they are engaged in state action. In the absence of legal relationship between the state and a private institution to administer a public program (*Powe v. Miles,* 1968), the courts have rejected student's claims regarding state action by private institutions and the student conduct system (e.g., *Albert v. Carovano,* 1988, *Cummings v. Virginia School of Cosmetology,* 1979; *Grossner v. Trustees of Columbia,* 1968). The courts instead consider the contractual relationship to determine what procedural rights must be afforded the private college student. Stoner and Lowery (2004) described the courts' expectations for the private colleges and universities:

Although twenty-first century courts no longer merely rubberstamp college or university decisions, as they once may have done under the doctrine of *in loco parentis*, courts continue to afford institutions of higher education a great deal of discretion. Nevertheless, when colleges and universities do specify the process they will follow for student discipline, courts expect them to follow the process they select. (p. 10)

A New York court limited its scrutiny of the disciplinary actions of a private college to "determining whether the university substantially adhered to its own published rules and guidelines for disciplinary proceedings so as to ascertain whether its actions were arbitrary or capricious" (*In re Rensselaer Soc. of Eng. v. Rensselaer Poly. Inst.*, 1999, p. 295) (see also *Boehm v. University of Pa. Sch. of Veterinary Med.*, 1990; *Holert v. University of Chicago*, 1990; *Nguyen v. University of Louisville*, 2006; *Slaughter v. Brigham Young University*, 1975). Furthermore, the courts have noted that these deviations from published rules must be substantial before the courts will intervene on behalf of students. Silverglate and Gewolb (2003) warned students considering lawsuits against institutions for failing to follow their own rules that "they [the courts] tend to give universities a certain leeway if they have followed their rules in a general way, even if not to the letter" (p. 37).

Private institutions are not required by the U.S. Constitution to provide the basic requirements of due process that public colleges and universities must offer. However, various authors (Kaplin & Lee, 2014; Pavela, 2000; Stoner & Cerminera, 1990; Stoner & Lowery, 2004) have argued that private institutions would be well advised to provide these basic rights including the following:

- The right to have your case heard under regular procedures used for all similar cases
- The right to receive notice of the charges against you
- The right to hear a description of the university's evidence against you
- The right to present your side of the story to an impartial panel (Silverglate & Gewolb, 2003, p. 6)

Stoner and Lowery (2004) noted that the private institutions should avoid using phrases such as due process or fundamental fairness, suggesting that "a better practice is to state exactly what process is provided without using such platitudes" (p. 11). In several cases (*Ackerman v. College of the Holy Cross*, 2003; *Fellheimer v. Middlebury College*, 1994; *Goodman v. Bowdoin College*, 2001), the courts have overturned campus disciplinary action by private institutions that promised to afford students *fundamental fairness* but failed to effectively define that term, after concluding that the institutions failed to meet the courts' expectations for fundamental fairness.

Federal Laws and Student Conduct

Unlike constitutional requirements that apply only to public institutions, compliance with federal laws that impact the practice of student conduct apply with equal force to both public and private institutions of higher education. Civil rights laws such as Title IX of the Educational Amendments of 1972 require compliance of all institutions of higher education, which are recipients of federal financial assistance. This includes both direct financial support from the federal government to the institution of higher education as well as the indirect support to institutions in the form of federal financial aid for students (*Bob Jones University v. Johnson,* 1974; *Grove City v. Bell,* 1984). Compliance with such laws as FERPA and the Campus Security Act is required of all institutions of higher education that are participants in Title IV programs of the Higher Education Act, which includes the various federal student aid programs. While Hunter and Gehring (2005) identified more than 185 federal laws that affect higher education institutions, this chapter will focus on a select group of federal laws that most directly impact the practice of student conduct, including Title IX of the Educational Amendments of 1972, the Jeanne Clery Disclosure of Campus Security Policy and Campus Crime Statistics Act, the Family Educational Rights and Privacy Act (FERPA), and the Drug-Free Schools and Communities Act.

Title IX of the Educational Amendments of 1972

Under Title IX of the Educational Amendments of 1972, institutions of higher education cannot exclude any person "from participating in, be denied the benefits of, or subjected to discrimination under any educational program or activity receiving federal financial assistance." The Supreme Court has ruled that sexual harassment is a form of discrimination under Title IX in several cases (*Davis v. Monroe County Board of Education,* 1999; *Franklin v. Gwinnett County Public Schools,* 1992; *Gebser v. Lago Vista Independent School District,* 1998). In *Davis* (1999), the U.S. Supreme Court addressed the question of student-on-student sexual harassment. The Court ruled that institutions could be held legally liable for student-on-student sexual harassment when the institution has "substantial control over both the harasser and the context in which the known harassment occurs" (p. 645) and the harassment is "severe, pervasive, and objectively offensive that it effectively bars the victim's access to an educational opportunity or benefit" (p. 633).

The Court further limited institutional liability by applying its standard from *Gebser* (1998), which limited liability to those cases in which a school official who has authority to take corrective action has actual knowledge of the harassment and responds with "deliberate indifference" (p. 290). Under these standards, Kaplin and Lee (2014) warned that the courts offer "scant opportunity for student victims of harassment to succeed with Title IX damages actions against educational institutions (p. 543). However, the U.S. Department of Education has established a much lower threshold for determining whether an institution has violated Title IX. An institution can be found to have violated Title IX "if the school knows or reasonably should know about the harassment, the school is responsible for taking immediate effective action to eliminate the hostile environment and prevent its recurrence" (Cantu, 2001, p. 12, internal citations omitted).

While the courts have not made significant changes in Title IX liability in recent years, the U.S. Department of Education's guidance and enforcement of Title IX represents the area that has changed most significantly since the publication of the first edition of this work. The U.S. Department of Education's Office for Civil Rights (OCR) demands that the grievance procedures for resolving sexual harassment and sexual violence must be "prompt and equitable" (Jackson, 2017b, p. 2). Institutions can use the student conduct process for this purpose as long as this standard and the other elements of the guidance are met. A fundamental expectation of OCR is that the resolution process must afford both parties the same rights.

In September 2017, Candice Jackson, acting assistant secretary for civil rights, issued a new Dear Colleague Letter on campus sexual misconduct. The Office for Civil Rights withdrew the 2011 Dear Colleague Letter on sexual violence (Ali, 2011) and the 2014 questions and answers on Title IX and sexual violence (Lhamon, 2014). In comments echoing those of Secretary of Education Betsy DeVos earlier in the month, Jackson (2017a) criticized the Obama Administration's guidance for depriving "many students—both accused students denied fair process and victims denied an adequate resolution of their complaints" (p. 2).

The U.S. Department of Education also announced plans to undertake a formal rulemaking process to develop new Title IX guidance, which includes an opportunity for public comment. The Notice of Proposed Rulemaking (NPRM) was published in the *Federal Register* more than a year later (Nondiscrimination on the Basis of Sex in Education Programs or Activities Receiving Federal Financial Assistance, 2018). When the comment period closed two months later, the Office for Civil Rights had received more than 120,000 comments on the proposed regulations.

Until the new regulations were finalized, institutions were instructed to follow the 2001 *Revised Sexual Harassment Guidance* (Cantu, 2001) and the *Q&A on Campus Sexual Misconduct* (Jackson, 2017b) issued with the letter. This document addressed a number of points relevant to the adjudication of sexual assault complaints:

- OCR moved from the 60-day time frame for the case resolution in the 2011 DCL to requiring that institutions make "good faith" (Jackson, 2017b, p. 3) efforts to resolve the cases in a timely fashion.
- The Q&A emphasized repeatedly that the investigatory process must be fair and impartial.
- In regard to training, OCR stressed, "Training materials or investigative techniques and approaches that apply sex stereotypes or generalizations may violate Title IX and should be avoided so that the investigation proceeds objectively and impartially" (Jackson, 2017b, p. 4).
- OCR specifically stated that upon opening an investigation that may lead to disciplinary action the responding party should be notified in writing of their alleged misconduct, "including sufficient details and with sufficient time to prepare a response before any initial interview. Sufficient details include the identities of the parties involved, the specific section of the code of conduct allegedly violated, the precise conduct allegedly constituting the potential violation, and the date and location of the alleged incident" (Jackson, 2017b, p. 4).
- OCR offered institutions the opportunity to resolve cases using informal resolution models, including mediation. However, mediation is still explicitly prohibited in sexual assault cases under the 2001 *Revised Sexual Harassment Guidance*. While there is considerable interest in the use of restorative justice within the field, greater clarity is clearly need in this area (Wilgus & Lowery, 2018).
- OCR also allowed institutions to use either a preponderance of the evidence or a clear and convincing evidence standard in sexual violence cases but prohibited institutions from using a lower standard for sexual violence cases than other student cases.
- OCR demanded that both parties must have equal access to information to be used in the hearing and that those involved in the investigation should be "free of actual or reasonably perceived conflicts of interest and biases for or against any party" (Jackson, 2017b, p. 4).
- The Q&A also offered institutions several options regarding appeals. Institutions could limit appeals to just the responding party or allow

both parties to appeal, in which case the right to appeal would need to be equal.

Few institutions made significant changes to policy in response to the *Q&A on Campus Sexual Misconduct* (Jackson, 2017b) and instead took a wait-and-see approach for the outcome of the rulemaking process.

The Notice of Proposed Rulemaking (Nondiscrimination on the Basis of Sex in Education Programs or Activities Receiving Federal Financial Assistance, 2018) largely followed the *Q&A on Campus Sexual Misconduct* (Jackson, 2017b). However, there were some significant differences. In the NPRM (2018), the U.S. Department of Education returned to a model that required the same appeal rights for both parties. The proposed regulations would require a live hearing with direct cross-examination by the parties' advisers in Title IX cases. In its comments, the American Council on Education (ACE, 2019) warned that the proposed rules would demand "highly legalistic, court-like processes that conflict with the fundamental educational missions of our institutions" (p. 8). Multiple higher education groups, including ACE (2019) and NASPA (2019), were dismayed by the repeated use of the term *due process* to describe the Title IX process at both public and private institutions. A number of groups also expressed concern that the NPRM significantly narrowed the definition of *sexual harassment* under Title IX for the purposes of the U.S. Department of Education's enforcement. Until the final regulations are issued, it is difficult to accurately predict what shape the final regulations will take; furthermore, advocacy groups will likely sue the administration in federal court, which may further delay implementation.

Jeanne Clery Disclosure of Campus Security Policy and Campus Crime Statistics Act

In 1990, Congress passed the Crime Awareness and Campus Security Act. The legislation was renamed in 1998 to the Jeanne Clery Disclosure of Campus Security Policy and Campus Crime Statistics Act, in memory of Jeanne Clery who was murdered in her Lehigh University residence hall room by another student in 1986. After her death, her parents, Howard and Connie Clery, formed security on campus and pushed for campus safety legislation at the state and federal level. A full consideration of the requirements of the Jeanne Clery Disclosure of Campus Security Policy and Campus Crime Statistics Act is beyond the scope of this chapter, and readers interested in learning more about all of the requirements of the law are encouraged to review *The Handbook for Campus Crime Reporting* (U.S. Department of Education, 2016). This chapter considers only those requirements of the law that have the greatest relevance to campus conduct practice. The Clery Act was significantly expanded by the 2013 Violence Against Women Act (VAWA) reauthorization.

One of the core requirements of the Jeanne Clery Disclosure of Campus Security Policy and Campus Crime Statistics Act is the publication of the Annual Security Report, which is distributed to all current students and employees and a summary is provided to prospective students and employees. The Annual Security Report contains summaries of a host of institutional policies relating to campus security including information regarding who on campus should report crimes. Institutions must provide specific information regarding sexual assault, domestic violence, dating violence, and stalking and the disciplinary procedures used to address these allegations, including the following:

- Notification to victims about options for, available assistance in, and how to request changes to academic, living, transportation and working situations or protective measures. The institution must make such accommodations or provide such protective measures if the victim requests them and if they are reasonably available
- A description of each type of disciplinary proceeding used by the institution; the steps, anticipated timelines, and decision-making process for each type of disciplinary proceeding; how to file a disciplinary complaint; and how the institution determines which type of proceeding to use based on the circumstances of an allegation of dating violence, domestic violence, sexual assault or stalking
- A description of the standard of evidence that will be used during any institutional disciplinary proceeding arising from an allegation of dating violence, domestic violence, sexual assault or stalking
- A list of all the possible sanctions that the institution may impose following the results of any institutional disciplinary proceeding for an allegation of dating violence, domestic violence, sexual assault or stalking
- A description of the range of protective measures that the institution may offer to the victim following an allegation of dating violence, domestic violence, sexual assault or stalking
- A provision that the proceedings will include a prompt, fair, and impartial process from the initial investigation to the final result
- Proceedings conducted by officials who, at a minimum, receive annual training on the issues related to dating violence, domestic violence, sexual assault and stalking and on how to conduct an investigation and

hearing process that protects the safety of the victims and promotes accountability

- A provision for the accuser and the accused to have the same opportunities to have others present during any institutional disciplinary proceeding, including the opportunity to be accompanied to any related meeting or proceeding by an adviser of their choice
- No limit on the choice of adviser or presence for either the accuser or the accused in any meeting or institutional disciplinary proceeding; however, the institution may establish restrictions regarding the extent to which the adviser may participate in the proceedings, as long as the restrictions apply equally to both parties
- Requirement of simultaneous notification, in writing, to both the accuser and the accused of
  - the result of any institutional disciplinary proceeding that arises from an allegation of dating violence, domestic violence, sexual assault or stalking;
  - the institution's procedures for the accused and the victim to appeal the result of the institutional disciplinary proceeding, if such procedures are available;
  - any change to the result; and
  - when such results become final. (U.S. Department of Education, 2016)

These requirements will demand that institutions ensure that their codes of conduct and practices for students and employees reflect these expectations.

Beyond the policy statements, the Annual Security Report must include statistical information regarding crimes on campus for the preceding three calendar years in the following geographic areas: on campus, residence halls, non-campus buildings and property, and public property. The statistics must include reports made to campus security authorities or local law enforcement of murder/non-negligent manslaughter; negligent manslaughter; sex offenses (rape, fondling, statutory rape, and incest); robbery; aggravated assault; burglary; motor vehicle theft; and arson. Furthermore, when these crimes were motivated by a bias (race, religion, sexual orientation, gender, gender identity, ethnicity, national origin, and disability) as well as larceny-theft, simple assault, intimidation, and destruction/damage/vandalism of property, they must be reported as hate crimes. Student conduct administrators are all considered campus security authorities as "official[s] of an institution who ha[ve] significant responsibility for student and campus activities, including, but not limited to, student housing, student discipline and campus judicial proceeding" (U.S. Department of Education, 2016, p. 4-2). Statistical information is also included regarding arrests and referrals for disciplinary action (not resulting in arrests) for violations of liquor laws, drug laws, and illegal weapons possession. The 2013 reauthorization of the Violence Against Women Act added a requirement for reporting statistics for domestic violence, dating violence, and stalking (U.S. Department of Education, 2016).

Institutions are required to maintain records to demonstrate their compliance with the Jeanne Clery Disclosure of Campus Security Policy and Campus Crime Statistics Act for a period of three years after compliance. Because statistics are included in the next three years' Annual Security Report, this effectively means that records to support the statistics must be maintained for seven years (U.S. Department of Education, 2016). It is important that the student conduct office have a system in place for maintaining records to support the statistics originating through the conduct system included in the Annual Security Report.

Family Educational Rights and Privacy Act (FERPA)

The Family Educational Rights and Privacy Act was passed in 1974 as part of the larger Educational Amendments of 1974. Under FERPA, *education records* were defined as "those records, files, documents, and other materials which contain information directly related to a student; and are maintained by an educational agency or institution or by a person acting for such agency or institution." FERPA created three primary rights for parents and eligible students:

1. Right to inspect and review/right to access education records
2. Right to challenge the content of education records
3. Right to consent to the disclosure of education records

It is important to recognize that there are numerous exceptions within the regulations to allow the release of a student's education records without consent. These include releases to school officials with legitimate educational interest, releases to parents of dependent students, and releases in compliance with subpoenas. Since 1974, FERPA has been amended numerous times and many of the recent amendments are directly related to student disciplinary records (Family Policy Compliance Office, 2002).

The first major amendment to FERPA related to student conduct came in 1990 when Congress passed the Student Right-to-Know and Campus Security Act. The legislation amended FERPA to clearly allow colleges and universities to share the final results of a campus disciplinary proceeding with the victim of an alleged crime of violence or nonforcible sex offenses

(Lowery, 1998, 2000, 2004). Congress again amended FERPA in 1992 to exclude campus law enforcement unit records from the definition of *education records*. Some groups argued that this change excluded student disciplinary records from the definition as well. In issuing regulations, the U.S. Department of Education clearly stated that disciplinary records were not excluded from the definition of education records.

Congress again made significant changes to FERPA when passing the Higher Education Amendments of 1998. The first of these changes allowed colleges and universities to release information to the parents of a student under the age of 21 when the institution determined that the student had violated any local, state, or federal laws or campus policy governing the use of alcohol or other drugs (Lowery, 2005). In the years following this change, many institutions revised their policies to allow for parental notification, and this remains an area needing further research (Gehring, Lowery, & Palmer, 2012, 2013; Lowery, Palmer, & Gehring, 2005; Palmer, Lohman, Gehring, Carlson, & Garrett, 2001; Palmer, Lowery, Wilson, & Gehring, 2003). The second, and much broader, change allowed the public release of the final results of a student disciplinary proceeding if the accused student was found responsible of a violation, which was a "crime of violence." The regulations define *final results* as

> means a decision or determination, made by an honor court or council, committee, commission, or other entity authorized to resolve disciplinary matters within the institution. The disclosure of final results must include only the name of the student, the violation committed, and any sanction imposed by the institution against the student.

While this amendment did not require the release, public institutions in many states could be compelled to release the information under open records laws (Lowery, 2000; also see *Board of Governors of Southwest Missouri State University* v. *Patrick M. Nolan,* 1999).

In the 1990s, lawsuits were brought in several state courts seeking access to student disciplinary records under state open records laws. In *John Doe v. Red & Black Publishing, Inc.* (1993) and *State ex rel The Miami Student v. Miami University* (1997), the Georgia and Ohio supreme courts ordered the release of student disciplinary records under those states' open record laws. However, courts in Louisiana (*Shreveport Professional Chapter of the Society of Professional Journalists and Michelle Millhollon v. Louisiana State University,* 1994), North Carolina (*DTH v. University of North Carolina at Chapel Hill,* 1998), and Vermont (*Burlington Free Press v. University of Vermont,* 2001) refused to grant access under those states' open records laws. These issues would move to federal court in 1998 when the U.S. Department of Justice brought suit against Miami University and The Ohio State University to block those institutions from complying with Ohio's supreme court decision from the previous year. Ultimately, the U.S. Court of Appeals for the Sixth Circuit would determine the following:

- FERPA prohibits the release of education records
- Disciplinary records are education records
- There is no First Amendment right of access to student disciplinary records
- Student disciplinary records are not criminal in nature
- Public access might be harmful to the disciplinary process
- The public interest in crime prevention does not require open records (*United States v. Miami University*, 2002)

The court also noted that the fundamental purpose of the campus conduct system was educational and public access would not support that goal. The court observed, "We find that public access will not aid in the functioning of traditionally closed student disciplinary proceedings" (p. 823). It is also important to note that the Supreme Court ruled that FERPA did not afford students a private right of action to sue for violations of the law (*Gonzaga v. Doe*, 2002).

Drug-Free Schools and Communities Act

Under the Drug-Free Schools and Communities Act, institutions are required to distribute an annual notification to current students and employees, which includes standards of conduct related to alcohol and other drugs and disciplinary sanctions for violations of those standards. These standards of conduct must "clearly prohibit, at a minimum, the unlawful possession, use, or distribution of illicit drugs and alcohol by students and employees" (U.S. Department of Education, 2006, p. 7). Institutions are also expected to state that the institution "will impose disciplinary sanctions on students and employees for violations of standards of conduct" (U.S. Department of Education, 2006, p. 7). In addition to the annual notification, institutions are required to complete a biennial review, which in part considers whether the institution "enforces sanctions for violating standards of conduct consistently" (U.S. Department of Education, 2006, p. 13). With the passage of the 2008 Higher Education Opportunity Act, institutions were also required to determine the number of alcohol- and drug-related deaths that occurred on campus and the sanctions imposed as a result of the biennial review. In order for an institution to meets it obligations under Drug-Free Schools and Communities Act, student conduct administrators must be involved in revising the annual notification as well as preparing the biennial review.

For most of the history of the Drug-Free Schools and Communities Act, the U.S. Department of Education's enforcement efforts have been limited (DeBowes, 2016). In 2012, the Inspector General concluded the U.S. Department of Education's "oversight was not appropriate, because OPE [Office of Postsecondary Education] did not perform any oversight activities" (p. 3). In the years after the Inspective General's report, the U.S. Department of Education has significantly increased its enforcement (Custer & Kent, 2019). Between 2014 and 2018, the department fined 36 institutions of higher education a combined $739,000 (Custer & DeBowes, 2019).

Conclusion

Since the U.S. Court of Appeals for the Fifth Circuit ruled in the landmark case of *Dixon v. Alabama State Board of Education* (1961), the courts have consistently held that students at public colleges and universities are entitled to due process protections, although these due process protections differ greatly from those enjoyed by criminal defendants. While there are differences between the requirements mandated by the various federal courts of appeals, the general requirements are the establishment of a student conduct system through which cases are adjudicated, notice to students of the charges they are facing, the right to know the evidence against them, and the opportunity to present their side of the story to an unbiased panel or hearing officer (Silverglate & Gewolb, 2003). Student conduct administrators should view these requirements as the framework on which the student conduct system is based. When considering additional rights to afford students, institutions should balance student rights with the need to maintain the core educational purpose of the student conduct system and avoid the creation of an adversarial system. The courts have noted that an adversarial system runs counter to this educational purpose (*Osteen v. Henley*, 1993). Private colleges and universities should strongly consider affording students at least the minimum rights required at public colleges and universities. Beyond these requirements, public and private colleges and universities must also ensure that all of the contractual obligations established through the conduct code are met. Beyond these procedural considerations, public and private institutions must also be concerned with meeting the institution's requirements under federal laws such as FERPA, the Clery Act, Title IX, and the Drug-Free Schools and Communities Act.

References

Ackerman v. College of the Holy Cross, 16 Mass.L.Rep. 108 (Super.Ct.Mass. 2003)

Albert v. Carovano, 851 F.2d 561 (2d Cir. 1988)

Ali, R. (2011, April 4). *Dear Colleague Letter.* Washington DC: U.S. Department of Education. Retrieved from https://www2.ed.gov/about/offices/list/ocr/letters/colleague-201104.pdf

Anthony v. Syracuse, 224 App. Div. 487 (N.Y. App. Div. 1928)

American Council on Education. (2019). *ACE comments to Education Department on proposed rule amending Title IX regulations.* Retrieved from https://www.acenet.edu/news-room/Pages/Comments-ED-2019-Title-IX-rule.aspx

Bob Jones University v. Johnson, 396 F.Supp. 597 (D.S.C. 1974), *affirmed,* 529 F.2d 514 (4th Cir. 1975)

Boehm v. University of Pa. Sch. of Veterinary Med., 573 A.2d 575 (Pa. Super. Ct. 1990)

Burlington Free Press v. University of Vermont, 779 A.2d 60 (Vm. 2001)

Cantu, N. V. (2001). *Revised sexual harassment guidance: Harassment of students by school employees, other students, or third parties.* Washington DC: U.S. Department of Education. Retrieved from https://www2.ed.gov/about/offices/list/ocr/docs/shguide.pdf

Cloud v. Boston Univ., 720 F.2d 721 (1st Cir. 1983)

Connally v. General Construction Co., 269 U.S. 385 (1926)

Cummings v. Virginia School of Cosmetology, 466 F. Supp. 780 (E.D. Va. 1979)

Custer, B. D., & DeBowes, M. M. (2019, February 18). The consequences of not complying. *Inside Higher Ed.* Retrieved from https://www.insidehighered.com/views/2019/02/18/colleges-are-facing-more-consequences-not-complying-drug-free-schools-and

Custer, B. D., & Kent, R. T. (2019). Understanding the Drug-Free Schools and Communities Act, then and now. *Journal of College and University Law, 44,* 137–158.

Dannells, M. (1977). Discipline. In W. T. Packwood (Ed.), *College student personnel services* (pp. 232–278). Springfield, IL: Charles C. Thomas.

Dannells, M. (1990). Changes in disciplinary policies and practices over 10 years. *Journal of College Student Development, 31*(5), 408–414.

Dannells, M. (1991). Changes in student misconduct and institutional response over 10 years. *Journal of College Student Development, 32*(2), 166–170.

Dannells, M. (1997). *From discipline to development: Rethinking student conduct in higher education,* ASHE-ERIC Higher Education Report, *25*(2). San Francisco, CA: Jossey-Bass.

Dannells, M., & Lowery, J. W. (2004). Discipline and judicial affairs. In F. J. D. MacKinnon & Associates (Eds.), *Student affairs functions in higher education* (3rd ed.) (pp. 178–217). Springfield, IL: Charles C. Thomas.

Davis v. Monroe County Board of Education, 526 U.S. 629 (1999)

DeBowes, M. M. (2016). *The resurgence of the Drug-Free Schools and Communities Act: A call to action.* Fishers, IN: STANLEY.

Dixon v. Alabama State Board of Education, 294 F.2d 150 (5th Cir. 1961)

Doe v. Alger, 175 F.Supp.3d 646 (W.D. Va. 2016)

Doe v. Baum, 903 F.3d 575 (6th Cir. 2018)

Doe v. Brown University, 166 F.Supp.3d 177 (D. RI. 2016)

Doe v. Ohio State University, 239 F.Supp.3d 1048 (S.D. Oh. 2017)

Doe v. Rector and Visitors of George Mason University, 149 F.Supp.3d 602 (E.D. Va. 2016)

Doe v. University of Cincinnati, 872 F.3d 393 (6th Cir. 2017)

Doe v. University of Southern California, 200 Cal.Rptr.3d 851 (2DCA 2016)

Donohue v. Baker, 976 F. Supp. 136 (N.D. NY 1997)

Drug-Free Schools and Communities Act, 20 U.S.C. § 1145g (1989)

DTH v. University of North Carolina at Chapel Hill, 496 S.E.2d 8 (N.C. App.1998)

Due v. Florida A&M Univ., 233 F. Supp. 396 (N.D. Fla. 1961)

Esteban v. Central Missouri State College, 290 F. Supp. 622 (W.D. Mo. 1968), *aff'd*, 415 F.2d 1077 (8th Cir. 1969)

Family Educational Rights and Privacy Act, 20 U.S.C. §1232g (1974)

Fellheimer v. Middlebury Coll., 869 F. Supp. 238 (D.Vt. 1994)

Franklin v. Gwinnett County Public Schools, 503 U.S. 60 (1992)

French v. Bashful, 303 F. Supp. 1333 (E.D.La. 1969)

Gabrilowitz v. Newman, 582 F.2d 100 (1st Cir. 1978)

Gebser v. Lago Vista Independent School District, 524 U.S. 274 (1998)

Gehring, D. D. (2001). The objectives of student discipline and the process that's due: Are they compatible? *NASPA Journal, 38*(4), 466–481.

Gehring, D. D., Lowery, J. W., & Palmer C. J. (2012). *Students' views of effective alcohol sanctions on college campuses: A national study.* Reno, NV: National Judicial College.

Gehring, D. D., Lowery, J. W., & Palmer C. J. (2013). *Students' views of effective alcohol sanctions on college campuses: A national study* (2nd ed.). Washington DC: The Century Council.

Gomes v. Univ. of Maine Sys., 304 F. Supp. 117 (D. Me. 2004)

Gonzaga University v. Doe, 536 U.S. 273 (2002)

Goodman v. Bowdoin College, 135 F. Supp. 2d 40 (D.Me. 2001)

Gorman v. University of Rhode Island, 837 F.2d 7 (1st Cir. 1988)

Goss v. Lopez, 419 U.S. 565 (1975)

Gott v. Berea College, 161 S.W. 204 (Ky. 1913)

Grossner v. Trustees of Columbia, 287 F. Supp. 535 (S.D.N.Y. 1968)

Grove City v. Bell, 465 U.S. 555 (1984)

Hannah v. Larche, 363 U.S. 420 (1960)

Herman v. University of South Carolina, 341 F. Supp. 226 (D.S.C. 1971), *affd.* 457 F.2d 902 (4th Cir. 1972)

Higher Education Centers. (2006). *Complying the Drug-Free Schools and Campuses Regulations [EDGAR Part 86]: A guide for university and college administrators.* Washington DC: Author. Retrieved from http://safesupportivelearning.ed.gov/sites/default/files/hec/product/dfscr.pdf

Hill v. Board of Trustees of Mich. State Univ., 182 F.Supp.2d 621 (W.D. Mich. 2001)

Holert v. University of Chicago, 751 F. Supp. 1294 (N.D. Ill. 1990)

Holmes v. Poskanzer, 2007 U.S. Dist. LEXIS 3216 (N.D.N.Y. 2007)

Hunter, B. & Gehring, G. D. (2005). The cost of federal legislation on higher education: The hidden tax on tuition. *NASPA Journal, 42*(4), 478–497.

Jackson, C. (2017a). *Dear Colleague Letter on Sexual Violence.* Washington DC: U.S. Department of Education, Office for Civil Rights. Retrieved from https://ed.gov/about/offices/list/ocr/letters/colleague-title-ix-201709.pdf

Jackson, C. (2017b). *Q&A on campus sexual misconduct.* Washington DC: U.S. Department of Education, Office for Civil Rights. Retrieved from https://www2 .ed. gov/about/offices/list/ocr/docs/qa-title-ix-201709.pdf

Jaska v. University of Michigan, 597 F. Supp. 1245 (E.D. Mich. 1984) *aff'd* 787 F.2d 590 (6th Cir. 1986)

Jeanne Clery Disclosure of Campus Security Policy and Campus Crime Statistics Act 20 U.S.C. §1092 (1990)

Jenkins v. Louisiana State Bd. of Education, 506 F.2d 992 (5th Cir. 1975)

Jones v. State Board of Education, 279 F. Supp. 190 (M.D. Tenn. 1968), *aff'd,* 407 F.2d 834 (6 Cir. 1969)

Kaplin, W. A., & Lee, B. A. (2014). *The law of higher education* (5th ed.). San Francisco, CA: Jossey-Bass.

Lhamon, C. A. (2014). *Questions and answers on Title IX and sexual violence.* Washington DC: U.S. Department of Education, Office for Civil Rights. Retrieved from https://www2.ed.gov/about/offices/list/ocr/docs/qa-201404-title-ix.pdf

Lowery, J. W. (1998). Balancing students' right to privacy with the public's right to know. *Synthesis: Law and Policy in Higher Education, 10,* 713–715, 730.

Lowery, J. W. (2000). FERPA and the Campus Security Act: Law and policy overview. *Synthesis: Law and Policy in Higher Education, 12,* 849–851, 864.

Lowery, J. W. (2004). Battling over Buckley: The press and access to student disciplinary records. In D. Bakst & S. Burgess (Eds.), *Student privacy review: An annual review and compendium for higher education leaders* (pp. 40–45). Palm Beach Gardens, FL: Council on Law in Higher Education.

Lowery, J. W. (2005). Legal issues regarding partnering with parents: Misunderstood federal laws and potential sources of institutional liability. In K. Keppler, R. H. Mullendore, & A. Carey (Eds.), *Partnering with the parents of today's college students* (pp. 43–51). Washington DC: NASPA.

Lowery, J. W., Palmer, C., & Gehring, D. D. (2005). Policies and practices of parental notification for student alcohol violations. *NASPA Journal, 42*(4), 415–429.

Matthews v. Eldridge, 424 U.S. 319 (1976)

Nash v. Auburn University, 812 F.2d 655 (11th Cir. 1987)

NASPA. (2019). *NASPA TIX Public Comments: Final.* Retrieved from https://www.naspa.org/images/uploads/posts/NASPA_TIX_Public_Comments_Final_20190130.pdf

Nguyen v. University of Louisville, 2006 U. S. Dist. LEXIS 20082 (W.D.Ky. 2006)

Nondiscrimination on the Basis of Sex in Education Programs or Activities Receiving Federal Financial Assistance, 83 Fed. Reg. 230 (proposed November 28, 2018) (to be codified at 34 CFR Part 106)

Osteen v. Henley, 13 F.3d 221 (7th Cir. 1993)

Palmer, C. J., Lohman, G., Gehring, D. D., Carlson, S., & Garrett, O. (2001). Parental notification: A new strategy to reduce alcohol abuse on campus. *NASPA Journal, 38*(3), 372–385.

Palmer, C. J., Lowery, J. W., Wilson, M. E., & Gehring, D. D. (2003). Parental notification policies, practices, and impacts in 2002 and 2003. *Journal of College and University Student Housing, 31*(2), 3–6.

Papachristou v. Univ. of Tenn., 29 S.W.3d 487, 489 (Tenn. Ct. App. 2000)

Pavela, G. (2000, Spring). Applying the power of association on campus: A model code of student conduct. *Synthesis: Law and Policy in Higher Education, 11,* 817–823, 829–831.

Pavela, G., & Pavela, G. (2012). The ethical and educational imperative of due process. *Journal of College and University Law, 38*(3), 567–626.

Powe v. Miles, 407 F.2d 73 (2d Cir. 1968)

Prasad v. Cornell University, 2016 WL 3212079 (N.D. NY 2016)

In re Rensselaer Soc. of Eng. v. Rensslaer Poly. Inst., 689 N.Y.S.2d 292 (N.Y.App. Div. 1999)

Schaer v. Brandeis Univ., 432 Mass. 474 (2000).

Shreveport Professional Chapter of the Society of Professional Journalists and Michelle Millhollon v. Louisiana State University, et al., Unpublished (La. Dist. Ct., Caddo Parish, March 4, 1994)

Silverglate, H. A., & Gewolb, J. (2003). *FIRE's guide to due process and fair procedure on campus.* Philadelphia, PA: Foundation for Individual Rights in Education.

Slaughter v. Brigham Young University, 514 F.2d 622 (10th Cir. 1975)

Soglin v. Kauffman, 418 F.2d 163 (7th Cir. 1969)

State ex rel. The Miami Student v. Miami Univ., 680 N.E.2d 956 (Ohio, 1997), cert. denied 522 U.S. 1022 (1997)

Sterrett v. Cowan, 85 F.Supp.3d 916 (E.D. Mi. 2015)

Stoner, E. N. (2000). *Reviewing your student discipline policy: A project worth the investment.* Chevy Chase, MD: United Educators.

Stoner, E. N., II, & Cerminara, K. (1990). Harnessing the "spirit of insubordination": A model student disciplinary code. *Journal of College and University Law, 17*(2), 89–121.

Stoner, E. N., II, & Lowery, J. W. (2004). Navigating past the "spirit of insubordination": A twenty-first century model student conduct code with a model hearing script. *Journal of College and University Law, 31*(1), 1–78.

Title IX of the Educational Amendments of 1972, 20 U.S.C. § 1681 et seq.

Trahms v. Columbia Univ., 245 A.D.2d 124 (N.Y.Sup.Ct.App.Div. 1997)

Travelstead, W. W. (1987). Introduction and historical context. In R. Caruso & W. W. Travelstead (Eds.), *Enhancing campus judicial* systems (New Directions for Student Services No. 39) (pp. 3–16). San Francisco, CA: Jossey-Bass.

United States v. Miami Univ., 294 F.3d 797 (6th Cir. 2002)

U.S. Courts. (2003). *Understanding the federal courts.* Washington DC: Author. Retrieved from https://www.uscourts.gov/sites/default/files/understanding-federal-courts.pdfU.S. Department of Education, Office of Postsecondary Education. (2016). *The handbook for campus safety and security reporting.* Retrieved from http://www2.ed.gov/admins/lead/safety/handbook.pdf

Weidemann v. SUNY College at Cortland, 592 N.Y.S.2d 99 (N.Y. App. Div. 1992)

Wilgus, J. K., & Lowery, J. W. (2018). Adjudicating student sexual misconduct: Parameters, pitfalls, and promising practices. In J. Jessup-Anger and K. E. Edwards (Eds.), *Addressing sexual violence in higher education and student affairs* (pp. 83–94). San Francisco, CA: Jossey-Bass.

Winnick v. Manning, 460 F.2d 545 (2d Cir. 1972)

Wood, N. L. (2004, June). *Due process in disciplinary proceedings: Classic cases and recent trends in case law.* Session presented at the ASJA Donald D. Gehring Campus Judicial Affairs Training Institute, Salt Lake City, UT.

Woodis v. Westark Community College, 160 F.3d 435 (8th Cir. 1998)

5

TYPES AND FORUMS
FOR RESOLUTION

Eugene L. Zdziarski II and Patience L. Bartunek

Introduction and Philosophy

The purpose of this chapter is to introduce the reader to the various types of resolution currently in use to resolve allegations of student misconduct on college campuses in the United States. Before exploring these different types of resolution, however, it is important to acknowledge the role and expectations of the student conduct administrator (SCA).

No matter what the forum of adjudication, the role of a SCA is to learn the answers to several very basic questions—who, what, when, where, and in most cases, why. In many instances, the answers to these questions may appear obvious on the various complaint documents, including reports from residence life, police (both internal and external), and reports from other sources such as university staff or faculty members. An experienced and skilled SCA, however, always keeps in mind that until the student who allegedly violated policy is heard, all may not be as it seems on paper. Individuals' perceptions of the same event can and will vary. Witnesses may not always be truthful, and in some cases, identities may be mistaken. Decisions concerning responsibility should be reserved until all documents have been carefully reviewed with the accused student and they have had the opportunity to respond fully to any other information and/or witnesses to be considered by the SCA.

While the primary goal of any resolution process is to determine whether it is more likely than not that the student is responsible for violating one or more specific sections of the student code of conduct and assign an appropriate sanction, the contemporary practice of student conduct administration includes an expectation that the SCA is holistically attending to the developmental needs of the student. For this reason, the SCA must take the time necessary to learn about the student's background, the student's status within the university, and the student's goals and aspirations beyond the university community. By engaging in a conversation with the student about these personal characteristics, opportunities often arise to assist students to use campus and community resources more effectively and efficiently to help them achieve those goals and aspirations.

To be truly developmental and educative, it is also critical that students understand how their behavior affects others and how engaging in that behavior may also affect students' futures, particularly in the context of career choice. If the student's career choice is unknown, then it is especially important to help them understand that without a specific career goal, maintaining a positive behavioral record on and off campus is essential to protect the student's interest for maximizing future employment and/or postgraduate opportunities.

With a basic understanding of the SCA's role in making objective and fully informed decisions, as well as their expectation to address the developmental needs of students, we can now turn our attention to the different forums used to resolve student conduct matters.

Typical Forums for Resolution Currently in Use Across the United States

The most prevalent forms of resolution in use to process complaints concerning student behavior on college campuses include informal resolution, one-to-one student conduct conferences (also called administrative hearings), the dual SCA model and board or panel hearings. Board hearings vary greatly. They may include student-only boards, student and faculty boards, and boards that may include students, faculty, and staff to represent all campus constituencies. Many campuses also utilize various forms of alternative dispute resolution (ADR). These may include mediation, restorative justice, and transformative justice. Following is a brief discussion of each of these types of resolution.

Informal Resolution

Often called educational conferences, informal resolution allows the conduct case to be resolved without a formal hearing. While a formal hearing should always follow the due process or fundamental fairness as is appropriate to the institution, there is a time and place for informally resolving a case. These instances are situations where the student has accepted responsibility for violating the potential violations and agrees to the educational outcomes of the resolution. This process allows for a more conversational approach to resolving the issue and finding the root cause of the behavior (Fischer et al., 2014).

Educational conferences should not be confused with a plea bargain or plea deal. They are not a shortcut or easy way out of the hearing process; rather, they allow students to resolve a case without the additional step of the formal hearing when they have already accepted responsibility. Educational conferences also allow for students to have an active role in selecting their sanctions or educational outcomes. As the educational conference outcome is an agreement between the student and the SCA, the student agrees to complete the assigned sanction giving that student ownership in the sanction. The educational conference allows for flexibility that cannot be found in the formal hearing process. This flexibility gives the SCA and student the ability to reach goals of growth that can sometimes be lost in the formal hearing process.

As the informal process is nonconfrontational, it allows for the SCA to become a resource for students rather than just the person who heard their case. In the educational conversation, the SCA can help students find resources they need on campus and can serve in a mentor role going forward. Often students in these settings share information that is deeper than just the behavior that brought them to that meeting, and this allows the SCA to help the student make appropriate connections on campus—such as with the counseling center, student support services, and the advising center. To make these connections, the SCA needs to look at the student holistically, not just as the incident report they have prior to meeting with the student. This means looking into the student's life outside of this incident report. How well is the student doing academically (GPA)? Have they been referred to the CARE or BIT team? Are there other contributory issues such as possible roommate conflicts within housing? Are they involved and connected on campus? These are insightful questions the SCA should know the answers to before the end of a meeting. Often, students identify the SCA from an educational conference as the person they go to on campus when they have questions, which results in an ongoing relationship with the student.

If students do not accept responsibility for their behavior, this process cannot go forward. The student should then be referred to one of the processes discussed next. The educational conference can also serve as the fact-finding meeting for a hearing in a case where students choose to not accept responsibility for the potential violations they are facing.

Administrative Hearing

Perhaps the most recognized method for resolving student conduct issues is the administrative hearing. In the administrative hearing, the SCA facilitates a one-on-one hearing process for the student that can look like a simple conversation or can be as complex as a process through which the reporting party, the student who allegedly violated policy(s), and any relevant witnesses share information about a situation and respond to clarifying questions before the SCA renders a decision and issues a sanction.

From an administrative point of view, conducting this type of conduct hearing has several advantages. First, the SCA is able to get a general overview of the student relatively quickly and to set the student at ease before entering the fact-finding portion of the hearing. Second, the student is viewed holistically; rather than focusing only on the student's negative behavior, the SCA is focusing on how the institution can assist the student in learning how their behavior affects others, and how their behavior may affect the student's future in the context of their particular major.

This is a very important part of today's conduct processes. More and more employers are conducting background checks on potential employees, while graduate institutions are also checking potential applicants (Liptak, 2006). Students may be unaware of these practices and may need assistance in learning how their conduct record and/or a criminal record may affect them in the context of particular majors, especially nursing, pharmacy, education, criminal justice, law, medicine, and others.

An administrative hearing allows for a one-on-one connection between the SCA and the student. A student being found responsible in an administrative hearing has had an opportunity to agree or disagree with the SCA in a safe and moderated situation. This should allow the student to have an opportunity to feel truly heard.

Administrative hearings can lead to a high degree of consistency over time, so that students in similar situations are treated in a similar manner, adjusting for their conduct records. This is particularly important so that the SCA and the office in which the SCA works is perceived as treating students fairly and consistently. Students may not always like the decisions that are reached, but having a sense of fairness is essential in maintaining the image of credibility with the institution's student body.

Some students prefer an administrative hearing because it allows greater preservation of their privacy, as fewer individuals learn about their misdeeds. In addition, administrative hearings can generally be scheduled and held more quickly, thus giving students a speedier resolution, allowing them quicker relief to their anxiety, while allowing administrators a more efficient work flow.

There are some limitations to using an administrative hearing. Because there is no other community involvement, the SCA may be vulnerable to accusations of bias and other forms of attack intended to deflect attention from the student's misconduct, especially if the conference is not recorded. While recordings can change the conversational atmosphere of the administrative hearing, formal hearings should be recorded to avoid these allegations.

Depending on the age of the student, the nature of the violation, and the policies of the institution, it can be beneficial to discuss whether the student has informed his or her parents or guardian about the current difficulties. Parents or guardians can be a positive source of support in assisting their sons and daughters to make a successful recovery from difficult conduct cases. Judgment must be used, however, as in some cases parents and guardians can be counterproductive and even enabling, refusing to believe that their offspring violated campus policies and, even if they did, that significant campus sanctions are warranted, particularly if separation from the campus is contemplated.

While the administrative hearing is more structured than the informal resolution, it should still allow for the connection between the SCA and student who potentially violated policy. Asking the same questions about the student's well-being should be part of the hearing process and also allow for the connection to be made between the SCA and student.

Duel SCA Model

Often campuses have more than one code of student conduct on campus. These can be academic, non-academic, fraternity and sorority, or even specific to a major or professional program.   Students can engage in behavior that violates more than one of these codes at the same time. Allowing for joint resolution in these cases can reduce the stress on the student, reduce redundancy in administrator workload, and allow for consistency in decision-making. It is important to make sure that the processes used to adjudicate these codes allow for a dual SCA model before initiating a joint resolution. This type of resolution is also contingent on people having previously built strong relationships that allow for the SCAs to work together and be comfortable with an outcome that they both must sign off on.

One of the authors of this chapter used this model in a case that spanned the academic and non-academic code of conduct at their institution. The adjudication team was composed of SCAs from both student conduct and academic affairs. This was a good strategy, as this allowed for an educational conversation with the student while addressing the academic issue of cheating as well as the non-academic issue of solicitation (of papers) without causing additional stress or confusion.

This dual SCA model can also be helpful when a case has potential bias concerns. In some cases a single SCA can give the appearance of bias, even if there is not any. If a student is before a female SCA and accused of vandalism that was misogynistic in nature, they could feel the SCA was automatically against them. In the same cases, they could perceive a male SCA as for them. A dual SCA model removes this bias concern. This style of adjudication is often used in the investigative stages of sexual harassment and misconduct cases.

Student Conduct Board

Student conduct boards are another common way for resolving student behavioral issues. Use of such boards is appealing because it resonates with our sense of justice and fairness. The concept of having students' fate determined by an impartial jury of their peers is something we are taught as schoolchildren when we learn about the Sixth Amendment to the Constitution. Having an impartial group of people review the facts of the situation, judge those facts based on a set of community standards, and determine a reasonable and appropriate response to one's behavior is what most U.S. citizens have come to expect as fair and just.

In addition to their common acceptance and inherent perceptions of fairness, student conduct boards provide significant educational benefits. Having members of the campus community judge the behavior of their peers and assign sanctions for behavior they find inappropriate is an important learning process for both the accused student and the members of the board. While a decision made by an administrator in an administrative hearing might simply be perceived as a customary institutional response, decisions made by peers in a board or panel can be very effective in communicating community standards of acceptable behavior within the campus community.

Types of Boards
There are many different types of student conduct boards in higher education. Boards can be used to conduct individual hearings concerning behavioral violations, academic integrity violations, or both. They can also hear organizational cases involving violations committed by student groups or clubs. Such organizational boards might hear cases involving alleged violation of university policies as well as alleged violation of organizational rules. For example, a common organizational board on many campuses is a Greek conduct board, which might address violations of university policies, such as alcohol or hazing policies and/or the policies of the campus Interfraternity Council, membership recruitment policies, or achievement standards. Student conduct boards may also be unique to different programs within

the campus community. For example, some campuses may have separate student conduct boards to address the unique needs and interests of a particular segment of the campus community. This most often involves professional programs such as medicine and law. Because of professional standards and ethics, certification and licensure requirements, or other legal requirements, the implications of some violations may be much different from those of other parts of the campus. Therefore, while these boards enforce the same code of conduct and use the same process for adjudication as other conduct boards within the campus community, how they might sanction a particular violation could be significantly different within the professional school environment.

Another type of student conduct board is an appellate board. While student conduct boards can be used as primary hearing bodies, they can also hear appeals. In some campus conduct systems, primary adjudication of student conduct cases is conducted through administrative hearings, and appeals are heard by a board. On other campuses, primary adjudication is conducted through boards, and appeals are heard by an administrative review process. On still other campuses a combination of administrative hearings and board hearings is available at both the primary and appellate levels.

The number and types of different boards used on any campus depends on the individual history and culture of each institution. At the same time, administrators should have a clear rationale and justification for the existence of each of the different boards. When a new board is created to address the needs of one group, others will surely seek to have a board created to address their needs. As the number of boards increases, it is more difficult to provide adequate training and maintain an appropriate level of consistency across the conduct system. Another approach to address the various needs of the campus community is through the composition of student conduct boards.

Board Composition
Much like the different types of boards, the composition of student conduct boards can take a variety of forms. Such boards can be composed entirely of students, faculty, or staff, or any combination. Again, the individual history and culture of each campus will play a role in how some boards are comprised.

As noted earlier, part of the allure of a board is the concept of having a decision made by a jury of one's peers. The primary question, however, becomes, "How does one define peers?" Students often define peers as other students. Student conduct boards comprised entirely of students can be very effective in adjudicating cases if they are trained properly. A former SCA, Diane Waryold (1998), notes, "Students dialoguing with students in a disciplinary hearing regarding the behavioral expectations of the university community can be the best method for redirecting behavior" (p. 228). Examples of student conduct boards composed solely of students can be found throughout the country.

Others might suggest that faculty are the primary determiners of institutional standards, so such decisions should be made by a faculty board. This is particularly true when dealing with academic honesty violations, where faculty feel a strong sense of responsibility for maintaining the institution's academic integrity.

Fundamentally however, student conduct boards should represent the campus community, which includes students, faculty, and staff, so one might argue that all are peers and should be represented in such campus decisions. Student conduct boards should also be representative of the campus makeup. Thus, board composition should consider such things as race, gender, classification, college, and so on.

While boards should be representative of the campus community and draw from a wide cross-section of the campus, we must be careful to ensure that the size of the board does not become unwieldy. Although it may be tempting for some campuses to comply with the U.S. concept of a jury comprised of 12 members, routinely getting a group of 12 together for campus hearings can be challenging, depending on the frequency of such hearings. Further, as the size of the board grows, the longer the hearing tends to be and the more difficult it is to reach consensus. In addition, an even number of members can lead to a split decision requiring added time in deliberations to break the tie or for the case be reheard altogether. It is for these reasons that boards consisting of five to seven members seem ideal; the number is sufficient to represent the campus community, while still making the group manageable in terms of scheduling and group processing.

Although you may require five to seven members to conduct a hearing, you will typically want to select and train a larger group of individuals to manage your caseload. Minimally, you will want to have alternate members to fill in when other members are unable to attend a particular hearing or when a member must be excused because of prior knowledge of the case or a relationship with the accused. Structural consideration must be considered to adequately address caseloads (volume), and boards should meet at varying times to accommodate class/work schedules of the board members, accused students, and witnesses who may need to be involved.

Another approach to managing caseload with a student conduct board is to develop a pool of individuals trained in the student conduct process from which members can be drawn for various hearings. This approach provides the greatest flexibility in both scheduling and board composition.

With thoughtful recruitment and selection of members, a pool of board members can be useful in ensuring that the composition of the student conduct board represents the community in which an infraction took place and that the members appreciate the unique needs and interests of that community. For example, it was noted earlier that because of professional standards and ethics, certification and licensure requirements, or other legal requirements, it is important to have involvement of members from a particular professional school in the hearing process. With a pool of board members, students and faculty from the particular professional school could be called on to participate in a hearing that involves a student from that school, and the nature of the case requires input from individuals in that particular discipline.

Recruitment and Selection of Members
The different types of boards and their size will affect the recruitment and selection process required to fill them. Members can be elected, appointed, nominated, or apply for seats on student conduct boards.

In some cases, board members may be appointed or even elected. For example, representatives from student government or the faculty senate may be elected to serve as members of a student conduct board. In other cases, board members may be appointed by the student body president or faculty senate chair. This approach to recruitment and selection of board members can provide a consistent and stable source of board members. On the other hand, when board members are elected or appointed, sometimes they can bring with them a particular "hidden" agenda. In these cases, student conduct board training must focus on creating an understanding of the process and the need for board members to maintain their objectivity in every case.

In other cases, board members may be nominated or may apply for positions. Particularly in situations where there is an application process, the SCA has a significant level of responsibility to recruit potential members. The campus community needs to be educated not only about the opportunity to serve on the student conduct board, but also about the benefits and advantages of doing so. It is during this recruitment phase that SCAs should give careful consideration to various constituencies within the campus community and ensure that representation is obtained from all parts of the institution.

In a process where individuals either apply or are nominated to serve on a board, there is usually some type of interview process. The primary purpose of such interviews is to ensure that the individuals who have applied or been nominated clearly understand what the time commitments will be, the training that will be required, and the types of decisions they will be asked to make. With this information, some individuals will choose to opt out on their own. The interview process also provides SCAs with an opportunity to evaluate whether potential members have hidden agendas that might be counterproductive to the student conduct process. To ensure a level of objectivity, this interview process may be conducted by one or two current board members in addition to the SCA.

An issue that sometimes arises in the selection process is whether a student who has previously been sanctioned for misconduct should be eligible to serve on a student conduct board. We would contend that a student should not be eliminated from the process simply because he or she has previously been sanctioned. Instead, factors such as the nature of the violation, how recently the violation took place, and the attitude or demeanor of the student concerning his or her own proceeding are more appropriate indicator of whether a student should serve on a board. Sometimes, a student who has been through the process can be one of its best proponents.

Board Training
Regardless of the type, size, or composition of student conduct boards, proper training is essential for them to operate effectively. All board members should undergo an initial comprehensive conduct board training program before participating in a hearing. A comprehensive training program should provide board members with an understanding of the educational philosophy behind campus conduct proceedings, a basic sense of fundamental due process rights and burden of proof, clear knowledge of specific campus procedures, and exposure to group process and decision-making skills. Often conducted over the course of a couple of days or several evenings, board training programs should involve a combination of lecture-style presentations, interactive discussion, and role-plays or mock hearings. It can be useful to include experienced board members in planning and implementing the board training, particularly in facilitating mock hearings so that they are realistic and relevant. In addition to the formal training program, it may be beneficial for new board members to observe an actual student conduct hearing before serving on the board.

In conjunction with the training program, it is important that all members of the student conduct board receive a procedures manual that includes a complete copy of the student conduct code and an outline of the hearing process. A good procedures manual also provides board members with a sample script to use at various stages of the hearing process.

Depending on the frequency of student conduct board hearings and the opportunity for all members to participate regularly, it is advisable to conduct periodic in-service training programs. Such programs can focus attention on areas in which boards have experienced difficulties or can clarify aspects of the process that may be the subject of frequent questions.

We have reviewed the types of conduct boards and the structural considerations of said boards commonly utilized on U.S. college and university campuses.

Alternative Dispute Resolution and Other Forums for Resolution

Thus far we have addressed common forums for the adjudication of student conduct violations. But not all types of situations fall under the jurisdiction of the institution or its neatly defined codes of conduct. Sometimes disputes arise between members of the campus community that fall outside the parameters of the campus conduct process, but if they are not addressed, they may become disruptive to other members in the community or might evolve into a conduct violation that might have been avoided. In these situations, we need alternatives to the traditional forums for adjudication.

In other situations, we may have a clear violation of the student code of conduct, but simply conducting a hearing and issuing a sanction that is part of a confidential student record isn't enough. Hurt and pain has been brought on the community and there is a need to repair the harm and heal that community. But at times there is also a need to address the inequalities and root causes of why a student committed a violation.

Beyond traditional forums of resolution, there are needs for alternative resolution processes. Such alternative forms of resolution include conciliation, mediation, restorative justice, and transformative justice. Chapter 9 offers a thorough explanation of alternative forums.

Conciliation

Conciliation is simply the involvement of a third party in the discussions and bargaining between other parties to assist in reaching a mutually agreeable resolution of their differences. As noted in the seminal work on campus dispute resolution, *Peaceful Persuasion: A Guide to Creating Mediation Dispute Resolution Centers on Colleges Campuses*, the third party attempts to bring the various parties together and share information between them to facilitate dialogue and encourage resolution (Girard, Rifkin, & Townley, 1985). In conciliation, the third party is not necessarily a true neutral party and often has some interest in resolving the situation. A common example of conciliation in the college and university environment is when a resident assistant helps two students involved in a roommate conflict. While the staff member plays an important role in helping to resolve the situation, he or she has a vested interest in the resolution because continuing the dispute may cause further disruptions to other residents on the floor or might force the resident assistant to take other actions, such as relocating the residents or making a student conduct referral.

Mediation

Mediation is another common form of alternative dispute resolution used in higher education, but administrators are well advised to have more specific training before implementing this approach. Like conciliation, mediation is a voluntary process that involves a third party; however, the third party is a neutral party who assists the disputing parties in satisfying their interests by guiding them through a semi-structured process (Waters, 2000). This process is typically described as a series of steps or stages (e.g., see Girard, Rifkin, & Townley, 1985; Goldberg, Sander, & Rogers, 1992; Lovenheim, 1989; Waters, 2000). These stages can be summarized as (a) opening statement; (b) storytelling; (c) identification of issues; (d) generation of options; and (e) agreement (Zdziarski, 1998). Each stage of the process builds on the previous stage and helps the parties focus on the issues central to the dispute rather than just on their positions. Ultimately, the goal of the process is to reach a mutually acceptable agreement that is a win for both parties.

This form of alternative dispute resolution is particularly advantageous in cases where individuals are reluctant to pursue the traditional forms of complaint resolution on campus. Take, for example, a relationship dispute in which a boyfriend and girlfriend break up. The ex-boyfriend repeatedly calls the ex-girlfriend, but she refuses to answer his calls. Despite being told she never wants to speak to him again, he persists. E-mail messages, cards, and flowers are sent. The ex-boyfriend's actions could be considered harassment, but the ex-girlfriend does not want him to face behavioral sanctions; she just wants him to leave her alone. Mediation may be an appropriate alternative in this situation.

Restorative Justice

Restorative justice is grounded in three principles: repairing harm, holding students accountable, and restoring the loss to the community. The basis of the process is to involve all of the parties that have been impacted by an incident, and as a group identify and address the damages done and how to heal the community that was harmed. Restorative justice gives voice to the impacted parties, including those who are often overlooked when a student goes through a standard conduct hearing. Restorative justice as an alternative forum of adjudication is not appropriate for all cases, and thus must be applied with intention and caution. In some types of incidents, such as assault or sexual misconduct, reporting parties or victims do not feel comfortable confronting the responding party. All parties must be willing to participate in the process for it to have its intended impact (Clark, 2014).

In a restorative process, the SCA needs to identify all of the involved parties. If it is an alcohol violation, this could be the student who consumed, the person they disrupted by yelling when they entered the hall, the resident assistant who had to get up and address the issue, and the housekeeper who had to come in and clean up their vomit. All those impacted by the behavior should be involved in the process—willingly and without expectation and with the intention that they forgive the student who caused the issue. Once the impacted people have been identified, they meet with the SCA and the student who caused the issue to create a restorative agreement. This conversation, often facilitated as a restorative justice circle, is open, honest, and often emotionally charged. It allows everyone in the situation to express their concerns as well as what they feel the redress should be (Clark, 2014; Derajtys & McDowell, 2014).

At the close of the meeting, the restorative agreement is put into place. This agreement is just that—an outcome that is agreed on by all who are impacted by the behavior. The SCA now has the responsibility to monitor the student's adherence to the agreement and ensure all sanctions agreed on are followed.

Restorative justice is often a great equalizer in the conduct process. It allows for a community to make a decision, often identifying bias in the behavior of the student as well as in the persons who addressed the issue. Having a community talk through an incident allows for each person to evaluate their bias in the situation and learn from the situation. It also takes away some sanctioning bias that can occur inherently in an administrative hearing or a board hearing where the member identity is homogeneous (Clark, 2014; Derajtys & McDowell, 2014; Pedrea, 2014).

Transformative Justice

Transformative justice focuses on systematic inequalities (e.g., socioeconomic conditions) that present roadblocks for students. It allows those who have allegedly violated community standards to undo harm without requiring emotional labor from those who have been harmed and also looks at the root cause of the concern. When resolving a conduct case involving a student who has harmed others or their community, finding a way to rehabilitate or fix the concern is in the best interest of all involved, but so is addressing the root cause for the student who violated policy. Unlike restorative justice, which often is resolved through a separate process, this can be done in an educational conference or administrative hearing (Evans, 2016; Stein, 2018).

Transformative justice can be helpful in resolving issues of theft, unauthorized access, and other issues where the student is violating policy to address a socioeconomic roadblock that has been placed before them. For example, a student who is stealing food from the cafeteria or vandalizing a vending machine to get food because they are living in poverty can be an excellent application for this type of resolution. Due to the unique relationship of the SCA and a student, the SCA is in the perfect position to address food insecurity. Using transformative justice, an SCA can address the behavior but also find the resources with which the student needs to connect. The transformative justice process allows the SCA to not only educate the student on behavioral concerns, but also advocate for the student in finding the assistance they need.

Similar to the discussion in the informal hearing section on connecting students to the appropriate resources on campus for their academic and behavioral success, this process connects the students to resources that help them fill their basic needs. It requires the SCA be knowledgeable about and build bridges to resources on campus and in their community that can meet the needs of students. This includes being aware of food pantries that will assist students, both on and off campus, and what is required of the student to utilize the services. This may also include knowing what transportation is available for the student to get to an off-campus location. Knowing where a student can get weather-appropriate clothes for free or at a reduced cost, especially if they have moved to the campus from a different climate, is needed. Knowing what housing or which shelters are available to students is necessary to assist those in need.

Transformative justice transforms students' accessibility to their needs and allows the student to leave the process educated on behavior but connected to the resources they need beyond the educational setting.

Additional Considerations

The following section provides some additional considerations for the reader to contemplate in creating connections with students.

Involvement of an Adviser

It can be intimidating for a student to be required to participate in a student conduct proceeding. For some students, regardless of the severity of the charges against them, the conduct process can be so anxiety producing that they find it difficult to talk or even think straight. For others, the idea of facing a professional SCA on their own seems fundamentally unfair. After all, most students are unfamiliar with the process and have a limited understanding of their rights and alternatives for resolving the situation. It is for these reasons that most student conduct systems offer students the opportunity to have an adviser in the process.

As suggested in the Model Student Code (Stoner & Cerminara, 1990; Stoner & Lowery 2004), most student conduct codes allow for both the complainant and the accused to be assisted by an adviser. Advisers are not permitted to speak or participate directly in a student conduct proceeding. The student is responsible for speaking on their own behalf and presenting relevant information in the proceeding.

Generally, students may select an adviser of their choosing. In some student conduct systems, an adviser must be a member of the college/university community and may not be an attorney. Many campuses provide a list of faculty, staff, and students who have volunteered to serve as an adviser to students. These individuals have some familiarity with the student conduct system and may have received some specific training on the process. This gives students a knowledgeable and impartial resource to help guide them through the process and helps to maintain a sense of fairness.

In most systems, however, an attorney may be allowed to serve as an adviser if the accused student is facing criminal charges off campus for the same instance, or in Title IX cases. Further, in some states, students have a right to an attorney in all conduct proceedings.

Use of Technology

Technology continually adds new challenges to adjudicating cases, yet also provides resources for resolving conduct cases. Social media has changed the way students communicate with others, and while this can help them connect with others, it can also create new spaces for conflict. Conduct issues often occur in the virtual setting as students frequently use apps such as Snapchat, Instagram, Finstagram, Twitter, and so on. Additionally, students often post pictures, videos, boomerangs, recordings, and so on of themselves or their peers and may violate the code of student conduct when doing so. Virtually constructed evidence in posts, texts, and e-mails can be included as part of an incident report or part of the information shared by the student who allegedly violated policy. It is important for the SCA to keep abreast of the rapidly changing virtual world and to understand social media platforms and the information they maintain.

While technology can pose challenges, it also can enhance the conduct process. Technology can be used to conduct hearings when students are in an off-campus location or to facilitate hearings where certain parties should not be in the same room. It can allow for witnesses to share information from afar or parties to question each other through a text-to-talk program, which can provide a safe space for all parties involved in an incident.

Conclusion

A variety of forums for resolution are available today in the administration of campus conduct systems. We have provided a description of the administrative hearing, student conduct board, and alternative methods of dispute resolution. As noted, each of these forums has advantages and disadvantages. How these forums fit into a comprehensive student conduct system and how they are applied on each campus depends on the unique history and characteristics of the institution. Administrators need to be familiar with these different forums and how they might be utilized in administering student conduct on campus and with learning the who, what, when, where, and, in most cases, why of an incident.

References

Clark, K. L. (2014). A call for restorative justice in higher education judicial affairs. *College Student Journal, 48*(4), 707–715.

Derajtys, K. J., & McDowell, L. A. (2014). Restorative student judicial circles: A way to strengthen traditional student judicial board practices. *Journal of Theoretical & Philosophical Criminology, 6*(3), 213–222.

Evans, M. (2016). Structural violence, socioeconomic rights, and transformative justice. *Journal of Human Rights 15*(1), 1–20. doi:10.1080/14754835.2015.1032223

Fischer, W., Lewis, W. S., Lowery, J. W., Schuster, S. K., Sokolow, B. A., & Swinton, D. C. (2014). A developmental framework for a code of student conduct: The NCHERM group model code project. Retrieved from https://cdn.tngconsulting.com/website-media/ncherm.org/unoffloaded/2013/09/PRIVATE-A-Developmental-Framework-for-a-Code-of-Student-Conduct-03-11-20143.pdf

Girard, K., Rifkin, J., & Townley, A. (1985). *Peaceful persuasion: A guide to creating mediation dispute resolution centers on college campuses.* Amherst, MA: Mediation Project, University of Massachusetts.

Goldberg, S. B., Sander, F. E., & Rogers, N. H. (1992). *Dispute resolution: Negotiation, mediation, and other processes* (2nd ed.). Boston, MA: Little, Brown & Co.

Liptak, A. (2006, October 17). Criminal records erased by courts live to tell tales. *New York Times.* Retrieved from http://www.nytimes.com/2006/10/17/uw/17expunge.html

Lovenheim, P. (1989). *Mediate, don't litigate. How to resolve disputes quickly, privately, and inexpensively—without going to court.* New York, NY: McGraw Hill.

Pedreal, M. L. B. (2014). Restorative justice programs in higher education. *Vermont Connection, 35*(5), 37–46.

Stein, S. (2018). Higher education and the im/possibility of transformative justice. *Critical Ethnic Studies, 4*(1), 130–153.

Stoner, E. N., II & Cerminara, K. L. (1990). Harnessing the "spirit of insubordination": A model student disciplinary code. *Journal of College and University Law, 17*(2), 89–121.

Stoner, E. N., II & Lowery, J. W. (2004). Navigating past the "spirit of insubordination": A twenty-first century model student conduct code with a model hearing script. *Journal of College and University Law, 31*(1), 1–77.

Waryold, D. M. (1998). Increasing campus judicial board effectiveness: Are two heads truly better than one? In B. G. Paterson & W. L. Kibler (Eds.), *The administration of campus discipline: Student, organizational and community issues* (pp. 227–235). Asheville, NC: College Administration Publications.

Waters, W. C. (2000). *Mediation in the campus community: Designing and managing effective programs.* San Francisco, CA: Jossey-Bass.

Zdziarski, E. (1998). Alternative dispute resolution: A new look at resolving campus conflict. In B. G. Paterson & W. L. Kibler (Eds.), *The administration of campus discipline: Student, organizational and community issues.* Asheville, NC: College Administration Publications.

6

BREAKING THE CYCLE

Embedding Social Justice Into
Student Conduct Practice

Ryan C. Holmes and Reyna M. Anaya

"Without addressing issues of injustice, we cannot truly value diversity"
Adams and Bell, 2016

As individuals living in the United States, we are influenced by socialization, "a pervasive (coming from all sides and sources), consistent (patterned and predictable), circular (self-supporting), self-perpetuating (intra-dependent), and often invisible (unconscious and unnamed)" (Harro, 2000, p. 15) process of constructing and maintaining an inequitable social system. The messaging we receive informs our lived experiences and social identities (e.g., disability, documentation status, ethnicity, gender, gender identity, race, religion, sexual orientation, social class) (Bell, 1997), and is enforced in ways that perpetuate injustice and devalue difference and/or diversity. Historically, U.S. society has upheld socialization patterns (e.g., racism, sexism, classism, heterosexism, ageism, etc.) through culturally created rules that give unearned power and control to individuals and groups with privilege (e.g., White, straight, upper/middle class, documented, Christian, able-bodied, cisgender, men) (Johnson, 2006). Privilege, however, cannot exist without oppression, the restriction of access to resources, and isolation of individuals because of their group membership (Johnson, 2006; McIntosh, 1990). While each individual who experiences oppression, marginalization, and/or minoritized status (e.g., people of color, lesbian/gay/bisexual, transgender, working/lower class, undocumented, non-Christian beliefs/faiths, disabled, and women) may individually experience oppression differently; each is marginalized systemically through socialization.

The perpetuation of socialization throughout history is responsible for the foundation of the student conduct profession. Specifically, on February 25, 1960, approximately 30 students who identified as Black/African American staged a sit-in at a local, segregated lunch grill in Montgomery, Alabama, and asked to be served (*Dixon v. Alabama*, 1961). Their service was refused, police were called, and the students were ordered outside where they remained in protest for over an hour. The governor of Alabama advised the president of Alabama State College, who identified as an African American man, to consider expulsion of the nine student organizers of the sit-in from the college. The injustice experienced by the nine students denied them of their constitutional rights because of socialization values (i.e., White supremacy) taught and reinforced in the Jim Crow South through multiple institutional and cultural systems (e.g., legal, educational). This unfortunate event was challenged and documented in the landmark case known as *Dixon v. Alabama State Board of Education* (1961) and ultimately led to the enforcement of due process in student conduct matters. For the students impacted and expelled in the incident, it took the Alabama State Board of Education 58 years to acknowledge the racist behavior, issue a public apology, and expunge their records (Haag, 2018). As student conduct administrators, it is important that we understand the impact of socialization, privilege, and oppression on our students and their experiences in and outside of the conduct process and higher education, while also examining our own socialization and how it influences our practice with students.

The Cycle of Socialization

The cycle of socialization (Harro, 2000) is one way of conceptualizing how individuals living in the United States are taught to be and act in their various social identities and differences while upholding systemic oppression. The cycle of socialization (Harro, 2000) has five components: (a) the beginning, (b) first socialization, (c) institutional/cultural socialization, (d) enforcements, and (e) results, which divides and provides an individual with the choice to interrupt or repeat the cycle. Infused within the cycle is the core, which holds an individual's value system and acts as a guide to navigate through the socialized realities being constructed around the individual. The core is often blocked and confused by myths and misinformation that can lead to feelings of fear, ignorance, confusion, and insecurity.

The movement within the cycle can shift as individuals deepens their development in systems of oppression and/or their experiences with systemic injustice.

In the beginning, almost immediately after a child is born they are "asked" by parents/family, teachers, and friends whom they love and trust to operate in a world where oppressive systems are already in place and functioning (Harro, 2000). These individuals influence a child's "self-concepts and self-perceptions, the norms and rules we must follow, the roles we are taught to play, our expectations for the future, and our dreams" at both intrapersonal and interpersonal levels (Harro, 2000, p. 17). For example, children may be told, "Girls belong in the kitchen"; "Boys should not cry. Why are you so sensitive?" and "You need to stop eating so much mi hija (my daughter), or you will never get a man to love you." Children may internalize these messages as truth and do everything they can to maintain status quo or adhere to privileged ideologies.

Once children begin school or *first socialization,* they fall into one of two categories: the group that benefits from the rules (privileged) or the group that is penalized by the rules (marginalized). The messaging they receive is also reinforced through interactions with media, places of worship, and other institutions (e.g., legal system, mental health, medicine, business), otherwise known as *institutional/cultural socialization* (Harro, 2000). A constant feeling of discomfort may develop in the marginalized individual or group, whereas the privileged group may not notice that the rules created are not fair or equitable. For children of color, this may show up in how they participate in the classroom based on the messages they have received about their intelligence from media, and/or respect for authority in the classroom, and how they are taught at home not to disagree or challenge their teachers or authority.

Enforcements (e.g., higher education admissions standards, ACT/SAT scores, financial aid), are in place to protect socialization and its rules throughout the cycle. Individuals who try to work against normative ideas and/or highlight the wrongdoings of others, a policy, or system "are accused of being troublemakers, of making waves, or of being 'the cause of the problem'" (Harro, 2000, p. 19). Racial microaggressions, "brief and commonplace daily verbal, behavioral, and commonplace indignities, whether intentional or unintentional, that communicate hostile, derogatory, or negative racial slights and insults to the target person or group" are a direct result of enforcements (Sue et al., 2007, p. 271). For instance, if a member of the privileged group confronts a person for using a racial microaggression such as assuming a Brown person speaks Spanish and asks them to translate something into Spanish, they risk losing benefits they have access to and receive because of their privilege.

The *results* of the cycle determine actions and whether individuals take the direction for social change. Learning the cycle of socialization is a system set up to oppress marginalized individuals and groups based on their social identities and is a hard reality for an individual to understand in spaces of both privileged and marginalized identities. In addition, there is a responsibility of advocacy and agency that comes along with the awareness of the cycle and the choice to engage with or interrupt socialization (Harro, 2000). For individuals with privileged identities, it is easy to remain unconscious or to perpetuate the cycle of oppression by maintaining the status quo because "it's not your problem." In addition, there are limited incentives to challenge oppressive assumptions, which can create guilt for privileged individuals and groups as they fail to interrupt and participate in socialization. Failure to act on this guilt becomes privileged individuals' consent for the cycle to continue. For others who are unaccepting of socialization, they often act as advocates and use their power and privilege to challenge the system and create hope alongside marginalized individuals and groups.

For individuals who identify with a marginalized identity or group, they may "experience anger, a sense of being silenced, dissonance between what the USA stands for and what they experience, low self-esteem, high levels of stress, a sense of hopelessness and disempowerment that can lead to crime and self-destructive behavior, frustration, mistrust, and dehumanization" (Harro, 2000, p. 19). These feelings can translate into a learned helplessness or internalized oppression, which makes individuals who identify with a marginalized identity or group victims of the cycle and oppression. Others may become tired of the discomfort and find agency to push against the power of the system. Their agency can be found in others who share their experience and/or advocates who want to work in solidarity with them to create change.

History Is Still Here

While there has been progress in many areas of the United States, when one looks closely, it is easy to see that many injustices carryover from the past. The United States at its core was founded as a White country and, as early as 1790, restricted naturalization to "white persons" only, and left this standard in place until 1952 (López, 2006, p. 1). In fact, to strengthen this notion, the law continued to change to support this ideology by allowing some court cases to justify Whiteness by skin color, other cases by country of origin, others by common knowledge, and yet others by scientific evidence (López, 2006). By having court cases play a part in creating the narrative, such cases not only legalize the decisions but also significantly drive thoughts of power and privilege, shaping later race relations (López, 2006).

The United States was also a male-oriented, male-dominated country. The fact that women did not receive the right to vote until 1920, upon the ratification of the 19th Amendment, confirms this notion. While the 14th Amendment (1868) gave citizens the right to vote, citizens were considered male. Even more, it was not until the 15th Amendment (1870) that Black men were given that right to vote. Regarding property ownership, originally a woman's belongings were the property of her father and, upon being married, the rights of her property transferred to her husband. In 1718, women were allowed to own property as long as their spouses were incapacitated. The Expatriation Act of 1907 called for an American woman to lose her citizenship if she married an "alien." *Muller v. Oregon* (1908) allowed women's working hours to be limited so that their health could be protected. We highlight these instances to display that the limits to personal control by women were not only community standards but were supported by the very laws of the country.

The United States was also, historically, a homophobic country. For this reason, the Society of Human Rights was founded in 1924 and produced the first newsletter highlighting gay interests. Later, because of harassment and poor treatment, the gay rights movement was started in the 1960s where the Stonewall riots of 1969 (Franke-Ruta, 2013) served as the movement's catalyst. Since then, there have been many movements and political and legislative victories, such as the election of Harvey Milk (the first openly gay elected official in the state of California), the Matthew Shepherd and James Byrd, Jr. Hate Crimes Prevention Act (2009), changes in the Boy Scouts (Leopold, 2015) and Girl Scouts (McLaughlin, 2015) to allow openly gay employees and leaders, and the 2015 U.S. Supreme Court ruling (*Obergefell v. Hodges*, 2015) requiring all states to grant same-sex marriage. These triumphs for LGBTQ interests occurred because the government mandated the general population accept the changes. Much progress still has to be made, however, as evidenced by the "bathroom bill," which was introduced and negatively targets transgender citizens (Drew, 2018).

As we examine the United States today, many of the scars we hope to forget still show themselves. Racially, the scars surface with the images of Walter Scott being gunned down by a South Carolina police officer (Schmidt & Apuzzo, 2015), Eric Garner whispering "I can't breathe" to his death at the hands of an officer in New York City (Goldstein & Schweber, 2014), Freddie Gray sustaining injuries and eventually dying in police custody in Baltimore, Maryland, (Hermann & Cox, 2015), and the emergence of the Black lives matter movement that has served to bring to light the violence and systemic racism that continues to pervade U.S. culture. Beyond Blackness, and while still connected to race, the images of Standing Rock Sioux protests opposing law enforcement and a pipeline through land held as sacred to this ethnic group were widespread (Harris & Gonchar, 2016). Reports and research recently display Latinx males being at the highest risk of police shootings (Everding, 2018) and brutality at the hands of authorities connected to the increase of anti-immigration rhetoric (Nittle, 2018). Additionally, research from the Pew Research Center (Horowitz, Brown, & Cox, 2019) shows that being Black, Latinx, Asian, or part of other non-White populations increases the likelihood of being impacted by racial slurs in the current political climate (Horowitz, Brown, & Cox, 2019).

Similar scars surface in regard to sex and gender when the #MeToo movement, founded by Tarana Burke, displays countless tragic stories of women who have continued to suffer in silence not knowing how to come forward to express the truth surrounding their instances of sexual harassment and/or assaults (North, 2018; Remnick, 2018; Zarkov &Davis, 2018). More so, with the emergence of the Larry Nassar scandal, women were again abused by a male in authority whom they did not know how to challenge until recently (Salam, 2019). Further, there have been reports that many women, in relation to Title IX, feel that the proposed rules will act to discourage women from sharing their experiences if they feel as if they have been discriminated against (Schwartz, 2018), even in a climate that suggests schools may still be underreporting sexual misconduct cases (Miller, 2018). Additionally, there has also been an increase of men stating they believe that processes are being skewed toward women who report instances of sexual misconduct (Avi-Yonah & Chaidez, 2018; Bauer-Wolf, 2018; Costello, 2018). Ironically, even today in 2019, lawmakers, the majority of whom are male, are making laws about women's bodies to include when a woman can have an abortion (Belluck, 2019).

Yet, there are still other marginalized communities and identities impacted in today's climate. Students with both mental and physical disabilities continue to express concerns of discrimination and disenfranchisement for not being afforded accommodations and/or resources due to them (Beja, 2009; Kadvany, 2018). Regarding religion, many reports of Islamophobia continue to surface, creating a chilly climate across the country, and there have been increases in political engagement of Muslim citizens, due to rhetoric connecting Islam to terrorism (Gray, 2018). Similarly, incidents of anti-Semitism through word and/or actions have increased concern in many Jewish communities and at the national level (Kesslen, 2019; Weise & Ellis, 2019). Finally, as many international visitors are getting familiar with new immigration practices, the current political climate, and mounting fears connected to the immigration process, many/potential students are electing to gain access to degrees elsewhere (Ellis, 2019; Johnson, 2019).

Differences Between the Legal System and the Student Conduct System

Why are the aforementioned aspects of United States history important? These points are important because all aspects of current events and climate affect the students who come to our campuses and who ultimately can enter our conduct systems. Further, depending on students' view of authority, their comfort and trust levels toward those they see as operators of a system may vary as well. While many publications in the last 15 years have sought to differentiate the legal system from the student conduct process, those differences are primarily understood by the student conduct practitioners. In 2004, Stoner and Lowery sought to remove the notion of the student conduct process as connected to the legal system when they presented their model code, which displayed that student conduct was steeped in policy not law, was between the student and institution not the state or federal governments, and that each process was specific to the institution of enrollment. Further, in 2006, the Association for Student Judicial Affairs (ASJA), now the Association for Student Conduct Administration (ASCA), created a guide detailing a brief history of student conduct practices (Loschiavo, Newman, & Kelly, 2006). It stated that a conduct violation is not necessarily a crime and that the student conduct process does not lead to a criminal record and explained how the Family Educational Rights and Privacy Act 1974 (FERPA) protects students' educational records from being shared except for limited circumstances. Yet, for students entering the conduct system, these nuances may not matter. They are entering a system whereby there is an authority figure, and potentially a system backing the authority, in place to negatively affect their lives.

How Students Enter the Student Conduct Process

Many students are introduced to the student conduct process through either being confronted by a person in authority: a police officer, residence hall staff, or another member of the institution's faculty or staff who is supported by institutional policy to do so. During or after the confrontation, a report of some kind is written and an account of the happenings is documented. The report is then given to an office responsible for investigations and the student is asked to converse with system personnel who are then charged with making decisions as to how the situation will be resolved. For students who have grown to see systems as their support, this may not be problematic. However, what about those who perceive themselves as being part of a marginalized social group? Studies show that not only are marginalized student groups systemically singled out more than majority populations, but also that those in the majority are believed to be unbiased in their actions (Solórzano, Ceja, & Yosso, 2000). On college campuses, this sentiment is prevalent in the relationships displayed with campus law enforcement. Some campus law enforcement officers have been accused of racial profiling in recent history, with a North Carolina campus instituting a bias reporting system for those who believe officers behaved in a discriminatory fashion (Schmidt, 2015). Yet, when a university president in Pennsylvania joined students in a protest against unfair treatment of students, the officers believed her actions were a disservice to every uniformed officer serving the institution (Schmidt, 2015). These sentiments connected to institutions of higher education seem to correlate with the sentiments in our larger communities. Students do not change their perceptions because they cross the threshold of the campus. The same societal perceptions and impacts associated with race, gender, ability, sexual orientation, nationality and other criteria remain with students as they interact with the campus environment.

Why Social Justice?

For our work in this chapter, we chose to use a social justice lens while understanding there are emerging terminologies that may be considered similar. "The goal of social justice is full and equal participation of all groups in a society that is mutually shaped to meets their needs. Social justice also includes a vision of society in which the distribution of resources is equitable and all members are physically and psychologically safe and secure" (Adams, Bell, & Griffin, 2007, p. 16). Such phrases such as "cultural competence," "cultural humility," "inclusive excellence," "intercultural competence," and others yet to be presented are used, sometimes interchangeably to affirm a much-needed acceptance of cultures toward increased diversity and inclusion (Foronda, Baptiste, & Reinholdt, 2015; Lum, 2011; Tervalon & Murray-Garcia, 1998; Williams, Berger, & McClendon, 2005). We give space to cultural humility later in this chapter. The social justice lens was selected because we believe higher education professions need to go beyond recognition and acceptance of difference to the dismantling and reconstructing of systems toward the equal distribution of access, excellence, and resources. Power, privilege, and oppression continue to impact our communities, to include higher education, through discriminatory practices such as racism, sexism, ableism, heterosexism, and so on, through our individual actions and via practices that remain unchecked on campuses. The principle problem of being on the margins, any margin, is that those on the margins can be made to feel that not only do they not belong, but that systems of support are not designed to support them. It is imperative to continue examination of unearned access and opportunities and work toward full and equal participation and physical and psychological safety and security on our campuses. We must eliminate socialization patterns that repeat historical harms lest we allow students to continue enduring what current systems are designed to produce: inequity. An abundance of research has shown that inequity not only negatively affects connectivity to campuses but can also impact behaviors and self-concepts of students both positively and negatively (Adams & Bell, 2016; Steele & Aronson, 1995). In other words, "Without addressing issues of injustice, we cannot truly value diversity" (Adams & Bell, 2016, p. 4).

Strategies to Embed Social Justice Into Student Conduct Process

Recognizing the influence of socialization, privilege, and oppression in the student conduct process is important to learning how to embed social justice into the student conduct process. Specifically, embedding social justice into the student conduct process allows a student conduct administrator to practice a culture of care and acknowledgment of difference while also maintaining a fair process. Strategies to promote social justices in the student conduct process are as follows.

Take Responsibility for Your Own Learning and Reflection

Engaging in social justice work requires commitment to individual reflection, learning, and responsibility. Specifically, it is valuable to embed critical self-reflection and self-critique of cultural values, beliefs, and biases into daily life and practice, otherwise known as cultural humility (Tervalon & Murray-Garcia, 1998). Cultural humility expands self-awareness beyond the notion of cultural competence, the ability to understand self, and developing positive attitudes toward difference and encourages individuals to commit to a lifelong process of inclusivity. In addition, cultural humility centers on individual reflection and growth versus othering individuals who are different. As a result, there is also individual and collective accountability in cultural humility. The accountability that occurs in cultural humility requires individuals to take responsibility for their actions and engage in work with their own social membership groups. For instance, in exploring racial identity, it is important that White people educate, reflect, and hold each other account-able for their actions and racist socialization versus relying on people of color to engage them in conversation on their behaviors.

Focus on Dialogue Not Debate

To understand others and receive their perspectives, there must be a transi-tion from debate to dialogue in our conversations with others. Compared to debate where there is a competitive notion that can create disagreement, frus-tration, harm, and confusion, dialogue expands communication and allows individuals to connect and build shared meaning through a collaborative exchange focused on mutual respect and understanding (Winbolt, 2010). Other characteristics and benefits of dialogue include the following:

- Fostering exploration when there are multiple perspectives to an answer that can be shared
- Encouraging an open-minded attitude and openness to change and being wrong
- Surfacing assumptions for discussion and evaluation
- Reexamining all positions and understanding values
- Providing space for acceptance that others can improve
- Treating communication as a relationship (Winbolt, 2010)

At the core of dialogue is active listening, a pattern of listening that encourages listening attentively while someone shares their perspective and reflects back what is shared without judgment and advice (Cunic, 2019). Listening first to understand an individual's experience can increase the impact and meaning of dialogue. Applying active listening to conversations with others takes practice as it may challenge authenticity and be difficult to maintain between individuals. However, with structure and guidance, the benefits of active listening dialogue can improve relationships and foster change.

Apply Intersectionality as a Framework

Intersectionality (Crenshaw, 1989, 1991) emerged in critical race theory (Bell, 1989), critical race feminism (Delgado, 1995), and Black feminist scholarship (Collins, 1990; hooks, 1984; Lorde, 1984) to illuminate the marginalization experienced by Women of color through an examination of multiple, intertwining social and cultural identities (e.g., race/ethnicity, gender, and social class). Since its unveiling, scholars acknowledge identity intersectionality is complex and it does not foreground individual identity experiences and stories (Collins, 2009). Rather, intersectionality highlights how individuals—as members of multiple groups—experience fluidity among their competing marginalized and dominant identities, even in movements where social justice and institutional change are present (Dill, McLaughlin, & Nieves, 2007). An intersectional perspective also creates a foundation for understanding how power and privilege dynamics influence the fluidity of intersectionality and which identity becomes most salient for an individual in the context of an experience (Torres, Jones, & Renn, 2009). Leading with an intersectional framework allows individuals to have agency over their salient identities, while also encouraging them to bring their whole selves and unique experiences into a space.

Practice Multipartiality

Bias in humans is inevitable. We have things and people that we like and dislike, prefer or not, and have associated with good and/or bad. Thorndike's (1920) study on the halo effect, that is still positively regarded, displayed that when a person forms an opinion in one area, there is still residual information that can impact future judgments. This implies that when a person makes a judgment about a perceived social group, that judgment/bias can be attached to anyone perceived to be connected to that group. For example, if a person assumes that a collegiate athlete gets special treatment, they may assume that all collegiate athletes receive advantages. Yet, in structures where professionals have had to decide an outcome or help participants through a conflict, for a significant amount of time neutrality was the standard (Olshak, 2001; Warters 2000). More recently, many have begun to accept that neutrality, while some semblance of it can be shown on the surface, is not actually attainable. Therefore, multipartiality is increasing in acceptance (Gadlin & Sturm, 2007). Through multipartiality, the third-party facilitator or process controller does not have to play the role of the unaffected but can ask questions and make statements to examine deeper meanings, oppression, and existence of power while honoring the realities of all involved (Gadlin & Sturm, 2007). As such, third-party professionals do not have to limit themselves, but need to be skilled enough to have all involved feel truly heard while being in line with the method used. In fact, it must be understood that the third party, while not a participant in the conflict, is involved in the conflict and has to be accounted for. Multipartiality can be used in all pathways of resolution; however, the way it is used in facilitated dialogue and its appearance in a more formal method of conflict resolution will differ. Student conduct work involves much more than decisions and outcomes;

education is central to this work. The more students can make sense of the process, the better educated they will become. Further, we contend that multipartiality helps to create a socially just environment because the unequal culture and structures will most likely come under scrutiny as a result of proper process management forcing the acknowledgement of surrounding inequities.

Create Brave Spaces

Creating spaces where students can share their lived experiences authentically without judgment and with a sense of safety is important for individual growth and reflection. However, safe spaces (Schapiro, 2016) are not guaranteed to be "safe" from harm and can mislead individuals about the goals of the space. For instance, a space designed to support the LGBTQ communities can easily be disrupted by someone who does not identify as LGBTQ without parameters for engagement for both individuals in and outside of the community. As a result, the idea of brave spaces (Arao & Clemens, 2013) has surfaced in an effort to reduce harm and strengthen guidance around honoring individual experiences. In a brave space,

- multiple perspectives are respected and shared;
- acknowledgement and discussion occur about intention and impact on the emotional well-being of another person;
- options to step in and out of challenging conversations are provided;
- respect for one another's personhood is valued; and
- there is agreement not to inflict harm intentionally on one another (Arao & Clemens, 2013; Ali, 2017).

Facilitating spaces with intentionality allows individuals to understand expectations of the space and choice about their engagement, which can increase confidence to participate and share. In addition, when guidelines are created in a community there is shared accountability that can be applied to refocus on the purpose of the space.

Other ways to create brave spaces is through displaying artifacts, effective nonverbal communication, and inclusive/culturally responsive practices. For instance, in your office, placing artifacts that represent your support for social justice, inclusion, and equity in areas that can be noticed such as your door, your walls, and your bookshelves can provide insight for individuals about who you are and how you may receive their stories. Being vulnerable about artifacts in your space humanizes you and shares insight into your personhood as both a practitioner and individual. Equally as important is the nonverbal communication received from facial expressions or body language. When listening to an individual's story, be mindful of how you are receiving the information and the messages you are sending about it. For instance, are your arms crossed? This could send a message that you are not open to receiving the other person's perspective. Others to be aware of are checking your phone or clock for time or typing/writing while someone is talking without telling them what you are doing. Active listening requires listening to understand versus listening to respond. These are all things to be mindful of in conversation with others.

In addition, it is important to embed inclusive/culturally responsive practices into your conversations with others. A few practices include the following:

- Asking about personal pronouns and sharing your own as a way to model support for individuals who identify as transgender or non-binary
- Providing choice for individuals entering your office around where they want to sit. There may be a need to sit in a space that provides access to a door or scan of the room for individuals with specific lived experiences (e.g., individuals with military connection, survivors of sexual assault)
- Displaying a variety of fidget figures to manipulate for individuals who you may perceive to be nervous while engaging in conversation. Model this by grabbing a fidget yourself and invite them to do so as well. Providing this option can support focus and reduction in anxiety

By engaging in these types of practices, you can begin to create brave spaces for individuals to share their stories and perspectives with you in authentic ways because there is comfort and a reduction for the possibility of harm.

Learn How to Apply Each of the Conflict Resolution Models

In 2009, Schrage and Giacomini edited *Reframing Campus Conflict*, a book that offered a variety of conduct and conflict resolution options known as the spectrum model. Along the spectrum, readers were made familiar with the following pathways by which student conflicts could be resolved: no conflict resolution, dialogue, conflict coaching, facilitated dialogue, mediation, restorative practices, shuttle negotiation, informal adjudication, and formal adjudication. While this chapter is not designed to train the audience on any or all of these pathways, we want to familiarize the audience with them while also displaying how social justice still takes station through all aspects of the spectrum.

1. Under the "no conflict management" pathway, institutional personnel do not get involved with the conflict when it is believed that the dissonance present can create an education space with no safety concerns and when those involved have no risk of marginalization.

2. The "dialogue" pathway is optimal with students have equal power and seek to gain an understanding independent of university professionals or third-party intervention. Those involved in this pathway understand that they are working together to craft a solution and are not competing, are collaborators trying to find meaning, have hope of reexamining all positions, and are hopeful of creating new opinions rather than seeking closure.

3. The "conflict coaching" pathway is the first pathway in which one or more students contact a third party to aid them in how to independently approach a situation in a more effective manner (Jones & Brinkert, 2007). The third-party person functions as a trained coach to aid in individual education and reflection for those who want to handle the situation on their own, when a timely response is needed and is simple enough to implement and is often done before accessing another pathway.

4. In "facilitated dialogue," students access the administration to facilitate the conversation so that they can hear each other better than they could alone while maintaining control of the decisions and outcomes. The facilitator uses sessions to prepare the participant while also outlining the flow of the upcoming meeting(s). These sessions should feel as if they are lower risk than more formal sessions while still allowing all voices to be heard toward an understanding rather than a concrete resolution. The sessions feature ground rules, questions, and a monitoring or airtime while remaining focused.

5. Through the "mediation" pathway, students understand that they are asking for a third-party professional to create a structured session in order to resolve a conflict they could not resolve independently. It is important to note that the mediator has received at least 40 hours of training in mediation and understands they can be asked to focus on solving problems or restoring relationships. This is the first station in the spectrum of resolution options where an outcome is desired, if possible.

6. "Restorative practices" can be used as a way to either avoid punishment for behaviors or as an added portion of the formal conduct process. In either case, students first take ownership of harmful actions while also allowing others who were directly and indirectly affected by the behaviors to join in creating an agreement toward community restoration.

A trained facilitator is also needed in this pathway, and participants identify the harm and how to repair it and also decide who will take ownership of the repairs. This pathway is used to develop empathy, gain a holistic view of the offense, and aid in transformation of all involved. All participants enter the process voluntarily and understand that the exchanges are less about finding and documenting fault and more about restoring the community to the best of everyone's ability.

7. "Shuttle negotiation" is used when parties involved cannot, or choose not to, directly engage each other while choosing not to become involved in the formal conduct/adjudication process. One party's positions are presented to another and vice versa until a workable solution is agreed on (if possible). This method is useful when future interactions are improbable or limited, a future relationship is not desired or needed, and there are definite objectives in mind.

8. "Adjudication" (formal and informal) is the most familiar pathway along the student conduct continuum and leaves the third-party entity in complete control of the process and the outcome.

In all pathways it is important to note that all student participants are seen as humans of good faith who desire to receive an education while remaining part of the community. The individuals and the social groups they belong to (real or perceived) are to be honored through the maintenance of respect and inclusion in either pathway. The personal, cultural, and systemic experiences are to be accounted for as they are all a part of the educational process as well. The educational process includes teaching, restoration, inclusion, and protection, while also allowing for stages of interpersonal development. When a pathway involves a facilitator or process owner, it should be understood that the professional fully comprehends multipartiality as described. All in all, as members of communities understand their own cultures and climates best, these community members are responsible for choosing the best pathways for educating members.

Implications for Practice

While there is much to contemplate about socialization, privilege, and oppression and its impact on students' experiences in institutions of higher education, it is important to offer implications for practice toward engaging difference in higher education. Throughout this chapter, we attempt to exhibit that our challenges and opportunities not only exist in the realm of the individual but at the communal, societal, operational, and structural levels as well. Therefore, we offer the following:

1. *Messages affirming that belonging, cultural understanding, equity, fairness, inclusion, and transparency should be featured in the overall mission of the institution and/or division, as well as connected to the student conduct process in easy-to-see ways.* Before students, and families for that matter, are introduced to any specific campus entity, they are given information about the overall institution. Much of this information is conveyed in communications prior to arriving to campus and during new student orientation. These contacts allow prospective students and families the opportunity to learn more about the campus culture and expectations and allow for them to begin building an understanding of the new environment. Once families understand the perceived campus atmosphere, any experiences with any campus entity, if not similar to the original messages about the larger entity, feel incongruent. Therefore, we believe that if prospective students and families are led to understand the institution as a socially just community, the same will be expected of the student conduct process and those operating it.

2. *It is helpful for the individual student to receive neutral information about the student conduct process, and the operators of the process, upon entering the campus community.* As discussed earlier in the chapter, individuals create meaning through lived experiences and the perceived experiences of others. First impressions, while they may not be the only impressions to be made, still matter significantly when assessing new surroundings. Therefore, it is important to afford students the opportunity to understand the purpose, operation, and impression of the student conduct process prior to interacting with it. To expect students to read the conduct code, or similar information, may not be realistic; however, passive marketing may increase familiarity so students have some level of understanding regarding the process and its actors.

3. *Individual students, when the situation allows, should be afforded avenues to aid them in decision-making prior to finding themselves in the student conduct process.* Not all students find themselves in the student conduct process because of a split-second decision. Some students interact with the process because they did not know how to handle a situation or did not understand what support may have been in place to assist them prior to making a poor choice. While situations of the sort are not limited to marginalized populations or first-generation students, studies

have shown there is a decreased likelihood of these students knowing how to access resources and assistance (Rubio, Mireles, Jones, & Mayse, 2017). With this said, we believe in a proactive approach that connects students to support systems and advocates and provides mentors who are available to coach students through interpersonal situations in an attempt to avoid violations of policy.

4. *Individuals should be able to see someone from their perceived social group at some level of authority in the student conduct process.* One of the best ways to feel connected to and accepted by a community is to see others from your perceived social group(s). In order for students to view the conduct process as fair and equitable, it is necessary for them to see others from their perceived social group as operators of the process in some way. For offices that have smaller staffs and may not be able to guarantee representation, it may be equally important to have messaging present as a method to show the importance of inclusion. The more comfortable students are in their surroundings, the most they can learn.

5. *Those operating the student conduct process should understand multipartiality and how it can be displayed based on the conduct method being used.* As discussed earlier, some methods in the student conduct process may have increased openings for multipartiality to be shown. However, for all parts of the spectrum of resolution connected to conduct, there is some opportunity for it to be displayed. The practitioner should be familiar with multipartiality, ways to exhibit it openly in the student conduct process, to ensure that students have an opportunity to feel heard at the deepest levels possible. Ensuring this can continue to transform students' perceptions of the process over time.

6. *Practitioners should seek and invest in ways to improve their cultural understanding to continue developing as professionals and community members.* Professional development is important. In student affairs work, there are numerous associations and for-profit entities whose major focus is to ensure professionals have the most up-to-date training and access to high-impact practices. As our campuses are becoming increasingly diverse, understanding how diversity, inclusion, cultural competence, and social justice affects our work and communities is no different. Professionals and institutions must commit to continue improvement in order to provide for the best service to student populations overall, including students entering the student conduct process.

7. *Individuals and offices responsible for confronting students and/or generating the reports introducing students to the conduct process should have meth-*

ods of building relationships with the general student population (or sub-communities they interact with frequently) prior to a situation. Beginning a trusting relationship in the midst of a confrontation is difficult. One service entity that understands this is law enforcement. As such, community policing has become a method by which community partnerships are formed and problems are solved before an incident occurs that warrants a law enforcement response. This proactive stance can increase trust in the police (United States Department of Justice, n.d.). We believe that the same method can be used to strengthen campus communities. Personnel responsible for policy enforcement and students expected to function within the policies are part of the same community. Creating more trust also increases educational opportunities.

8. *Offices responsible for the student conduct process should offer an avenue for students to express how they encounter the student conduct process both as an individual and as a member of their perceived social group(s).* Assessment is crucial in determining the impact and satisfaction levels of experiences with the conduct system. Depending on how the assessment is conducted, both objective and subjective feedback can be gained. Sometimes, there is a disconnect between those who experience office cultures and functions from the receiving end and the perceptions of services offered by personnel in student conduct offices. As we seek to build partnerships with our students in their educational journey, we also need to gather feedback and information from them to help maintain standards and to improve service.

9. *Any part of the conduct process that is perceived to be oppressive should be changed.* Many students may not give their opinions, because they do not want to bring possible negative attention to themselves. Yet, there are others who have no problem being vocal about campus aspects (e.g., interactions, organizations, traditions, and campus structures) they consider to be oppressive in nature. The student conduct process may be one to review. Listen to the students. In recent higher education history, there are many examples of problems to make national news that surfaced as a result of students feeling unheard. While students are resilient and are excellent problem solvers, our students increasingly see education as a commodity in which administrators owe them a product (Keenan, 2015). Therefore, students are demanding campus aspects that cause inequity to be removed; they are also expecting campus professionals to do so or else they will make it an issue on a larger scale.

Conclusion

Many aspects of United States history are still visible in the present. Institutions of higher education and the practices associated within academia are not separate from this truth; there are various parts of the academy that have proven to be beneficial over time such as scholarly discourse, transparent policy manuals, and support services, to name a few. Yet other aspects of history remain and need to be challenged, both in structure and in practice. Examples of such are unequal access and traditions that further marginalize populations and campus climates that cause students to feel less than accepted based on real or perceived social groups. While we believe it important for all portions of institution of higher learning to be free of the latter, we also believe it paramount for offices and professionals dealing with conduct and conflict resolution to take the lead in this effort. Conduct and conflict resolution professionals are in positions to affect students through decisions and interpersonal facilitations and are seen by many students as the holders of the campus moral compass. The United States, in its short history, was seen as a country steeped in the beliefs of human rights and the pursuit of equity. Many countries aspired to those same standards. However, as portrayed earlier in this chapter, the social climate in the United States and the international view of the United States has become more critical and informed (Codevilla, 2018; Lanktree, 2018). More appropriately, the same skepticism is becoming attached to institutions of higher education, specifically by those who believe that these colleges and universities are not contributing to what matters (Smith, 2018). Behavior and conflict management are of great importance, especially in today's contentious society. Students learn from their experiences. Additionally, students learn more in fundamentally fair situations and when they believe they are accepted. Students feel accepted when transparency is abundant, information is accessible, their voice is given space to be heard, they are challenged for the better, they are given the opportunity for strengthened relationships, and they have the ability to offer feedback. All of these aspects, at the core, should occur in a socially just conduct process.

References

Adams, M., & Bell, L. A. (Eds.). (2016). *Teaching for diversity and social justice* (3rd ed.). New York, NY: Routledge.

Adams, M., Bell, L. A., & Griffin, P. (Eds.). (2007). *Teaching for diversity and social justice* (2nd ed.). New York, NY: Routledge.

Ali, D. (2017, October). Safe spaces and brave spaces: Historical context and recommendations for student affairs professionals. NASPA Policy & Practice Series, 2. Retrieved from https://www.naspa.org/images/uploads/main/Policy_and_Practice_No_2_Safe_Brave_Spaces.pdf

Arao, B., & Clemens, K. (2013). From safe spaces to brave spaces: A new way to frame dialogue around diversity and social justice. In L. Landreman (Ed.), *The art of effective facilitation: Reflections from social justice educators* (pp. 135–150). Sterling, VA: Stylus.

Avi-Yonah, S. S., & Chaidez, A. A. (2018, October 26). Student alleges in suit that Harvard discriminated against him in Title IX case. *Harvard Crimson*. Retrieved from https://www.thecrimson.com/article/2018/10/26/title-ix-discrimination-lawsuit/

Bauer-Wolf, J. (2018, May 21). Student wants to "end affirmative action for women." *Inside Higher Ed*. Retrieved from https://www.insidehighered.com/news/2018/05/21/yale-being-investigated-discrimination-against-men-unusual-title-ix-complaint

Beja, M. (2009, July 2). Advocates for the blind sue Arizona State U. over Kindle use. *Chronicle of Higher Education*. Retrieved from https://www.chronicle.com/blogs/wiredcampus/advocates-for-the-blind-sue-arizona-state-u-over-kindle-use/7252

Bell, D. (1989). *And we are not saved: The elusive quest for racial justice*. New York, NY: Aspen Law and Business.

Bell, L. A. (1997). Theoretical foundations for social justice education. In M. Adams, L. A., Bell,

& P. Griffin (Eds.), *Teaching for diversity and social justice: A sourcebook* (pp. 3–15). New York, NY: Routledge.

Belluck, P. (2019, May 9). What do new state abortion laws really mean for women? *New York Times*. Retrieved from https://www.nytimes.com/2019/05/09/health/state-abortion-laws.html

Codevilla, A. M. (2018, June 26). America has the world's envy, but no longer its respect. *Washington Examiner*. Retrieved from https://www.washingtonexaminer.com/opinion/america-has-lost-the-worlds-respect

Collins, P. H. (1990). *Black feminist thought*. New York, NY: Routledge.

Collins, P. H. (2009). *Another kind of public education: Race, schools, the media and democratic possibilities*. Boston, MA: Beacon Press.

Costello, B. (2018, December 11). Lawsuit: IU violated Title IX by suspending male student accused of rape. *WFYI Indianapolis*. Retrieved from https://www.wfyi.org/news/articles/lawsuit-iu-violated-title-ix-by-suspending-male-student-accused-of-rape

Crenshaw, K. (1989). Demarginalizing the intersection of race and sex: A Black feminist critique of antidiscrimination doctrine, feminist theory and antiracist politics. *University of Chicago Legal Forum, 1989*(8), 139–167.

Crenshaw, K. (1991). Mapping the margins: Intersectionality, identity politics, and violence against women of color. *Stanford Law Review, 4*, 1241–1299.

Cunic, A. (2019, July 16). How to practice active listening. *Very Well Mind.* Retrieved from https://www.verywellmind.com/what-is-active-listening-3024343

Delgado, R. (Ed.). (1995). *Critical race theory: The cutting edge.* Philadelphia, PA: Temple University Press.

Dill, B. T. McLaughlin, A., & Nieves, A. D. (2007). Future directions of feminist research: Intersectionality. In S. Hesse-Biber (Ed.), *Handbook of feminist research, theory, and praxis* (pp. 629–638). Thousand Oaks, CA: SAGE.

Dixon v. Alabama State Board of Education, 294 F.2d 150 (5th Cir. 1961)

Drew, J. (2018, June 25). North Carolina's transgender rights battle isn't over. *USA Today.* Retrieved from https://www.usatoday.com/story/news/nation/2018/06/25/north-carolina-bathroom-bill-transgender/729791002/

Ellis, L. (2019, June 3). China is warning it students about going to college in America. Here's why that matters. *Chronicle of Higher Education.* Retrieved from https://www.chronicle.com/article/China-Is-Warning-Its-Students/246427?cid=wcontentlist_hp_latest&cid=db

Expatriation Act, H.R. 24122, Chap. 2534, 59th Cong. (1907)

Everding, G. (2018, March 29). Young Hispanic men may face greatest risk from police shootings, study finds. *The Source.* Retrieved from https://source.wustl.edu/2018/03/young-hispanic-men-may-face-greatest-risk-from-police-shootings-study-finds/

Family Educational Rights and Privacy Act, 20 U.S.C. § 1232g; 34 CFR Part 99 (1974)

Foronda, C., Baptiste, D., & Reinholdt, M. M. (2015, June 28). Cultural humility: A concept analysis. *Journal of Transcultural Nursing, 27*(3), 210–217. doi:10.1177/1043659615592677

Franke-Ruta, Garance (2013, January 24). An American revolution: An amazing 1969 account of the Stonewall uprising. *The Atlantic.* Retrieved from https://www.theatlantic.com/politics/archive/2013/01/an-amazing-1969-account-of-the-stonewall-uprising/272467/

Gadlin, H., & Sturm, S. P. (2007). Conflict resolution and systemic change. *Journal of Dispute Resolution, 2007*(1), 1–65.

Goldstein, J., & Schweber, N. (2014, July 18). Man's death after chokehold raises old issue for police. *New York Times.* Retrieved from https://www.nytimes.com/2014/07/19/nyregion/staten-island-man-dies-after-he-is-put-in-chokehold-during-arrest.html

Gray, A. (2018, August 10). Islamophobia is driving more US Muslims to become politically engaged, suggests report. *World Economic Forum.* Retrieved from https://www.weforum.org/agenda/2018/08/muslims-in-united-states-more-politically-engaged-islamophobia/

Haag, M. (2018, May 30). An Alabama sit-in in 1960, an apology, and the lifetimes between. *New York Times.* Retrieved from https://www.nytimes.com/2018/05/30/us/alabama-students-sit-in-apology.html

Harris, K., & Gonchar, M. (2016, November 30). Battle over an oil pipeline: Teaching about Standing Rock Sioux protests. *New York Times.* Retrieved from https://

www.nytimes.com/2016/11/30/learning/lesson-plans/battle-over-an-oil-pipe-line-teaching-about-the-standing-rock-sioux-protests.html

Harro, B. (2000). The cycle of socialization. In M. Adams, W. Blumenfeld, R. Castaneda, H.

Hackman, M. Peters, & X. Zuniga (Eds.), *Readings for diversity and social justice* (pp. 16–21). New York, NY: Routledge.

Hate Crimes Prevention Act, H.R. 2647, 18 U.S.C. § 249 (2009)

Hermann, P., & Cox, J. W. (2015, April 28). A Freddie Gray primer: Who was he, how did he die, why is there so much anger? *Washington Post.* Retrieved from https://www.washingtonpost.com/news/local/wp/2015/04/28/a-freddie-gray-primer-who-was-he-how-did-he-why-is-there-so-much-anger/

hooks, b. (1981). *Ain't I a woman: Black women and feminism.* Boston, MA: South End Press.

Horowitz, J. M., Brown, A., & Cox, K. (2019, April 9). Race in America 2019. *Pew Research Center.* Retrieved from https://www.pewsocialtrends.org/2019/04/09/race-in-america-2019-methodology/

Johnson, A. G. (2006). *Privilege, power, and difference* (2nd ed.). New York, NY: McGraw Hill.

Johnson, S. (2019, May 29). Visa woes, politics, and fears or violence are keeping international students away, report warns. *Chronicle of Higher Education.* Retrieved from https://www.chronicle.com/article/Visa-Woes-PoliticsFears/246398?utm_source=at&utm_medium=en&cid=at

Jones, T. S., & Brinkert, R. (2007). *Conflict coaching: Conflict management strategies and skills for the individual.* Thousand Oaks, CA: SAGE.

Kadvany, E. (2018, May 25). Lawsuit: Stanford violated students' rights in mental health response. *Palo Alto Online.* Retrieved from https://www.paloaltoonline.com/news/2018/05/18/lawsuit-stanford-violated-students-rights-in-mental-health-response

Keenan, J. F. (2015). *University ethics: How colleges can build and benefit from a culture of ethics.* Lanham, MD: Rowman & Littlefield.

Kesslen, B. (2019, April 30). Anti-Semitic assaults in the U.S. more than doubled in 2018, ADL reports. *NBC News.* Retrieved from https://www.nbcnews.com/news/us-news/anti-semitic-assaults-u-s-more-doubled-2018-adl-reports-n1000246

Lanktree, G. (2018, January 18). Global respect for U.S. leadership dropped sharply under Trump—The opposite happened under Obama. *Newsweek.* Retrieved from https://www.newsweek.com/global-respect-us-leadership-dropped-sharply-under-trump-opposite-happened-784298

Leopold, T. (2015, July 28). Boy Scouts change policy on gay leaders. *CNN.* Retrieved from https://www.cnn.com/2015/07/27/us/boy-scouts-gay-leaders-feat/index.html

Loschiavo, C, Newman, A., & Kelly, M. T. (2006). The student conduct process: A guide for parents. *Association for Student Judicial Affairs (ASJA).* Retrieved from https://www.theasca.org/files/Publications/Student%20Conduct%20Process%20Guide%20for%20Parents%202006.pdf

López, I. H. (2006). *White by law: The legal construction of race.* New York, NY: New York University Press.

Lorde, A. (1984). *Sister outsider: Essays and speeches.* Berkeley, CA: Crossing Press.

Lum, D. (Ed.). (2011). *Culturally competent practice: A framework for understanding diverse groups and justice issues* (4th ed.). Belmont, CA: Brooks/Cole.

McIntosh, P. (1990). White privilege: Unpacking the invisible knapsack. *Independent School, 49*(2), 31–36.

McLaughlin, J. (2015, March 27). Boy Scouts and Girl Scouts take different paths to LGBT inclusion. *LawStreet.* Retrieved from https://lawstreetmedia.com/issues/entertainment-and-culture/boy-scouts-vs-girl-scouts-lgbt-policies-show-different-paths-modernization/

Miller, K. (2018, November 2). Schools are still underreporting sexual harassment and assault. *American Association of University Women.* Retrieved from https://www.aauw.org/article/schools-still-underreporting-sexual-harassment-and-assault/

Muller v. Oregon, 208 U.S. 412 (1908)

Nittle, N. K. (2018, February 20). Brutality against Hispanics: Anti-immigration rhetoric has put Latinos at risk. *ThoughtCo.* Retrieved from https://www.thoughtco.com/racial-profiling-police-brutality-against-hispanics-2834820

North, A. (2018, October 11). The #MeToo movement and its evolution, explained. *Vox.* Retrieved from https://www.vox.com/identities/2018/10/9/17933746/me-too-movement-metoo-brett-kavanaugh-weinstein

Obergefell v. Hodges, 576 U.S. ___ (2015)

Olshak, R. T. (2001). *Mastering mediation: A guide for training mediators in a college and university setting.* Horsham, PA: LRP.

Remnick, D. (2018, October 10). One year of #MeToo. *The New Yorker.* Retrieved from https://www.newyorker.com/news/news-desk/one-year-of-metoo

Rubio, L., Mireles, C., Jones, Q., & Mayse, M. (2017). Identifying issues surrounding first-generation students. *American Journal of Undergraduate Research.* Retrieved from http://www.ajuronline.org/uploads/Volume_14_1/AJUR_Vol_14%20Issue_1_04192017_pp5-10.pdf

Salam, M. (2019, May 3). How Larry Nassar "flourished unafraid" for so long. *New York Times.* Retrieved from https://www.nytimes.com/2019/05/03/sports/larry-nassar-gymnastics-hbo-doc.html

Schapiro, M. (2016, January 15). I'm Northwestern's president. Here's why safe spaces for students are important. *Washington Post.* Retrieved from https://https://www.washingtonpost.com/opinions/how-to-create-inclusive-campus-communities-first-create-safe-places/2016/01/15/069f3a66-bb94-11e5-829c-26ffb874a18d_story.html

Schmidt, M. S, & Apuzzo, M. (2015, April 7). South Carolina officer is charged with murder of Walter Scott. *New York Times.* Retrieved from https://www.nytimes.com/2015/04/08/us/south-carolina-officer-is-charged-with-murder-in-black-mans-death.html

Schmidt, P. (2015, January 9). Campus police departments struggle with issues of race. *Chronicle of Higher Education, 61*(17), A16–A16.

Schrage, J. M., & Giacomini, N. G. (Eds.) (2009). *Reframing campus conflict: Student conduct practice through a social justice lens.* Sterling, VA: Stylus.

Schwartz, G. (2018, November 29). The proposed Title IX rules will further discourage victims from coming forward. *Boston University School of Public Health.* Retrieved from https://www.bu.edu/sph/2018/11/29/the-proposed-title-ix-rules-will-further-discourage-victims-from-coming-forward/

Smith, C. (2018, January 9). Higher education is drowning in BS and it's mortally corrosive to society. *Chronicle of Higher Education.* Retrieved from https://www.chronicle.com/article/Higher-Education-Is-Drowning/242195

Solórzano, D. G., Ceja, M., & Yosso, T. J. (2000). Critical race theory, racial microaggressions, and campus racial climate: The experiences of African American college students. *Journal of Negro Education, 69*(1), 60–73.

Steele, C. M., & Aronson, J. (1995). Stereotype threat and the intellectual test performance of African-Americans. *Journal of Personality and Social Psychology, 69*(5), 797–811.

Stoner, E., & Lowery, J. W. (2004). Navigating past the "spirit of insubordination": A twenty-first century model student conduct code with a model hearing script. *Journal of College and University Law, 31*(1), 1–78. Retrieved from https://learn.uvm.edu/wordpress_3_4b/wp-content/uploads/stoner___lowery_JCUL_2004_cropped.pdf

Sue, D.W., Capodilupo, C. M., Torino, G. C., Bucceri, J. M., Holder, A. M., Nadal, K. L., & Esquilin, M. (2007). Racial microaggressions in everyday life: Implications for clinical practice. *American Psychologist, 62*(4), 271–286.

Tervalon, M., & Murray-Garcia, J. (1998). Cultural humility versus cultural competence: A critical distinction in defining physician training outcomes in multicultural education. *Journal of Health Care for the Poor and Underserved, 9*(2), 117–125.

Thorndike, E. L. (1920). A constant error in psychological ratings. *Journal of Applied Psychology, 4*(1), 25–29. Retrieved from http://web.mit.edu/curhan/www/docs/Articles/biases/4_J_Applied_Psychology_25_(Thorndike).pdf

Torres, V. R., Jones, S. R., & Renn, K. A. (2009). Identity development theories in student affairs: Origins, current status, and new approaches. *Journal of College Student Development, 50*(6), 577–596.

United States Department of Justice. (n.d.). Community policing defined. *Community Oriented Policing Services.* Retrieved from https://ric-zai-inc.com/Publications/cops-p157-pub.pdf

Warters, W. C. (2000). *Mediation in the campus community: Designing and managing effective programs.* San Francisco, CA: Jossey-Bass.

Weise, E. & Ellis, N. T. (2019, April 30). Rising anti-Semitic hatred is changing Jewish life across the United States. *USA Today.* Retrieved from https://www.usatoday.com/story/news/nation/2019/04/30/holocaust-remembrance-day-arrives-us-jews-under-attack/3616318002/

Williams, D. A., Berger, J. B., & McClendon, S. A. (2005). Toward a model of inclusive excellence and change in postsecondary institutions. *Association of American Colleges and Universities (AAC&U)*. Retrieved from https://www.aacu.org/sites/default/files/files/mei/williams_et_al.pdf

Winbolt, B. (2010). *Dialogue vs. debate*. Retrieved from https://www.barrywinbolt.com/dialogue-vs-debate/

Zarkov, D., & Davis, K. (2018). Ambiguities and dilemmas around #MeToo: #ForHowLong and #WhereTo? *European Journal of Women's Studies, 25*(1), 3–9.

7

ETHICS AND
DECISION-MAKING

James A. Lorello and Jeffrey A. Bates

Life is a self-renewing process through action upon the environment
Dewey, 1921, p. 2

Know Thyself

Know thyself. It is a phrase espoused often among student affairs practitioners as we help students navigate the complex world of college. We have theory such as Baxter Magolda's self-authorship devoted to better understanding one's self through self-reflection and developing authenticity. We ask the "big" questions in life to help us make meaning and better understand ourselves and the path ahead. We are great at lecturing from our soapbox to students in an effort to help them transform their understanding of self through cognitive dissonance. But how good are we at understanding ourselves as student conduct practitioners? In order to provide learning for our students we need to have our own sense of self to engage with students in an authentic and compassionate way. "We cannot give [students] what we do not have ourselves; what we do have, we cannot keep from them" (Kaplan, 1991, p. 33). In today's world of student conduct, there are too many high-stakes campus issues to sort through that need our best selves. Issues of sexual violence, free speech, campus shootings, and the rise of mental health concerns have made our work more complex than it was a decade ago when the last edition of this book was released. These complex issues also make it more difficult for student conduct administrators to sustain and persist in their roles. Professionals continue to exit early from their student affairs roles, and this trend has continued to be a concern, as demonstrated by much recent research in the field (Lorden, 1998; Tull, 2006; Marshall, Gardner, Hughes, & Lowery, 2016). Perhaps an increased focus on understanding of self, meaning-making, and ethical decision-making can help foster growth for both ourselves as professionals as well as the students we serve.

The Importance of Sense of Self

In the world of student conduct we bring all of who we are to our work with students. Our stories follow us. We carry them with us. Just as we carry the stories of our students. Many of us know that when a student walks through our doors for a simple alcohol violation it can often turn out to be far more complex as the layers of the onion begin to be peeled. It would be naive of us as professionals to think that we were somehow indifferent or immune to our own stories as we work with students. We must recognize our stories and experiences, make meaning of them, and use them in our work moving forward as though we were a researcher in a qualitative research project.

When conducting qualitative research, it is the researchers themselves who serve as the instrument for the study, as opposed to a survey or data set used for quantitative research (Reeves, 2019)Whether by being in the room, deciding which questions to ask, navigating how to clarify a response, or determining what documentation to review, the presence of the researcher alone can and will influence the research study. In an effort to address this inherent influence, many researchers choose to include a positionality statement in their research. A positionality statement both describes individuals' world views and defines the position they have chosen to adopt in relation to a specific research task. "The positionality that researchers bring to their work, and the personal experiences through which positionality is shaped, may influence what researchers may bring to research encounters, their choice of processes, and their interpretation of outcomes" (Foote & Bartell, 2011, p. 46). Recognizing the researcher's particular world view in a positionality statement helps support the validity and applicability of the research findings.

As student conduct administrators, it can be helpful to view the work we do in hearing conduct cases for alleged misbehavior as a type of qualitative research. In the same way that qualitative research seeks to understand social phenomena within their natural setting by focusing on the "why," a student conduct administrator should seek an understanding of what specific behavior occurred focusing particularly on the "why" in order to sanction appropriately within a developmental framework. To be clear, we do not mean this to be a judgmental "why!?" but instead a glimpse behind the curtain of a student's life. What values and understandings of the world might this student hold that are contributing to the behavior in question? It is the similarities between qualitative research and the hearing of conduct cases that should compel student conduct administrators to develop a student conduct positionality statement of their own. In viewing conduct administrators as researchers and hearing cases as a type of research, "it is important for all researchers to spend some time thinking about how they are paradigmatically and philosophically positioned and for them to be aware of how their positioning—and the fundamental assumptions they hold—might influence their research related thinking and practice" (Sikes, 2004, p. 15).

A few examples of questions to consider in developing a student conduct positionality statement include the following:

- How are my personal identities and characteristics sources of power and privilege?
- How do my social identities impact the lens through which I see the world?
- How do the decisions I made in college impact how I view specific violations now?
- How has my upbringing influenced the opportunities available to me?
- Where could I miss information based on my bounded life experiences?
- How do my values influence the types of people I gravitate toward?

An "awareness of how identities, experiences, and biases can inform and influence data collection, analysis, and interpretation" (Schuh, Biddix, Dean, & Kinzie, 2016, p. 167) will allow student conduct administrators to identify their positionality in hearing cases and thereby better serve the needs of the students who sit across from them. Whether drafted individually, as an office, or as a student conduct board, a well-crafted positionality statement forces us to examine and know ourselves in order to better serve others and make the difficult decisions inherent in student conduct work.

Decision-Making From the Heart

Without recognizing our positionality and sense of self, decision-making becomes more difficult as a student conduct practitioner. Without this recognition we have no frame of reference for our decision-making. We have no compass to go back to when we face a difficult decision in front of us. It makes us less likely to be consistent and to give students our best when we don't even know what our best is.

A lack of sense of self also makes it easy for us to rely on overly legalistic decision-making. While our codes of student conduct may be black-and-white documents, we must know that we live in a very gray world. While law and policy are important and essential to student conduct processes, a sense of self allows us to resist the temptation of making decisions grounded only in law and policy. This is crucial for newly minted conduct administrator who are seeking to balance law and policy in their practice. With a proper sense of self, we can be more comfortable operating in the gray and make decisions that are informed by law and policy but rooted in ethical considerations and our personal values. When we write "decision-making from the heart," we do not mean this to make decisions solely on the basis of emotion, but instead to combine our emotions, our positionality, our lived experiences, and our legal understanding to do our best for students.

The following story reflects the experience of one practitioner in this regard. A student in this person's office had several alcohol-related situations in a row, all during the fall semester. These situations included the student passing out from alcohol consumption and high blood alcohol content readings. Normally behavior like this would result in a separation from the university in order for the student to get back on his feet and prioritize school. In each meeting with the student he would brush off the incidents as being a one-time mistake in which he just had "a little too much." The final meeting occurred just before winter break, so the case could not be resolved before he left for the break. During his time away for the break, he completed loads of community service with a local rehabilitation facility and attended counseling sessions on his own. The practitioner felt like they connected with the student during their meetings and that the student would change if given one more chance. Given his work during the break, the practitioner discussed it with his supervisor and felt like the right decision was to not suspend the student just yet, and to give him one more chance, while also putting some accountability in place such as continued meetings with the conduct administrator and continued reflection on his actions and behavior. The student made it until the end of April in the spring semester before he mysteriously did not show up for one of his follow-up meetings with the conduct administrator. The next day they received a report that he again was caught with alcohol and this time even attempted to run from the campus police officers. The student avoided his meeting with the conduct administrator for about a full week. When he finally came in, he broke down in tears because he shared that he knew he had disappointed them and messed up and knew he was going to be suspended. He also shared that his mom had been diagnosed with cancer that month, and he was overwhelmed with the end of the semester, all of this leading him to drink again. The student accepted his suspension for the next year and returned home to continue to get help with his drinking.

We share this story as it is one in which the practitioner could have made a number of decisions along the way. Should the practitioner have suspended him earlier? Does he regret giving him another chance? Would he have learned the same way if the conduct administrator hadn't given him another chance? These questions can't really be answered. We don't know that there was a right and a wrong decision here. This was one of those student conduct moments that can continue to help shape our own decision-making. In that moment the practitioner believed the student deserved grace. The practitioner believed he deserved another chance. He were well aware of the fact that he could be lying and that no one can change behavior during a month-long break but he felt there was limited risk in showing him compassion in the form of additional support versus a suspension (though suspensions can be compassionate too!). The practitioner gave him that chance and it didn't work out, but this time he understood at the deepest level that he had messed up because he knew that the conduct administrator was invested in him. The practitioner chose to help and support him, and he unfortunately made another mistake, but this time he would learn from it. He showed him that they cared about him, and in return when he made a mistake he knew it right away and owned up to it. Without the practitioner's sense of self, he may have made a different decision. With more experience today the practitioner might have gone about his conversations differently or have suspended him earlier.

Early decisions in a conduct career, such as this example, help to inform all future decisions in student conduct, just as every case does along the way. This example has helped to shape the "heart" portion of the practitioner's decision-making—the part that can only be learned from experience and can't be taught in a master's program. Each case along the journey provides new perspective and informs decisions moving forward. We as practitioners need to make meaning from all of them and infuse them into our future work with students.

Meaning-Making in Student Conduct

Zittoun and Brinkmann (2012) define *meaning-making* as "the process by which people interpret situations, events, objects, or discourses, in the light of their previous knowledge and experience" (p. 1707). How we make meaning is directed by our previous experiences, positionality, and values. This is true for us as practitioners as well as for our students. For us as practitioners, we need to make meaning of each student experience we have. Each investigation report, each student story, can provide us new fuel for learning. Each story gives us new information to inform our future decisions and how we interact with future students in our offices. Without these stories we would have trouble balancing our different sensitivities. For instance, perhaps you are someone who gets absorbed in a student's story. The student is emotional and upset about being caught with drugs in their room. They promise to never do it again if you just let them off this one time. Without any prior knowledge or experience you may think, "Sure, let's give them a pass." But by making meaning of a variety of experiences with other students in similar situations you can make a more thoughtful decision on how to handle this student behavior. You can read if students are being truthful, or if they really are daily users of a substance who need more help. Perhaps you have made your own mistakes in the past and have learned from them. Upon further reflection, all of these different experiences help to build a thoughtful response to our students.

In student conduct we address student behavior and help students make meaning of the sometimes complicated situations in which they find themselves. How they reflect and how they make meaning of their experience with us can help to alter their future path and inform their own decision-making moving forward. The conversation we have and the sanctions we implement for a first-time cheating violation could have lasting impacts on students' experience. If they felt that they were treated unfairly by our office, what might that do for how they make meaning of the experience? Will they walk away saying "Wow that person really tried to help me! Maybe a need to take another look at this," or "What a jerk! They clearly don't understand me, and I am still going to continue my behavior." In student conduct we have a prime place to give students space for reflection. In a world filled with instant gratification and social media scrolling, student conduct can be a space to stop and reflect—a place to help center ourselves and our students and make meaning of life, to help us in our journey.

Domain Approach to Decision-Making

For student conduct administrato rs to encourage the development of moral capacity within students, it is important to first understand how different domains influence how individuals determine right from wrong. Research on social cognitive domain theory has shown that students as young as five distinguish between moral, social conventional, and personal domains when considering what types of behaviors are acceptable in specific situations and what types of behaviors are not (Nucci, 2001; Turiel, 2002). This discovery pushes against a common assumption that students are constantly taking away an intended moral message from a text or video on social media. "In reality, students' understanding is filtered through their intellectual, moral, and social development levels" (Vozzola, 2014, p. 114). Explicit definitions of each domain adapted from Vozzola (2014) and examples through a student conduct lens are the following:

1. Moral domain: Actions and issues categorized into this domain are based on a perception of how one's actions will affect others, not because a specific rule prohibits an action (e.g., using a roommate's identification to purchase alcohol without their permission or knowledge).
2. Social conventional domain: Actions and issues categorized into this domain are right or wrong based solely on a rule or social norm (e.g., violating a housing policy by storing a bicycle in a room).
3. Personal domain: Actions and issues categorized into this domain only affect the individual and are about our sense of self as opposed to right or wrong (e.g., the friends a student chooses to spend time with).

One of the focuses of a domain approach to moral development stresses the importance of domain-appropriate responses to student transgressions (Nucci, 2008). For student conduct administrators, this suggests the ability to identify which domain a behavior fits into and being able to sanction appropriately in consideration of that domain. It is important to keep in mind that some behaviors involve several domains of thinking simultaneously and most incidents consist of overlaps in domains. A student's choice of friends would not inherently constitute a policy violation but may contribute to the environment a student was in when a policy was violated. Being able to unpack how choices in each domain relate to one another can be a powerful tool during a student conduct hearing.

Considering the domain approach to morality in addressing behaviors allows student conduct administrators to use their discretion when making decisions on policies that appear to be more black and white. For example, at an institution with a zero-tolerance policy for weapons, a student conduct administrator can still have discretion regarding sanctioning depending on the type of code-violating weapon a student was in possession of. Although all weapons may be prohibited in a policy, it may be problematic to give students with more severe weapons (e.g., firearm or combat knife) and students with less severe weapons (e.g., nerf gun or pocketknife) identical sanctioning (e.g., suspension or expulsion). This kind of domain-inappropriate response would do very little to encourage students' understanding of community standards and their role in upholding them in the future. Although assessing and responding in domain-appropriate ways can be challenging as a result of how domains can often overlap, "anyone willing to take the time to explore this approach in more detail will find real value in integrating knowledge about social domains into their teaching practice" (Vozzola, 2014, p. 115). A student conduct administrator's role as a moral educator (Kiss, 2003) implores a greater understanding and application of domains in order to encourage an ethical life for students as global citizens.

The Path to Ethical Decision-Making Steps

Each day in our personal lives and in our work lives we are presented with opportunities for ethical decision-making. Consider the daily ethical decision fathers and mothers face with their children. Often a decision can revolve around what age their children might be on a given day. For context, many sporting events are free for kids under 3 years old. So, perhaps the parent will simply say that she's 3, instead of 5, and save the extra cost; after all, who wants to pay $20 for a seat your child probably won't sit in? Student affairs practitioners may face much more complex and challenging decisions in their daily work, often having to decide between competing goods as opposed to simple right and wrong questions. For a conduct administrator, this could be the decision to remove a student from campus (justice) or to give the student another chance (mercy). Or, perhaps the decision is to change the code of student conduct to have language that is more student friendly or resort to more "legalistic" language to help with fending off the increasing likelihood of potential lawsuits as more lawyers engage in the process. If and when Title IX, or other regulations, change, do we choose to follow policy strictly (justice), or do we do what we believe is best for our students (mercy)? For a student leader, the dilemma could be the decision to report a code violation by a friend (truth) or to give the friend a warning and choose not to report (loyalty). In order to move through these decisions and answer them appropriately, both practitioners and students alike need to develop a process for making ethical decisions. Following is a potential framework for making ethical decisions.

1. Recognize the problem: This step puts the entire process of ethical decision-making into motion since there is no hope in effectively solving an ethical dilemma if one fails to recognize its existence to begin with. Recognition of the problem includes the ability to separate moral

questions from social conventions, utilizing the domain approach to morality discussed previously in this chapter. For example, a friend showing up late to a party may violate social conventions about punctuality but would not in and of itself constitute a moral problem involving right and wrong.

2. Gather relevant facts: This step involves seeking out and putting together information that relates to the ethical dilemma. Careful consideration concerning the best individual to address or act on an ethical concern should be present in the fact-gathering process as well. Finally, it is important to recognize individual positionality during the fact-gathering process. This recognition will beg questions such as, "What details am I most likely to seek out and why? What details do I tend to miss? How have my own past experiences shaped what information I seek to gather?"

3. Identify values and principles: During this step, individuals should identify which values or principles are at play in a particular decision. This includes taking into account important duties or loyalties one may hold (Potter, 1972) as well as what one's intention is when making ethical choices (Nash, 1989). Recognizing that many ethical dilemmas may not have a distinct, clear resolution, testing for both right-versus-wrong issues and right-versus-right issues (Kidder, 1995) becomes essential in identifying the principles at play in a decision. A few strategies to consider when contemplating an ethical dilemma are the stench test (what is your gut reaction?), the front-page test (how would you feel if your decision appeared on the front page of tomorrow's newspaper?), and the mom test (does the decision violate the moral code of someone you greatly admire?).

4. Seek alternatives: Before rushing into a final decision, it can be helpful to consider any alternative solutions. Alternative solutions for seemingly irreconcilable values will typically manifest themselves either through a compromise or the development of a creative solution (Johnson, 2009).

5. Decide and act: All of the previous steps culminate into this final step, making a decision and taking action. Despite potentially being less time consuming than previous steps in this model, the step to take action can often be the most challenging because it is the transition from theory to application—a transition from considering potential consequences to actualizing those consequences. "Many of us like to think that we are rational thinkers who decide based on the facts. In reality we often make choices based on stories. A good narrative [even if inaccurate] is more persuasive than statistical evidence" (Johnson, 2009, p. 222). In making

a final decision and taking action, it is important to recognize this innate human tendency to make choices based on stories in order to properly make ethical decisions in our daily work.

Principles to Consider

In order to inform these decision-making steps, it is important to consider Kitchener's (1984) five ethical principles for counseling psychology; autonomy, do no harm (nonmaleficence), do good for others (beneficence), justice and faithfulness (fidelity). While we as practitioners are not usually acting as counseling psychologists, the principles have much benefit to the work we do in student conduct.

1. Autonomy: People have autonomy and freedom of action and choice over their behavior. It is the right of our students to make their own decisions even when we are holding them accountable for their mistakes. We must also know that as autonomous individuals we must equip them with tools for responsible decision-making.

2. Do no harm: Rooted in medical practice, do no harm is espoused through professions as an ethical principle. Our goal in student conduct is to help our students, not to knock them down. This includes helping our community. Behavior that compromises community and personal safety must be addressed while also balancing the needs of the autonomous individual.

3. Do good for others: We not only should be preventing harm but also doing good for others. We should be promoting positive growth of our students through our conversations with them and the ways in which we hold them accountable. Much good can come from conduct, if we are intentional in watering the seeds for growth.

4. Justice: We have a duty to create fair processes and procedures for our students. This includes taking into account populations or people who may be treated unfairly or differently in our process. It means providing equity, not just the same thing for everyone.

5. Faithfulness: If we want our conversations with our students to be fruitful, we must enter into them with expectations for ourselves and for our students of respect and trust. Students should not be afraid that we are lying to them or out to get them. They should be able to trust that we are there to help them in their journey, even if they are being held accountable for inappropriate behavior. When we say we will do something, we must do it.

Conclusion

As we endeavor to make ethical decisions we must recognize that humans often fall short of acting based completely on their ideals and expressed values. To apply this knowledge in our everyday work, we need to be held accountable by those around us to be our best selves and aspire to meet our ideals and values. Our effort can provide an example for the very students we work with every day. Student conduct plays a vital role on a college campus, and we must be partners with our students on their journey through their college life and beyond. As practitioners we need to analyze our own positionality and frame our work as if we were qualitative researchers aiming to learn more about the participants of our study. We must reframe and refocus when we drift away from our values and ideals. We must stay on the path to ethical decision-making. Each story along the way provides us new meaning and clarity for the next student who walks through our door. One meeting, or one decision, can plant a seed that grows throughout a student's life journey. A field of student conduct practitioners committed to instilling the practices discussed in this chapter into their daily work will be uniquely positioned to support students as they identify who they are, where they want to go, and how to get there in an effort to make a lasting impact on the world around them. We believe the future is bright.

References

Dewey, J. (1921). *Democracy and education*. New York, NY: Macmillan

Foote, M. Q., & Bartell, T. G. (2011). Pathways to equity in mathematics education: How life experiences impact researcher positionality. *Educational Studies in Mathematics, 78*(1), 45–68.

Johnson, C. E. (2009). *Meeting the ethical challenges of leadership: Casting light or shadow*. Thousand Oaks, CA: SAGE.

Kaplan, A. (1991). Moral values in higher education. In D. L. Thompson (Ed.), *Moral values and higher education: A notion at risk* (pp. 11–45). New York, NY: New York University Press.

Kidder, R. M. (1995). *How good people make tough choices: Resolving the dilemmas of ethical living*. New York, NY: Fireside.

Kiss, E. (2003). The courage to teach practice and learn: Student affairs practitioners as moral educators. In J. M. Lancaster and Associates (Eds.), *Exercising power with wisdom: Bridging legal and ethical practice with intention* (pp. 77–95). Asheville, NC: College Administration Publications.

Kitchener, K. S. (1984). Intuition, critical evaluation and ethical principles: The foundation for ethical decisions in counseling psychology. *Counseling Psychologist, 12*(3), 43–55.

Lorden, L. (1998). Attrition in the student affairs profession. *NASPA Journal, 35*(3), 207–216.

Marshall, S. M., Gardner, M. M., Hughes, C., & Lowery, U. (2016). Attrition from student affairs: Perspectives from those who exited the profession. *Journal of Student Affairs Research and Practice, 53*(2), 146–159.

Nash, L. L. (1989). Ethics without the sermon. In K. R. Andrews (Ed.), *Ethics in practice: Managing the moral corporation* (pp. 243–257). Boston, MA: Harvard Business School Press.

Nash, R. J., & Murray, M. (2010). *Helping college students find purpose: The campus guide to meaning-making.* San Francisco, CA: Jossey-Bass.

Nucci, L. P. (2001). *Education in the moral domain.* Cambridge, UK: Cambridge University Press.

Nucci, L. P. (2008). Social cognitive domain theory and moral education. In L. P. Nucci & D. Narvaez (Eds.), *Handbook of moral and character education* (pp. 291–309). New York, NY: Routledge.

Potter, R. B. (1972). The logic of moral argument. In P. Deats (Eds.), *Toward a discipline of social ethics* (pp. 93–114). Boston, MA: Boston University Press.

Reeves, M. (2019, February 10).). *Positionality in student conduct.* Paper presented at the ASCA National Conference, Jacksonville, FL.

Schuh, J. H., Biddix, J. P., Dean, L. A., & Kinzie, J. (2016). *Assessment in student affairs.* San Francisco, CA: Jossey-Bass.

Sikes, P. (2004). Methodology, procedures and ethical concerns. In C. Opie (Ed.), *Doing educational research: A guide for first-time researchers* (pp. 15–33). Thousand Oaks, CA: SAGE.

Tull, A. (2006). Synergistic supervision, job satisfaction, and intention to turn over of new professionals in student affairs. *Journal of College Student Development, 47*(4), 465–480.

Turiel, E. (2002). *The culture of morality: Social development, context, and conflict.* New York, NY: Cambridge University Press.

Vozzola, E. C. (2014). *Moral development theory and applications.* New York, NY: Routledge.

Zittoun T., & Brinkmann S. (2012). Learning as meaning making. In N. M. Seel (Ed.), *Encyclopedia of the sciences of learning* (pp. 1089–1811.) Boston, MA: Springer.

8

ASSESSMENT AND STUDENT CONDUCT

Matthew T. Stimpson and Brent E. Ericson

Introduction

Observers of higher education can reasonably speak to the challenges faced by institutions. For example, the rising cost of higher education and diminishing sources of aid raise questions on the value of an education and the return on investment (Seltzer, 2017). Additionally, students who are attending institutions of higher education are more diverse than ever, and the modes of educational delivery are diverse as well. Put simply, the demographics of a "traditional" college student have changed, and with the changes in our student populations, professionals must stay current on the educational needs of students, the content and delivery of the lessons taught, and how to effectively assess and report the value of practice.

As a significant factor in overall learning, individual student affairs units contribute to the overall education of students, as well as support the mission of an institution (Henning & Roberts, 2016). For audiences of this publication, our focus will be on how student conduct professionals assess the efficacy and outcomes of our interventions. As Goldstein and Stimpson (2013) assert, student conduct professionals should view themselves as professional educators, playing a role in student learning and development, who are also engaged in the assessment of the teaching-learning process inherent in their work.

We will begin by reviewing the history and current issues around assessment practices within higher education and those specific to student conduct. The chapter will then focus on assessment plans, outcomes development, the measures used to understand student learning, and data analysis. We conclude with a discussion of using assessment results.

Current Context

While literature including assessment can be seen as early as the 1937 American Council on Education's *The Student Personnel Point of View* and traced throughout the twentieth century, the concept appears more prevalently in the 1990s and early 2000s (Goldstein & Stimpson, 2013; Henning & Roberts, 2016) as professionals were called to balance the gains and benefits of an education against the rising costs of college and university attendance.

In 1994, the American College Personnel Association (ACPA) (1996) published *The Student Learning Imperative* that discussed moving the student affairs profession toward a focus on student learning and not simply student services. Not only were student affairs professionals expected to be competent in student learning, but there also developed a need to be proficient in assessment of student learning. In essence, the practice of assessment was moving from an understanding of student services and satisfaction to that of student learning (Henning & Roberts, 2016).

In 2004, the National Association of Student Personnel Administrators (NASPA) and ACPA published *Learning Reconsidered: A Campus-Wide Focus on the Student Experience* (Keeling & Dungy, 2004) that explored the transformative nature of student learning and argued that the college experience should be comprehensive and integrated, combining both academic learning and student development. *Learning Reconsidered* lent credibility to the important work of student affairs professionals in terms of cocurricular learning and the development of life skills. Additionally, Keeling and Dungy (2004) state that educators should establish routine methods to listen to student voices and opinions and to report the quality of their learning experience.

While the Council for the Advancement of Standards in Higher Education (CAS) was created in 1979 with an emphasis on quality in functional units, CAS published specific standards for assessment practices in 2006 in recognition of the growing field (Henning & Roberts, 2016). Additionally, following the economic recession of the early twenty-first century, Goldstein and Stimpson (2013) state that accountability for fiscal management in higher education was as acute as any point in history.

While the proceeding provides a brief historical perspective, several forces are currently at play that demonstrate the importance of assessment in higher education. First, policy makers remain concerned with accountability of higher education. For example, members of the Obama Administration placed an emphasis on degree attainment and career readiness and also encouraged students to enroll in some form of postsecondary education, including two-year institutions and community colleges (Henning & Roberts, 2016). Second, state legislators are accountable for the allocation of public resources

and must also examine issues of retention and persistence, time to graduation, and containing costs (Richardson & Smalling, 2005). Finally, accreditation agencies also determine the appropriateness of missions, resources
dedicated to those missions, and if the objectives of institutions are measured. Institutions may be placed on notice that their accreditation is in dan-
ger should they fall short of external standards (Henning & Roberts, 2016).

As stated, as professional educators, student conduct professionals play
a vital role in student learning and, in turn, the assessment program of an
institution. For example, Goldstein and Stimpson (2013) report on the educational value of student conduct practices and note that assessment is a critical competency for professionals. Additionally, Heiser, Gauthier, DiCato,
and Bartholomew (2018) most recently furthered the discussion on assessment practices in ASCA's *Conduct and Community* publication that explores
assessment within campus residential communities. In 2015, the Council for
the Advancement of Standards in Higher Education published standards for
student conduct programs that specifically includes competencies related to
assessment. Perhaps best summarized by Waryold (2013), "The survival of
student conduct as a profession depends upon competent, student conduct
professionals who attach importance to and possess a skillset that will capture
learning outcomes" (p. 13).

Within this context, the goal of this chapter is to further the literature
on this valuable aspect of our profession. We focus on assessment plans, outcomes development, measures used in student conduct assessment, and the
use of assessment data.

Key Skills Related to Assessment

Assessment is the process of gathering data related to a set of outcomes, analyzing that data, making a conclusion related to outcome attainment, and
then making decisions to improve practice, where appropriate. Viewed in
that context, assessment is simply a set of skills that student conduct administrators must become familiar with to improve student learning (formative
assessment) and to demonstrate the value and worth of their program (summative assessment). The view we articulate here is not new and has been
espoused by a number of authors.

Goldstein and Stimpson (2013) argued that assessment in student conduct was based on four key principles: articulating what students should
be learning, identifying ways to gather data about student learning, analyzing data, and feeding results back into the system to make improvements.
As they acknowledge, "These principles are not unique to student conduct"

(Goldstein & Stimpson, 2013, p. 43). Indeed, Suskie (2009), Banta and Palomba (2015), Henning and Roberts (2016), and countless others all identify these basic components as critical aspects of assessment that, when articulated, form the basis for an assessment plan.

Assessment Plans

Assessment plans form the foundation of assessment activities; plans should be forward looking and self-contained and should undergo regular evaluation and updating. When beginning the process of developing an assessment plan, a good starting point is making a list of available resources on campus. This may include individuals working in institutional research offices, dedicated campus assessment professionals (at the divisional and institutional level), and sympathetic faculty with training in social science research. It is important to note that while these individuals may not have subject matter expertise relative to student conduct, individuals with assessment and research experience can help operationalize many of the concepts and approaches in the context of student conduct administration.

When starting the process of planning for assessment, a list of stakeholders, both internal and external, should be developed. Stakeholders are any person or group of persons who have an interest in the student conduct system. These may include faculty, staff, university police, general counsel, students, student organizations, parents, and governing boards. Given the recent prevalence of high-profile student conduct incidents, stakeholders may also include media, legislators, and members of the broader society at large. As the assessment plan is developed, it is important to consider these stakeholders in determining the types of outcomes each group may be interested in and the types of data that would be most meaningful.

We conceptualize assessment plans in student conduct administration as having six critical elements: the population(s) being assessed, the learning experience being assessed, outcomes, measures, outcome achievement, and timeline. The population is the group of individuals being assessed and, consequently, the group to which the developed outcomes apply. There are a number of different populations that student conduct administrators might decide to assess and may include accused students, student board members, hearing officers, and complainants. More often than not, assessment in student conduct seems to focus on accused students, and it is with this population that our examples and discussion will focus, though other populations should be considered in developing actionable plans.

Student conduct administrators also oversee a variety of learning experiences, including conduct hearings (both administrative and board), passive sanctioning exercises (e.g., probation), and active sanctioning exercises (e.g., alcohol education classes), just to name a few. Each of these learning experiences can have outcomes assigned, and comprehensive assessment plans should be inclusive of all potential learning activities.

We divide outcomes into two categories, student learning outcomes and programmatic outcomes. Outcomes are the "knowledge, skills, and habits of mind that a student takes with them from a learning experience" (Suskie, 2004, p. 75). Operational outcomes encompass all of the other outcomes (recidivism, satisfaction with process, timeliness of process) that conduct administrators are concerned with but do not relate directly to student learning (Heiser et al., 2018).

Measures are the means by which evidence of outcome achievement are collected and are classified in a number of ways. One way to consider measures is distinguishing direct measures from indirect measures. Direct measures provide clear, convincing evidence the outcome is or is not being achieved, while indirect measures provide evidence that the outcome is or is not being achieved, but it is not as clear or convincing (Suskie, 2009). Direct measures are outcome specific. For instance, if an outcome involves a student synthesizing information, then the measure would involve evaluating a student synthesizing information. If the outcome focused on students being able to articulate community standards, then the measure would involve students articulating community standards. Meanwhile, indirect measures would include questions where students provide their opinion on what they have learned.

As we detailed earlier, assessment is undertaken for two purposes. Formative assessment is conducted to improve student learning, while summative assessment is used to demonstrate accountability. For both of these purposes, it is important to set a standard point an outcome is considered met. The standard that is set is largely up to the discretion of individuals, but it should be defensible. One option is that a percentage of students should be able to perform at a specific level.

The final aspect of an assessment plan is the timing of the assessment. Included in this information should be when assessments are going to be administered, and attention should be given both to the annual assessment cycle and when in the process a student will complete the assessment. In terms of an assessment cycle, care should be given to determining the number of outcomes to be assessed in a given year and the frequency of assessing outcomes on a year-to-year basis. Identifying a regular schedule of when outcomes should be assessed helps to facilitate a manageable process, and a cyclical pattern where outcomes are being measured on a regular basis (but not necessarily the same outcomes every year) should be identified (Suskie, 2009).

Identifying the timing in which a student will complete an assessment is also an important consideration. Generally speaking, we encourage assessments to be administered as close to the end of the learning experience as possible. We encourage this approach for two reasons. The first reason is to assist in making the assessment process more manageable. Conducting assessments close to the end of the learning process provides opportunities for conduct administrators to incorporate assessment into the workflow of the student conduct process. Second, the further out from the learning experience an assessment is administered, the less likely it is to draw inferences about outcome obtainment as a result of the learning experience. Maturation is a threat to internal validity (does Y happen because of X?) (Pedhazur & Schmelkin, 1991), and the more time that transpires between the conclusion of a learning experience and the assessment, the more likely that other experiences and growth influence outcome attainment. We recognize that many conduct administrators feel that meaningful and important changes may not happen for significant periods of time after a student interacts with a conduct system, and we acknowledge the many anecdotal stories of such changes. However, and as we detail in the next section, writing outcome statements that are measurable and that a conduct administrator has a reasonable and expected chance of influencing is paramount to a successful assessment process.

Outcomes Development

Outcomes form the foundation of assessment efforts, and as previously discussed, outcomes can be broken down into two types: student learning outcomes and programmatic outcomes. Student learning outcomes are the "knowledge, skills, and habits of mind that a student takes with them from a learning experience" (Suskie, 2004, p. 75). Meanwhile, programmatic outcomes encompass all other outcomes a conduct administrator is concerned with but are not directly learning related. We begin the discussion of outcomes development with student learning outcomes.

Anecdotally, we have observed that the development of student learning outcomes can be a difficult task, especially for professionals new to student conduct administration. During a period of six years, we developed a specific process for writing learning outcomes used at the ASCA Donald D. Gehring Academy for Student Conduct Administration. The process involves breaking a learning outcome into its three component parts: the population being assessed; the behavior a student will engage in as part of the assessment; and the skill, habit of mind, or knowledge being measured. Figure 8.1 presents a sample learning outcome appropriate for student conduct administrators, broken into the three component parts.

Populations were discussed previously, and the population is the group of individuals being assessed. In the example, the population is students who violated the alcohol policy. Next, consider that learning outcomes are inherently action oriented, and it is helpful to consider Bloom's taxonomy when considering appropriate behaviors students might engage in as part of the assessment. Composed of six domains, the cognitive domain of Bloom's (1956) taxonomy concerns itself with classifying "the changes produced in individuals as a result of educational experiences" (p. 12). The six domains (knowledge, comprehension, application, analysis, synthesis, and evaluation) are presented and defined in Figure 8.2 and included are behaviors tied to each domain area, as articulated by Palomba and Banta (1999).

Bloom's taxonomy is developmental in nature and the domains build on each other. The taxonomy, along with Palomba and Banta's (1999) operationalization of behaviors accompanying each domain can be helpful in identifying the types of behaviors that can be employed in the development of student learning outcomes. Conduct administrators may choose to have these behaviors present as they go about crafting learning outcome statements.

The knowledge, skills, and habits of mind that a student should take from the conduct process speak to the specific gains that students are expected to take away from interactions with the conduct process. While not replete with examples, the literature does aid in helping conduct administrators identify areas in which learning should be occurring. Howell (2005) found that students report learning in at least three broad categories: consideration of

Figure 8.1. Elements of a learning outcome.

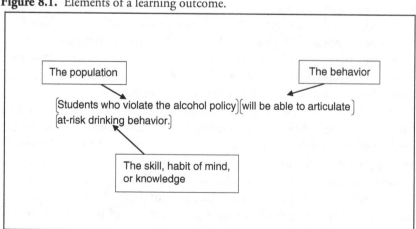

Figure 8.2. Bloom's taxonomy.

Knowledge	Focuses on the recall and recitation of facts and information	Describing, listing, identifying, and labeling
Comprehension	Ability to understand and use information that is communicated	Explaining, discussing, and interpreting
Application	Able to use previously obtained information, skills, and knowledge in new situations and scenarios	Demonstrating, showing, and making use of information
Analysis	Breaking down material into components and recognizing the relationships between the components	Differentiating, comparing, and categorizing
Synthesis	Ability to combine information in a manner that creates something new	Composing or designing something new
Evaluation	Assignment of value-based judgments to ideas, concepts, and products	Concluding, criticizing, prioritizing, and recommending

consequences, empathy, and familiarity with conduct procedures (p. 381). In a series of articles using data collected as part of the NASCAP project, a multi-institution project focused on outcomes assessment in student conduct systems, learning in areas of academic, legal, and emotional consequences; influence of behavior on others; knowledge of community standards; and learning skills for future use were explored as important outcomes of conduct systems (Janosik & Stimpson, 2009, 2017; Stimpson & Janosik, 2011, 2015). Other work included evaluation of rules, external influences, knowledge and reference of rules in relation to behavior, evaluating how to behave, and consideration of risks and benefits of alcohol consumption (Nelson, 2017).

An important consideration should be given to the likelihood that an outcome can be influenced, given the learning experience being assessed. Great care should be exercised in deciding which outcomes should be assessed, especially given the tremendous emphasis placed on summative assessment. While certainly some student conduct practices are deeply immersive and impactful, many are not, and conduct administrators should be mindful of targeting areas that can reasonably be affected.

Up to this point, we have focused our attention on student learning outcomes, and we endorse the view that the majority of assessment activities should focus on student learning outcomes. However, there are critical operational outcomes that are also deserving of attention and should be incorporated into assessment plans. We categorize these operational outcomes into two broad categories: system input and outputs and system efficacy.

System input and outputs focus on the mechanics of the conduct system. Number of referrals, cases resolved, time taken to resolve cases, and sanctions assigned and completed would fall under this category. These are important components to track and help to demonstrate the workload, efficiency, and potential burden placed on the conduct system and those charged with its management. System inputs and outputs are also mainstays of traditional conduct reporting practices (Janosik & Stimpson, 2009).

System efficacy focuses on the hallmarks of fundamental fairness but does so in a way that focuses on student perceptions. System efficacy entails measuring the degree to which students perceive the process as fair, timely, and comprehensible (Stimpson & Janosik, 2015). The importance of measuring this construct should be emphasized as close to 50% of the variance in reported learning is due to student perceptions of the conduct system (Janosik & Stimpson, 2017; Stimpson & Janosik, 2015). (Janosik and Stimpson (2017) and Stimpson and Janosik's (2015) findings on the importance of measures of perceived fundamental fairness are broadly consistent with King's (2012) findings.) As was noted, "How a conduct system is perceived by students has a dramatic influence on how much is learned" (Stimpson & Janosik, 2015, p. 64).

Measures

With outcomes identified, the next point of focus should be on identifying measures for each outcome. A full discussion of every conceivable measure is beyond the scope of this work, and as such, we focus on three measures that we believe are of most utility to conduct administrators: objective tests, rubrics, and surveys.

Objective tests are commonly found in classroom settings and provide students an opportunity to demonstrate knowledge, as well as the application of knowledge. Objective tests involve students being asked a series of questions and then indicating the correct answer in some manner or form (Banta & Palomba, 2015). Objective tests come in both commercially available forms, as well as those developed by local constituencies.

Outcomes affiliated with defined curricular experiences are good candidates to be measured by objective tests. For instance, student learning outcomes associated with alcohol education classes/programs, honor code seminars, or decision-making seminars would all be viable options. These curricular experiences typically have finite objectives, tied to specific types of misconduct that lend themselves to the construction of student learning outcomes measurable through objective tests.

Rubrics are the second measure we find of significant value to conduct administrators. Stevens and Levi (2013) define *rubrics* as tools that "divide an assignment into its component parts and provide a detailed description of what constitutes acceptable or unacceptable level of performance for each of those parts" (p. 3). We will substitute "assignment" for "outcome" given our purposes and proceed with this definition.

Rubrics are flexible and can be incorporated into many of the existing conduct system structures. For instance, rubrics can be incorporated into hearings or used to evaluate reflection exercises. Rubrics will almost always have to be locally developed, and conduct administrators interested in developing their own rubrics should consider four key elements (Stevens & Levi, 2013):

1. Reflecting: Identify what you are trying to assess with the rubric and why.
2. Listing: Draft the specific details of the outcome.
3. Grouping and labeling: Using the details listed in the second element, group the elements together to form the individual dimensions of the rubric.
4. Application: Apply the dimensions and descriptions into the rubric format.

Surveys are the final measure we will discuss and are often used to gauge the opinion, attitudes, or perceptions of participants (Banta & Palomba, 2015). Surveys, albeit overused, are a valuable tool for assessment purposes when used appropriately, and for good reason. Surveys are easily and quickly managed, affordable to conduct, and require little infrastructure to support.

Surveys should be employed by conduct administrators when outcomes focus on perceptions and experiences. Outcomes focusing on student views of the conduct system, for instance, would be a good topic for a survey. Great care should be placed in crafting understandable, accurate questions that yield the type of information needed.

Dillman (2005) proposes a list of 23 guiding principles in the construction of survey questions. While all 23 are useful, we have selected the 10 that we see as being most relevant to conduct administrators:

1. Choose simple over specialized words.
2. Use as few words as possible in each question.
3. Use complete sentences.
4. In response options, use an equal number of positive and negative categories.
5. Avoid bias from unequal comparisons.
6. State both sides of attitude scales in the question stems.
7. Make response categories mutually exclusive.
8. Ensure each item is technically accurate.
9. Avoid double-barreled questions.
10. Soften the impact of potentially objectionable questions.

Once each measure has been identified and data collected, the next step is to consider the type of analysis that will be used.

Analyzing Data

Data analysis related to assessment data should be aligned to the stated objective with the goal of determining if an outcome was met. To that end, it is important to have identified the point at which data indicate an outcome was met. We touched on this briefly when discussing assessment plans, and there are multiple ways to set a performance indicator. A common approach would be to set a percentage of students who perform at a specified level (Heiser et al., 2018). For instance, if data being analyzed comes from a rubric, setting the goal that 70 or 80% of students will score at least a 4 or higher on each dimension of the rubric might serve as the performance indicator. A similar type approach can be taken with Likert item data. If, for instance, students were asked to respond to a question on the timeliness of the process (using a five-point scale), the performance indicator might be set at "80% of students respond with a 4 or 5."

Using frequencies is preferred to using mean values since mean values are dependent on the distribution of scores. As a result, it would be possible to have relatively high mean values and small percentages of students who perform at the benchmark. Using frequency distributions removes this concern and provides you a more robust measure of performance. In many instances, the calculation of frequency distributions will be a sufficient enough process to determine if outcomes have been achieved. However, in some instances inferential statistics are needed.

Inferential statistics allow for the drawing of conclusions from a sample to a population (Howell, 2005) and encompass an array of analytical approaches. In most cases, inferential statistics are not required for assessment purposes, but they should be considered in cases where there is group comparison, benchmark comparisons, and in some pre- and post-test data cases. While highly useful to researchers, inferential statistics often go beyond the scope of assessment practice in student conduct.

Using Results

Using assessment results, or closing the loop, is the final and perhaps most critical component of the assessment process. As Henning and Roberts (2016) note, "Assessment does not happen if results are not used" (p. 215). Yet, using results can be difficult and is often times not an intuitive process.

The first and perhaps most altruistic way of using data is to use it to improve student learning and experience. Formative assessment (Suskie, 2009) focuses on assessment to improve student learning and involves making changes to student conduct programs and services to better student learning. When evidence points to the lack of outcome achievement, it is then incumbent upon student conduct administrators to make appropriate changes in an attempt to improve student learning.

Part of the process of using assessment results also involves making informed decisions about when a change is warranted. There are times when an outcome is not achieved and a decision to make no changes is reached. Perhaps it is decided to collect more data for another year to determine if what was observed is truly an issue. The key consideration is making defensible decisions.

When decisions are warranted, changes should be made in a thoughtful and informed manner. It is best to accept disappointing results and not attempt to hide or cover them up. Similarly, disappointing assessment results should not be used to take punitive action (Suskie, 2009). We embrace a model of making changes where key stakeholders are involved in revising processes and procedures collectively. By involving a number of constituencies, changes are more likely to take root and become effective means of promoting student outcome achievement.

One way to ensure that assessment results are being used is to engage in a regular cycle of program review. Program review, long a staple of academic programs, is becoming commonplace in student affairs units, too (Henning & Roberts, 2016), and is the process of intentionally and systematically reviewing all facets of a program; developing a written self-study of the program; and identifying areas of success, weakness, and recommendations for improvement.

The Council for the Advancement of Standards (CAS, n.d.), outlines a six-step program review process that includes the following:

1. Planning the process: Including steps, timeline, and who will be involved
2. Assembling and educating the team: Comprised of three to five people who are trained on the program review process
3. Identifying, collecting, and reviewing evidence: Collecting all assessment data, as well as other data points relative to the unit's objectives and goals
4. Conducting and interpreting ratings using evaluative evidence: The development of team member ratings of each area being evaluated as part of the program review process
5. Developing an action plan: List of strengths, weaknesses, areas of improvement, and steps to make improvements
6. Preparing a report: Drafting of the self-study

Program reviews typically take place every five to seven years and are viable means of ensuring that assessment and other forms of evaluative data are being used. However, student conduct administrators should not wait until program review to use assessment results to make improvements in programs and services. At a minimum, results should be reviewed on an annual basis and changes should be made as warranted and needed.

Conclusion

Assessment in all areas of higher education has seen sustained interest and attention in the last two decades. A near countless number of volumes on the subject are now available, and many of these texts focus on assessment in student affairs specifically. Yet, assessment of student conduct systems remains in an infancy. There is a dearth of resources and best-practice examples, and our hope and attempt in this chapter was to provide a discussion of the assessment process and its corresponding elements in the context of student conduct administration.

References

Banta, T. W., & Palomba, C. A. (2015). *Assessment essentials: Planning, implementing, and improving assessment in higher education* (2nd edition). San Francisco, CA: Jossey-Bass.

Bloom, B. S. (Ed.) (1956). *Taxonomy of educational objectives: The classification of educational goals, handbook 1: Cognitive domain.* New York, NY: David McKay.

Council for the Advancement of Standards in Higher education (n.d.). *Program review.* Retrieved from https://www.cas.edu/programreview

Council for the Advancement of Standards in Higher Education. (2015). *CAS professional standards for higher education* (9th ed.). Washington DC: Author.

Dillman, D. A. (2005). *Mail and Internet surveys: The tailored designed method* (2nd ed.). Hoboken, NJ: Wiley.

Goldstein, A., & Stimpson, M. (2013). Competency nine: Assessment. In D. M. Waryold & J. M. Lancaster (Eds.), *The state of student conduct: Current forces and future challenges: Revisited* (pp. 42–44). College Station, TX: Association for Student Conduct Administration.

Heiser, C. A., Gauthier, A. P., DiCato, K. A., & Bartholomew, K. M. (2018). Assessing conduct student behavior. In J. Hudson, A. Acosta, & R. C. Holmes (Eds.), *Conduct and community: A residence life practitioners guide* (pp. 256–287). Columbus, OH: Association of College & University Housing Officers-International (ACUHO-I).

Henning, G., & Roberts, D. M. (2016). *Student affairs assessment: Theory to practice.* Sterling, VA: Stylus.

Howell, M. T. (2005). Students' perceived learning and anticipated future behaviors as a result of participation in the student judicial process. *Journal of College Student Development, 46*(4), 374–392.

Janosik, S. M., & Stimpson, M. T. (2009). Improving outcomes assessment in student conduct administration. *Journal of Student Conduct Administration, 2*(1), 46–56.

Janosik, S. M., & Stimpson, M. T. (2017). The influence of the conduct system and campus environments on student learning. *Journal of Student Affairs Research and Practice, 54*(1), 28–41.

Keeling, R. P., & Dungy, G. J. (2004). *Learning reconsidered: a campus-wide focus on the student experience.* Washington, D.C: ACPA.

King, R. H. (2012). Student conduct administration: How students perceive the educational value and procedural fairness of their disciplinary experiences. *Journal of College Student Development, 53*(4), 563–580.

Nelson, A. R. (2017). Measure of development for student conduct administration. *Journal of College Student Development, 58*(8), 1274–1280.

Palomba, C. A., & Banta, T. W. (1999). *Assessment Essentials: Planning, implementing, and improving assessment in higher education.* San Franciso, CA: Jossey-Bass.

Pedhazur, E. J., & Schmelkin, L. P. (1991). *Measurement, design, and analysis: An intergrated approach.* Hillsdale, NJ: Lawrence Erlbaum.

Richardson, R. C., Jr., & Smalling, T. R. (2005). Accountability and governance. In J. C. Burke (Ed.), *Achieving accountability in higher education* (pp. 55–77). San Francisco, CA: Jossey-Bass.

Seltzer, R. (2017, October 25). Net price keeps creeping up. *Inside Higher Ed.* Retrieved from https://www.insidehighered.com/news/2017/10/25/tuition-and-fees-still-rising-faster-aid-college-board-report-shows

Stevens, D. D., & Levi, A. J. (2013). *Introduction to rubrics: An assessment tool to save grading time, convey effective feedback, and promote student learning.* Sterling, VA: Stylus.

Stimpson, M. T., & Janosik, S. M. (2011). Variability in reported student learning as a result of participating in a student conduct system. *College Student Affairs Journal, 30*(1), 19–30.

Stimpson, M. T., & Janosik, S. M. (2015). The conduct system and its influence on student learning. *Journal of College Student Development, 56*(1), 61–65.

Suskie, L. (2004). *Assessing student learning: A common sense guide.* Bolton, MA: Anker.

Suskie, L. (2009). *Assessing student learning: A common sense guide* (2nd ed.). San Francisco, CA: Jossey-Bass.

Waryold, D. (2013). The student conduct administrator. In D. M. Waryold & J. M. Lancaster (Eds.), *The state of student conduct: Current forces and future challenges: Revisited* (pp. 10–14). College Station, TX: Association for Student Conduct Administration.

9

BIAS INCIDENTS
ON CAMPUS

Patience D. Bryant and Derrick D. Dixon

Bias Incidents on Campus

Over the years, institutions have placed emphasis on increasing access for individuals who, in the past, were denied admittance to higher education (Pope, Torres, & Arminio, 2012). Unfortunately, as Pope and colleagues (2012) reveal, although institutions have been successful in creating increased access, they still face the challenge of creating an environment that is welcoming, accepting, affirming, and engaging once those individuals have arrived on campus. Managing the increased level of different identities, opposing opinions, and so on within communities has proven to be more complex than simply focusing on assimilation and seeing everyone through a similar lens, as not every student is the same (Pope et al., 2012). These differences and increased diverse student populations need to be properly addressed and not focus on a strategy that tries to "fit" every student into the same box within an institutional community. Our students are very different, and each student and groups have unique needs that we have to work to support (Pope et al., 2012).

As a result, institutions must also work to ensure that an environment has been created in which differences are not only welcomed, but are intentionally sought as part of building a fully inclusive culture within the institution (Pope et al., 2012). This is not a simple task. Often times this goal is only achieved through dialogue and the willingness to be uncomfortable. Watt (2007) drives home this point by insisting that welcoming campus environments are created through dialogue and that educators should constantly ask and evaluate ways in which they have initiated a dialogue that promoted human dignity, equality, and community. Pope and colleagues (2012) state that "a truly welcoming and inclusive environment is one where difficult conversations are the norm, and individuals are empowered to notice, question, and stop inequality" (p. 4).

Although creating an environment with open dialogue is ideal, it is not always an easy task. In many cases, faculty, staff, and students are reluctant to participate in difficult conversations due to the tensions that are involved with the examination of themselves and becoming more self-aware (Pope et al., 2012). More specifically, increasing one's self-awareness involves a profound exploration of one's beliefs, attitudes, values, and behavior that can facilitate the personal change required to create an inclusive environment. This period of self-exploration forces individuals to understand and gauge the potential for incongruence between who they are and who they think they are (Pope et al., 2012). Understanding self allows individuals to fully engage in the work of promoting inclusivity by moving past the politically correct responses and on to deeper responses that we may or may not be ready to accept (Pope et al., 2012).

In many cases, entering college is the first time that many of our community members (who could be students of traditional entry college age, as well as faculty and staff who may have been isolated from diverse cultures) are exposed to the most diverse populations that they have ever experienced (Pope et al., 2012). As a result, individuals are provided prime opportunities to learn about belief systems, values, and world perspectives different than their own. Despite these opportunities for growth and learning, in many cases, the mixture of diverse populations often leads to individual and community responses in the form of bias-related incidents or worse, incidents of hate (LePeau, Snipes, Morgan & Zimmerman, 2018). "When college students experience incidents of bias based on social identities such as gender, race, and religion, these incidents reinforce the minoritized status of oppressed and underrepresented students" (LePeau, Snipes, Morgan & Zimmerman, 2018, p. 681). This chapter provides readers with the opportunity to think about how to address bias incidents that occur on campus and cause an impact on the community, as institutions are working to create diverse learning environments.

Responding to a growing number of identity-based bias-related incidents has been an expanding and necessary area of focus for colleges and universities in recent years. For the most part, almost all public institutions have processes and procedures in place to respond to policy and law violations including but not limited to the areas of affirmative action, equal opportunity, human resources, university/city police regulations, and various student affairs programs (primarily student conduct) (LePeau, Morgan, Zimmerman, Snipes & Marcotte, 2016).

One of the most egregious forms of bias incidents come in the form of hate crimes. *Hate crimes* are defined as "a crime of violence, property damage, or threat that is motivated in whole or in part by an offender's bias based on race, religion, ethnicity, national origin, gender, physical or mental disability, or sexual orientation" (Wessler & Moss, 2001, p. 17) Unfortunately, in many cases, confirming that a hate crime occurred is a challenging task for both institutions and law enforcement agencies due to First Amendment protections (Schuster, Bird, & Mackin, 2006). Typically, First Amendment issues are not apparent until a thorough investigation is conducted. This is primarily because speech can take many forms beyond spoken words (issues of speech, religious expression, student press, or right to assembly) (Schuster et al., 2006). The advancement of technology and online resources has also added to the challenges of navigating speech and first amendment issues (Schuster et al., 2006). As a result, not all incidents rise to the "hate crime status" that would warrant a criminal or institutional policy violation.

Despite not rising to the level of a hate crime, these acts of bias still have a major impact on the institutions' members and overall climate (Miller, Guida, Smith, Ferguson, & Medina, 2018b). Miller and colleagues (2018b) further explain that these incidents still may cause impacted parties to feel physically and psychologically unsafe. As a result of this impact, institutions are scrambling to find alternative ways to respond, educate, and provide healing to the community and its members (U.S. Department of Justice, 2001, 2003). As defined by Teaching Tolerance (2019) in "Identifying and Responding to Bias Incidents," "A *bias incident* is conduct, speech or expression motivated, in whole or in part, by bias or prejudice. It differs from a hate crime in that no criminal activity is involved" (emphasis added).

Miller and colleagues (2018b) highlight that bias incidents include but are not limited to microaggressions, protests, displays, and incidents that create hostile environments. Often times, bias incidents include conduct, speech, or expressions that are motivated by the prejudice of the individual(s) causing the harm (Wessler & Moss, 2001). Livingood (2007) discusses the various types of biases that occur and can result in conflict, in particular, learned bias. Biases are often learned and can be viewed through the lens that the person who carries the bias has preferences or strong beliefs. Learned biases can come from socialization, environment, education and other experiences that the person has been exposed to. These experiences can impact how people view others. This all can lead to conflict occurring in situations that would not normally happen. Identity-based conflict often stems from learned biases. Livingood (2007) states that "special attention should be accorded to identity-based conflicts, which are rooted in complex and multidimensional psychological, historical, cultural, ethnic and/or religious associations"

(p. 54). Within the college or university community, bias-related incidents often manifest in the form of microaggressions, protests, displays, and events that are hostile to various diverse groups that negatively impact the campus community (Miller, Guida, Smith, Ferguson, & Medina, 2018a).

Microaggressions are one of the most common forms of bias that are reported on college campuses. Rollock (2012) defines *microaggressions* as brief, subtle, and insidious everyday interactions that send denigrating messages to members of oppressed groups. Microaggressions can be broken down into three subtypes: microassaults, microinsults, and microinvalidations (Boysen, 2012). Sue and colleagues (2007) defined the former as the following:

A *microassault* is an explicit racial derogation characterized primarily by a verbal or nonverbal attack meant to hurt the intended victim through name-calling, avoidant behavior, or purposeful discriminatory actions. A *microinsult* is characterized by communications that convey rudeness and insensitivity and demean a person's racial heritage or identity. Microinsults represent subtle snubs, frequently unknown to the perpetrator, but clearly convey a hidden insulting message to the recipient of color. *Microinvalidations* are characterized by communications that exclude, negate, or nullify the psychological thoughts, feelings, or experiential reality of a person of color. (p. 1, emphasis added)

However, it is important to note that whether the actions be intentional or unintentional, they can have similar impacts, and unintentional actions are often used as an excuse to get away from accountability.

Microaggressions occur throughout the university community in various forms. As a result, institutions have been constantly searching for ways to respond to these incidents, especially the incidents that do not rise to the level of a policy violation (Miller et al., 2018a). Schrage and Giacomini (2009) highlight that one of the primary functions of student conduct/student affairs administrators are supporting and ensuring that the campus climate is welcoming to all members of the community. If our systems do not evolve to include all members of the community, we are failing to model what we are expecting our students to learn. As a result of these challenges, and the emphasis institutions are placing on creating equitable processes, many institutions have created and implemented bias incidents response teams to serve as an educational unit to respond to bias incidents (Hughes, 2013).

Campus Bias Response Teams

Bias incidents appear on college campuses in a variety of ways, often leaving practitioners to wonder what, if anything, they can do to respond. It often feels as though a week cannot go by without an institution being placed in headlines because of a bias-related incident. Miller and colleagues (2018a) pinpoint the following incidents as some of the more recent major occurrences of bias that have occurred on college campuses:

- Yale university turning women of color away from a party (Brown, 2015)
- Black students being subjected to verbal racial slurs at the University of Missouri (Supiano, 2015)
- Members of a fraternity at the University of Oklahoma singing a chant featuring the N-word (Stripling & Thomason, 2015)
- Vandalism of the University of Mississippi's on-campus statue of James Meredith (WAPT, 2014; Journal of Blacks in Higher Education, 2016)

Such incidents often result in an institution releasing a statement in which the students' actions are denounced and that the students' actions may be referred to their department of student conduct. The students involved with the bias-based incident often must leave their institution while the public demands punishment of some sort. The overall result is a kind of public shaming of the students without any regard for meaning-making and learning. Others within the institution and the overall community are left without any overall context on the incident and wondering how they can go back to normal after such an occurrence on their campuses and in their community.

LePeau and colleagues (2016) reveal that "organizing bodies" such as community groups and student organizations are calling on campus educators to be responsive to bias incidents on college campuses and connect those responses to ultimately improving campus climate for diverse students, faculty, and staff (Council for the Advancement of Standards, 2012; U.S. Department of Justice, 2001, 2003: Worthington, Stanley, & Lewis, 2014). As a result, there has been a rapid increase in numbers of bias response teams on campuses across the nation. These teams have been crafted as a response to the calls for the development of processes and procedures to respond to the increased number in bias-related incidents that do not constitute a policy violation (Anthony & Johnson, 2012).

McDermott (2013) defines *bias response teams* as "institutional committees designed to receive and respond to reports of bias incidents, hate speech, and/or hate crimes on college campus" (p.317). Anthony and Johnson (2012) highlight the following key functions of bias response teams: supporting those targeted by hate or bias; referring students to resources and services; educating the campus community about the impact of incidents;

and promoting initiatives and new ideas that further an inclusive and welcoming environment. Wessler and Moss (2001) highlight that bias teams also help to resolve incidents and facilitate the appropriate communication between the institution and the community members.

Institutions that are hoping to craft and implement a bias response team will require buy-in from institutional leadership and the institutional community as a whole. As a result, such efforts will require a great deal of research and preparation prior to the development of the team. Despite being created with purpose and positive intentions, Lepeau and colleagues (2016) highlight that there is minimal empirical evidence about the process that campus educators employ when crafting bias response teams. One process example that can be utilized is taken from the University of Mississippi in their development of the Bias Incidents Response Team in 2013. Their plan of action in developing the team included the following:

- Developing a committee charged with exploring the establishment of the Bias Incident Response Team. The team included staff members from student housing; university police; a faculty member from the women and gender studies program, the counseling center, the office of international programs, student disability services, student organization professional, multicultural affairs and volunteer services; and two graduate students.
- Researching journal articles and benchmarking institutions with established bias response teams.
- Crafting the structure of the Bias Incidents Response Team including the following:
  ○ Defining the purpose of the committee
  ○ Developing and crafting the objectives that the committee would utilize to fulfill its outlined purpose
  ○ Outlining how bias incidents would be routed once reported
  ○ Developing a standard university definition for *bias incidents*
  ○ Identifying the makeup of the Bias Incidents Response Team, including the following:
    ▪ Primary group representatives (student conduct, university counseling, university police department, equal opportunity for regulatory compliance, appointed student representative, multicultural affairs, and chair)
    ▪ Specialty/ad hoc representatives (chosen based on need/area of expertise) (violence prevention, Student Disability Services, international programs, Title IX, Veteran Affairs, gender studies, LGBTQ)

- Developing the initial marketing and advertisement for the team
- Developing a short- and long-term plan for the team and their place within the institution

The proliferation of bias response teams across the nation has illustrated a focus on providing a response avenue when institutions are unsure how to respond to incidents that do not constitute a violation of established institutional policy (McDermott, 2013). As a result, due to the potentially serious nature of bias-related incidents, it has become important for institutions to utilize a diverse group of students and professionals, as suggested, to ensure that the team is serving the overall needs of the community (Miller et al., 2018a).

Using Alternative Approaches to Address Bias Incidents

Despite their success in providing institutions with an avenue of responding to bias-related incidents, bias response teams also come with their own unique set of challenges (LePeau et al., 2016). LePeau and colleagues (2016) further reveal that if institutions are not careful, their teams "may paradoxically serve as mechanisms to publically distance an institution from negative incidents and to shift attention away from underlying exclusionary cultures that require sustained, long-term effects and organizational change" (p. 318). McDermott (2013) also reveals that, in some cases, students are disappointed in the responses issued by bias response teams and instead prefer a punitive or disciplinary action. As a result, institutions should have multiple avenues to respond to bias incidents.

In addition to utilizing policies and bias response teams to respond to bias-related incidents, institutions should also consider infusing conflict-resolution practices into their community and processes. As outlined by Schrage and Giacomini (2009) traditional adjudication processes, in many cases, are limited to the extent to which they can resolve incidents. This is especially true when dealing with situations that result from oppressive social structures both within and outside the institution. Often time's students view the formal adjudication process through an adversarial lens and question whether the institution is actively working within its best interests or actively protecting those of the institution (Schrage & Giacomini, 2009). Therefore, institutions are constantly challenged to ensure that the policy and procedures that are developed are equitable and inclusive (Schrage & Giacomini, 2009). Unfortunately, as Schrage and Giacomnini (2009) further explain, despite the increased focus in this area, students still may perceive the formal adjudication process as oppressive.

Additionally, although formal adjudication processes are designed to reach a resolution for incidents, in some cases it overlooks the root causes of the dispute (Schrage & Giacomini, 2009). As a result, the likelihood of the behavior recurring remains high as the conflict at the root of the incident has yet to be resolved. Ultimately, as described by Schrage and Giacomini (2009), adjudication only models present challenges for institutions in their attempt to respond to the bias-related incidents:

1. Adjudication-only models fail to address conflicts that often underlie the behavior that is reported to student conduct administrators.
2. Adjudication seldom acts to intentionally restore a community harmed by a student's actions.
3. The single-process option does not appreciate the diversity of the student population it attempts to serve.

When bias incidents occur on a college campus, the campus community must not only deal with the incident, but they must also look at the impact the incident has had on others, directly or indirectly (Schrage & Giacomini, 2009). Addressing bias incidents and community impact can often occur when conflict resolution is introduced into the process. Schrage and Giacomini (2009) bring alternative approaches to student conduct together to create the spectrum of resolution options model. Since its inception, the spectrum of resolution options has provided support to institutions across the nation in their process of infusing conflict resolution into their university processes and procedures.

As defined by Schrage and Thompson (2009) "the *Spectrum Approach* assumes that a majority of incidents on campus can be managed through alternative conflict resolution methods where parties are presented with a menu of options and a review of their rights before being asked to articulate their story" (p. 66, emphasis added). Understanding that not all institutions may have the resources to provide students with the full alternative approaches that the spectrum model offers, giving students or student groups access to a menu of options and reviewing student rights provides students with a level of comfort that increases the likelihood of them being open and honest about the conflict (Schrage & Giacomini, 2009). Ultimately, the most effective and efficient time frame to resolve a conflict is the time between an incident occurring and the selection of the pathway of resolution. This period is known as the "magic real estate" (Schrage & Giacomini, 2009). Schrage and Thompson (2009) further explain that "once a dispute moves beyond the magic real estate and decides to bypass other informal venues to file a complaint under a formal conduct code process the stakes are higher. Rather than conflict, the incident is now framed as an alleged violation" (p. 66).

The spectrum of resolution option model outlines the following forms of alternative dispute resolution that staff and students can utilize to tailor the learning experiences for each unique incident that may occur. The informal side of the spectrum begins with no need for informal conflict management from administrators. Ideally, through proactive education, educators should strive to provide community members with tools and resources they can use to effectively resolve conflict at the moment without having the need for a third party or the likelihood of the incident being unresolved. Additionally, to effectively resolve conflict, individuals must have a thorough understanding of the differences that exist among dialogue, debate, and discussion. Often times when locked in conflict, individuals revert to debating their stance with little intention of hearing or understanding the stance of the opposing individual (Schirch & Campt, 2007).

Schirch and Campt (2007) further explain that when dealing with debate individuals may treat the interaction like a contest where there are winners and losers involved. In other instances, individuals approach the conflict with the hopes of discussing the incident. Discussion is often viewed as the midpoint between debate and dialogue (Symphony Orchestra Institute, 2005). However, it still focuses primarily on persuading others (Winchell, 2004). For the most part, the discussion provides a space for surface-level conversations. However, it limits the ability to have deeper conversations (Winchell, 2004).

Ideally, as the research has suggested, the most effective way to resolve a conflict is through the use of dialogue. As outlined by Schirchand Campt (2007), during a dialogue, "listeners find ideas they can agree with and combine them with their own for the purpose of building a larger truth than any side has on its own" (p. 8). Wilmot and Hocker (2001) further explain that dialogue allows participants to "explore different assumptions, develop an objective view and description of the conflict, give up persuasion in favor of exploration of different perspectives, look critically at all sides of the controversy, and express hope and belief in the goodwill of the other person and [the] intention to work out differences" (p. 257).

Next, Schrage and Giacomini (2009) emphasize the art of conflict coaching. More specifically, they emphasis that coaching is not to be mistaken for counseling. Instead, it is structured to provide a one-on-one opportunity for administrators to gain insights and the additional information needed to help students overcome specific obstacles in their current and future paths. Coaching can be utilized and effective during and/or after a formal disciplinary process. Despite that formal resolution, individuals can be coached through the underlying conflict. Essentially, "conflict coaching can help a student resolve his or her own conflict issues at the lowest level, handle an active conflict in a timely way, and engage another person who has not opted for formal resolution" (Giacomini, 2009. p. 101).

When in situations in which two or more students are actively seeking to engage in the process, facilitated dialogues may be appropriate. Facilitated dialogue is a form of early intervention that starts the process of resolving incidents by increasing the opportunity for all voices to be heard (Schrage & Thompson, 2009). It "refers to a conversation between two or more individuals or groups in which a trained multi-partial facilitator (a neutral party that gives opportunity for all parties to have a voice in the process) helps parties overcome communicative barriers and engage in productive conversations regarding issues of mutual concern" (Wilgus & Holmes, 2009, p. 113). Although similar in nature to mediation, the primary difference is that facilitated dialogue is not necessarily designed to produce an outcome (Folger, Poole, Stutman, 2005). Often times, facilitated dialogues are effective because the involvement of the third-party facilitator helps to create opportunities for peace and relationship-building while also helping to transform competition into collaboration (Schrage & Giacomini, 2009). Mediation, on the other hand "refers, in the broadest sense, to conciliatory interventions by an acceptable third party who works with individuals or groups in conflict to facilitate the development of a shared and mutually acceptable solution to their problem(s)" (Warters, 2009. p. 126)

Another option outlined in the spectrum of resolution model is restorative justice/practices. "Restorative justice views crime as more than breaking the law [or violating institutional policies;] it also causes harm to people, relationships, and the community. So a just response must address those harms as well as the wrongdoing. If the parties are willing, the best way to do this is to help them meet to discuss those harms and how to about bring a resolution" (Center for Justice and Reconciliation, 2019). Restorative justice focuses on repairing the harm that was caused by the offense; it looks at bringing the parties together to figure out what that looks like; and the process allows for the people, relationships, and communities to be transformed (Goldblum, 2009).

Additionally, shuttle diplomacy is a vital tool that can be utilized to resolve conflict (Schrage & Goldfarb, 2009). The essence of shuttle diplomacy is the use of a third party to convey information back and forth between the parties, serving as a reliable means of communication less susceptible to the grandstanding of face-to-face or media-based communication. The intermediary serves not only as a relay for questions and answers but can also provide suggestions for moving the conflict toward resolution and does so in private (Schrage & Goldfarb, 2009). The ability to work with the parties in private allows the participating parties to not spend their time debating each other and acting defensively (Schrage & Goldfarb 2009).

Finally, Giacomini (2009) reiterated the most common form of accountability: the informal and formal adjudication process. Adjudication generally refers to processes of decision-making that involves a neutral third party with the authority to determine a binding resolution through some form of judgment or award. Adjudication is carried out in various forms but most commonly occurs in the court system. Adjudication is an involuntary, adversarial process. This means arguments are presented to prove one side right and one side wrong, resulting in win-lose outcomes (Schrage & Giacomini, 2009; Spangler, 2003).

In addition to having a menu of resolution options to respond to incidents, Thorne (2014) wrote about the importance of including students in the planning processes of addressing bias incidents on campus. Even though students often are the population most directly affected by such incidents, students are often left out of the resolution process. Restorative justice offers a way that all impacted parties can be heard when incidents are addressed and when resolutions are decided (Goldblum, 2009). Getting student buy-in helps to increase the accountability level for other students. Students often complain that institutions only talk about diversity, inclusion, and acceptance, but that they don't act on it and don't hold parties who commit bias incidents responsible.

Conflict resolution allows for there to be action behind the words that students are used to hearing in conduct processes. It also helps institutions create a culture of acceptance and inclusion on their campuses. Livingood (2007) reveals that "bias can contribute to the creation of conflict and increase its duration. Conflict, in turn, can create and intensify bias. Left unchecked, bias distorts how we communicate and interpret communications. Consequently, it complicates the process of conflict resolution. Thus, understanding the relationship between conflict and bias can assist in developing approaches to resolve conflict" (p. 54). Once bias arises, it has an impact on communication.

Conclusion

Bias-related incidents are a growing concern for institutions of higher education. Because of this concern, institutions must constantly work to develop processes and procedures to address these issues with processes that ensure that their communities are safe and welcoming to students from all backgrounds. Having pre-established plans for responding to bias incidents on college campuses is very important (Thorne, 2014). However, if there is no plan to repair the harm that has been caused to the campus community and only a plan to react to it, campus community members could feel left out of the process. It could also make them wonder if their institution only cares about addressing these issues after they happen. Faculty and staff of the institution may feel ill-equipped to handle such issues when they come and lean on the "experts" on campus to handle them. Practitioners who want to be proactive in addressing bias on their campuses should consider using some of the following techniques:

1. Create opportunities to educate the campus community on communication so that they could work on improving their listening, reflection, and reactionary skills. In doing so, participants could also learn how to pay attention to verbal and nonverbal cues, a skill that could be used in mediations or shuttle negotiations. This skill could also be beneficial to parties who are in the middle of a conflict that resulted from a bias incident, as it creates an opportunity for them to learn from other perspectives.

2. Developing relationships within the campus community before incidents occur can help when practitioners are responding to bias incidents. These relationships can help build trust with the campus community under positive circumstances. The trust and relationships that are created help assist the practitioners leading the parties into developing an understanding and is key to conflict-resolution practices such as mediation and restorative justice.

3. If a student who committed a bias act on campus will remain a student on that same campus, practitioners also have to think about how they will address the incident with that person who has caused harm to the campus community. Utilizing conflict resolution practices when addressing bias helps to prevent repeated behavior and allow the community to be involved in decision-making.

Ultimately, in addition to having processes in place, institutions also have to identify their stance on ensuring an inclusive community that allows them to create a philosophical approach to how they resolve bias incidents based on values, ethics, and justice for all. Throne (2014) insists that this can be achieved through institutional practitioner self-evaluation and considering these questions:

1. What is our responsibility as practitioners when it comes to addressing bias incidents?
2. What role do we play in making sure that the community is safe, but also that students who commit the acts are held accountable and learn from their actions?
3. How do we show support for opposing groups, ensuring that we are not leaving students out?

Addressing bias incidents on campus is no easy task. However, in order to hold institutions accountable to uphold their mission and value statements it requires institutions to actively address these issues when they occur. It is only by addressing these issues will individuals learn that these sorts of incidents are not acceptable on college campuses.

References

Anthony, M. D., & Johnson, J. L. (2012). *Creating and sustaining bias incident response teams: From inception to execution* [Webcast]. Retrieved from http://studentaffairs.com/webinars/

Boysen, G. A. (2012). Teacher and student perceptions of microaggressions in college classrooms. *College Teaching 60*(3), 122–129.

Boysen, G. A., Vogel, D. L., Cope, M. A., & Hubbard, A. (2009). Incidents of bias in college classrooms: Instructor and student perceptions. *Journal of Diversity in Higher Education, 2*(4), 219–231.

Brown, S. (2015). At Yale, painful rifts emerge over diversity and free speech. *Chronicle of Higher Education.* Retrieved from http://chronicle. com/article/At-Yale-Painful-Rifts-Emerge/234112

Center for Justice and Reconciliation. (2019). Lesson 1: What is restorative justice?. Retrieved from http://restorativejustice.org/restorative-justice/about-restorative-justice/tutorial-intro-to-restorative-justice/lesson-1-what-is-restorative-justice/#sthash.Bj0G4Gmo.dpbs

Chesler, M. A., Lewis, A. E., & Crowfoot, J. E. (2005). *Challenging racism in higher education*. Lanham, MD: Rowman & Littlefield.

Council for the Advancement of Standards. (2012). *Council for the Advancement of Standards professional standards for higher education* (8th ed.). Washington DC: Author

DeKeseredy, W., Nolan, J. J., & Hall-Sanchez, A. (2019). Hate crimes and bias incidents in the ivory tower: Results from a large-scale campus survey. *American Behavioral Scientist.*

Giacomini, N.G. (2009). Incorporating principles of conflict resolution and social justice into formal student conduct code pathways. In Schrage, J. M., & Giacomini, N. G. (Eds.), *Reframing campus conflict: Student conduct practice through a social justice lens* (pp. 181–196). Sterling, VA. Stylus.

Giacomini, N.G. (2009). Providing a spectrum of resolution options. In Schrage, J. M., & Giacomini, N. G. (Eds.), *Reframing campus conflict: Student conduct practice through a social justice lens* (pp. 65–86). Sterling, VA. Stylus.

Goldblum, A. (2009). Restorative justice from theory to practice. In Schrage, J. M., & Giacomini, N. G. (Eds.), *Reframing campus conflict: Student conduct practice through a social justice lens* (pp. 140-149). Sterling, VA. Stylus.

Folger, J. P., Poole, M. S., & Strutman, R. K. (2005). *Working through conflict: Strategies for relationships, groups, and organizations* (5th ed.). Boston, MA: Pearson Education.

Hughes, G. (2013). Racial justice, hegemony, and bias incidents in U.S. higher education. *Multicultural Perspectives, 15*(3), 126–132.

Journal of Blacks in Higher Education. (2016). *More racist incidents on college campuses*. Retrieved from https://www.jbhe.com/2016/11/more-racist-incidents-on-american-college-campuses/

Lancaster, J., & Waryold, D. (Eds.). (2008). *Student conduct practice: The complete guide for student affairs professionals* (1st ed.). Sterling, VA. Stylus

LePeau, L. A., Snipes, J. T., Morgan, D., & Zimmerman, H. (2018). Campus educators deploying cultural and social capital: Critically examining a bias response team. *Journal of College Student Development, 59*(6), 681–697.

LePeau, L. A., Snipes, J. T., Morgan, D., Zimmerman, H., & Marcotte, B. A. (2016). Connecting to get things done: A conceptual model of the process used to respond to bias incidents. *Journal of Diversity in Higher Education, 9*(2), 113–129.

Livingood, J. (2007). Addressing bias in conflict and dispute resolution settings. *Dispute Resolution Journal, 62*(4), 54–61.

McDermott, C. (2013). As slurs and offenses multiply, colleges scramble to respond. *Chronicle of Higher Education*. Retrieved from https://www.chronicle.com/article/As-SlursOffenses/141479

Miller, R. A., Guida, T., Smith, S., Kiersten Ferguson, S., & Medina, E. (2018a). A balancing act: Whose interests do bias response teams serve? *Review of Higher Education, 42*(1), 313–337.

Miller, R. A., Guida, T., Smith, S., Kiersten Ferguson, S., & Medina, E. (2018b). Free speech tensions: Responding to bias on college and university campuses. *Journal of Student Affairs Research and Practice, 55*(1), 27–39.

Pope, R. L., Torres, V., & Arminio, J. (2012). Are we there yet? In Pope, R. L., Torres, V., & Arminio, J. (Eds.). *Why aren't we there yet? Taking personal responsibility for creating an inclusive campus* (pp.1–8). Sterling, VA. Stylus.

Prutzman, P. (1994). Bias-related incidents, hate crimes, and conflict resolution. *Education and Urban Society, 27*(1), 71–81.

Prutzman, P., & Johnson, J. (1997). Bias awareness and multiple perspectives: Essential aspects of conflict resolution. *Theory Into Practice, 36*(1), 26–31.

Robinson, T. (2009). Moving toward a healthier climate for conflict resolution through dialogue. In Schrage, J. M., & Giacomini, N. G. (Eds.), *Reframing campus conflict: Student conduct practice through a social justice lens* (pp. 87–99). Sterling, VA. Stylus.

Rollock, N. (2012). Unspoken rules of engagement: Navigating racial microaggressions in the academic terrain. *International Journal of Qualitative Studies in Education, 25*(5), 517–532. doi:10.1080/09518398.2010.543433

Schirch, L., & Campt, D. (2007). *The little book of dialogue for difficult subjects: A practical, hands on guide.* Intercourse, PA: Good Books.

Schrage, J.M., & Giacomini, N.G. (2009). Building community in the current campus climate. In Schrage, J. M., & Giacomini, N. G. (Eds.), *Reframing campus conflict: Student conduct practice through a social justice lens* (pp. 7–21). Sterling, VA. Stylus.

Schrage, J.M., & Goldfarb, M. (2009). Using shuttle diplomacy to resolve campus conflict. In Schrage, J. M., & Giacomini, N. G. (Eds.), *Reframing campus conflict: Student conduct practice through a social justice lens* (pp. 175–180). Sterling, VA. Stylus.

Schrage, J.M., & Thompson, M.C. (2009). Providing a spectrum of resolution options. In Schrage, J. M., & Giacomini, N. G. (Eds.), *Reframing campus conflict: Student conduct practice through a social justice lens* (pp. 65–86). Sterling, VA. Stylus.

Schuster, S. K., Bird, L. E., & Mackin, M. B. (2006). *The first amendment on campus: A handbook for college and university administrators.* Washington DC: NASPA.

Spangler, B. (2003). *Adjudication.* Retrieved from https://www.beyondintractability .org/essay/adjudication

Stripling, J., & Thomason, A. (2015). Oklahoma president's swift action on racist video carries risks. *Chronicle of Higher Education.* Retrieved from https://www .chronicle.com/article/Oklahoma-President-s-Swift/228389

Sue, D. W. (2015). *Race talk and the conspiracy of silence: Understanding and facilitating difficult dialogues on race.* Hoboken, NJ: Wiley.

Sue, D. W., Capodilupo, C. M., Torino, G. C., Bucceri, J. M., Holder, A. M. B., Nadal, K. L., & M. Esquilin. (2007). Racial microaggressions in everyday life. *American Psychologist, 62*(4), 271–286.

Supiano, B. (2015). Racial disparities in higher ed: An overview. *Chronicle of Higher Education.* Retrieved from http://chronicle.com/article/ Racial-Disparities-in-Higher/234129

Symphony Orchestra Institute. (2005). *Dialogue.* Retrieved from http//www.soi .org/reading/goodpractice/dialogue.shtml

Teaching Tolerance. (n.d.). *Identifying and responding to bias incidents.* Retrieved from https://www.tolerance.org/professional-development/identifying-and-responding-to-bias-incidents

Thorne, A. (2014). Stages emergencies: How colleges react to bias incidents. *Academic Questions, 27*, 28–47.

U.S. Department of Justice. (2001). *Hate crimes on campus: The problem and efforts to confront it.* Washington DC: Author. Retrieved from https:// www.ncjrs.gov/ pdffiles1/bja/187249.pdf

U.S. Department of Justice. (2003). *Responding to hate crimes and bias-motivated incidents on college/university campuses.* Washington DC: Author. Retrieved from https://www.justice.gov/archive/crs/pubs/university92003.pdf

WAPT. (2014, February 18). *Meredith statue defaced at Ole Miss.* Retrieved from https://www.wapt.com/article/meredith-statue-defaced-at-ole-miss/2087391

Watt, S. K. (2007). Difficult dialogues, privilege and social justice: Uses of the privileged identity model (PIE) model in student affairs practice. *The College Student Affairs Journal, 26*(2), 114–126.

Wessler, S., & Moss, M. (2001). *Hate crimes on campus: The problem and efforts to confront it.* Washington DC: U.S. Department of Justice. Retrieved from https:// www.ncjrs.gov/pdffiles1/bja/187249.pdf(

Winchell, P. (2004). *The power of dialogue.* Retrieved from http://thedialoguegame .net/thedialoguegame/wordpress/wp-content/uploads/2012/06/Power-of-Dialogue.pdf

Wilgus, J., & Holmes, R.C. (2009). Facilitated dialogue. In Schrage, J. M., & Giacomini, N. G.

(Eds.), *Reframing campus conflict: Student conduct practice through a social justice lens* (pp. 112–125). Sterling, VA. Stylus.

Wilmot, W., & Hocker, J. (2001). *Interpersonal conflict* (6th ed.). New York, NY: McGraw-Hill.

Worthington, R. L., Stanley, C. A., & Lewis, W. T. (2014). National Association of Diversity Officers in Higher Education standards of professional practice for chief diversity officers. *Journal of Diversity in Higher Education, 7*(4), 227–234. doi:10.1037/a0038391

SEXUAL MISCONDUCT

Kristen A. Harrell and Michael R. Gillilan

The current, intense conversations about sexual misconduct are new enough that this book's first edition (Lancaster & Waryold, 2008) contained multiple references to sexual misconduct but not a dedicated chapter. Looking at the historical record available to us, there is little to help us understand the prevalence and nature of sexual misconduct. Not until the mid-1980s, after *Ms. Magazine* sponsored a study of campus date rape, did we begin to have a comprehensive sense of what was happening among our students. This study identified that one in four college women were victims of rape or attempted rape (Koss, Gidycz & Wisniewski, 1987). This is not to mention the assaults we knew were happening to students who did not identify as women or those that were unreported. The Koss, Gidycz, and Wisniewski (1987) study brought to light campus gang rapes, the impact of rape on victims, and much more about the role of alcohol as it relates to sexual misconduct (Ehrhart & Sandler, 1985). In 1991, campus sexual assault came to the cover of *Time* magazine after Katie Koestner began telling her story of being sexually assaulted while in college (Gibbs, 1991).

Decades later, sexual misconduct on the college campus seems to have finally captured greater attention. This chapter will focus on how we have arrived at this point, the scope and nature of sexual misconduct and related offenses (e.g., stalking) on college campuses, and critical considerations for addressing sexual misconduct. We will end with thoughts about the future given the anticipated and imminent changes in the legal landscape.

How We Got Here

Since April of 2011, the discussion about multiple forms of interpersonal violence, including sexual harassment, sexual assault, dating violence, domestic violence, and stalking in the United States has grown (Poole, 2014). The prevalence and problem of sexual assault is at the forefront of this discussion. Employees at institutions of higher education are doing everything they can to keep up with state and federal laws, case law, federal guidance, and public opinion. In an ever-changing landscape, it is easy to lose sight of how we got here. This section provides a brief overview of key federal regulations and guidance that have led us to where we are now on the topic of interpersonal violence. A timeline is provided in Figure 10.1.

Title IX of the Educational Amendments of 1972

"No person in the United States shall, on the basis of sex, be excluded from participation in, be denied the benefits of, or be subjected to discrimination under any education program or activity receiving federal financial assistance" (Title IX of the Education Amendments of 1972). Title IX applies to any educational entity that receives funding from the United States federal government. As noted by Lowery in chapter 4 of this text, "compliance with federal laws apply with equal force to public and private higher education institutions" as nearly every institution receives federal financial assistance that supports students and institutional research. It was made clear through the Civil Rights Restoration Act 1987 that Title IX applies to all portions of the institution, not just to the program receiving federal funding.

It is important to keep in mind that Title IX is a prohibition on sex discrimination, not just a prohibition on discrimination against women. Although there have been several cases addressing sexual harassment in the court of law, a lower threshold exists when Title IX is enforced by the U.S. Department of Education's Office for Civil Rights (OCR) (Lowery, 2008). In 1997, the OCR published *Sexual Harassment Guidance: Harassment of Students by School Employees, Other Students, or Third Parties.* This guidance made it clear that sexual harassment, which includes sexual assault, could be considered a form of discrimination under Title IX. This "was grounded in long-standing legal authority establishing that sexual harassment of students can be a form of sex discrimination covered by Title IX" (Office for Civil Rights, 2001, p. i).

Sexual harassment as defined under this 1997 guidance followed case law regarding quid pro quo harassment and the creation of a hostile environment (*Franklin v. Gwinnett County Public Schools*, 1992). As it pertains to hostile environments, the behavior must be "sufficiently severe, persistent, or pervasive to limit a student's ability to participate in or benefit from an education program or activity, or to create a hostile or abusive educational environment" (Sexual harassment guidance, 1997, p. 12038). In 2001 the OCR

Figure 10.1. A timeline of significant influences on the landscape of sexual violence issues in the United States.

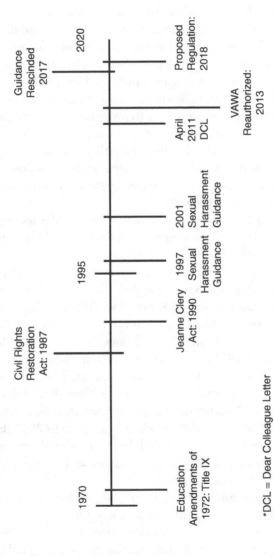

1970

Education
Amendments of
1972: Title IX

Civil Rights
Restoration
Act: 1987

1995

Jeanne Clery
Act: 1990

1997
Sexual
Harassment
Guidance

2001
Sexual
Harassment
Guidance

April
2011
DCL

VAWA
Reauthorized:
2013

Guidance
Rescinded
2017

2020

Proposed
Regulation:
2018

*DCL = Dear Colleague Letter

published revised sexual harassment guidance. The 2001 guidance did not differ substantially from the 1997 guidance, but, as included in the preamble, the guidance provided clarity after Supreme Court decisions on sexual harassment in educational environments (Office for Civil Rights, 2001). (Refer to chapter 4 for specific case law.) Both documents include the expectations that schools take action when they know or reasonably should have known about sexual harassment. Readers are encouraged to read the 2001 guidance, which provides context and understanding of both documents.

Ten years later, the OCR published a "Dear Colleague" letter in April (Ali, 2011). Unlike the guidance published in 1997 and 2001, the April 2011 letter caught the attention of higher education and resulted in a push to focus on resolution procedures. In response to this letter, and other federal action, institutions of higher education evaluated and changed their policies, designated and publicly identified Title IX coordinators responsible for the administration of Title IX on campuses, bolstered training and education, and became increasingly aware of the potential consequences for not following OCR's guidance (Poole, 2014).

OCR began posting the names of schools under review for alleged violations of Title IX. This caught media attention. A raging battle ensued between advocates pushing for a greater response to complaints of sexual harassment, particularly sexual assault, and individuals who felt individuals' due process rights were being trampled, and this battle continues as we write this chapter (Bauer-Wolf, 2018; Brodsky, 2015; End Rape on Campus, n.d.; Foundation for Individual Rights in Education (FIRE), 2018; Friedersdorf, 2019; Joyce, 2017; Kissel, 2011; Know Your IX, n.d.; McGowan, 2017; McWilliams, 2019; New, 2016; Patel, 2018; White House Task Force to Protect Students From Sexual Assault, 2014a). The 2016 presidential election brought a significant change to the leadership of the United States. Changes in the Department of Education and increased scrutiny of the April 2011 "Dear Colleague" letter resulted in a notice in 2017 that the guidance provided in the letter was rescinded. In the interim, the government directed schools to rely on the 2001 revised guidance and interim guidance provided by the Department of Education.

While much attention has been given to Title IX, it is important not to ignore the impacts of the Jeanne Clery Disclosure of Campus Security Policy and Campus Crime Statistics Act of 1990 (the Clery Act) and the Violence Against Women Reauthorization Act of 2013 (VAWA), which codified some aspects of the April 2011 "Dear Colleague" letter. The Clery Act (1990) provided early expectations about information that must be available to campus populations regarding sexual misconduct. VAWA (2013) provides the requirement to allow participants to have an adviser of their choice at all meetings throughout the resolution of a complaint and for schools to publish a definition for *consent* in their annual security reports (Clery Act, 1990). These regulations have more extensive impacts beyond those referenced on the work that we do as it pertains to interpersonal violence. (Chapter 4 provides further analysis and information.)

Ultimately each of these influences has contributed to pushing higher education into a focus on legalistic processes. This shift toward legalistic processes has seemingly diminished some of the focus on institutions' educational missions where it comes to sexual misconduct. This is a primary reason the faculty of the ASCA Gehring Academy's Advanced Sexual Misconduct track (Harrell, Morehead, Akin, Gillilan, & Wade, 2018) made an effort to provide a multidisciplinary lens in the curriculum provided to participants. While it is important to stay vigilant of the legal influences outlined in this section, practitioners should not forget the breadth of knowledge and expertise that comes from an educational student conduct foundation.

Forms of Sexual Misconduct

It is important to consider *sexual misconduct* in its broadest definition. Many people seem to default to thinking of sexual misconduct as analogous to sexual assault. So far in this chapter we have mentioned the issues of sexual harassment, dating violence, domestic violence, and stalking. The following sections provide brief explanations of what is encompassed in these varying forms of interpersonal violence. While not discussed here, we would also encourage the reader to consider how hazing may fall into this category as well.

Before diving into some basic definitions and considerations, it is important to provide context for the language and words we use to talk about sexual misconduct within the national framework. Sexual assault means a lot of different things to different people. For example, under the Colorado Revised Statutes (2016) and Texas Penal Code (2017) sexual assault of an adult must include some form of penetration, whereas in other states the statutes would refer to this act as rape (California Penal Code, 2013; Washington Revised Code,1998). Federal regulations contain yet a different set of definitions. Conduct administrators must ensure that policies and codes are clear when discussing these issues. Failure to do so creates challenges in student conduct work as students, parents, attorneys, and others come in with preexisting frameworks for these topics that may or may not align with our institution's rules and regulations.

Sexual Harassment

The Office for Civil Rights (2001) revised guidance on *sexual harassment* and defined it as "unwelcome conduct of a sexual nature" and noted that it could "include unwelcome sexual advances, requests for sexual favors, and other verbal, nonverbal, or physical conduct of a sexual nature" (p. 2). The guidance offered numerous examples of what behavior constitutes sexual harassment. It is worth noting that the Supreme Court cases that contributed to the revisions involved a teacher having sex with a student (*Gebser v. Lago Vista Independent School District,* 1998) and a fifth-grader making sexual advances to a classmate (*Davis v. Monroe County Board of Education,* 1999). The guidance noted that school employees, students, and non-affiliated parties could be harassers and, thus, any "person" could be the subject of the harassment. This case established that there is no requirement that the subject be a student or employee, that both female and male students are protected from harassment (at the time there was little to no conversation regarding non-binary and gender-identity, which is different from sex identification), and that a harasser could be the same sex as the target of harassment.

Colleges and universities must respond to two types of sexual harassment under Title IX, quid pro quo harassment and hostile environment (Office for Civil Rights, 2001). Examples of quid pro quo harassment include a coach who conditions a starting position on whether the student-athlete submits to unwelcome sexual conduct and a faculty member who threatens to assign an unsatisfactory grade to a student who refuses sexual advances. In both cases, quid pro quo harassment has occurred. Whether the students submitted or not, their opportunity to fairly participate in the educational program has been limited or denied by the demand or threat.

Hostile environment harassment occurs when the unwelcome sexual conduct is "sufficiently serious to deny or limit a student's ability to participate or benefit in the school's program based on sex" (Office for Civil Rights, 2001, p. 5). In *Davis v. Monroe County Board of Education* 1999, one fifth-grader's constant sexual advances toward a classmate led to a hostile environment claim. In the university context, a college student who leaves school after non-consensual sexual penetration by a classmate easily could be imagined to have experienced a hostile environment.

As sexual harassment can be of a verbal or otherwise expressive nature, practitioners, particularly those in public institutions, need to be mindful of the fact that not all offensive, crude, sexual language constitutes actionable harassment. In 2003, the Office for Civil Rights affirmed that its guidance was not meant to conflict with First Amendment rights. The assistant secretary indicated that a single statement would not create a hostile environment, and furthermore, the harassment "must include something beyond the mere expression of views, words . . . that some person finds offensive" and must be sufficiently "severe, persistent, or pervasive" (Reynolds, 2003, p. 1) to limit a student's educational participation. This is not to suggest that student conduct professionals should ignore or refuse to become involved in these conflicts; instead, formal action is better replaced by educational conversations.

Sexual Misconduct

While the name of this chapter is "Sexual Misconduct" with the intent to cover a breadth of interpersonal violence issues, sexual misconduct, as referenced here, is narrower. This specific focus emphasizes the various ways that individuals define these issues of interpersonal violence. In addition to the terms already used in this chapter, and the other terms identified later, some also use *sexual violence* as an umbrella term. The following are specific types of interpersonal violence that are sexual in nature (excluding sexual harassment, which was previously discussed). Unless otherwise noted, the definitions were created by the authors based on experience and expertise in this area.

Sexual assault
- Basic definition: Unwanted touching of a sexual nature without consent
- Other terms: *Sexual contact* (Texas A&M University, 2019; Tufts University, 2019; Northwestern University, 2018); *unwanted sexual touching and fondling* (Gordon College, n.d.)

Rape
- Basic definition: Unwanted penetration of the anus or genitals without consent. Unwanted penetration of the mouth with genitals without consent. Using someone else's genitals to penetrate one's own mouth, anus, or genitals without consent
- Other terms: *Sexual assault* (Colorado Revised Statutes, 2016; Texas Penal Code 2017); *non-consensual/forced intercourse* (Ball State University, 2017; Tufts University, 2019); *sexual penetration without consent* (Northwestern, 2018); *sexual abuse* (Texas A&M University, 2019)

When discussing sexual assault and rape, particularly when developing policies and engaging in prevention education, it is important to ensure there are clear definitions and understandings of what constitutes consent when consent is part of the policy. This includes defining and understanding incapacitation and other statuses, such as age, that may automatically indicate consent is not present. Further discussion of consent may be found in the critical considerations portion of this chapter.

Sexual exploitation
- Basic definition: Taking sexual advantage of another person for one's own benefit
- Examples of sexual exploitation:
  - Stealthing (indicating one is going to use protection, such as a condom, and then removing or not using it without the other person's knowledge)
  - Human trafficking
  - Voyeurism
  - Filming sexual activity without involved parties' consent
  - Sharing images and/or recordings of sexual activity without involved parties' consent
  - Allowing viewing of sexual activity without involved parties' consent
  - Exhibitionism
  - Sexual activity with individuals who are not of a legal age to consent
  - Solicitation of a minor
  - Knowingly transmitting a sexually transmitted infection
  - Causing or attempting to cause incapacitation for purposes of an assault

Dating and Domestic Violence

The April 4, 2011 "Dear Colleague" letter focused on sexual violence. However, while this letter made little reference to dating and domestic violence, it did encourage institutions to "adopt comprehensive, coordinated responses to domestic violence, dating violence, sexual assault, and stalking" (Ali, 2011, p. 19). The 2013 Violence Against Women Reauthorization Act codified this recommendation into law, thus requiring institutions to prohibit dating and domestic violence (DDV) and to report DDV statistics in their Clery Act annual security reports. In addition, this mandate requires institutions to provide information about their programs to prevent dating and domestic violence.

DDV may affect more college students than sexual assault. In 2011, Knowledge Networks published its college dating and abuse poll. Forty-three percent of college women reported experiencing violent and abusive dating behaviors and over 52% of college women reported knowing a friend who had experienced those behaviors, which ranged from physical abuse (including sexual) to verbal abuse and controlling behavior, sometimes via technology. Iconis (2013) reported similar rates of physical dating violence among male and female students. Addressing these problems with students is complex; the Knowledge Networks study found that 57% of participants said it was difficult to identify dating abuse, with 38% saying they did not know how to find help if they were a victim. The number-one reason for students staying in an abusive relationship was the threat of self-harm or suicide by the partner.

Dating and domestic violence can have similar presentations but are distinguished by spousal relationships, cohabitation, and children (among other characteristics) (U.S. Department of Education, 2016), with variation among states. DDV reports can be highly complicated, and they require patience and a comprehensive approach. Complex cases like that of Lauren McCluskey, a University of Utah student killed by her boyfriend (Pettit, 2019), warrant a full-blown threat assessment.

Stalking

"*Stalking* is defined as engaging in a course of conduct directed at a specific person that would cause a reasonable person to—

- Fear for the person's safety or the safety of others; or
- Suffer substantial emotional distress" (U.S. Department of Education, 2016, p. 3, emphasis added).

For the individuals responsible for the collection and dissemination of campus Clery Act statistics, this definition can encompass many types of issues on a campus, including roommate conflicts, hazing, and disputes between friends. Policy makers might consider adopting a definition for *substantial emotional distress*, if using the Clery Act definition of *stalking*, and having conversations with relevant stakeholders (including the Clery Act help desk) about how you are interpreting this definition.

Related Retaliation

Title IX also prohibits retaliation and requires administrators "not only take steps to prevent retaliation but also take strong responsive action if it occurs" (Ali, 2011, p. 5). Retaliation is typically understood in sexual misconduct proceedings as action taken against someone who has made a complaint, protested discriminatory actions by a school, or has testified or otherwise participated in proceedings (Coveney, 2016). Retaliation can take the form of firing someone, denying them a position, intimidating them, and so on, "because of the individual's complaint or participation" (Galanter, 2013, para. 3). Retaliation against students can include bullying (Ali, 2011); we've seen in our work where students have been denied access to desirable social events or been subject to threats and intimidation. Coveney (2016) pointed out that retaliation claims under Title IX require three elements: participation in a protected activity (e.g., making a complaint); an adverse action, that is, one that "produces injury or harm" (para. 14); and causation, a showing that the protected activity was a guiding factor in the adverse action. Retaliation reports should be investigated separately from the investigation of the original conduct report and should be a high priority. The Supreme Court considers retaliation an egregious, intentional form of Title IX discrimination and thus individuals have a private right of action including seeking monetary damages by private persons (*Jackson v. Birmingham Board of Education*, 2005).

Critical Considerations

Practitioners who engage in sexual misconduct issues manage many considerations. It takes years to be proficient on this topic and requires constant attention to frequently changing laws, research, and societal viewpoints relating to sexual engagement. The following sections provide a brief overview of some of the most critical considerations.

Policy Development

By now, every institution should have a sexual misconduct policy. However, those policies should be reviewed and revised on a regular, routine basis. There are a number of considerations in revising sexual misconduct policies, ranging from institutional fit to support from the general counsel's office. A primary consideration for sexual misconduct policies is to address all the elements required for compliance with Title IX, the Clery Act, and the Violence Against Women Act. In addition, practitioners need to be mindful of any state laws that may require additional elements.

Two excellent "checklists" are provided by the White House Task Force to Protect Students from Sexual Assault (2014b) and ASCA 2014 white paper (2014) on practices for resolving sexual misconduct cases. The checklists are similar in that they both recommend including (a) an introduction, (b) a statement of the policy's scope or jurisdiction, (c) an outline of options for assistance including confidential support, (d) definitions, (e) reporting options, (f) investigation procedures, (g) adjudication procedures, (h) outcomes, and (i) information about the Title IX coordinator. The White House checklist was shorter and its authors recommended statements about prevention programs and training. This checklist also contains suggestions for who should participate in policy revision, target audience(s), and other documents to consider. The ASCA checklist is a comprehensive resource and includes many useful details. It has been authored by practitioners in the field who are knowledgeable of compliance requirements. Using one or both checklists to audit a current policy, coupled with benchmarking peer institutions and similar in-state schools, will be prudent.

Balance of Equity and Due Process

In watching the ever-evolving conversation around Title IX and interpersonal violence, there has been frequent discussion about providing equity for complainants in a system that has typically been constructed to favor respondents. In fact, this was an apparent focus in the April 2011 "Dear Colleague" letter. At the same time, concerns have been raised that the focus on equity for complainants has resulted in an abridgment of due process rights of respondents. This puts institutions of higher education in a precarious place to balance these concerns.

The following are some critical questions to ask about how your processes are conducted:

- If you are a state actor, are you following basic procedural due process rights outlined for higher education through case law?
- If you are not a state actor, what rights have you afforded contractually to students and are you following those?
- Are you staying up to date on emerging case law, state laws, and federal regulations that guide conduct practice relating to sexual misconduct issues?
- When providing a service or courtesy for one involved party, are you providing that service or courtesy to the other involved parties?
- Are you engaging in ongoing assessments of your process?
- Are you engaging in deliberate and thoughtful evaluation of your sexual misconduct policy on a regular schedule?
- Are your policies clear, easily available, and understood by your campus population?
- Do students, faculty, and staff understand possible outcomes for violations of your sexual misconduct policy?

Standards of Evidence

The 2011 "Dear Colleague" letter (Ali, 2011) caused a stir for a number of reasons, not the least of which was to prescribe that schools use a preponderance of evidence standard in resolving sexual assault complaints. The preponderance of evidence standard can be understood as "the proof need only show that the facts are more likely to be than not so" (as cited in Loschiavo & Waller, 2016, p. 1). In doing so, the Office for Civil Rights cited the use of preponderance of evidence in its own proceedings and the Supreme Court's application of the same standard in regard to Title VII complaints (Title VII prohibits discrimination on the basis of sex in employment). The rationale for using the preponderance standard was that using a higher standard (e.g., clear and convincing) was inequitable and advantaged respondents. While a minority of institutions used a higher standard (including the "beyond a reasonable doubt" standard used in criminal cases) for sexual misconduct complaints prior to 2011 (FIRE Staff, 2011), the Association of Student Conduct Administrators has long considered the preponderance standard to be the appropriate standard for resolving student misconduct complaints, including sexual misconduct (ASCA, 2014; Loschiavo & Waller, 2016). Loschiavo and Waller's 2016 treatise on the preponderance standard provided a comprehensive historical and legal context for the standard's use and concluded, in application to sexual assault allegations, that preponderance is "the only standard that treats all parties equitably," and recommends it not only because its use is legally supported but because "it is the only standard . . . which treat[s] all students with respect and fundamental fairness" (p. 4).

Consent

While we have heard claims that *consent* should be easy to define, it is a very complicated consideration. The Violence Against Women Reauthorization Act of 2013 makes it clear that higher education institutions must publish a definition for *consent* in the applicable jurisdiction in their annual security report. However, where that definition comes from for each campus is different. Many states do not define *consent*. It is interesting to note that when there is some kind of direction, it is usually about what consent is not, not about what constitutes consent. If working from an affirmative consent framework (yes means yes) versus a non-consent framework (no means no) it is important to define consent.

The following are some questions to take into consideration:

- Does your institution philosophically support an affirmative consent framework?

- Is nonverbal communication a sufficient way to communicate consent?
- Are you utilizing research to develop your *consent* definition? For example, Simon and Gagnon's (1984) sexual script theory suggests sex is a socially constructed interaction and thus can change over time. Given this knowledge, are you engaging current students in the creation of your definition of *consent*? Have you reviewed research about constitutes consent?
- Do you include coercion in your policy and how is that defined?
- Are you including age requirements in your definition of *consent*?
- What does incapacitation mean if included in your policy? (see "The Role of Alcohol and Other Drugs")

Trauma-Informed Processes

Trauma-informed responses have become buzz phrases. There is much emphasis on trauma-informed care, trauma-informed interviewing, and generally being trauma-informed. In the context of interpersonal violence issues and conduct processes, being trauma-informed equates to understanding the impacts of trauma that stem from reported events. For individuals working on sexual misconduct cases, it is important to display great sensitivity and to be trauma informed. This includes being aware of how questions are worded and the approach to our processes. These considerations will affect what information we are able to gather. It should be noted that sometimes a genuine response to trauma does not always look the way we are socialized to believe that it does. An example of seemingly incongruent behaviors is an individual who uses humor when discussing a traumatic event. Some may interpret this behavior to mean that the event was in fact not traumatic to that individual.

Some questions for consideration include the following:

- Do campus investigators and decision makers, at all levels, receive adequate training and education on the neurobiology of trauma including, but not limited to, fear responses, emotional impacts, as well as possible short- and longer-term behavioral impacts? And, related to this, does the institution have a way to engage investigators and decision makers in authentic dialogue about socially constructed ideas about how a stereotypic complainant and/or respondent should act?
- Do hearing panels and "officers" receive training on the manner in which questions are asked during an investigation and/or hearing process and how that may be received by someone who has experienced trauma related to the incident?
- How does staff remain up to date with current research and trauma-informed care?

The Role of Alcohol and Other Drugs

Few student conduct professionals will be surprised to learn that alcohol and other drug use is significantly associated with sexual violence among college students (DeGue, 2014). Research suggests that of the women who experienced sexual assault while in college, most of them were assaulted when incapacitated due to substance use, alcohol being the primary but not only substance abused (Krebs, Lindquist, Warner, Fisher, and Martin, 2007). Those who are tasked with the responsibility of resolving sexual misconduct cases will require a deeper understanding of alcohol-and-other-drug-facilitated sexual assault. For instance, let us say that a complaint alleged that a respondent sexually penetrated the complainant without consent for the reason that the complainant was too drunk to consent. Under some policies, establishing responsibility for a violation of sexual misconduct would require that the facts of the case support that the complainant was incapacitated, that is, without the ability to know or judge the "who, what, when, where, why, and/or how of a sexual interaction" (Ball State University, 2017, p. 13). In addition, the facts also must support the finding that the respondent knew or reasonably should have known that the complainant was unable to consent (Black et al., 2017). Although this seems to be an easy concept to understand, in practice, cases involving alcohol can be very difficult to evaluate. Thus, the decision may hinge upon witnesses who share that a complainant's throwing up, inability to stand, and other behaviors are signs of incapacitation.

Conduct administrators will need to understand the factors that play into a student's BAC (blood alcohol content), but with that said, there is no easy calculus to determine how much alcohol prevents the ability to consent (Scalzo, 2007). An understanding of the physiological impact of alcohol abuse and different types of "blacking out" (Milton & Canaff, 2017) is necessary to reach an accurate conclusion.

Identity Considerations

As with all good conduct work, being keenly aware of the identities that complainants and respondents hold and their interaction with the incidents is of utmost consideration in sexual misconduct cases. Given sexual interactions are socially constructed (Simon & Gagnon, 1984) and identities influence social interactions, the identities of individuals likely impact sexual interactions and how others perceive those actions. Thus, lesbian, gay, bisexual, transgender, and queer folks, plus other identities that do not fit within the heteronormative and gender normative frameworks, may regularly experience additional barriers when engaging in our systems.

The following are some questions to take into consideration:

- Does institutional policy include language that contains assumptions about gender?
  - Are gendered pronouns used?
  - How are genitals referenced, if at all?
- Is there a mechanism in place for complainants, respondents, and witnesses to identify their pronouns?
- Are gender binaries reinforced by using honorifics in correspondence (i.e., Mr. or Ms.)?
- Are investigators, conduct officers, and/or administrators properly trained on identity considerations?
- What assumptions and implicit biases are evident in our processes?
  - Are assumptions about gender roles and who initiated a complaint prominent?
  - Are there assumptions about identities based on the reported behavior?
- For example, if the case involves a same-sex assault or assault involving non-binary individuals, what questions are being asked? And, are unnecessary questions being asked that would not be asked in the case of a male-to-female assault?
- How might our own identities affect a complainant or respondent when engaging with us in our processes?

Training

Throughout this chapter, the reader will find numerous references to the need for education and training. The main reason is that learning how to effectively investigate and resolve the complexity and nuances of the various forms of sexual misconduct takes an immense amount of time and effort. Training is important so that practitioners can be effective in administering student conduct systems, and regular training on multiple topics is required, initially by guidance (Ali, 2011) and eventually by federal law (Violence Against Women Act Reauthorization of 2013).

This chapter provides a start to the list of topics to be included in a comprehensive training program for investigators and adjudicators. Appendix C of the ASCA "Gold Standard Practices" (2014) document provides a longer list of training requirements, some of which are core competencies for any adjudicator while others are specific to resolving sexual misconduct complaints. There are numerous, excellent training opportunities including ASCA's regional sexual misconduct institutes and training conducted by large, national law firms.

Resolution Models

There are a number of ways to resolve sexual misconduct complaints. The fine details differ by campus and some states regulate this. For instance, as we write this chapter, Missouri's legislature is seeking to amend how universities there will handle Title IX complaints, sending appeals to administrative court judges, among other changes (McKinley, 2019). There are three categories of sexual misconduct resolution models described by the Association of Student Conduct Administrators (ASCA) 2014 white paper.

The hearing model is a traditional model in student conduct practice. The resolution is determined (finding of "responsible," "not responsible," and/or sanctions) by a panel of students, faculty, and or administrators. Some hearing models feature a single administrator making the decision. Student conduct professionals may be involved in scheduling and advising the board, conducting investigations, and, in some cases, serving as the complainant on behalf of the institution.

The investigation model eliminates the hearing in favor of one investigator (or more) taking in a complaint, sometimes implementing interim remedies, and interviewing the complainant, respondent, and other witnesses. Once the investigation is completed, the investigator prepares a complaint for review by the parties and then sends the final report with an analysis to an adjudicator who determines the outcome, including sanctions, based on the report. A controversial and highly litigated version of this model has the investigator playing a dual role by also rendering an outcome that can be appealed to a separate administrator or panel (*Doe v. Baum,* et al., 2018).

The ASCA 2014 white paper also acknowledged hybrids of these two approaches, noting that some institutions may have an investigation process conducted by an equity/compliance office with cases being referred to a student conduct office for adjudication. At other institutions, different staff members in the same office play different roles, one conducting an investigation while another handles adjudication. Resolution practices can include alternative dispute resolution, informal resolutions, mediation (except, at least as of this writing, for sexual assault), and restorative justice practice. When deciding what model to use and how to implement it, the critical question to ask is "Does it provide equitable participation for both the respondent and the complainant?"

Compassion Fatigue and Secondary Trauma

We have known for some time the reactions of sexual misconduct victims do not fit into a narrow range. In the short term, some complainants may experience nightmares, sleeplessness, feelings of helplessness and loss of control, guilt, hypervigilance, shame, calm and denial, anger, physical pain, and changes in sexual functioning (Lonsway & Archaumbalt, 2019). Long-term impacts can include depression, post-traumatic stress disorder (PTSD), changes in relationships—and with support—ways of coping and healing (Lonsway & Archaumbalt, 2019). The effects of sexual misconduct may have a ripple effect on family and friends who experience their own denial, guilt, anger, and frustration and may respond in harmful ways, such as blaming or disempowering the victim. Even those who work through their own feelings and do all the prescribed, "right things" to be supportive can become worn out and feel ineffective (Ahrens & Campbell, 2000).

Professionals who work with students involved with sexual misconduct complaints feel effects as well. Over time, compassion fatigue, a secondary traumatic stress disorder, also known as vicarious trauma or secondary trauma, can set in. The Office for Victims of Crime (2019) notes that compassion fatigue can become a problem for victim advocates, law enforcement, prosecutors, and medical personnel, with symptoms ranging from stress and negativity to hopelessness. Chapter 1 of this text speaks to the importance of recognizing compassion fatigue as a consequence of this demanding work.

Peters (2016) found a similar phenomenon among campus investigators of sexual violence: "Ultimately, working with repeated graphic sexual detail, victimization, and trauma of others comes at an emotional cost to the investigator" (p. 142). This is difficult and complex work. Not everyone is well suited for it, and those who have a special affinity for this work should pay attention to their self-care. Supervisors need to pay attention as well and work to construct a supportive environment around those who work regularly with sexual misconduct. Employee burnout, lessened performance, and frequent turnover are the unfortunate outcomes associated with the intensity of this work. Those seeking to plan for and mitigate compassion fatigue can start with the Office for Victims of Crime (n.d.) and its vicarious trauma toolkit. Consulting with colleagues and acquaintances in counseling and other social services work can also be an excellent start.

The Forecast

As we write this chapter, we are keenly aware that much of what we have written may be thought of as "old news" very soon. Traditionally, courts have allowed higher education institutions much leeway in creating and implementing rules and processes with little oversight. This hands-off approach is evaporating, specifically in regard to handling sexual assault cases. In *Doe v. Baum* et al., (2018) the Sixth Circuit Court of Appeals ruled against the University of Michigan, requiring a formal hearing with live questioning if cases rest on the parties' credibility.

We also await a new round of final rules from the Department of Education. These rules likely will regulate jurisdiction, hearing procedures, standards of evidence, and more. While these may be issued prior to this book's publication, implementation may be delayed by litigation (Johnson, 2018). In addition to federal expectations, states are also influencing how we engage in sexual misconduct work. Some states are considering new rules that affect handling of sexual misconduct cases: Texas Governor Greg Abbott recently signed a bill requiring higher education employees to report sexual harassment and assault and making failure to do so a criminal offense (Husch Blackwell LLP, 2019); Michigan's legislature, driven in part by the Larry Nasser gymnastics scandal, is currently working on bills to expand reporting and training requirements, prohibit interference with reporting, and provide more prevention resources (Gibbons, 2019). While these changes will be welcomed by some and criticized by others, institutions that revert to older practices will continue to face pressure from students who have learned a great deal in the last few years about their rights and institutions' current obligations regarding handling complaints of sexual misconduct. This knowledge has come from their institutions and advocacy groups like KnowYourIX, End Rape on Campus, and SurvJustice, to name a few (Hartocollis, 2017).

As we reflect on the current landscape of sexual misconduct on college and university campuses, it is evident that laws and mandates have changed the way we conduct our work. And so, we offer a few practical considerations. First, accept that this already difficult work will continue to be difficult. Keep listening, keep learning, and keep advocating for fair and equitable practices. Continue to seek resources and training to help practitioners manage the complexities of the work and support their emotional and physical welfare. Seek audiences with decision makers to educate them on the increased complexities of this work and advocate for increased capacity not only in investigation and adjudication, but also in sexual violence prevention. Look at sexual misconduct from a multidisciplinary lens; individuals in many fields are focused on this topic and have a great deal to bring to the table. Finally, keep in mind that increased attention to campus sexual misconduct is considered progressive. While the focus is on court decisions and changing mandates, student conduct professionals remain in excellent position on their campuses to ensure that the increased attention results in education and support for students.

References

Ahrens, C. E., & Campbell, R. (2000). Assisting rape victims as they recover from rape: The impact on friends. *Journal of Interpersonal Violence, 15*(9), 959–986.

Ali, R. (2011, April). *Dear Colleague letter.* Washington DC: United States Department of Education, Office for Civil Rights.

Association of Student Conduct Administrators (ASCA). (2014). *ASCA 2014 white paper: Student conduct administration and Title IX: Gold standard practices for resolution of allegations of sexual misconduct on college campuses.* College Station, TX: Author.

Ball State University (2017). *Code of student rights and responsibilities: Appendix K— Sexual harassment and misconduct policy.* Muncie, IN: Ball State University.

Bauer-Wolf, J. (2018, September 10). An "unprecedented" director for Title IX. *Inside Higher Ed.* Retrieved from https://www.insidehighered.com/news/2018/09/10/appeals-court-ruling-opens-door-boosted-due-process-rights

Black, N., Henry, M., Lewis, W. S, Morris, L., Oppenheim, A., Schuster, S. K., Sokolow, B. A., & Swinton, D. C. (2017). *The 2017 ATIXA whitepaper: The ATIXA rubric for addressing campus sexual misconduct.* Lancaster, PA: Association for Title IX Administrators.

Brodsky, A. (2015, January 21). Fair process, not criminal process, is the right way to address campus sexual assault. *American Prospect.* Retrieved from https://prospect.org/article/fair-process-not-criminal-process-right-way-address-campus-sexual-assault

California Penal Code §261, 2013

Civil Rights Restoration Act of 1987

Colorado Revised Statutes §18-3-401 (2016)

Coveney, C. E. (2016, June 14). How teachers and coaches can defend against sexual harassment. *Katz, Marshall, & Banks.* Retrieved from https://www.kmblegal.com/employment-law-blog/how-teachers-coaches-can-defend-against-sexual-harassment

Davis v. Monroe County Bd. of Ed., 526. U.S. 629 (1999)

DeGue, S. (April 2014). *Preventing sexual violence on college campuses: Lessons from research and practice. Part one: Evidence-based strategies for the primary prevention of sexual violence perpetration.* Washington DC: White House Task Force to Protect Students from Sexual Assault.

Doe v. Baum et al., No. 17-2213 (6th Cir. Sept 7, 2018)

Ehrhart, J. K., & Sandler, B. R. (1985). *Campus gang rape: Party games?* Washington DC: Association of American Colleges, Project on the Status and Education of Women.

End Rape on Campus (n.d.). *Mission and vision.* Retrieved from https://endrapeoncampus.org/our-team-1

Foundation for Individual Rights in Education FIRE. (2018, July 13). *Title IX: History & implications.* Retrieved from https://www.thefire.org/issues/title-ix/

Foundation for Individual Rights in Education (FIRE) Staff. (2011, October 28). *Standard of evidence survey: colleges and universities respond to OCR's new mandate.* Retrieved from https://www.thefire.org/standard-of-evidence-survey-colleges-and-universities-respond-to-ocrs-new-mandate/

Franklin v. Gwinnett County Public Schools, 503 U.S. 60, 75 (1992)

Friedersdorf, C. (2019, February 8). The ACLU moves to embrace due process on Title IX. *The Atlantic.* Retrieved from https://www.theatlantic.com/ideas/archive/2019/02/aclu-title-ix/582118/

Galanter, S. M. (April 24, 2013). Dear Colleague letter. *Office for Civil Rights.* Retrieved from https://www2.ed.gov/about/offices/list/ocr/letters/colleague-201304.html

Gebser v. Lago Vista Independent School Dist., 524 U.S. 274 (1998)

Gibbons, L. (2019, March 19). Nassar-inspired bills reemerge in Michigan legislature. *M Live.* Retrieved from https://www.mlive.com/news/2019/03/nassar-inspired-bills-reemerge-in-michigan-legislature.html

Gibbs, N. (1991, June 3). When is it rape? *Time, 137*(22). Retrieved from http://content.time.com/time/magazine/article/0,9171,973077,00.html

Gordon College (n.d.). *Sexual misconduct policy: Prohibited behavior.* Wenham, MA: Author.

Harrell, K. A., Morehead, M., Akin, H., Gillilan, M., & Wade, A. (2018). *Advanced sexual misconduct track.* Donald D. Gehring Academy, Indianapolis, Indiana. Program held July 8, 2018–July 12, 2018.

Hartocollis, A. (2017, February 18). Universities face pressure to hold the line on Title IX. *New York Times.* Retrieved from https://www.nytimes.com/2017/02/18/us/college-campuses-title-ix-sexual-assault.html

Husch Blackwell LLP (2019, June 20). Texas legislature passes comprehensive sexual assault legislation. *JDSUPRA.* Retrieved from https://www.jdsupra.com/legalnews/texas-legislature-passes-comprehensive-21214/

Iconis, R. (2013). Dating violence among college students. *Contemporary Issues in Education Research,* 6(1). Retrieved from https://files.eric.ed.gov/fulltext/EJ1073179.pdf

Jackson v. Birmingham Bd. Of Ed., 544 U.S. 167 (2005)

Jeanne Clery Disclosure of Campus Security Policy and Campus Crime Statistics Act (1990), 20 U.S.C. § 1092(f)

Johnson, S. (December 21, 2018). The fight over Title IX has reached the comments section. Here's what people are saying. *Chronicle of Higher Education.* Retrieved from https://www.chronicle.com/article/The-Fight-Over-Title-IX-Has/245380

Joyce, K. (2017, December 5). The takedown of Title IX. *New York Times Magazine.* Retrieved from https://www.nytimes.com/2017/12/05/magazine/the-takedown-of-title-ix.html

Kissel, A. (2011). Standing up for due process on campus = "sticking up for penises everywhere?" *Huffpost.* Retrieved from https://www.huffpost.com/entry/standing-up-for-due-proce_b_940352

Koss, M. P., Gidycz, C. A., & Wisniewski, N. (1987). The scope of rape: Incidence and prevalence of sexual aggression and victimization in a national sample of higher education students. *Journal of Consulting and Clinical Psychology, 55*(2), 162–170.

Know Your IX. (n.d.). *Fair process in campus discipline.* Retrieved from https://www.knowyourix.org/issues/fair-process-campus-discipline/

Knowledge Networks. (2011). *2011 College dating violence and abuse poll: top-line report.* San Francisco, CA: Author.

Krebs, C. P., Lindquist, C. H., Warner, M. A., Fisher, B. S., & Martin, S. L. (2007, December). *The campus sexual assault (CSA) study.* Washington DC: National Institute of Justice.

Lancaster, J. M., & Waryold, D. M. (Eds.). (2008). *Student conduct practice: The complete guide for student affairs professionals.* Sterling, VA: Stylus.

Lonsway, K. A., & Archaumbalt, J. (2019). *Victim impact: How victims are affected by sexual assault and how law enforcement can respond.* Colville, WA: End Violence Against Women International.

Loschiavo, C., & Waller, J. L. (2016). *The preponderance of evidence standard: use in higher education campus conduct processes.* College Station, TX: Association for Student Conduct Administration.

Lowery, J. (2008) Laws, policies, and mandates. In J. M. Lancaster & D. M. Waryold (Eds.), (2008). *Student conduct practice: The complete guide for student affairs professionals.* (pp. 71–96). Sterling, VA: Stylus.

McGowan, C. (2017). The threat of expulsion as an unacceptable coercion: Title IX, due process, and coerced confessions. *Emory Law Journal, 66*(1175), 1175–1207.

McKinley, E. (2019, January 30). Proposed Missouri Title IX changes would give accused more power than any other state. *Kansas City Star.* Retrieved from https://www.kansascity.com/news/politics-government/article225240190.html

McWilliams, J. (2019, February 22). Victims of campus sexual assault and the accused stand to lose from DeVos proposed changes to Title IX. *Pacific Standard.* Retrieved from https://psmag.com/education/devoss-proposed-title-ix-changes-could-harm-both-due-process-and-victims-rights

Milton, M. & Canaff, R. (2017). A dangerous defense: "Blackout" in alcohol-facilitated, non-stranger sexual assault cases [Video file]. Colville, WA: End Violence Against Women International.

New, J. (2016, October 13). A Title IX win for accused students. *Inside Higher Ed.* Retrieved from https://www.insidehighered.com/news/2016/10/13/us-says-wesley-college-violated-rights-students-punished-over-sexual-misconduct

Northwestern University. (2018). *Comprehensive policy on sexual misconduct.* Evanston, IL: Author.

Office for Civil Rights. (2001). *Revised sexual harassment guidance: Harassment of students by school employees, other students, or third parties.* Washington DC: United States Department of Education.

Office for Victims of Crime. (n.d.). Vicarious trauma toolkit. Retrieved from https://vtt.ovc.ojp.gov/

Office for Victims of Crime. (2019). *Compassion fatigue.* Retrieved from https://ovc.ncjrs.gov/topic.aspx?topicid=79#tabs1

Patel, S. (2018, April 9). Don't believe Betsy DeVos. Title IX already has a fair process for students accused of sexual assault. *Rewire.News.* Retrieved from https://rewire.news/article/2018/08/09/dont-believe-betsy-devos-title-ix-fair/

Peters, T. M. (2016) *The phenomenology of investigating campus sexual violence* (Unpublished doctoral dissertation). Ball State University, Muncie, IN.

Pettit, E. (2019, June 21). In plain sight. *Chronicle of Higher Education, 65*(35), A12–A16, A19.

Piper, G. (2019, April 20). NAACP suspends St. Louis leader for his support of Title IX due to process legislation. *The College Fix.* Retrieved from https://www.thecollegefix.com/naacp-suspends-st-louis-leader-for-his-support-of-title-ix-due-process-legislation/

Poole, K. M. (2014). *University response to the dear colleague letter on sexual violence: A case study* (Doctoral dissertation). Retrieved from All Dissertations. (1287).

Reynolds, G.A. (2003, July 28) *First Amendment: Dear colleague.* Washington DC: Office for Civil Rights.

Scalzo, T. (2007) *Prosecuting alcohol-facilitated sexual assault.* Arlington, VA: National District Attorneys Association.

Sexual harassment guidance: Harassment of students by school employees, other students, or third parties, 62 Fed. Reg. 12,034 (final policy action March 13, 1997), (codified at 34 C.F.R. pt. 106).

Simon, W., & Gagnon, J. H. (1984). Sexual scripts. *Society, 22*(1), 53–60.

Texas A&M University. (2019). *Student Conduct Code.* College Station, TX: Author.

Texas Penal Code § 22.011 (2017)

Title IX of the Education Amendments of 1972, 20 U.S.C. A§1681

Tufts University. (2019). *Sexual misconduct policy.* Medford, MA: Author.

U.S. Department of Education (2016). *The handbook for campus safety and security reporting: 2016 edition.* Washington DC: Author.

Violence Against Women Reauthorization Act of 2013, 42 U.S.C. §13925-14045

Washington Revised Code § 9A.44, 1998

White House Task Force to Protect Students from Sexual Assault (2014a). *Not alone: The first report of the white house task force to protect students from sexual assault.* Retrieved from https://www.nccpsafety.org/assets/files/library/NOT_ALONE_Report.pdf

White House Task Force to Protect Students from Sexual Assault. (2014b). *Checklist for campus sexual misconduct policies.* Retrieved from https://www.justice.gov/archives/ovw/page/file/910271/download

II

THE FIRST AMENDMENT ON CAMPUS

Lee E. Bird, Mackenzie E. Wilfong, and Saundra K. Schuster

First Amendment Controversy and the Changing Climate on Campus

As a new student conduct administrator, issues surrounding the applicability of the First Amendment on your campus vis-a-vis your code of conduct and campus policies may not be of great concern to you—but perhaps they should be. Over the last three years, political rhetoric has heightened tensions on campus, with some students (across the political chasm) feeling targeted and threatened and leaving institutional administrators frustrated. Such incidents may involve offensive White nationalist posters in residence halls and elsewhere; campus preachers spewing their version of religion at passersby; controversial speakers that ignite protests and counter-protests; and offensive fraternity and sorority theme parties perceived as racist or degrading, to name a few.

So, What Has Changed?

The short answer is student tolerance for speech they find marginalizing, disturbing or inconsistent with their own values. Julie Winokur, creator of Bring it to the Table, a program designed to promote civil political and ideological discourse says, "Democracy is founded on robust dialogue" (J. Winokur personal communication, June 23, 2019). Many of our students, who historically aggressively supported the notion of "the marketplace of ideas," including good, bad, and ugly ideas, now feel that sociopolitical protectionism exceptions to free speech should be considered on campus. Among other things, they do not want to believe that hate speech is largely protected speech. Noted First Amendment scholars Edwin Chermerinsky and Howard Gillman (2017) wrote,

> The historic link between free speech and the protection of dissenters and vulnerable groups is outside the direct experience of today's students, and it was too distant to affect their feelings about freedom of speech. They were not aware of how the power to punish speech has been used primarily against social outcasts, vulnerable minorities, and those protesting for positive change-the very people toward whom our students are most sympathetic. . . . Still, they remain unconvinced of the value of defending hateful or discriminatory speech. They acknowledge that one could adopt a "more speech" solution rather than an "enforced silence" or punishment solution, but they doubted that this would protect their peers from psychological distress. (pp. 11–12)

A study conducted by Yale University (Chermerinsky & Gillman, 2017) found that 30% of students polled say that physical violence can be justified to prevent someone from using hate speech. Eight-one percent of students polled believed that words can be a form of violence and 31% said that hate speech is not protected under the First Amendment. Similar results were gleaned from the Knight Foundation's (2018) study of 3,000 college students, which reported that while students say they generally support an open learning environment, 69% of college students say colleges should enact policies to restrict slurs and offensive language; 63% say that policies could extend to restricting Halloween costumes based on stereotypes; and 27% of students say colleges should be able to restrict speech expressing political views that might offend or upset certain groups. It appears that while students support the idea of free speech, they favor limiting hurtful speech in hopes of creating a more inclusive learning environment.

Chermerinsky & Gillman (2017) notes that students in the United Kingdom as early as 1974 created a "no platform" policy (meaning that students in the UK would not provide a platform for fascist speakers to appear on college campuses), but the list of banned speakers has grown beyond this initial target group. One must ask if avoiding "haters" is the best strategy to change society. Students may indeed feel safer, but are they? Exposing lies with more speech would seem preferable to silence and avoidance.

As Pen America stated in "Chasm in the Classroom, Campus Free Speech in a Divided America" (2019), "Failures of political leadership, persistent racism and bigotry, the weaponization of speech on digital platforms, and gaps in civic education are combining to undermine the consensus for an open marketplace for ideas" (p. 9). In addition, President Trump, through an executive order issued in March 2019, has tied receipt of federal research dollars to an institution's obligation to protect First Amendment rights campus. It remains unclear who will arbitrate such funding decisions going forward. No doubt the decisions will be made through a political, rather than a legal lens. In 2017–2018, 28 states proposed new state laws aimed at ensuring public colleges and universities will protect the First Amendment on campus. Well-publicized controversies such as the "disinvitation" of conservative speakers and protests have prompted such legislation, with many legislators fearing that public, left-leaning colleges and universities have not adequately protected the First Amendment on campus.

The First Amendment to the Constitution of the United States reads, "Congress shall make no law respecting an establishment of religion, or prohibiting the free expression thereof; or abridging the freedom of speech or of the press; or the right of the people peaceably to assemble, and to petition the Government for a redress of grievances." As public institutions, we represent the government and are held to the standards set forth for a governmental entity.

Robert M. O'Neil (1997), founder of the Thomas Jefferson Center for the Protection of Free Expression and author of *Free Speech in the College Community*, wrote,

> The starting point is that all public colleges and universities are bound by the First Amendment. That means they must tolerate much speaking and writing that may not be pleasing to many of their students, faculty, alumni, trustees, and others. Case after case has reaffirmed this principle with regard to student protest, campus newspapers, radical student groups and outspoken faculty. While private campuses are not directly governed by the Bill of Rights, many pride themselves on observing standards of expression at least as high as those their public counterparts must meet. Thus, the guiding principle for virtually all institutions of higher learning is that free speech must be protected, even when the speech for which freedom is sought may be offensive or disruptive or at variance with the campus mission. (p. 15)

Administrators generally support the educational benefits of preserving the "marketplace of ideas" where students may listen and judge for themselves the credibility of the speaker and the value of the ideas expressed. However, when the proverbial "tug-of war" begins between preserving First Amendment rights and protecting widely accepted institutional values, such as civility or respect for individual differences, administrators may find themselves in a conundrum, questioning just what the right thing is to do. Legally the answer is easy—protect the First Amendment; yet, in practice, standing up for the First Amendment may create an unintended maelstrom of conflict. Hateful words and images hurt. No one wants to see students hurting, but too often, well-intended responses to stop or prevent perceived harmful expression on campus results in a clear violation of the First Amendment. The best weapon against hurtful speech is better speech. Educating ourselves and our students about their rights under the First Amendment is critical.

Watchdog groups, such as the Foundation for Individual Rights in Education (FIRE), have roundly criticized higher education for failing to honor the First Amendment on campuses. Kermit Hall (2017), writing for the First Amendment Center website, said, "[Speech codes] are the most controversial ways in which universities have attempted to strike a balance between expression and community order" (p. 2). "Efforts to restrict the viewpoint or message of anyone on a campus puts the institution at odds with its primary educational mission: to give students the opportunity to sort through opposing ideas" (Hudson, 2018, p. 5).

Public-Private Distinction

Succinctly stated, "a state university is, legally, an arm of the government and is constrained by the First Amendment" (Paulsen, 2008, p. 104). A private college or university, however, stands upon a different footing in relationship to the state and to their constituencies, thus affecting limits they can place on expression. Such an institution is not an instrument or arm of state government. "Even though such an institution may operate identically to its state-operated counterparts and, in terms of educational purposes and activities, may be virtually indistinguishable from a public institution, a private college or university does not thereby either operate under or exercise the authority of state government." (McKay, 1968, p. 558). The modern similarities between public and private institutions often leads to student confusion. A recent poll of students at Elon University found 44% were unaware that private universities have different regulations than public schools, allowing them to restrict students' freedom of expression to a far greater extent (Ardinger, 2011).

As a student affairs professional, understanding a student's perspective on these issues is important and can inform programming and educational opportunities. How are students made aware of these distinctions? A private institution may promise or guarantee First Amendment–type freedoms via promotional materials and may solidify these in contracts with students in a student code of conduct, with faculty in a faculty handbook, and with staff in an employee handbook or manual. At a public institution the parameters are set by law and cases interpreting these laws, and public institutions often attempt to rearticulate these concepts using non-legalistic language in student codes of conduct, facilities use policies, campus access policies, and faculty/staff handbooks.

California's Leonard Law, passed in 1992 and amended in 2006, applies the First Amendment of the United States Constitution and the California Constitution's protections of freedom of speech to students at private secular colleges and universities in California. California is the only state to grant federal First Amendment protections to students at private postsecondary institutions. The law also has a private right of action provision, which means that students may file civil lawsuits against their private institutions and may also recover any attorney's fees related to the case if successful (Cal. Stat. 1992). Notably, California is the only state that has this type of statute; however, numerous other states, 28 by current count, have added state law protections for expressive outdoor activity since early 2018. (In *State v. Schmid* (1980), the New Jersey Supreme Court held that state constitutional protections applied to a private institution of higher education, in this case Princeton University. See *Princeton University v. Schmid*, 1982; *State v. Schmid*, 1980.) The most prevalent campus free-speech legislation being introduced in state legislatures today is drafted from model bills produced by the Goldwater Institute, which typically states that all outdoor "green space" should be a public forum. See the American Association of University Professors (AAUP, n.d.) toolkit for information about the numerous state laws.

Guidelines for Policy Development and Analysis

Faced with the dichotomy of providing an educational environment that represents the "marketplace of ideas," rich in challenge, discourse, and, of course, disagreements, alongside a commitment to diversity and acceptance, college educators and administrators often seek guidance in developing, applying, and analyzing their policies in a manner that balances competing rights and interests while minimizing the risks of legal challenge. Creating policies that incorporate the college mission, support free expression, address access, and balance competing interests pose great challenges. The U.S. Supreme Court has held, time and time again, that the mere fact that someone might take offense at the content of expressive activity is not sufficient justification for prohibiting it.

Private colleges and universities have broader latitude in restricting both access to campus property and topics for public speech, because they generally are not bound by First Amendment limitations that are imposed on government entities.

Although First Amendment restrictions are not a factor in the development and implementation of private school's policies, private institutions are, nevertheless, bound by federal nondiscrimination laws, which are imposed on all institutions that receive federal funding. Therefore, these nondiscrimination laws must be a consideration in policy development related to inclusion, exclusion, and public speech, often posing similar confounding challenges to private institutions as those presented to public institutions.

The standard by which the constitutionality of a policy that regulates speech or other forms of expressive activity on a public college or university campus must be evaluated is based on the character of the "property" at issue (for purposes of this article, "property" refers to both physical space and the conceptual space represented by other venues of expressive activity, such as student press, student organization regulations, and campus policies).

The Supreme Court, through many First Amendment decisions, has created an analysis framework, referred to as "forum analysis," as a means to determine the nature or special characteristics of the "property" or location on campus in question in relation to the degree of restrictions that may be imposed on expressive activity for that specific "property." The concept of forum analysis concedes that not all government property is equally open for expressive use by everyone. Thus, a public college or university must apply a forum analysis for each policy that involves regulation of speech or other forms of expressive activity.

The extent to which the First Amendment permits a college or university to restrict speech or other forms of expression protected under the First Amendment depends on the character of the forum at the institution. In applying the forum analysis, a public college or university must first identify the type of forum, based on special characteristics. The type of forum establishes the appropriate category of "scrutiny" that must be applied to any limitation or restriction that is imposed by the institution. "Scrutiny" refers to the level of analysis required by law to the "governmental interest" impacted by the expressive activity in establishing a limitation on a constitutionally protected right—such as speech. The courts apply an analysis to the decision process related to the nature of the forum, identifying three levels—a rational basis standard, an intermediate standard, and a strict scrutiny standard—as a part of a hierarchy to weigh the asserted government interest in limiting expression against an individual or group's right to speak, organize, or engage in any other form of expressive activity. Once the category of forum and level of appropriate scrutiny is identified, colleges and universities may impose content neutral "time, place, and manner" limitations to expressive activities consistent with forum type. The various categories of forum follow.

Traditional Public Forum

A traditional public forum is a place that has "immemorially been held in trust" for use by the public and has always been used for purposes of assembly and to communicate thoughts between citizens and in discussion of public questions (*Hague v. Committee for Industrial Organizations,* 1939). Examples include public streets, sidewalks, and parks. Restrictions on expression in this type of forum are subject to the highest level of scrutiny (i.e., limitation on the expression); any time, place, and manner regulations imposed on expressive activity in this type of forum must be "content neutral" and "narrowly tailored" to serve a compelling government interest. "Content neutral" means that one cannot impose limitations on expressive activity based on the topic, and "narrow tailoring" means that any limitations the college imposes on expression must be sufficiently limited to achieve the compelling government interest involved without encompassing more expression than is necessary in doing so. A "compelling governmental interest" refers to something necessary or crucial, as opposed to something merely preferred or imposed as a preference or convenience. Any restrictions must also leave open ample alternative channels of communication. Public colleges and universities may never prohibit all expressive activity in this type of forum, and any content-based limitations must be drawn narrowly to meet the compelling government interest standard. For example, the public sidewalks surrounding a campus, a public parking lot adjacent to the campus, and sidewalks or paths that are primary routes of travel through the campus and are used by the public and the campus community are considered a traditional public forum. In areas such as this, any limitation on expression must meet the compelling government interest standard, such as protecting the educational process from disruption in support of the college's mission, or by ensuring the public safety of the college community's members. The college cannot regulate the topics for discussion, but it can apply regulations that are content neutral and narrowly tailored to time, place, and manner restrictions such as no amplified sound (which might disturb classes in session) or restrictions on groups convening in a way that limits ingress or regress of the campus buildings or walkways.

Designated Public Forum

A designated public forum is created specifically by the government entity (college or university) as a place for expressive activity that generally is not by its inherent nature identified for this purpose and is not by default a traditional public forum. Designated public forum areas are not created by inaction or simply permitting limited discourse in the designated area; instead, they must be created by the institution's policy and practice. In the designated public forum area, there is an automatic assumption that expression may only be restricted when it meets the high standards of scrutiny as applied in the traditional public forum in balancing the right of the institution to create limitations with the rights of the speaker.

Common descriptors for designated public forum areas include the "free speech zone," the "gazebo," and the "oval." (The courts have not definitively addressed the standard of evaluation speech in college or university subsidized newspapers. See Hunker (2007) and Student Press Law Center, n.d.) This type of forum is not required to remain so designated indefinitely, but as long as it is designated as a public forum, all restrictions on expressive activities are subject to the same analysis as a traditional public forum.

Designated Limited Public Forum

This type of forum is created by the government entity (college or university) for public expression, but is not the same as a "designated public forum" because this type has additional limitations related to restricting expression based on the specific and unique elements of the space. Although the institution may not discriminate on the basis of viewpoint, it may implement content-neutral parameters for use of a particular space. Examples of this type of forum are student organizations, athletic arenas, indoor meeting spaces, or auditoriums. (Note: This is not an exhaustive list.) In this type of forum, the institution may give priority for use to one form of expression over another based on the unique characteristics of the facility or space (e.g., a college auditorium may have priority for campus theater productions, or meeting space may be limited to student or faculty groups only).

Designated limited public forum areas must be governed by a written use policy that includes the stated purpose of the forum and the basis for any limitations on that use. The limitations on the use must be rationally related to the space (forum). The standard to be applied for creating limitations is "reasonableness." That is, the restriction or limitation must be consistent with the purpose of the location, the college mission, or the historical use to meet the reasonableness test. However, the institution cannot impose more limitations than are necessary to reasonably support the purpose of the forum. In this type of forum, the college may give priority to college entities over noncollege entities as long as that standard is applied consistently.

Nonpublic Forum

Any public property that is not, by designation or tradition, a public forum is, by default, considered a nonpublic forum. This type of forum is created when there is clear evidence that the public body did not intend to create a public forum, or where the nature of the property at issue is inconsistent with expressive activity. One example is where a public college or university is acting as a "proprietor," managing its internal operations. In this type of forum, the public body may restrict expressive activity for its intended purposes as long as the restrictions do not contain viewpoint-based expression. Limitations on expression must only be "reasonable" and may not limit the expressive activity based on a disagreement with the speaker's viewpoint. Examples of nonpublic forum areas include campus offices, classrooms, and residence hall rooms. These locations have the lowest standard for restricting expression. These forum areas may have limitations imposed on expression as long as the limitations are reasonable in nature and do not limit expression based simply on viewpoint. For example, a college may restrict all posters on residence hall walls because of the environmental impact but may not restrict posters to those that communicate a certain message even if it's an offensive one.

The most important point is that in the past decade courts have been clear about the fact that public college and university campuses should not consider themselves entirely public forums in nature for the efficient functioning of the institution; however, neither can they identify themselves as completely nonpublic or limited in nature. Therefore, college administrators are faced with the challenging task of identifying the appropriate forum areas for their specific campus and applying the appropriate level of "scrutiny" when creating the limitations that will establish the legal balance between the type of forum and the rights to expression.

Categories of Unprotected Speech

Not all speech is permitted at all times and in all places. The previous sections discussed *where* speech and expression may occur. The courts are the ultimate arbiters of forum analysis and will consider campus facility use policy and practice in their decision-making should it be required. It behooves conduct officers to familiarize themselves with their campus policies that may give rise to First Amendment issues on campus. This section covers categories of speech (broadly defined) that do not enjoy First Amendment protection regardless of where it takes place. Six such categories will be discussed: fighting words, obscenity, true threats, incitement of imminent lawless action, racial and sexual harassment, and defamation. The intersection of free speech and professional standards will also be discussed briefly. It should be noted that court decisions that framed the categories discussed are narrowly and specifically defined. Your understanding of the specific defining elements within each category is critical in guiding your practice.

You will not find a category called "hate speech." Hate speech, and to some degree the fighting words doctrine, have been used to justify the creation of speech policies (codes) beginning in the 1980s. In an article in the *New York Times*, Erwin Chemerinsky (2017) discussed the best-known case involving the creation of a speech code at the University of Michigan:

> The law under the First Amendment is clear: Hate speech is protected speech. Over 300 colleges and universities adopted hate speech codes in the early 1990s. Every one to be challenged in court was ruled unconstitutional. And there are good reasons for that.

After some really ugly incidents at the University of Michigan in the late 1980s, the school adopted a hate speech code that was undoubtedly well intentioned. But a federal court declared it unconstitutional, in part, because it was so vague. It said that there could not be speech that "demeans or stigmatizes" anyone based on race or gender. But what does that mean? A sociobiology student who challenged the law said, "I want to study whether there are inherent differences between women and men. What if my conclusions are deemed stigmatizing on the basis of gender?" And during the years Michigan's speech code was on the books, more than 20 black students were charged with racist speech by white students. There wasn't a single instance of a white student being punished for racist speech, even though that was what had prompted the drafting of the Michigan speech code in the first place. (p. 2)

Fighting Words

Perhaps the most misunderstood category of unprotected speech on the college campus is that of *fighting words*. In reality, the concept of fighting words is so narrow that it would be difficult to comprehend what truly meets that definition in modern society.

The "fighting words" doctrine was defined by the Supreme Court in the 1942 case *Chaplinsky v. New Hampshire* (1942), where Chaplinsky was arrested for calling someone "a God-damned racketeer" and "a damned Fascist." The Court reaffirmed that the right of free speech is "not absolute at all times and under all circumstances" and that "fighting words" represented a class of speech that could be prevented and punished. The Court in *Chaplinsky* (1942) defined *fighting words* as "those which by their very utterance inflict injury or tend to incite an immediate breach of the peace" (pp. 571–572). Inherent in this definition is the notion that such words, when spoken, would be so inflammatory that a reasonable person hearing them would have no recourse but to react with immediate physical violence. The Court also clarified additional limitations on so-called fighting words. In the Supreme Court decision, the courts said that speech must be "said to the person of the hearer." This implies a toe-to toe encounter. While students sometimes claim that online, hateful communication is tantamount to fighting words, it does not fit the old and narrow definition provided by the courts. No court has affirmed or supported this doctrine since its inception.

Obscenity

Modern college campuses are fraught with profane messages on clothing, tasteless cheers at sporting events, political cartoons of a sexual nature, and a host of other messages that some people find offensive. It is rare, however, that any of these give rise to the level of true *obscenity* as defined by the Supreme Court.

The 1973 Supreme Court case *Miller v. California* (1973) related to sexually oriented adult materials and provided the test for measuring obscenity by modifying the formerly used *Roth* test. According to the Court, the determination of obscenity must take into account whether "the average person, applying contemporary community standards" would find that the work, taken as a whole, appeals to the prurient interest; whether the work depicts or describes, in a patently offensive way, sexual conduct specifically defined by the applicable state law; and whether the work, taken as a whole, lacks serious literary, artistic, political, or scientific value. This has been referred to the as the SLAPS test. Given this very narrow definition, the majority of offending messages on college campuses do not constitute obscenity and thus do not lose their First Amendment protection.

In 2011, California sought to have extreme violence in video games deemed obscenity but failed when the court stated in *Brown v. Entertainment Merchants Association* that "violence is not part of the obscenity that the Constitution permits to be regulated." Pornography is widely protected by the courts, but child pornography is illegal and has no protection under the law. The U.S. Department of Justice (2018) has a "Citizen's Guide to U.S. Federal law on Obscenity," which is brief and informative. Internet obscenity is additionally complicated by the myriad of federal laws and previous precedent which, when overlaid on obscene Internet content, becomes particularly hazy (*Nitke v. Gonzales*, 2005).

Student conduct administrators should become familiar with their campus Internet use policies. This document should educate students about what they can and cannot post on a university-hosted website. Faculty may also dictate appropriateness on the Internet related to class on platforms such as D2L and others.

Threats

Administrators often grapple with complaints by students and staff alike that they have been threatened or felt threatened on campus. "True threats" certainly may be prohibited or punished, but it may be difficult to discern between a casual or sarcastic statement and a "true threat." Several court cases have attempted to define such a threat, and the common thread running through all of them seems to be the intent of the speaker and the interpretation of a "reasonable person." In *Virginia v. Black* (2003), the Supreme Court said, "Intimidation in the constitutionally proscribable sense of the word is a type of true threat, where a speaker directs a threat to a person or group of persons with the intent of placing the victim in fear of bodily harm or death" (p. 360). The intent in this language is to protect a victim from the fear of violence and does not rely on the speaker's plan to carry out the threat. The Court, in *Planned Parenthood v. American Coalition of Life Activists* (2002), defined a *threat* as "a statement which, in the entire context and under all the circumstances, a reasonable person would foresee would be interpreted by those to whom the statement is communicated as a serious expression of intent to inflict bodily harm upon that person" (p. 1077). Thus, such a statement that is made in an offhand fashion, is uttered as a joke or prank, or does not seem likely to be carried out may not rise to the level of unprotected speech.

In 2015, the U.S. Supreme Court decided a case involving Internet threats, in this case a Pennsylvania man posted long tirades in the form of music lyrics on Facebook. *Elonis v. United States* (2015) (see Harvard Law Review, 2015; whether music lyrics constitute "true threats" when posted on the Internet continues to be litigated; see Harvard Law Review, 2019) *is the* first time that the Supreme Court of the United States has agreed to hear a case involving the constitutionality of prosecuting potential threats in a social media context. The man posted that he would like to see a Halloween costume that included his estranged wife's "head on a stick" and would be "making a name for myself" with a school shooting, saying, "Hell hath no fury like a crazy man in a kindergarten class." He also stated that he fantasized about killing an FBI agent: "Pull my knife, flick my wrist, and slit her throat." The man was convicted under a federal law that makes it a crime to communicate "any threat to injure the person of another." He appealed the conviction. The Supreme Court has said that "true threats" are not protected by the First Amendment, but what counts as such a threat has not been clear. In that case, Chief Justice Roberts characterized the statements as "crude, degrading and violent."

The question for the Supreme Court in this case was whether prosecutors had done enough to prove threatening intent. The Court's decision in this case did not clarify as much as many hoped. Chief Justice Roberts said a criminal conviction requires more than consideration of how the posts would be understood by a reasonable person; prosecutors had to prove that the accused was aware of wrongdoing. Justice Alito disagreed and wrote that recklessness should be enough. Alito also addressed the First Amendment question, which the majority opinion avoided, and held that "lyrics in songs that are performed for an audience or sold in recorded form are unlikely to be interpreted as a real threat to a real person." Whereas "statements on social media that are pointedly directed at their victims, by contrast, are much more likely to be taken seriously." Justice Thomas wholly disagreed with his colleagues and said the majority's approach was unsatisfactory. "This failure to decide," he wrote, "throws everyone from appellate judges to everyday Facebook users into a state of uncertainty." Hopefully as these types of cases reach the court, we will see clarification of these issues. For now, student affairs professionals should proceed with caution if relying on a threat analysis when addressing Internet-related speech concerns.

Incitement

Just as difficult to determine a "threat," "incitement" can be an unprotected category of expression and may be difficult to precisely identify. In *Brandenburg v. Ohio* (1969), a Ku Klux Klan leader was arrested after a KKK rally featured a speaker who said, "if our President, our Congress, our Supreme Court, continues to suppress the white, Caucasian race, it's possible that there might have to be some revengeance [*sic*] taken" (pp. 446). The Court said that the arrest in Brandenburg punished the mere advocacy of violence, as well as assembly with others to advocate, rather than actual incitement of violence. The Court did define *unprotected expression*, however, when it stated, "of speech and press do not permit a State to forbid advocacy of the use of force or of law violation except where such advocacy is *directed to inciting or producing imminent lawless action and is likely to incite or produce such action*" (*Brandenburg*, 1969, p. 434, emphasis added). Thus, expression that actually incites or produces lawless action is prohibited, while expression that simply advocates violence or lawless action is protected.

Racial and Sexual Harassment

Much confusion has arisen regarding *racial harassment* and *sexual harassment*, as those concepts intersect with First Amendment freedoms of expression. Muddled expectations and directives from the Office of Civil Rights (OCR), along with imprecise language in Title VI and Title IX, have made these terms difficult to define. In a 2003 "Dear Colleague" letter (Reynolds, 2003), however, the Office of Civil Rights attempted to provide clarity regarding expectations for dealing with harassment and in defining such. As stated in the letter, harassment of students, which can include verbal or physical conduct, can be a form of discrimination prohibited by the statutes enforced by OCR. Thus, for example, in addressing harassment allegations, the OCR has recognized that the offensiveness of a particular expression, standing alone, is not a legally sufficient basis to establish a hostile environment under the statutes enforced by OCR. In order to establish a hostile environment, harassment must be sufficiently serious (i.e., severe, persistent, or pervasive) and objectively offensive as to limit or deny a student's ability to participate in or benefit from an educational program or activity. OCR has consistently maintained that schools, in regulating the conduct of students and faculty to prevent or redress discrimination, must formulate, interpret, and apply their rules in a manner that respects the legal rights of students and faculty, including those court precedents interpreting the concept of free speech. The OCR's regulations and policies do not require or proscribe speech, conduct, or harassment codes that impair the exercise of rights protected under the First Amendment (Reynolds, 2003).

The letter further states that prohibited harassment

> must include something beyond the mere expression of views, words, symbols or thoughts that some person finds offensive. Under OCR's standard, the conduct must also be considered sufficiently serious to deny or limit a student's ability to participate in or benefit from the educational program. (Reynolds, 2003)

In addition, the letter clarifies that the questionable conduct must be "evaluated from the perspective of a reasonable person in the alleged victim's position, considering all the circumstances, including the alleged victim's age." Given this more precise definition, it is incumbent on the administrator to determine if the expression in question is truly so severe, persistent, or pervasive and objectively offensive as to "limit the student's ability to participate in or benefit from the educational program." Since this test must also be applied from the "perspective of a reasonable person," it does not depend simply on the reaction of the specific victim, especially one who might be overly sensitive. Racial and sexual harassment are serious concerns on campus, and their impact is significant. To combat such intolerance, many institutions have implemented speech codes that prohibit hate speech and other expression that offends, marginalizes, or stigmatizes others. It is important to note that *hate speech* has no substantive legal definition and, in and of itself, is not a category of unprotected speech. Many such speech codes have been found to be unconstitutional in that they are either vague (a reasonable person could not easily discern exactly what is prohibited) or overbroad (they prohibit constitutionally protected speech in their sweep). Incorporating words and phrases such as "offends," "denigrates," or "belittles an individual" in a sexual harassment policy makes the institution vulnerable to challenges of having a policy that is vague (the student must guess at how this would translate to their actions) and overbroad (the language encompasses a substantial amount of protected speech along with prohibited speech).

Although there are many effective ways to deal with such intolerance on campus, implementing a speech code is generally not one of them. Institutions anticipate receiving additional guidance when the U.S. Department of Education finalizes and publishes its final Title IX regulations (anticipated in the fall of 2019), which will include and require standard definitions for *sexual harassment.*

Defamation

A final category of speech that is not constitutionally protected is defamation. Generally speaking, defamation is a state civil law issue, with the definition varying between states. Most states define *defamation* in a similar manner. (Many states have repealed their criminal defamation laws and most others have stopped prosecuting them; however, there has been a recent revival of using criminal defamation laws to prosecute people for their conduct online. See Carter, 2004.) Typically, defamation requires that a false factual statement be made about a person (either orally or in writing) to someone other than the person to whom it is likely to cause harm. In *New York Times v. Sullivan* (1964), the Supreme Court further stated that if the victim is a public official, actual malice must be present.

Defamation takes two forms of libel, which covers written published statements, and slander, which covers spoken statements. The Supreme Court has consistently ruled that laws against defamation are not unconstitutional and do not violate the First Amendment (*Beauharnais v. Illinois*, 1952; *United States v. Stevens*, 2010). According to a 2015 study by United Educators, approximately 72% of accused students who file a Title IX-related lawsuit against their university also sue their individual accuser for defamation.

Defamation cases in higher education, take many forms:

- A former University of Michigan student leader successfully sued a former Michigan assistant attorney general for making defamatory comments about him (*Armstrong V. Shirvell*, 2015; *Shirvell v. Department of Attorney General*; *Shirvell v. Gordon*, 2015; State of Michigan Attorney Discipline Board, 2018)
- Three respondent student athletes sued their private institution for defamation following a conduct proceeding resulting in sanctions and transcript notations. (Three student athletes were removed from the football team and sanctioned by Liberty University following an accusation from a female student that they had sexually assaulted her at an off-campus party. Following depositions in the case the three plaintiffs dismissed their claims with the institution stating that the matters were "resolved to the parties' mutual satisfaction." See Liberty Champion, 2018.)
- An associate dean at the University of Virginia (UVA), a fraternity, and its individual members sued both *Rolling Stone* magazine and its reporter for defamation regarding a now retracted and discredited 2014 story involving sexual violence on campus. After losing at the trial of the former associate dean, Rolling Stone settled the remaining claims. (In late 2016, a federal jury awarded the UVA associate dean $3 million in damages ($1 million from *Rolling Stone* and $2 million from the reporter); a later confidential settlement headed off an appeal. *Rolling Stone* came to a $1.65 million settlement with the fraternity itself and an undisclosed settlement with individual fraternity members. See Gardner, 2018.)
- A terminated faculty member brought a defamation claim against colleagues both at and outside his institution who accused him of sexual harassment, participated in an internal investigation, and discussed concerns regarding his behavior at a professional conference, which precipitated his termination (*Fogel v. University of the Arts*, 2019).
- Following his termination, a former chief academic officer brought a defamation claim against his public institution and an employee at the institution who accused him of sexual harassment (Stewart v. Florida Southwestern State College, 2019).
- A University of Florida horticultural faculty filed a defamation lawsuit against the *New York Times* (*Folta v. The New York Times Company*,

2017) and one of its reporters after the newspaper published an article about his ties to agricultural biotechnology companies including Monsanto. The court dismissed the claim.

These cases have varied outcomes from settlements to dismissals by the court; regardless, it's important to recognize that these claims are becoming more frequent and highlight the sometimes competing notions of the First Amendment and defamation.

Professional Standards

Professional schools, such as nursing, have professional codes of conduct or professional standards separate from the institution's student code of conduct. These codes or standards have been developed to ensure that those who are preparing for the profession have not only completed their academic studies but also conducted themselves in a manner consistent with the expectations of the profession. Courts are hesitant to intervene in academic decisions and show great deference toward academic judgment, creating a tension point between free speech (including online speech) and professional standards. One such case was *Keefe v. Adams* (Hall, 2017) which involved a nursing student making Facebook posts that were perceived as inappropriate and potentially threatening to other students. The behavior was reported to faculty who, using the professional standards code, removed him from the nursing program following a meeting with the director of the nursing program. The Eighth Circuit Court of Appeals upheld the decision of the nursing program to dismiss Keefe from the nursing program. Had the case been heard by student conduct rather than the college, it is unclear whether the student would have been found responsible at all. It is likely his speech would be protected under the First Amendment. True threat has a fairly high threshold.

By hearing the case in the college based on long-standing but somewhat vague professional standards, the court upheld the decision on appeal. In his law review of the case Maxamilian Hall (2017) wrote,

> The balance of First Amendment protections with campus climate concerns is an ongoing topic of fierce debate in academic communities. Colleges, particularly public institutions, must protect freedom of expression while also providing a safe and welcoming environment to students. Commentators often prioritize one over the other due to inherent conflicts between allowing all speech and placing limitations on speech in pursuit of benefits for the broader community. Note that whether a school *can* restrict

student speech is distinct from whether a school *should* restrict speech. The impact of speech restrictions on the learning environment and quality of public discourse are central to the broader discussion of First Amendment rights on college campuses. (p. 2)

Some observers worry about the use of professional standards to dismiss students when there is a possibility that the behavior in question would be protected speech in any other context. If behavior is being evaluated based on a code of professional standards rather than the institution's code of conduct proper, the case should be managed by academic affairs rather than student conduct.

How to Respond: The Educator's Challenge

If there is a time when speaking with one voice institutionally is critical, a First Amendment issue is that time. Student conduct administrators are capable of determining if an incident is actionable under their college or university code of conduct or is protected under the First Amendment. Regardless of the decision reached, as it becomes public on social media or other venues, your campus community may be negatively impacted. It is important that your supervisor and the administration be aware of the facts that are known in the moment, so faculty, staff, administration, and student leaders can work collaboratively to respond appropriately to the needs of the community. Impacted students who feel targeted are loathe to hear a lecture about protected speech under the First Amendment and why the campus cannot take disciplinary action against the alleged perpetrator if indeed their identity is known.

PEN America (2019) provides sound advice to administrators dealing with First Amendment crises:

Campus leaders should forcefully condemn hate crimes, slurs, and the display of manifestly hateful symbols or slogans, making clear that such expression violates their institutional values of inclusion. They should also offer support and assistance to those affected by the incidents in question. (p. 18)

Responding properly to these situations is not without challenges. Administrators must be conscientious about when to simply denounce hate and when to touch on the nuances of protected speech. This dilemma arises particularly when there are calls for discipline for offensive speech. When speech violates an anti-harassment policy or includes a threat, legal recourse may apply. In other instances, though, the noxious speech may be fully protected by the First Amendment or the free speech policies of a private university. In those cases, genuine and forceful messages of condemnation and solidarity can go a long way toward blunting calls for punishments that may be legally prohibited or inconsistent with university rules. In some instances, offensive but protected speech, followed by calls for harsh reprisals, may force the university to both condemn the offensive speech and vociferously defend the rights of the speaker. Campus personnel have to be prepared to respond on multiple fronts: in internal campus emails, press releases, and public statements as well as through presidential communications with board members, donors, and concerned alumni. Through such multipronged strategies, administrators can help ease tensions, reassure stakeholders that the administration is mounting an appropriate response, and avoid a situation where university board members or other leaders inadvertently send mixed messages. (p. 21)

One of the most common First Amendment issues seen on campus are those on social media. A photo or caption is shared and students who feel targeted or are alarmed by the post make their feelings known and seek a response from administration. There are some promising practices being used to defuse First Amendment crises, but most are predicated on well-established, positive relationships with students and student leaders. Healthy campus culture and strong leadership are critical to the success of various strategies. The first is talking, really talking, about the impact of hateful posts. Campuses need to think carefully about the right person or persons to engage the student(s) or organization involved. Even if disciplinary action is not possible, hard conversations with the student(s) involved should take place. This is a teachable moment that should not be missed. Often, inappropriate posts are alcohol fueled and born of privilege, ignorance, arrogance, and ethnocentrism. Others are simply malicious. Students are often shocked to learn that their racist, sexist, homophobic, or xenophobic posts on social media have spread across campus and often beyond and that they have had an impact. Helping student(s) involved understand this is a necessary first step.

Following the initial discussion with administrative staff well versed in the First Amendment and the impact of hateful speech, involving student leaders willing to discuss the impact on their peers can be extremely powerful. Having student leaders who are willing and able to engage in this type of conversation is a blessing. Restorative justice strategies are available from numerous texts and from the International Institute for Restorative Practices (2003). They require that (a) participation be achieved through cooperation rather than coercion—both sides must want to engage in the conversation; (b) participation of those directly affected should be face to face; (c) those directly affected should determine the outcome; and (d) there must be a fair process including equal access and informed consent (International Institute for Restorative Practice, 2003, p. 1).

One example of putting this into practice comes from a four-year, predominantly White campus. The strategy first involved a meeting with the students who posted the photo with a caption about Martin Luther King Jr. Day. The purpose of the meeting was to discuss the impact of their post and to determine how the post came into being. Two student leaders from the African American Student Association had agreed to meet with several students involved in a Blackface picture that went viral. Participation was voluntary and consensual. There was little small talk. The student leaders calmly and passionate talked about how they felt when they saw the picture. They explained they felt like during their tenure on campus that they were climbing a great wall. It was built of classes, tests, friends, and uncertain but promising futures after graduation. For them, this journey was a tough, seemingly endless climb, and the photo made them feel like they were losing their grip and sliding back down the wall. One more insult, one more slight made them question whether their struggle was all worth the effort. The student leaders asked the students involved in the post about their lives, previous contact with minority students at their high schools, their majors, their interests. They then invited the students to attend their weekly meeting. They attended that meeting. Fear was diminished, and the students better understood the impact of their careless behavior on their peers and the community at large. The grace and strength of the student leaders who participated in the discussion was amazing.

Another strategy is to use educational programs such as Better Angels (2019) and Bring it to the Table, which can help bridge political and social divides by teaching students and others how to talk to one other about their beliefs and values in a civil and respectful manner. While both programs are primarily focused on the bridging the political divide, the lessons and skills are readily transferable to all social issues that require self-understanding and better communication that focuses on listening to one another. Better Angels provides their programs for free. Programs such as these should be ongoing and not necessarily introduced during a crisis.

General crisis management principles apply to First Amendment crises as well. Many campuses have dealt with difficult, even deadly, issues the past two years including major protests and counter-protests, controversial speakers, and smaller but difficult issues such as the racist song sung by the SAE Fraternity at the University of Oklahoma. Much can be learned from other campuses. "Popular" responses that disregard the First Amendment are irresponsible and can lead to lawsuits and reputational issues. "Legalistic" responses that disregard the human impact of racist or other similar behavior are equally inadequate and irresponsible.

Campuses must uphold the First Amendment and compassionately respond to the needs of the community. Educating students about the First Amendment and helping them understand its importance in sustaining our democracy is also vitally important. Training students to listen and engage in dialogue to fight bad speech with better speech is still needed.

Crisis management tips are readily available on the Internet and all are somewhat similar. Most focus on thoughtful planning and communication. Sterling Communication (n.d.), a public relations firm, summarized the three most important crisis management tips:

1. Disseminate accurate information as quickly as possible.
2. Respond to incorrect information that may be circulating.
3. Activate appropriate mechanisms to keep the public, media, and stake-holders informed on an ongoing basis.

Talking about what has happened and how it impacts the community is an important first step. Campus leaders can and should speak frankly, not only about the behavior and expectations of the community, but also, and as appropriate, about the power of the First Amendment. Students who are most impacted by the behavior and the campus as a whole need to have care provided to them. Rumors will likely abound and therefore it's necessary to create a method of ascertaining whether the information being shared is accurate and to respond to concerns in a timely way. Media outlets will typically pick up these stories and often want to know what the campus "is going to do about it." Disciplinary action is typically, but incorrectly, assumed to be the immediate institutional response. "No comment" is not an appropriate response. Finding the right spokesperson (if not the president) is critical. That person should be well versed in the First Amendment and the impact of such incidents on students. Students unfamiliar with the First Amendment may wrongly believe that the campus *could* take disciplinary action regarding hateful speech if it wanted to, unaware of the legal constraints of doing so. Students should be encouraged to talk about the impact of said behavior both privately and publicly. Involving faculty and staff in these conversations is important, as they all interact with students daily.

> Speech is powerful. It can stir people to action, move them to tears of both joy and sorrow, and . . . inflict great pain. . . . [W]e cannot react to that pain by punishing the speaker. As a Nation we have chosen a different course—to protect even hurtful speech on public issues to ensure that we do not stifle public debate. (*Snyder v. Phelps*, 2011)

We need to remember that campuses grow into vibrant communities by confronting their "warts" and by developing, articulating and living shared values of a learned community. Students, like those in several recent studies, who prefer banning hateful speech to protect themselves and their peers, do not recognize the rich history of the First Amendment in winning important battles for human rights and dignity in the United States. The fight is clearly not over. We need to encourage our students to listen to the views they find offensive and find their own voice.

References

American Association of University Professors. (n.d.). *Campus free-speech legislation: History, progress, and problems.* Retrieved from https://www.aaup.org/report/campus-free-speech-legislation-history-progress-and-problems

American Civil Liberties Union. (n.d.) *Speech on campus.* Retrieved from https://www.aclu.org/other/speech-campus

Ardinger, A. V. (2011) Private universities and freedom of expression: Free speech on Elon University's Campus. *Elon Journal of Undergraduate Research in Communications, 2*(1), 94–102. Retrieved from https://www.elon.edu/docs/e-web/academics/communications/research/vol2no1/10Ardinger.pdf

Armstrong v. Shirvell, 596 Fed Appx 433 (CA 6, 2015)

Beauharnais v. Illinois, 343 U.S. 250 (1952)

Better Angels Project. (2019). Depolarize America from south Lebanon, Ohio to all fifty states. *Better Angels.* Retrieved from https://www.better-angels.org/our-story/

Bird, L. E., Mackin, M. B., & Schuster, S. K. (Eds). (2006). *The First Amendment on campus: A handbook for college and university administrators.* Washington DC: National Association of Student Personnel Administrators.

Brandenburg v. Ohio, 395 U.S. 444 (1969). (n.d.). *Oyez.* Retrieved from https://www.oyez.org/cases/1968/492

Brown v. Entertainment Merchants Association, 564 U.S. 786, 131 S. Ct. 2729 (2011)

Carter, E. L. (2004). Outlaw speech on the Internet: Examining the link between unique characteristics of online media and criminal libel prosecutions. *Santa Clara High Technology Law Journal, 21*(2), 289–319.

Chemerinsky, E., & Gillman, H. (2017). *Free speech on campus.* New Haven, CT: Yale University Press.

Chemerinsky, E. (2017, September 13). The free speech-hate speech trade-off. *New York Times.*

Elonis v. United States, 575 U.S., 135 S. Ct. 2001 (2015)

First Amendment Watch. (2019). As promised, Trump signs contentious executive order on campus free speech. Retrieved from https://firstamendmentwatch.org/trump-promises-executive-order-compelling-free-speech-on-campus/

Fogel v. University of the Arts, CV 18-5137 (E.D. Pa., 2019)

Folta v. The New York Times Company, CV 17-02102 (M.D. Fl 2017)

Gardner, E. (2017, December 21). *Rolling Stone* settles last remaining lawsuit over UVA rape story. *Hollywood Reporter*. Retrieved from https://www.hollywoodreporter.com/thr-esq/rolling-stone-settles-last-remaining-lawsuit-uva-rape-story-1069880

Hall, M. (2017). *Keefe v. Adams:* Overregulating off-campus speech under professional codes of conduct. *Minnesota Law Review, 101*. Retrieved from http://www.minnesotalawreview.org/2017/04/keefe-v-adams/

Hague v. Committee for Industrial Organiza*tions*, 307 U.S. 496, 515 (1939)

Harvard Law Review. (2015, November 10). *Elonis v. United States*. Retrieved from https://harvardlawreview.org/2015/11/elonis-v-united-states/

Harvard Law Review. (2019, March 8). *Commonwealth v. Knox*. Retrieved from https://harvardlawreview.org/2019/03/commonwealth-v-knox/

Hudson, D. L. (2018, March). Free speech on public college campuses overview. *Freedom Forum Institute*. Retrieved from https://www.freedomforuminstitute.org/first-amendment-center/topics/freedom-of-speech-2/free-speech-on-public-college-campuses-overview/

Hunker, C. J. (2007). From *Hazelwood* to *Hosty*: Student publications as public forums. *Communication Law Review*. Retrieved from http://www.commlawreview.org/Archives/v7i1/From%20Hazelwood%20to%20Hosty%20Student%20Publications%20as%20Public%20Forums.pdf

International Institute for Restorative Practices (August 2003). *Restorative practices—principles and practice standards*. Found at http://www.iirp.edu/pdf/beth06_davey7.pdf

Liberty Champion. (2018, April 9). Former Liberty football players drop defamation lawsuits. Retrieved from https://www.liberty.edu/champion/2018/04/former-liberty-football-players-drop-defamation-lawsuits/

Keefe v. Adams, 840 F.3d 523 (8th Cir. 2016)

Knight Foundation. (2018, March 11). College students show strong support for First Amendment, but some say diversity and inclusion is more important to democracy than free speech Gallup-Knight Foundation shows [Press release]. Retrieved from https://knightfoundation.org/press/releases/college-students-show-strong-support-for-first-amendment-but-some-say-diversity-and-inclusion-is-more-important-to-a-democracy-than-free-speech-gallup-knight-survey-shows

McKay, R. B. (1968). The student as private citizen. *Denver Law Journal, 45*(4), 558–570.

Miller v. California, 413 U.S. 15, 93 S. Ct. 2607 (1973)

Nitke v. Gonzales, 413 F., Supp. 2d, 262, U.S. District Court (2005)

New York Times v. Sullivan, 376 U.S. 254 (1964)

O'Neil, R. M. (1997). *Free speech in the college community*. Bloomington, IN: Indiana University Press.

Paulsen, M. S. (2008). Freedom of speech at a private religious university. *University of St. Thomas Journal of Law and Public Policy, 2*(1), 104–108. Retrieved from https://ir.stthomas.edu/cgi/viewcontent.cgi?article=1022&context=ustjlpp

Pen America. (2019). *Chasm in the classroom: Free speech in a divided America.* New York, NY: Author. Retrieved from https://pen.org/chasm-in-the-classroom-campus-free-speech-in-a-divided-america/

Planned Parenthood v. American Coalition of Life Activists, 290 F.3d 1058 (2002)

Reynolds, G. (2003, July 28). Dear Colleague First Amendment. Retrieved from https://www2.ed.gov/about/offices/list/ocr/firstamend.html.

Schuster, S. K. (n.d.). Sexual harassment and the First Amendment: Will your policies hold up in court. *NCHERM.* Retrieved from https://cdn.tngconsulting .com/website-media/ncherm.org/unoffloaded/2017/08/SexualHarassmentFirst AmendmentArticle.pdf

Shirvell v. Department of Attorney General, 308 Mich App 702 (2015)

Shirvell v. Gordon, 602 Fed Appx 601 (CA 6, 2015)

Shutler, A. (2017, September 13). The free speech-hate speech trade off. *New York Times.* Retrieved from https://www.nytimes.com/2017/09/13/opinion/berkeley-dean-erwin-chemerinsky.html

Snyder v. Phelps, 562 U.S. 443, 131 S. Ct 1207, 1220 (2011)

State of Michigan Attorney Discipline Board. (2018, May 8). *Board opinion.* Retrieved from http://www.adbmich.org/coveo/opinions/2018-05-08-15o-49. pdf

Sterling Communications. (n.d.). *Ten tips for effective crisis management* [Blog post]. Retrieved from https://sterlingpr.com/2012/10/crisis-communications-plan-a-must-have/

Stewart v. Florida Southwestern State College, CV 19-00053 (M.D. Fl. 2019)

Student Press Law Center. (n.d.). *Who we are.* Retrieved from https://splc.org

U.S. Department of Justice. (2018). *Citizen's guide to U.S. federal law on obscenity.* Retrieved from https://www.justice.gov/criminal-ceos/citizens-guide-us-federal-law-obscenity

United States v. Stevens, 559 U.S. 460 (2010)

Virginia v. Black, 538 U.S. 343, 123 S. Ct. 1536 (2003)

12

THREAT ASSESSMENT AND BEHAVIORAL INTERVENTIONS

Jonathan M. Adams

Threat Assessment and Behavioral Interventions

With college campus shootings increasing at high rates (Rock, 2019), a common question has emerged with each incident among media and the public: Was the individual on the university's radar? This common question related to the institution's knowledge, coupled with institutions developing strategies to proactively prevent any future incidents, demonstrates the importance of student affairs professionals understanding the need, use, and approaches of threat assessment and behavioral intervention teams for a variety of incidents involving serious and potentially dangerous student and nonstudent behaviors.

Understanding the Approaches

In the aftermath of the 2007 campus shooting at Virginia Tech, university administrators recognized the need for development and implementation of a behavioral threat assessment process. Randazzo and Plummer (2009) noted the process of development and implementation at Virginia Tech which included

> creating a multi-disciplinary threat assessment team; strengthening and developing necessary policies and procedures to enhance and support the team's efforts; training the team; identifying and harnessing key resources on and off campus to intervene where necessary; securing case manage-

ment personnel to implement and monitor intervention efforts; and raising awareness on campus regarding the team's existence, its purpose, and the role that everyone on campus shares in reporting troubling behavior to the team. (pp. 5–6)

Since 2007, numerous resources related to threat assessment and behavioral intervention have emerged, including publications from the National Behavioral Intervention Team Association (NaBITA) and from SIGMA Threat Management Associates. While each resource is based on the organization's philosophy and ethos, the central values of approaches to threat assessment and behavioral intervention are constant: consistency, multidisciplinary, collaboration, support, and awareness.

Consistency

Consistency provides the opportunity for a team to approach an incident/concern in an individualized, objective manner that is rooted in the mission, vision, and values of the institution. Consistency can be created through two components: the team's mission and purpose and assessment strategies for the exhibited behaviors and risks.

Mission and Purpose

Depending on the type of team being utilized (threat assessment or behavioral intervention), the mission and purpose will reflect different and somewhat unique goals. While a threat assessment team may be solely focused on "responding to existing threats" from students, employees, and noncommunity members, a behavioral intervention team tends to have a broader, more preventative focus, identifying and supporting students in distress before the behaviors become a threat (Van Brunt, Reese, & Lewis, 2015, p. 4). Regardless of the type of team, the mission and purpose must be grounded in the culture of the institution and should be understood by all members of the team so that the goals are clear and the most appropriate resources, referrals, and action steps are utilized.

Assessment

An additional component to ensuring consistency relates to objectively assessing the behaviors and associated risks. Sokolow and colleagues (2019) highlighted that starting with an established standardized instrument aids in three key phases of "data gathering, assessment, and intervention" by providing an objective mechanism to "identifying the safety concerns and deploying the appropriate intervention measures needed to address these concerns"

(p. 4). These rubrics create a foundation for the work done by teams so that the developed strategies are grounded in institutional culture, based on best practice, and utilized in a consistent and fair manner, removing opportunities for potential bias or for consideration of extraneous factors that are unnecessary or could be perceived as discriminatory.

Multidisciplinary

Threat assessment and behavioral intervention cannot be the responsibility of one single office or entity. While it is important to have a centralized mechanism to receive and triage concerns, the collective perspectives of campus community members provide a more comprehensive, holistic approach to assessing the behaviors and determining the most appropriate intervention strategies.

Dependent on the type of team and the individuals who may be discussed by the team, the membership will vary. At its core, student-focused teams should include representatives from student affairs, student conduct, mental health (e.g., campus counseling centers), campus law enforcement/public safety, health services, residential life, and disability services. Based on the function of the team, the type of reports received, and the campus culture, additional departments may include, in either secondary or ad hoc roles, legal counsel, faculty, academic affairs, media relations, human resources (for faculty and staff), athletics, international student services, hospital staff, and graduate/professional schools (Deisinger, Randazzo, O'Neil, & Savage, 2008; Sokolow, Lewis, Van Brunt, Schuster, & Swinton, 2014). Ultimately, teams should include those who know what is occurring on campus, those with expertise in managing students in distress and threats, and those who have the power to take action (Higher Education Mental Health Alliance [HEHMA], 2013).

Collaboration

Collaboration is not only critical to assessing the behavior; it is also vital to developing a comprehensive postintervention plan that mitigates the behaviors and that supports the individual. The collective expertise of the team members provides a knowledge base of resources that assists in addressing the presenting behaviors and the underlying issues or stressors that may be leading to the behavior. This is evidenced in the continual emergence of mental health issues among behavioral intervention and threat assessment teams (Raleigh, 2015). By having resources available through campus counseling or mental health providers, support can be available to address both the exhibiting behaviors and the underlying causes of those behaviors, hopefully leading to prevention of future occurrences.

Collaboration for intervention strategies should not be limited to only those resources available on campus. Community partnerships provide an even more robust toolbox for teams to utilize in developing intervention strategies. An example of this can be seen regarding basic needs, which many times can lead to stressors academically and mentally (Bruening, Argo, Payne-Sturges, & Laska, 2017). Access to community agencies that address food security, homelessness, and financial assistance provides additional networks to create an impactful web of support for a student.

Support

While multidisciplinary, collaborative approaches provide opportunities for accurate assessment and appropriate intervention strategies, the approaches cannot work unless there are also mechanisms to create individualized opportunities for support postintervention. These postintervention supports may be managed through campus counseling, health services, or student conduct. Depending on the behaviors, follow-up with subjects initiating the concern is critical to answering the following questions:

1. Has the behavior stopped or become less disruptive?
2. Have new problematic or disruptive behaviors arisen?
3. How are they complying with medication regimens?
4. How are they reacting to situational stressors, relationship issues, or other trauma-activating occurrences?
5. Are they coping effectively?
6. What additional supports may they need? (Van Brunt et al., 2015, p. 7)

Post Virginia Tech, one strategy many institutions have implemented to provide the most comprehensive postintervention is the adoption of case management models. As the Higher Education Case Managers Association (2013) described, "Higher Education Case Managers serve their University and individual students by coordinating prevention, intervention, and support efforts across campus and community systems to assist at risk students and students facing crises, life traumas, and other barriers that impede success," further noting that case managers

- arrange for appropriate medical or mental health care;
- monitor compliance with treatment plans and/or university behavioral expectations;

- evaluate threat and assess risk to self and/or the community;
- maintain contact and meet with students to address needs;
- foster self-advocacy in students to manage their academic, personal, and fiscal responsibilities; and
- advocate for students individually and systemically (HECMA, 2013).

The emerging field of case management services has not only been recognized within individual institutions but has been recognized nationally as a standard function of higher education. In April 2019, the Council for the Advancement of Standards in Higher Education (CAS) released a newly created set of standards for case management services providing nationally recognized standards and guidelines for the management and operations of case management functions at college and universities (Council for the Advancement of Standards in Higher Education [CAS], 2019b). These standards were followed by the July 2019 release of CAS's "Cross-Functional Framework for Identifying and Responding to Behavioral Concerns," "designed to guide development, review, and quality improvement of behavioral intervention and threat assessment teams" (CAS, 2019a, para. 2).

Awareness

For an institution to accurately respond to threats and appropriately intervene in concerning behavior, a culture of care among all members of the institutional community must be promoted among all facets of leadership. Students, faculty, and staff must

- be able to identify behaviors that may be concerning or threatening,
- be aware of campus resources that are available to assist both students in distress and those reporting the behavior, and
- know how and where to report, including understanding when it is appropriate to seek the assistance of emergency and law enforcement personnel.

An institutional culture of reporting is paramount to not only seeking the most information possible but also to providing the most comprehensive assessment, allowing the team to accurately "connect the dots" in order to determine if the behavior is an isolated incident or a broader concern. Reporting also provides the team a better sense of the individual's support networks so that the most appropriate and impactful outreach mechanisms can be identified.

Institutions have utilized a variety of strategies to promote a culture of awareness and reporting, many of which can be found through an online search. Some notable strategies have included incorporating reporting as part of bystander training, providing faculty strategies and coaching to proactively intervene in classroom management issues, developing emergency or "red folders" so that faculty and staff have access to strategies and resources at their fingertips, and incorporating the institution's behavioral intervention model into orientation sessions (student, new faculty, new staff, and departmental) and as part of educational programs in collaboration with student organizations, centers for teaching and learning, and human resources learning and development.

Student Conduct Professionals' Role in Threat Assessment and Behavioral Interventions

Student conduct professionals play a critical role in an institution's threat assessment and behavioral intervention strategies. First, student conduct professionals provide a unique skill set developed through experiences addressing inappropriate behaviors that naturally align with the processes utilized by threat assessment/behavioral intervention approaches. Student conduct professionals are well versed in being able to objectively assess a situation through a consistent standard (e.g., code of student conduct), develop strategies for ascertaining information that is comprehensive and in depth (e.g., investigations), and create individualized opportunities for addressing behavior that balances the needs of the individual with the needs of the institutional community (e.g., sanctioning). Second, due to the legal, compliance components that have emerged in student conduct practices, student conduct professionals are knowledgeable of issues and pitfalls that may develop due to the intersections of student care, due process, and safety and security. Third, through sanctioning approaches, student conduct professionals typically have well-established, collaborative partnerships that are beneficial to the team, developing a comprehensive intervention plan that utilizes all available resources. Finally, given some of the issues that emerge through threat assessment/behavioral intervention, which falls under the institutional code of student conduct, student conduct professionals' participation in behavioral teams can provide a seamless transition of processes to either formal conduct proceedings or alternative forms of resolution.

While student conduct professionals provide a valuable set of knowledge, skills, and abilities to threat assessment and behavioral intervention, it is vital for student conduct professionals to remain well versed in the trends and issues that are emerging within behavioral intervention. Professional development within individual plans or as part of continued team training provides student conduct professionals opportunities to continue to refine knowledge bases and skill sets that improves all facets of their job responsibilities.

Conclusion

The field of threat assessment and behavioral intervention at colleges and universities has emerged over the past decade; however, many of the practices and approaches utilized in threat assessment and behavioral intervention have been utilized in student conduct practices for decades. Policies and practices that are rooted in consistency, collaboration, support, and awareness are not new to student conduct practices and are engrained in the daily work done by student conduct professionals. Student conduct professionals provide a valuable addition to threat assessment and behavioral intervention approaches based on their professional experiences addressing behavior, and their participation is vital to teams being most successful. It is also critical for student conduct professionals to understand the values and functions of threat assessment and behavioral intervention so that all facets of the behavioral intervention models can support both the students and the university community.

References

Bruening, M., Argo, K., Payne-Sturges, D., & Laska, M. N. (2017). The struggle is real: A systematic review of food insecurity on postsecondary education campuses. *Journal of the Academic of Nutrition and Dietetics, 117*(11), 1767–1791. doi:10.1016/j.jand.2017.05.022

Council for the Advancement of Standards in Higher Education. (2019a, July 5). *CAS releases the cross-functional framework for identifying and responding to behavioral concerns* [Web log]. Retrieved from https://www.cas.edu/blog_home .asp?display=90

Council for the Advancement of Standards in Higher Education. (2019b, April 18). *New standards released for case management services* [Web log]. Retrieved from https://www.cas.edu/blog_home.asp?display=88

Deisinger, G., Randazzo, M., O'Neil, D., & Savage. J. (2008). *The handbook for campus threat assessment and management teams*. Boston, MA: Applied Risk Management.

Higher Education Case Managers Association. (2013). *About us*. Retrieved from https://www.hecma.org/about-us/

Higher Education Mental Health Alliance. (2013). *Balancing safety and support: A guide for campus teams.* Retrieved from https://www.jedfoundation.org/wp-content/uploads/2016/06/campus_teams_guide.pdf

Raleigh, M. J. (2015). Mental health. In B. Van Brunt, D. Denino, M. J. Raleigh, & M. Issadore, *The prevention and management of mental health emergencies: Fifteen scenarios for student affairs professionals* (pp. xv–xxvii). Berwyn, PA: NaBITA.

Randazzo, M. R., & Plummer, E. (2009). *Implementing behavioral threat assessment on campus: A Virginia Tech demonstration project.* Blacksburg, VA: Virginia Polytechnic Institute and State University.

Rock, A. (2019, January 15). College campus shooting statistics you should know. *Campus Safety Magazine.* Retrieved from https://www.campussafetymagazine.com/university/college-campus-shooting-statistics/

Sokolow, B., Lewis, W. S., Van Brunt, B., Schuster, S., & Swinton, D. (2014). *The book on behavioral intervention teams (BIT)* (2nd ed.). Malvern, PA: National Behavioral Intervention Team Association (NaBITA).

Sokolow, B. A., Van Brunt, B., Lewis, W. S., Schiemann, M., Murphy, A. & Molnar, J. (2019). *The NaBITA risk rubric: The NaBITA 2019 whitepaper, college and university edition* [White paper]. Retrieved from https://cdn.nabita.org/website-media/nabita.org/wp-content/uploads/2019/08/02122749/NaBITA-2019-Whitepaper-Final.pdf

Van Brunt, B., Reese, A. C., & Lewis, W. S. (2015). *The NaBITA 2015 whitepaper: Who's on the team? Mission, membership, and motivation* [White paper]. Retrieved from https://cdn.nabita.org/website-media/nabita.org/wp-content/uploads/2018/09/04141954/2015-NaBITA-Whitepaper.pdf

13

STUDENT ORGANIZATIONS THROUGH THE STUDENT CONDUCT LENS

Kathleen A. Shupenko and Jane A. Tuttle

S tudent organizations are a representation of the world beyond the collegiate academic experience. Students engage in organizations that relate
to personal growth, cultural connections, legacy status, academic interests, and physical engagement. Each institution will need to address the challenges posed by social expectations, operational decision-making, and the
"traditions" of their student organizations. In doing so, institutional personnel may find the activities of student organizations can result in violations of
institutional codes of student conduct.

In investigating alleged violations, be prepared to address the violations
or explain why there is no conduct action being taken. Addressing organizational misconduct establishes accountability for the organization. It allows
students to have an opportunity to examine and develop their beliefs and
values while assessing whether they are congruent with their professed values
and the values of the institution. This chapter invites administrators to pose
questions about the institution's current policies and practices related to student organization conduct and provide insights on new pathways to address
questionable behaviors on the campus. Its focus is on the education, accountability, and development of the student organizations on campus.

What Is an Organization?

The First Amendment of the U.S. Constitution gives students the right to
freedom of association. The U.S. Supreme Court Case of *Healy v James* (1972)

gives the institution the right to discipline organizations in most cases. The organization must agree to follow the institution's reasonable and lawful rules as well as state and federal laws. In exchange, the institution agrees to provide registration and certain privileges. Without the commitment to adhere to policies and laws, the institution is not obligated to recognize an organization.

As simple as the concept may seem, all organizations on campus are not created equally. Some organizations are an affiliate of a national organization; some have a mixture of students, faculty, and staff, plus community members with no association with the institution; and some are for students only. Besides membership, how does a campus acknowledge the existence of an organization? Some universities register organizations while others have a more formalized recognition process. The various categories of organizational type can impact the organizations' level of privileges. All of these factors can go into what constitutes an organization on a college campus. Do you know what your campus definitions are? Do you know what responsibilities and privileges come from being an organization on your campus?

For the sake of simplicity, the chapter assumes an organization is comprised of student members and is somehow acknowledged by the college with responsibilities and privileges of use. While the notion of a student organization seems straightforward, the relationships within and of the organization may matter. Is it an academic honorary, an affiliate of a national service organization, a chapter of a social fraternity or sorority or a sports club through a university program? Does it matter? Are the college's policies, practices, and guidelines applied universally? There should be, as fundamental fairness is the foundation for student conduct administration (Lake, 2011; Council for the Advancement of Standards in Higher Education [CAS], 2019, Association of Student Conduct Administration [ASCA], 2017).

Consistently institutions have used two main terms to denote an organization, *registered* and *recognized*. There seems to be no true difference and the terms are used interchangeably, although some would argue that *recognized* creates a stronger relationship. That has yet to be seen. Whichever term the institution uses, be certain it is the term used in all conduct administration documentation. Throughout this chapter we will use the word "recognized."

Considering Organizational Conduct

The authors would argue that a student conduct administrator should be involved in the management of any organizational conduct process, even if only as a consultant. Because student conduct professionals know the institution's policies and practices, they can best meet the goals of student conduct: education, accountability, and the development of the organization. The philosophical questions have already been addressed as the mechanism for dealing with misconduct is already established. While community standards are set by the institution's policies as well as its culture, those standards are best enforced by the student conduct office.

Policy Development (Individual Versus Organization)

Any practitioner seeking to build equitable due process for individual conduct need only look to the model conduct code for adequate guidance (Stoner & Lowery, 2004). However, a practitioner seeking to build on the model code to appropriately address organizational misconduct would need more. Managing organizational misconduct needs to account for the complex multifaceted decision-making that occurs over a length of time when an organization engages in a violation of the code of conduct.

Organizational violations may be comprised of a multitude of individual violations leading up to and including the organizational event. You may not have enough information to support individual charges in each organizational event. If you are examining the organization, you should consider the following analysis as a tool to support and challenge your decision-making.

Student organizations may be found responsible for violations when behaviors include, but are not limited to, the following:

- The conduct is endorsed by the student organization (SO) or any of its officers including, but not limited to, active or passive consent or support, having prior knowledge. That the conduct was likely to occur and not taking any substantive action to prevent it (e.g., canceling the event, notifying the Office of Student Conduct or university or local police, etc.), or helping to plan, advertise or promote the conduct.
- The conduct is committed during an activity paid for by the SO, or paid for as a result of one or more members of the SO contributing personal funds in lieu of organizational funds to support the activity or conduct in question.
- The conduct occurred on property owned, controlled, rented, leased, or used (on or off campus) by the SO or any of its members for an organizational event.

- The purpose of the activity was related to initiation or admission into, affiliation with, or as a condition for continued membership in the SO.
- Nonmembers of the SO learned of the activity through members, advertisements, or communications associated with the SO or otherwise formed a reasonable belief that the conduct or activity was affiliated with or endorsed by the SO.
- Members of the SO attempted to conceal the activity of other members who were involved.
- One or more officer(s) of the SO had prior knowledge or reasonably should have known that the conduct would take place (Pennsylvania State University, 2019; University of Kentucky, 2016).

This analysis was first published in *Student Conduct Practice: The Complete Guide for Student Affairs Professionals* (Lancaster & Waryold, 2008) and has been adopted in many conduct codes throughout the country. Each adaptation proves to be a valued addition in the assessment for conduct professionals managing organizational conduct issues.

An organizational violation is often a collection of individual decisions/violations that lead to single organization event. At the event multiple people may also violate the code of conduct. The (potentially) volatile behavior may be repeated over several months or years. For example, organizations may violate an academic integrity policy by amassing and distributing past test materials within the group.

In the case of a single organization event, a violation may result from the summation of many individual actions. For example, one member may purchase the alcohol with funds provided by other members, and another member might arrange the use of an off-campus location. While any or all of the aforementioned members may not attend the event or consume the alcohol, a "but for" analysis may still result in their shared responsibility for the actions of a single member who engaged in the verbal direction of hazing through forced consumption of alcohol. In other words, "but for" the other individual's actions, the hazing behavior may not have occurred.

Understanding the link and difference between collective and individual responsibilities is the first step in managing organizational conduct. In evaluating an organizational conduct case, it will be important to determine whether the organization can alone be held responsible (i.e., insufficient information exists to support individual charges); whether both organizational and individual charges are justified; or if the incident cannot be linked to the organization and was truly the behavior one or more individuals operating independent of the organization. It is possible to hold an organization accountable, as well as individuals, but only if the code and procedures allow for this.

The protections of due process are elegant in their simplicity and complex in implementation. Students are entitled to even minimal due process in both private and public institutions. Both private and public universities must follow their written rules of procedure. Public institutions have a greater responsibility to ensure due process procedures are followed. Kaplin and Lee (2014) remind private institutions, in the area of student misconduct, that procedural protections must be provided. Even minimally the following elements of due process are needed in student conduct administration:

- To be told the charges against the organization
- To hear the information about the alleged violation
- To present their explanation of the alleged violation
- To have an impartial factfinder

The need for clearly articulated, readily available procedures for student organizations' misconduct is evident; however, the procedures may look different than those of an individual student. Some institutions prefer their procedures are part of the student code of conduct while others have their procedures in a separate document but are referenced in their student code of conduct. Both approaches are adequate if the procedures are established and followed.

Gary Pavela (2018) in "Ten Principles for Members of Student Conduct Hearing Boards," cautions "Due process is more than a prescribed set of procedures; it also entails the 'internal control of impulse' grounded in a determination to hear cases before deciding them" (p. 1). By allowing for full examination of the facts, organization officers, members, and advisers may be more accepting of the outcome.

Many institutions are transitioning from a self-governance model to institutional oversight. Self-governance refers to an organization's ability to hold itself responsible for its actions. Making the transition to institutional oversight can still incorporate students in decision-making. Students could serve as decision makers in cases with lower-level outcomes. They could also serve, along faculty and staff, as decision makers in cases with higher-level outcomes. However, the ultimate responsibility for monitoring and adjudicating organizational misconduct resides with the institution (i.e., institutional oversight).

Partnerships (Internal and External)

Because some organizations are an affiliate or chapter of a national organization, they may have a different relationship with the campus. This is most obvious for the social fraternities and sororities. The partnership between the host institution and the national organization is two-fold: an educational partnership and an adjudication partnership in organizational conduct.

We suggest active engagement in partnerships for all student organizations, especially with organizations that are an affiliate or chapter of a national organization. Patterns of unresolved conflict are costly in student retention, in university resources and, perhaps most significant, student well-being. Unresolved conflict can lead to greater dysfunction in the organization. If misbehavior is looked at as a continuum and the minor violations of the code of conduct are not addressed, the misbehavior is likely to accelerate.

In the cases of social fraternities and sororities there are many players: the students and their guests, the advisers, the corporation board, the alumni, the sorority and fraternity life offices on campus, the office for student conduct, and possibly public affairs. It is vital to remember that the goal of student conduct is education and accountability. It is easy to get distracted by the competing entities. Do not ignore them but do not cater to them either.

The purpose of the offices related to sorority and fraternity life is not to control behavior; rather, they serve as liaisons between the national organization and the host institution. They understand the expectations and priorities of both entities. They advise the student officers in peer/self-governance and member development. The students need to know they have an ally and an expert resource on understanding the purpose, structure, policy, and process of the university and national organization. The conduct office needs a strong relationship with this office.

The keys to partnering with a national organization and their local chapter are simple but require good communication:

- Awareness of the knowledge and experience each party brings to the relationship
- Willingness to hear and honor all voices and address the issues they raise
- Assumption of best intentions among all parties
- Recognition of strengths and acceptance of limitations while addressing needs
- Shared decision-making, risk-taking, and accountability

The "how" of investigating and adjudicating organizational misconduct are addressed later in the chapter. Keeping the keys to this partnership in mind as one investigates and adjudicates organizational misconduct will lead to better results.

Organizations and FERPA (Size of the Organization Matters)

There are many federal laws institutions must comply with, and the one most often cited is the Family Educational Rights and Privacy Act (FERPA). The fundamental question is "Does FERPA apply to an organization?" The simple answer is no, *but* it is important to protect the FERPA rights of the individuals involved in the organization. If student development and learning is the overarching priority, is there a difference between what must be shared and what may be shared? As a matter of practice, most new members of a social fraternity and sorority and members of a business fraternity, a student organization, or a roster for club sports or athletic teams, may all be public record. Thus, if detailed information about organizational misbehavior is reported, the individual members could be easily identified and perhaps traumatized. If an organization is small, its members can easily be identified, thus making the disclosure all the more problematic.

This is why a number of schools that do publicly disclose an organization's conduct status report only report the provision of the code of conduct that was violated and not the behaviors that constituted the violation. (For examples see Student organization conduct status report [n.d.] or University of Kansas [2019].)

However, there are many institutions that are or will be providing data about organizational conduct outcomes either because of state legislation that require outcomes to be published or because of a commitment to provide great transparency.

Intersection of Antihazing Laws and Organization Misconduct

The 2017 death of Pennsylvania State University student Timothy J. Piazza has accelerated the pace of changes to organizational conduct, particularly for social sororities and fraternities. Most obvious are the state laws enacted to increase transparency in reported hazing violations, with penalties for failure to comply with a given law. While Pennsylvania's law was not the first to require institutions to disclose hazing violations, it has been the most visible. The nonprofit organizations HazingPrevention and Stop Hazing have interactive maps with antihazing legislation by state. Currently there are 44 states with laws against hazing. Most of these states classify hazing as a misdemeanor, while 12 states provide for felony hazing charges (StopHazing, n.d.). Besides state laws, federal legislation has been introduced that would amend the Higher Education Act of 1965 to add hazing violations to annual security reports.

These laws are a reaction to tragic student deaths from hazing and frustration with the inability to stop these deaths. Each law and those proposed by other states require information on outcomes. The transparency is intended to inform parents/families and their students as they make decisions on which organization they may want to join. In some ways these laws are based in consumer protection, much like the 1990 Clery Act in its effort to inform about crime and safety policies and practices.

This consumer protection approach also provides an opportunity for the institutions to invite stakeholders to engage in more meaningful ways around organizational conduct. It is designed to encourage stakeholders (parents/families, community members, recent alumnus, current undergraduate and graduate students, and others) to take part in the oversight, growth, and development of the organization. When the institutions provide clear information on the conduct outcomes, the institutions also acknowledge areas of concern on campuses.

Yet the push for more accountability, transparency, and education for student organizations must be handled with respect for the individual members of an organization. As mentioned earlier, individual students' educational records need to be protected. It is possible to report outcomes, preserve individual confidentiality, and have meaningful and possibly restorative conversations, although it requires commitment from all stakeholders.

The trend toward antihazing legislation for consumer protection is not going away. The laws already passed in Pennsylvania and other states can provide the practitioner a roadmap to expectations. Those working in these states and possibly others need to be aware of the detailed requirements for reporting and adjudicating. While these laws may set standards, education is always the guiding principle and compliance is the floor.

Steps to Adjudicating Organizational Misconduct

Here we have outlined some commonly used steps in adjudicating organizational misconduct.

Investigation Guidelines

Investigations are a strategic, dynamic, and variable practice. You should have a trusted colleague to assist in decision-making about the steps of the investigation along the way. No two investigations are alike; you will not always get the same information in each case. Investigations should focus on finding information about the experiences individuals had with the organization to include any exculpatory evidence. Investigative reports should establish the facts of the case to include timeline, behaviors, individuals involved, polices that may have been violated, and areas of dispute or inconsistencies. Investigators should establish good rapport with students, engage student leaders in dialogue about the future of the organization, and share on-campus and off-campus resources for students through the student affairs practitioner lenses.

Referrals/Reporting

The two prevailing considerations for those reporting or referring misconduct are how to report and how to remain anonymous. Other items to be addressed in the processes are if/when the institution will notify the police (internal or external), how retaliation will be addressed, how involved the reporter needs to be with your process, and how confidentiality of the reporting party can be maintained. Other important items to communicate include information on who will contact the reporter next.

Knowing if your institution is willing to accept and address anonymous reports will frame the rest of your investigative and conduct process. There are institutions that are not willing to address reports that are anonymous. If that is the case, you may want to allow for forwarding anonymous reports, if received, to other entities, such as national headquarters, the offices of fraternity and sorority life, or other partners to encourage education or conversations with the organization's leadership.

Credibility Assessment

Each time a report comes to your office, you will need an easy and effective set of questions to ask yourself concerning the credibility of the report. Following is a list of questions you should ask and be able to answer for each report. This information forms the basis of your investigative path or your transition into a conduct process without an investigation.

> Timeline: Does the report match the timeline of events for your institution? For example, are reported behaviors coincident with known campus events like student organization fair, new member recruitment, social activities, homecoming, probate, or spring break?
> Motivation for the report: Why did the person say they are reporting? Motive, interest, and potential bias are all considerations in evaluating the validity of a report. A complainant who has no personal gain in

reporting the concern may have more credibility than, for example, a member of a rival fraternity. Importantly, however, credibility and motive are not mutually exclusive; the allegation can be both true as well as submitted by a reporter with an ulterior motive.

Proximity: Are they reporting a direct experience/observation or hearsay? Specificity and accessibility of the information: Is the reporter providing detailed, verifiable information, such as names of actors, locations of activities, dates and times, and specific descriptions of the concerning behaviors? Would the information only be accessible to those with direct knowledge or interaction with the organization, or even only to individuals who were present at the event? Frequency: Have multiple reports come in for the same organization from varying sources, or have other trends in reports been identified (e.g., the same or similar reported behaviors around the same time[s] each year)? Corroborating evidence: Is there documentary information submitted in support of the claim (e.g., photographs, screenshots, medical records, e-mails)?

These initial considerations will inform your next steps. It is important the initial credibility assessment does not, however, undermine the impartiality required in any subsequent fact finding.

Interview Preparation

You should spend time searching for information that may be publicly available, as well as that which your institution retains in reference to the student organization. Seek out information about connections within the organization. Have an understanding as to whether any of the parties with which you are going to meet have been in your office before through an individual or organizational conduct case. Based on the allegations, consider what information you might ask of the parties that can be easily corroborated later. For example, if there is a report of hazing by means of requiring that new members relinquish their ID cards, you can gather evaluative information by requesting an audit of the new members' ID card swipes (e.g., to access buildings or make purchases).

Before you meet with students to ask about their experience, especially in a hazing-related investigation, take some time to reflect on their perspective. There are many barriers for individuals to report their own experience (e.g., the fear of social rejection, the loss of the sense of belonging, the fear of retaliation, the loss of investment, the loss of the future they envisioned).

During the Investigation

Set up the interviews in a neutral space (if possible). Ensure that each investigator has the information they need to conduct the investigation (e.g., access to the referral, information gathered in advance of the individual interviews, the parties they will be meeting with, the questions they are expected to ask, the resources on and off campus they should refer students to, the alternative pathways to reporting, how to follow up with your office). Make sure you have time to reflect on your notes and, if there is a team, time to reflect with the team on the information gathered. Create time to record your notes and know your own shorthand. Be prepared for the unexpected.

After Your Investigation

Corroborating information helps to address any question of confirmation bias in your process. Providing robust information from different sources can help the organization take ownership of its actions and understand this is not an "us-versus-them" situation. The investigative report should include all relevant information collected, including exculpatory evidence, as well as references to the policies the organization is alleged to have violated. Documenting the cooperation, or lack thereof, of members and student leaders may also be valuable for sanctioning and determining next steps for the organization; and, in the case where a national organization is involved, the information could inform their process.

For more information on methods of gathering information for investigations, see Appendix 13.A.

Education and Sanctioning

In the absence of foundational education, the organizations will educate on their own, often using misinformation. Cocurricular learning experiences can assist in building life skills for students. Our students learn valuable skills outside of the classroom. However, left to their own devices they may miss the mark on risk analysis, and these high-risk behaviors can lead to significant life-long consequences. Many high-risk behaviors such as alcohol/drug use, hazing, and financial mismanagement occur as a result of a type of group-think leadership. Highlighting these areas isn't to take away from the concern of behaviors such as harassment or sexual assault that can occur or be pervasive within organizations. It is simply to focus on the areas that are more often organization violations versus individual behaviors.

Student affairs professionals, along with advisers and national partners, should seek to provide continuous education to new and returning students on the following subjects:

- Code of conduct expectations
- Application of the code of conduct on campus and, in some instances, off campus
- Financial literacy
- Executive leadership
- Ethical decision-making
- Hazing policies
- Alcohol/drug use
- Sexual assault/gender-based violence
- Bystander intervention

Student organization turnover is high, with little time focused on transition of roles. Students need a continuous foundation in order to thrive and change the culture. Students have a finite amount of time at the institution and we need to be creative and focus on technology and messaging that is easy to understand and relatable to our students.

Sanctioning (Restorative Practices, Long-Term Education)

Sanctioning an organization requires a methodical approach that encompasses creativity and collaboration. Similar to sanctioning individual students, sanctioning of organizations should prompt reflection, remedy problematic behaviors, and create opportunities for moral and ethical growth.

Considerations for Sanctioning an Organization

Conduct history Consider if there have been repeat violations of the same nature and/or additional violations within the same academic semester. If so, consider if those violations should be used in recommending new sanctions. It would also be critical to examine whether previous sanctions have been completed and compare the completion of those sanctions (or lack thereof) to the timeline of the recent violation. This may help shape future sanctions and clarify if recidivism is occurring before educational interventions or after.

Allegation date There are various aspects of an allegation's timeline that should be considered. How you respond to an allegation that is an ongoing concern will be different than addressing an allegation that occurred last semester, last year, or three years ago. Within understanding the allegation date, it is important to analyze the awareness that current leadership and members have of the incident. This could be something current members have no knowledge of, or thought was simply a rumor from years ago. However, more recent incidents, or those founded in "tradition," are likely known by membership or leadership. Addressing the severity of allegations will change depending on the knowledge of those currently in the organization.

When addressing previous conduct consider the length of time since the incident occurred, the composition of the organization, the relevant steps the organization has taken in order to address the previous violation, as well as any educational programs, initiatives, or corrective action the organization has implemented.

Composition of the organization   It may be helpful to first assess the organization's executive board by understanding how many executive board positions exist and what those positions include. Consider whether there are positions that are vacant as well as the experience level of those executive board members. When assessing the time line of the allegation, take into consideration when the executive board members took their roles and what the organization's conduct history was. For general membership, understanding the ratio of leaders to members will be important in creating specialized sanctions, and evaluating the class year composition will assist in long-term planning and sanctioning.

Campus connections   Advisers and national organizations serve a powerful role for student organizations. It could be important to include advisers in educational programming so that they receive the same information as the students. While it is not an easy conversation, a university should challenge advisers to be introspective of their positions and how their interactions with the organization impact the organization's decisions. Not all adviser relationships are positive. Through creative sanctioning and relationships with campus partners, adviser behavior can be addressed so the organization is receiving the most beneficial assistance for its growth. Ask the organization and the adviser to reflect on the adviser's relationship with the organization and the organization's connection to campus partners.

Organizational values   Sanctions should not only address behavior but should connect with the organization's values. By understanding the role of advisers and the composition of current leadership, it is much easier to understand what organization's values are, what the stated values are, any incongruence between stated values versus lived values, and what steps are needed to set them on the path toward value-based decision-making. Assess the organization's mission and values and have the organization's members reflect on the reason the organization exists on your campus and the purpose it should serve in the future, long after the current students have left the institution.

Organizational feedback   Whenever possible, engage the organization's members in the active design and implementation of all sanctioning.

Remediation plan   A remediation plan, also known as a mutual agreement, is a written proposal, by the organization, to address the conduct violation(s), taking into consideration the resources on and off campus and the commitment of all members and any relevant partners such as national headquarters, organization advisers, and your campuses partner offices (fraternities and sororities, student activities, campus recreation, athletics). If an organization has national headquarters, they may already have language in place for a remediation plan. When explaining what a remediation plan is to organizations who may not have national headquarters, make sure it is explained to those students in a way that connects with their learning styles since it could be their (and their adviser's) first time in the conduct process.

A remediation plan should take a frame of reference for change over the next academic year, and address SMART goals created by the organization, with support from advisers and stakeholders, so that sustainable change can be created. The plan could include any of the following:

- Membership review
- The transition of executive board members or other group members
- Loss of on-campus housing
- Educational workshops or initiatives in consultation with campus or national partners
- Benchmarking with other like organizations on campus or at other institutions
- Measurable goals that address accomplishments over a period of time
- A calendar of events the organization intends to hold that focus on the purpose of the organization, including fundamental learning outcomes for events
- Assignment of any service activities
- Activities to foster healthy relationship building

When an organization submits the remediation plan, the conduct practitioner should assist in finalizing the plan and then incorporate it into the official outcome and sanctions for the organization. The remediation plan should be the "make-or-break" moment for the organization. If violations persist, the organization should no longer have recognition at your institution.

Even if your institution does not require it, for a nationally affiliated social fraternity or sorority, consider partnering with the national headquarters on the following:

- Closing the chapter house for a period of time to redirect the focus of the organization
- Conducting a membership review for all undergraduate members and alumnus who have graduated in the last five years
- Changing current alumni advisers

Many organizations are not nationally affiliated. However, each organization is affiliated with your campus and therefore all the resources of your institution. In addition to using your campus resources, you should use your professional networks, and your local community to create sanctions that are meaningful and engage the students in change.

Suspension or Loss of Recognition for an Organization
There may be instances where the organization loses recognition at the institution. Careful consideration should be taken for any plan to renew recognition. The length of the suspension should address the graduation of the culture and may need to be for no less than four years.

When an organization loses recognition at an institution, the students need support on how they can maintain a healthy identity and how they can maintain the relationships they've built, even if the foundation of how they built these relationships were violations of the code of conduct. (For more on sanctioning and restorative justice see chapter 5.)

Rogue Organizations
Loss of recognition for some organization could create new concerns for the institution. Consider the following: The organization loses recognition from the institution, but the national headquarters allows the organization to maintain recognition. Now you have an organization operating with the support of the national organization, which will often defer to the word of the undergraduate students. The students no longer have an organizational connection to the institution. They are supported at best from afar.

When a rogue organization exists, you need to lean into your partnerships. Consider sending joint letters to the families of the students who were registered with the organization. Provide clear information on why the organization has lost recognition, the time frame, and resources on campus and offer partnership with them to address any other residual issues related to the code of conduct, their housing arrangements, and their connection on campus. Encourage families to reach out now and in the future if there are concerns. Take time to help them revisit the liability for their students and for them.

Inform, through a letter, your local partners (e.g., alumni groups, landlords, local government, and local police). Do not assume they will know the organization's new status. In the letter address the behaviors, the organizational status, and how to address any ongoing concerns. Provide a letter similar to that provided to the families, addressing the behaviors, the current status, and the length of time the organization will be away.

Inform your new and returning students of the organizational change. Publish the outcome in your online communications. Be sure to address it during new student orientation with students and their families.

Staffing and Capacity (Case Management, Investigations)

Unlike many areas of student services, there is no set standard for staffing in conduct offices. This leads to issues of personnel capacity as well as burnout from intensity of work. The following are areas to consider.

Personnel

Just as student organizations vary in size and character, offices of student conduct vary in size and responsibilities. Unlike other student service areas, student conduct administration does not have a recommended number of student conduct officers per enrolled student. It behooves one to routinely run caseload summaries, complete with time from notice to adjudication. This data can help inform staffing needs. If the office has only one staff person and is responsible for both academic and nonacademic misconduct, the idea of adjudicating organizational misconduct may seem daunting. Even for seemingly well-staffed offices, organizational misconduct can be a challenge. The process of investigating, writing a report to determine if a violation may have happened, to consult with the organization and then to actually adjudicate takes time. While one is occupied with an organizational misconduct situation, the other conduct-related issues also continue.

Because of the ongoing nature of conduct administration, time management plays a key role in success. The administrative tasks, also called case management, are more than who has responsibility for what case. It is outlining a workflow that gives adequate time for each element of the process, including time for legal review. Because organizational conduct can be complicated and often litigious, legal review is prudent, and that takes time.

Most conduct administrators have found the use of a commercial database system vital to case management. These products offer a system for centralized reporting and record keeping and a scheduler/reminder system. Absent of having a commercially based system, every office must have a way to ensure each allegation is reviewed and addressed. Take an opportunity to meet with the Information Technology Department staff to talk through secure ways to keep received information, document a response, and comply with all federal regulations related to retention of educational records.

Every student conduct officer would benefit from the network of fellow professionals found in the Association for Student Conduct Administration (ASCA). The confidential nature of the work makes talking with other local colleagues impossible. Yet, sometimes it helps to talk with conduct professional at another institution. This exchange can help process the organization's misconduct while keeping the situation confidential. It is likely others have faced similar situations and can share their approach. A word of caution about using e-mail for such conversations: E-mails may be subject to open records requests or possible subpoena should the case go to court; hence, a phone call may be preferable.

While infrequent, some organizational misconduct cases do enter the legal system. This can be a stress-inducing event; however, in most instances the conduct officer will have legal representation provided through the school's in-house legal office, the state's attorney general for state-supported institutions, or an outside law firm. It is important to remember the legal team is representing you as an employee in the course of your responsibilities and assumes you were acting within your job description and were following institutional policies. One should not fear the threat of legal action when properly performing professional responsibilities.

Additionally, most professional associations provide access to economically priced professional liability insurance. Such coverage may protect you from alleged work-related errors as well as criminal allegation defense. These types of policies can be a comfort even if one never needs to use them.

Self-Care

Besides needing professional colleagues as a sounding board, the vicarious trauma, also known as compassion fatigue, one can experience in this work is indeed real. Much has been written about compassion fatigue, but one must be aware of it because it can impact one's personal life, including personal relationships, as well as one's physical health and emotional well-being. Most university employers provide an employee assistance program though the Human Resource Department, which can provide free or discounted counseling services.

Conclusion

As many institutions around the country are calling into question the value of student organizations, the authors suggest you remember the foundation of these organizations. The sense of belonging, the desire to come together on common ground, and the skills students develop outside of the classroom are some of the heritage of student organizations. Their ability to navigate challenging situations, provide peer accountability, and to form relationships around common interests are all worthy aspirations. Providing a solid foundation for organizations to include institutional accountability, guidance, and redirection should be at the forefront of how the organizational conduct process is constructed.

Perhaps the most important word to consider in student organization misconduct is "when" and not "if." Now is the time to review and refine the student organization misconduct policies, procedures, and practices. When engaged in organization misconduct cases, there are many influences and challenges, and that is not the time to be considering changes to the process or understanding the process. This chapter has given the basic considerations of organization misconduct and possible solutions to its adjudication. The possibilities to help change an organizational culture are endless, as student learning is the guiding principle of student conduct.

References

Andrew's Law S.B. 1080, 2019 Regular Session 2019 (Fla. 2019).

Association of Student Conduct Administration (ASCA). (2017). *ASCA bylaws.* Retrieved from https://www.theasca.org/files/Governing%20Documents/ASCA%20Bylaws%20Final%20Member%20Approved%2004-29-2017.pdf

Healy v. James, 408 U.S. 169 (1972)

Council for the Advancement of Standards in Higher Education. (2019).*CAS professional standards for higher education* (10th ed.). Washington DC: Author.

Kaplin, W. A., & Lee, B. A. (2014). *The law of higher education* (5th ed.). San Francisco, CA: Jossey-Bass.

Lake, P. F. (2011). *Foundations of higher education: Law and policy.* Washington DC, NASPA.

Lancaster, J. M., & Waryold, D. M. (2008). *Student conduct practice: The complete guide for student affairs professionals.* Sterling, VA: Stylus.

Library of Congress. (2018, June 27). *14th Amendment to the U.S. Constitution: Primary documents in American history.* Retrieved from https://www.loc.gov/rr//program/bib/ourdocs/14thamendment.html

Pavela, G. (2018). *Ten principles for members of student conduct hearing boards.* Retrieved from https://integrityseminar.org/wp-content/uploads/2018/05/Ten-Principles-Student-Conduct.pdf

Pennsylvania State University. (2019). *The code of conduct.* University Park, PA: Author.

Stoner, E. N., III, & Lowery, J. W. (2004). Navigating past the "spirit of insubordination": A twenty-first century model student conduct code with a model hearing script. *Journal Of College and University Law, 31*(1), 1–78.

StopHazing. (n.d.). Retrieved from http://www.stophazing.org/

Student organization conduct status report (n.d.). Retrieved from https://www.northwestern.edu/student-conduct/conduct-records/student-organization-conduct-status-report/index.html

University of Kansas. (2019). *Conduct status report for registered student organizations and university sponsored organizations.* Retrieved from https://studentconduct.ku.edu/conduct-status-report-registered-student-organizations-and-university-sponsored-organizations

University of Kentucky. (2016). *Code of student conduct.* Lexington, KY. Author.

Appendix 13.A

Methods of Gathering Information

The list that follows includes common methods for gathering information related to an organizational allegation. It is recommended, before you gather any information, you discuss with your in-house counsel or your senior administrators if your institution would require students to sign to affirm that they will provide truthful and accurate information as it relates to the investigation and clarify if information found to be inaccurate would the individual face an individual conduct process.

- *Questionnaire:* Students are provided a written questionnaire regarding the behaviors related to the allegation.
- *Phone/video interview:* Students may be unable to be present for an interview due to physical, emotional, or geographic constraints, or it may be more convenient to conduct a phone or virtual meeting.
- *In-person interviews:* When students are in your community, investigators can schedule the entire group to come in at one time and then proceed with individual interviews or schedule each student for an interview time. When scheduling a group to come in at one time

this method requires advanced planning to identify an appropriate block of time and to give the students enough notice to attend an interview and requires multiple investigators.

- *Follow-up interviews:* With any kind of interview or questionnaire, it may be necessary to follow up with students in regard to what they reported and/or because new information has been discovered.

Other considerations for gathering the information from students are to standardize the questions, which can include open-ended questions; to randomize a proportional sample of the members of a large group; and to use a participant form prior to an interview. The participant form can provide information on resources and the process as well as gauge how much information individual students are comfortable sharing (i.e., how detailed their written answers are in advance of the individual interview).

Single Investigator or Team

At times it is best to have a single investigator rather than a team. This is most beneficial in a case where there is a very limited number of students who need to be interviewed or when a more informal interview is conducted. Be sure to check on your institutional policies and if your policies dictate two-member interview teams. It is recommended to always have two in a room when resources allow it—one as lead and another for notetaking/back-up. Given limited resources, having a single investigator is acceptable. For those with limited staffing, you can train an investigative team that can be called on in order to investigate.

14

ACADEMIC INTEGRITY

Kara E. Latopolski and Tricia L. Bertram Gallant

Academic Integrity

As students develop into adults, they are bound to make choices while in college that may not always represent themselves to the best of their abilities. Just as in other endeavors, students may experience pitfalls in the classroom due to the actions they engage in that may at times constitute a violation of the college or university's policy on academic dishonesty. At many colleges or universities, academic dishonesty is primarily addressed through a student conduct system. This chapter is written for student conduct professionals in those institutions, rather than for student conduct professionals who work in institutions with separate honor codes or academic integrity offices within which there is little to no student conduct involvement. In such institutions where academic integrity falls under the student conduct policy or code, the student conduct professional plays a vital role in supporting the mission of the university in maintaining the integrity of academic work.

This chapter will equip these student conduct professionals to play this role in the academic integrity process. We will do this by reviewing the nature of academic integrity and why violations of academic integrity are different than nonacademic student misconduct. After a review of the factors that are shaping contemporary trends in academic misconduct, we will overview preferred practices for working with instructional staff and navigating the challenging conversations when meeting with students about academic violations. This chapter will conclude with some case studies that can be used in professional development sessions for student conduct professionals. It may be important to note here that the advice we give in this chapter should always be considered in the context of specific institutional policies that should ultimately guide behavior.

The Nature of Academic Integrity

According to the *Fundamental Values of Academic Integrity* (Fishman, 2014) "Integrity is strengthened within academic communities when community standards are aligned with the fundamental values and supported by its institutional policies and procedures" (p. 17). The role of the student conduct professional is to support the values of the university by supporting the institutional policies and procedures related to academic dishonesty. By doing this, the student conduct professional serves a critical role in achieving the mission and overall success of the university.

Student conduct professionals often work with students on a wide variety of issues that violate institutional policies. Many policy violations (the sale, distribution, or use of illegal narcotics, fighting, underage drinking, etc.) may constitute behavior that reflects poorly on the individual, may harm other students or the community, or may even be embarrassing to the university. While many of these policy violations may impact multiple members of the campus community, in the experience of the authors, these types of policy violations rarely have the same long-term impact on the university community as academic integrity violations because each incident of academic dishonesty diminishes the value of the degrees that students are earning and the pervasiveness of academic dishonesty undermines the morale of the entire student body and the faculty.

Academic integrity violations negatively impact other students by creating unfair advantages for those who engage in dishonest behavior in the classroom. These violations also negatively impact the faculty as the violation creates a breach of trust between the faculty member and the student, who have formed a relationship. Academic integrity violations cause additional harm as the faculty member's materials may have become compromised; faculty members frequently prohibit students from distributing classroom materials (e.g., assignments, exams, homework, and even notes) in an effort to deter academic integrity violations and encourage student learning. Course materials created by faculty for any course are the intellectual property of that faculty member. When this intellectual property is distributed without the permission of the faculty member, it also causes harm to the faculty member's reputation as an instructor and diminishes the value of the work the faculty member has done.

Essentially, when students engage in academic dishonesty the reputation of the institution is in peril, as the value of the degree decreases. Imagine how ocean waves erode a beautiful beach little by little over an extended period of time. What seems minimal, like the loss of a few grains of sand with each wave, can actually be highly impactful when the loss is compounded over an extended period of time. The same concept applies when considering academic integrity, as each incident of academic dishonesty erodes the value and credibility of the degree. Student conduct professionals must begin to think about the larger picture pertaining to academic integrity cases.

Issues and Trends

Academic integrity violations take many different forms. It is not possible to list all of the forms, nor is it necessary since most student conduct professionals will be aware of traditional types of cheating (e.g., homework copying, plagiarism, exam cheating). However, there are new violation types that do warrant discussion, as do the forces that are shaping them.

Contemporary student cheating is shaped by three main forces: technology, shifting definitions of *help*, and the educational landscape. Technologically smart devices (e.g., phones, watches) make cheating easier and more tempting for students (Bain, 2015; Marsh, 2017). Students are also using social media services to socially group in ways they never have before, which can be empowering, but these services also provide a platform for cheating that has not previously existed. Students can crowdsource (i.e., seek group input through the use of technology) answers to their homework questions, access answer keys to previously distributed exams, collude with other students on assignments, or access previously inaccessible solution manuals. These latter strategies have been enabled by "the cloud" (remote server storage), transforming fraternity or sorority "test banks" into file-sharing sites available to paying members and the completion of assignments by "tutors" that are available for a price.

This leads to a second force shaping cheating—a shifting definition of *help*. Parents have always "helped" their children with their schoolwork, and there has always been a fine line between helping and cheating. The shifting definition of help became apparent during the 2019 college admissions scandal, known as Operation Varsity Blues by law enforcement. In this scandal, the hired consultant and wealthy parents were simply "helping" their children gain admission to top-tier universities (Medina, Benner, & Taylor, 2019). Additionally, because of technology, as well as the desire of parents for their children to be successful, this notion of "help" has transformed social-circle cheating into a lucrative contract cheating industry (more on this later).

Finally, the landscape of higher education itself has shifted in the twenty-first century and reshaped cheating. Increasing class sizes in large universities and moving to hybrid or online courses make it easier and more tempting to cheat because students are, or feel, more anonymous. While Ullah, Xiao, and Barker (2016) overview the multiple ways that online exams can be corrupted, we know that plagiarism, contract cheating, copying, and collusion are common in both online and face-to-face classes (Alessio, Malay, Maurer, Bailer, & Rubin, 2017; Mellar, Peytcheva-Forsyth, Kocdar, Karadeniz, A., Yovkova, 2018; Peled, Eshet, Barczyk, & Grinautski, 2019).

The three forces outlined have instigated a revolution in the nature of cheating. *Contract cheating*, first termed by Thomas Lancaster and Robert Clarke (2016), is a booming business and probably the least familiar form of cheating. Contract cheating occurs when students arrange for another (the "provider") to complete their assessments (whether papers, tests, homework, etc.) for them that they then submit as their own work (Lancaster & Clarke, 2016). The forces have shifted this type of extreme cheating from rare and local (i.e., restricted to social circles) to increasingly common and global. In 2014, Owings and Nelson estimated that the contract cheating provider industry "has annual revenues somewhere upward of $100 million" (p. 2) and Ellis, Zucker, and Randall (2018) confirm that the contract cheating industry is very well organized and established with sophisticated and seductive strategies for luring in their customers. Newton (2018) estimates that there could be at least 31 million students worldwide engaging in paid contract cheating.

In contract cheating, the relationship between the client and the provider can look very formalized (e.g., providing the assignment prompt to another under contract for them to complete it) to informalized (e.g., engaging with a "tutor" for help on a particular question, which they solve and the student submits for credit). In fact, some companies will complete an entire class for a student. Either way, the providers present their services as a solution to a problem that the student has, whether that be a skill or time deficit (Rowland, Slade, Wong, & Whiting, 2018).

Student conduct professionals working with students—either to prevent violations or respond to them—should help students understand the risks they take in working with providers. It's not just the risk of cheating, but the risk of identity fraud, credit card theft, and selling personal information (Rowland et al., 2018; Sutherland-Smith & Dullaghan, 2019).

Working With Faculty and Instructional Assistants

Faculty and teaching or instructional assistants (IAs) are integral to ensuring academic integrity in the academy. Without faculty and IAs, preventing, detecting, and responding to academic integrity violations would be impossible. Cheating happens in direct relation to the teaching and learning environment—to the classroom—and it is the instructional staff who designs the course and the assessments, teaches the classes, gives instructions on how to complete assessments, monitors the completion of assessments, and grades the assessments. Since academic integrity falls under the domain of teaching and learning, it is primarily the responsibility of the faculty and, under their tutelage, the IAs. On most campuses, student conduct professionals are also involved and therefore must develop an awareness of the best practices for working with faculty and IAs in the preventing cheating and responding to academic integrity violations. (In some institutions, in fact, student conduct professionals might not be involved in academic integrity cases at all, such as in honor code schools or in institutions with academic integrity offices or with decentralized policies in which faculty and the academic administration primarily deal with academic integrity violations. See the first edition of this chapter (Drinan & Bertram Gallant, 2008) for more information about these different types.)

Student conduct professionals must be sensitive to the fact that most faculty and IAs do not want to be police officers, judges, or juries. They want to teach, assess learning, and maybe mentor. So, talk of preventing and responding to cheating can leave them with a feeling of dread and a disconnect with their own chosen profession. Therefore, student conduct professionals should avoid using legal-related language in the student conduct code and in conversations with faculty and IAs.

Student conduct professionals should also help faculty and IAs understand that when they are responding to cheating (by reporting), they are not functioning as police officers but as educators. Do this by conveying that faculty can shape student learning by responding to cheating; in other words, the faculty can use the "cheating moment as a teachable moment" (Bertram Gallant, 2017). For example, when an instructor or IA detect cheating and respond according to institutional policy, the student learns (a) that the institution cares about integrity; (b) that cheating is not a good strategy; and (c) that other people follow institutional policies and conduct codes (i.e., the instructor and IA). In this one interaction, a faculty member who doesn't normally teach ethics has taught the student about justice, fairness, responsibility, respect, and trustworthiness and about the courage to stand up for these values.

Along this same line, if faculty get the impression that employing technical or technological strategies (e.g., creating multiple versions of exams, checking IDs at exams, or using programs to detect potential issues in programming or narrative assignments) is the only way to prevent cheating, they'll feel less like educators and more like police officers. So, when talking about preventing cheating, student conduct professionals should not only provide faculty with strategies focused around the use of technology, but with ways in which they can teach and modify assessments to enhance integrity and learning (Bertram Gallant, 2017). Partnering with your campus teaching center would be helpful to develop teaching-for-integrity advice for your faculty.

It is also important to keep in mind that, in most institutions, faculty and IAs are not rewarded for attending to academic integrity. When they are asked to take time to prevent and respond to cheating, they are being asked to spend less time on the things for which they are rewarded (e.g., research, teaching evaluations, service). Finally, faculty may resist reporting because they worry about being accused of discrimination or fear retaliation by the student, such as through a poor evaluation or a lawsuit. Therefore, many faculty and IAs may resist reporting cheating and those who do report may be unhappy with the time they have to spend. The resolution process should take as little time from faculty and IAs as possible, while still ensuring due process and fairness for the students. The student conduct professional should expect to spend the time speaking with the student about the referral the faculty member has made and should inform the faculty member of the outcome. This will help the faculty member feel comfortable in making a referral for a student. Student conduct professionals should share their appreciation of the time faculty and IAs do have to spend; this could be as simple as an appreciation line in e-mails or as personal as an annual letter to individual faculty and IAs that they can use in their job, tenure, and promotion files.

Student conduct professionals can support faculty and IAs in other ways. They can provide educational support by holding annual awareness campaigns on the academic integrity policy and process, being available to give in-class presentations, and collaborating with faculty in other ways as they request.

Finally, given that academic integrity is a teaching and learning issue, faculty may question why there is a need for reporting to a central office, providing students due process, or meeting certain evidentiary standards. Student conduct professionals, who are required to be hyper attentive to such standards, must be prepared to explain these concepts in ways that educators can digest. Use the language of fairness and education. For example, a centralized process consistent for each student enhances fairness, which will make the process conducive for student learning. On evidentiary standards, convey that they are needed just as they are needed in research; as researchers would not draw conclusions on one piece of data but on the connections between points of data, we do not draw conclusions based on anything less than a "more likely than not" standard. Faculty need to be reassured that lawsuits are more unlikely if they follow institutional policy than if they do not, and if they do follow policy, they will be supported by the institution in the unlikely event of a lawsuit.

Navigating Challenging Conversations

It has been well researched and documented that students recognize that academic dishonesty is an issue that plagues the atmosphere at colleges and universities. In fact, more than two-thirds of college students acknowledged being involved in scholastic activity that constitutes academic dishonesty (McCabe, Trevino, & Butterfield, 2012). Despite this fact, having a conversation related to academic dishonesty with a student is one of the most challenging conversations a student conduct professional can have. This is due to the cognitive dissonance that exists within the act of engaging in academic dishonesty. Students understand that cheating is wrong but choose to engage in the behavior despite this knowledge (Stephens, 2017). Students also acknowledge that they would feel a great deal of shame should their peers and faculty find out that they have engaged in academic dishonesty; however, the pressure to obtain a needed grade may outweigh the risk of being caught and their behavior becoming exposed (McCabe et al., 2012). Given this information, it is important to be conscious regarding these facts when having a conversation about academic dishonesty allegations with a student, as a variety of factors may influence the student's reaction and perspective.

Due to the close connection students make with academic dishonesty being related to their character, students often have a challenging time having conversations about the actions in which they may have engaged. This is in stark contrast to the lack of connection to character that a student makes when engaging in other types of misconduct (e.g., drug use, alcohol consumption, fighting). The social norming surrounding academic integrity exists and greatly impacts the perspectives that students take regarding academic dishonesty (Stephens, 2017). Naturally, this then greatly influences how students are able to discuss academic dishonesty and how they view their own behavior (McCabe et al., 2012).

It is also critical to consider that student development impacts these conversations. Utilizing and understanding "A Framework for Addressing Academic Dishonesty," published by William Kibler (1993), may assist the student conduct professional in better understanding the student's perspective during some of the challenging parts of the conversation. By doing this, the student conduct professional may be able to have a conversation with a student that is more productive and educational in nature.

A more productive and educational conversation may also be facilitated by incorporating into the conversation the fundamental values of integrity honesty, trust, fairness, respect, responsibility, and the courage to uphold these values even when it is difficult (Fishman, 2014). By interweaving these values into the seams of the conversation that the student conduct professional has with each student, student understanding and connection with the topic at hand can improve. Think of the difference between talking to a student using phrasing like "It is alleged that you violated academic integrity" versus "The professor referred this case to us because of concern that the fairness of the assessment was compromised."

Once rapport has been established, the student conduct professional should provide an overview of the purpose of the meeting. If student conduct professionals are working in a system where they are the decision maker, it is important to provide students an overview of their procedural guarantees and possible outcomes of the meeting before the case is discussed and to allow students to ask any questions. Be sure to ask the student if they have any procedural questions. Take the time to go slowly, as different people process information at different speeds. By helping the student to understand the system, you are assisting the student to feel more at ease during the meeting.

Speak with the student about the incident that allegedly occurred. It is important that the student conduct professional be transparent with the student. Many students look at academic dishonesty as a he said/she said, "where's the proof?" situation. Simply because there is no police report, photos, and so on does not make what occurred any less real. The student conduct professional should gather all of the information from the instructor in advance and be aware of any related conversations that occurred between the student and instructor. These conversations between instructors and students are relevant to gather regardless of whether the institutional policy requires the instructor to meet with the student before reporting. The student conduct professional should share all of the documentation provided by the faculty with the student and give the student an opportunity to read the documentation. The student conduct professional should be prepared to redirect the conversation back to the documents provided by the faculty if the student becomes confrontational regarding what they perceive as a lack of evidence. Provide the student with the opportunity to review the college or university policy. Be cognizant of the student's needs; if the student needs additional support in having the documentation read to them, or a larger print copy, be prepared to meet these accommodations.

It is important that the student conduct professional be prepared to accept and understand the initial reaction of the student, which may be anger, defensiveness, or frustration. Students may have this reaction regardless of whether they are responsible for the academic integrity violation. While the student is speaking, it is important that the conduct professional stay quiet and allow the student the space to express their feelings. Many students will react by exclaiming that they aren't bad people, there is nothing wrong with their characters, they aren't cheaters, and so on. It is perfectly appropriate to reiterate that you are there to talk about allegations, that no decision has been made or will be made until the student has had an opportunity to share their position. It is also appropriate to state that even when students make mistakes, the mistake does not define who they are, and that they have an opportunity to grow as an individual and learn from the mistake. Human emotion simply does not prepare individuals to effectively communicate; persuasion and attentiveness are more effective tools than simply responding to an emotional reaction from a student (Patterson, Grenny, McMillian, & Switzler, 2002). The student conduct professional should be careful not to react emotionally to anything the student has said and to remain neutral.

Following the student's initial reaction, it is important that the student conduct professional demonstrates respect for the student. Listen attentively to the student; allow the student to share their full perspective on the incident in question. Provide the student with the space to speak by allowing for a long pause before you respond to ensure that they have completed their thoughts. It is critically important during this step that the student feel as though they have been heard. Acknowledge what the student is saying by summarizing what they have stated and allow the student to add additional or correct information.

If what the student shares does not match what the faculty member has shared, refer back to the information the faculty member has provided and ask appropriate questions; be neutral in approach. Give the student time to respond; ask a question and sit in silence to give the student time to gather their thoughts and answer. If what the student shares is in congruence with what the faculty member has shared in the documentation, thank the student for their honesty and their transparency. If the student continues to disagree with the information shared by the instructor, reinforce that you appreciate the student's discussion and perspective and that you will consider what they have shared with you.

At times, the student may express that they feel their instructor is prejudiced or biased against them or has a personal issue with the student. Do not dismiss these allegations but listen with care. Sometimes, what the student has alleged may hold some kernel of truth and so you should listen with discernment, not judgment. Faculty members are simply people with expertise in a particular field; they may or may not have engaged in the behavior the student is describing. Although there may be underlying issues between the faculty member and the student, these issues may not have influenced the referral they have made to the office regarding the allegations of academic dishonesty. Instead, let the student know that you are concerned about their experience and consider asking how what they have shared relates to the allegations the faculty member has made. Keep the focus of the conversation on the allegations as much as possible, while being careful not to dismiss or invalidate the concerns of the student. If the student's concerns may potentially fall under another university policy, provide the student the appropriate information on how to make a report. If the information the student has shared with you falls under your obligations as a mandatory reporter, tell the student that you are required to report the information that they have shared and explain that they will likely receive follow-up from the appropriate office. If this occurs, be sure to intentionally redirect the conversation back to discussing the referral the faculty member has made.

In closing the meeting, it is perfectly acceptable to share with the student that you may need time to reflect on the conversation and to consider what they have said before making a decision if you need additional time. Provide the student with a timeline as to when they can expect to reach a resolution and any rights of appeal to the decision that may result from that resolution. Thank the student for engaging in the conversation with you, recognizing that their time is valuable. Consider making any personal notes that reflect an objective view on the conversation, keeping in mind that these notes may not remain private and should be written as if others may read these notes in the future. Follow up with the student in the timeline you said that you would; be willing to answer any questions the student may have in the interim of time or after a resolution has been reached.

Conclusion

Maintaining the integrity of the degree is critical to the success of any college or university. On many campuses, the student conduct professional plays a vital role in supporting institutional success with integrity. By understanding academic dishonesty cases, working with faculty and instructional assistants, and navigating challenging conversations with students accused of cheating, the student conduct professional is playing a critical role in maintaining academic integrity as a university value that all students are expected to demonstrate.

References

Alessio, H. M., Malay, N., Maurer, K., Bailer, A. J., & Rubin, B. (2017). Examining the effect of proctoring on online test scores. *Online Learning, 21*(10), 1–14.

Bain, L. Z. (2015). How students use technology to cheat and what faculty can do about it. *Information Systems Education Journal, 13*(5), 92–99.

Bertram Gallant, T. (2017, April 1). Academic integrity as a teaching and learning issue: From theory to practice. *Theory Into Practice, 56*(2), 88–94.

Drinan, P. & Bertram Gallant, T. (2008). Toward a model of academic integrity institutionalization: Informing practice in postsecondary education. *Canadian Journal of Higher Education, 38*(2), 25-43.

Ellis, C., Zucker, I. M., & Randall, D. (2018). The infernal business of contract cheating: Understanding the business processes and models of academic custom writing sites. *International Journal for Educational Integrity, 14*(1), 1–21.

Fishman, T. (Ed.) (2014). *The fundamental values of academic Integrity* (2nd ed.). Des Plaines, IL: International Center for Academic Integrity. Retrieved from https://academicintegrity.org/wp-content/uploads/2017/12/Fundamental-Values-2014.pdf

Kibler, W. L. (1993). A framework for addressing academic dishonesty from a student development perspective, NASPA Journal, *31*(1), 8–18.

Lancaster, T., & Clarke, R. (2016). Contract cheating: The outsourcing of assessed student work. In T. Bretag (Ed.), *Handbook of Academic Integrity* (pp. 639–654). Singapore: Springer.

Marsh, S. (2017, April 10). More university students are using tech to cheat in exams. *The Guardian.* Retrieved from https://www.theguardian.com/education/2017/apr/10/more-university-students-are-using-tech-to-in-exams

Medina, J., Benner, K., & Taylor, K. (2019, March 12). Actresses, business leaders and other wealthy parents charged in U.S. college entry fraud. *New York Times.* Retrieved from https://www.nytimes.com/2019/03/12/us/college-admissions-cheating-scandal.html

Mellar, H., Peytcheva-Forsyth, R., Kocdar, S., Karadeniz, A., & Yovkova, B. (2018). Addressing cheating in e-assessment using student authentication and authorship checking systems: Teachers' perspectives. *International Journal for Educational Integrity, 14*(2), 1–21.

McCabe, D. L., Trevino, L. K., & Butterfield, K. D. (2012). *Cheating in college: Why students do it and what educators can do about it.* Baltimore, MD: Johns Hopkins University Press.

Newton, P. M. (2018). How common is commercial contract cheating in higher education and is it increasing? A systemic review. *Frontiers in Education, 3*(67), 1–18.

Owings, S., & Nelson, J. (2014). The essay industry. *Mountain Plains Journal of Business Economics and General Research, 15*, 1-21. Retrieved from http://www.mountainplains.org/articles/2014/General%20Research/Mountain_Plains_

Journal_of_Business_and_Economics_Volume_15_2014_1-21_General_ Research_Owings.pdf

Patterson, K., Grenny, J., McMillian, R., & Switzler, A. (2002). *Crucial conversations: Tools for talking when the stakes are high.* New York, NY: McGraw-Hill.

Peled, Y., Eshet, Y., Barczyk, C., & Grinautski, K. (2019). Predictors of academic dishonesty among undergraduate students in online and face-to-face courses. *Computers & Education, 131,* 49–59.

Rowland, S., Slade, C., Wong, K., & Whiting, B. (2018). "Just turn to us": The persuasive features of contract cheating websites. *Assessment & Evaluation in Higher Education, 43*(4), 652–665.

Stephens, J. M. (2017, April 1). How to cheat and not feel guilty: Cognitive dissonance and its amelioration in the domain of academic dishonesty. *Theory Into Practice, 56*(2), 111–120.

Sutherland-Smith, W., & Dullaghan, K. (2019). You don't always get what you pay for: User experiences of engaging with contract cheating sites. *Assessment & Evaluation in Higher Education, 44*(8), 1148–1162.

Ullah, A., Xiao, H., & Barker, T. (2016). *A classification of threats to remote online examinations.* IEEE 7th Annual Information Technology, Electronics and Mobile Communication Conference (IEMCON), Vancouver, BC.

Appendix 14.A: Case Studies

There are a number of pitfalls that new student conduct professionals can fall into when working with academic dishonesty cases. We will use case studies to illustrate common pitfalls such as the politics of working with faculty, working with influential and challenging students/parents, recognizing and adjudicating contract cheating, and issues with due process and appeals.

Case Study #1: Contract Cheating: Documentation and Talking About It

You are processing a new case of plagiarism. As you go through the case and the documentation, you begin to suspect that the student did not plagiarize but rather contracted someone else to complete the assignment for them. The paper has the telltale signs of contract cheating: unusual document properties, template headers, fabricated citations, sophisticated language, off-topic ideas, a Turnitin report that indicates the paper has matches to multiple papers submitted to multiple other schools, and bibliographic sources that are obscure or unassigned by the professor.

Thinking Critically
Consider the following questions:

- How would you go about documenting the evidence in this case?
- How would you start the conversation with the student when you meet to discuss?
- What are some key questions you would ask the student?
- If the student admits to contract cheating, how would you move the conversation?

Case Study #2: Faculty Resisting Reporting and Due Process

You are approached by a faculty member who wants to discuss a pervasive academic dishonesty issue that he has uncovered. The faculty member provides documentation that a group of 10 students have been engaging in academic dishonesty through at least a total of four 300–400 level courses. The faculty member is stating that these students utilized other students' work and submitted it as their own. This is made clear by the fact that the work is identical; one student even submitted the assignment of another student with that student's name still attached. The faculty member also discloses that the other faculty members in their department are reluctant to make a referral to your office for fear of ruining the students' lives; this case came to his attention because one of the teaching assistants alerted him. The faculty member shares with you that faculty members who do not refer students to your office for academic dishonesty have been either lowering the course grade of a student or giving them a zero on the assignment. Your campus has a policy that requires all faculty members to report academic integrity violations to the student conduct office.

Thinking Critically
Consider the following questions:

- How would you go about investigating and then adjudicating this case?
- What due process issues are present?
- How do you navigate the faculty politics? What pitfalls have you identified?
- How do you work with faculty members who are reluctant to refer students to your office for academic integrity violations?

Case Study 3: Lack of Clarity in Rules and Faculty-Administration Disconnect on Sanctions

You are approached by a faculty member who believes that two students have engaged in academic dishonesty because their homework appears identical.

The faculty member has not placed a policy regarding collaboration or academic dishonesty in their syllabus. The faculty member is upset and insists that something severe (e.g., expulsion) must be done because this has been happening all semester long. When you speak with the student, the student shares with you that they didn't know they couldn't work with others on their homework, that they have been doing their homework the same way all semester long, and the faculty member hasn't said anything indicating there is a problem.

Thinking Critically
Consider the following questions:

- What issues have you identified, and which is the most important?
- How would you go about resolving this case?
- Should the student be found responsible, what sanction is appropriate? If it is less than expulsion, how do you explain the outcome to the faculty member?
- What resources can you provide to the faculty member and to the student?

Case Study 4: Severity of Behavior/Sanctions

Your office is contacted by a faculty member regarding a dispute they recently had with a student that they are concerned about. After failing the course, the student approached the faculty member stating that their grade was incorrect. The student sends the faculty member what appears to be a screenshot of their grades for the course online. The faculty member keeps fastidious records both in their online module and privately, as well as retains electronically dated copies of the work that was turned in and is sure that the student is being dishonest. The faculty member tells the student that they have different grades recorded elsewhere. After learning this, the student tells the faculty member "Never mind, I'll just retake the class." You have checked, and the student does not have any prior conduct records, and has the class standing of a junior.

Thinking Critically
Consider the following questions:

- Are there other university offices that you should contact?
- How do you reconcile first-time violations with egregiousness of violation?
- Why is this behavior more severe than other incidents?
- How does this get explained to other university stakeholders that may contact your office?
- How would you talk to the student about this?

15

THOUGHTS ON THE FUTURE

John D. Zacker

What Does the Future Hold?

Looking into the future of higher education and the field of student conduct administration is an increasingly daunting task. Increasing proceduralism will continue to cause us to evaluate our current codes of conduct to determine how best to meet the educational and developmental needs of our students while balancing procedural requirements for due process and fairness. Legislative and regulatory intervention continues to increase every year and with it comes more work for undersized staffs to respond to reporting requirements. Parents and guardians have become immersed in their student's education and there is no sign of letting up. A growing number of students present behavior inside and outside the classroom that creates concern while the number of students with diagnosed and undiagnosed mental health issues continues to climb. And the "big four"—alcohol, drugs, sexual assault, and hazing—continue to be among our most vexing challenges.

In responding to so many pressing issues it seems that we hire more staff to respond to burgeoning caseloads and to pressing needs, but less time devoted to proactively preparing students for ethical decision-making in an increasingly complex society. It seems imperative that as a profession we should consider how to spend more time educating students on ethics, integrity, and developing character, with less time spent on adjudication. This will become more apparent as this "final" chapter proceeds.

Proceduralism

A critical question before us is "How much process is due in disciplinary proceedings?" I have observed over the past 40 years of practice in student affairs

258

a steady increased reliance on the adversarial model; thus, to some degree we are of our own making. With this increase in adversarialism comes a corresponding increase in procedures. While the use of alternative models such as restorative justice and mediation practices has increased, the vast majority of institutions base their adjudication models on a quasi-adversarial approach. Of course, elements of procedural fairness must be followed, but it would behoove us to undertake a careful evaluation of our codes of conduct to determine how they have grown in (excess) proceduralism and to determine how much is actually required in order to ensure fundamental fairness. Our first and foremost concern should be for the development and well-being of college students. Procedural fairness is a framework through which we administer rules and regulations of the campus, not the end goal.

Ever-increasing proceduralism does not necessarily promote educational and developmental goals. In my experience, many students seem willing to admit some degree of responsibility for misconduct and are accepting of consequences. Such cases should be resolved expeditiously and with particular attention to progressive disciplinary approaches, recognizing human fallibility while addressing developmental progression. Most misconduct cases are not suspension or expulsion cases and do not require the same level of proceduralism. Thus, more time should be spent in student conduct meetings discussing student success, wellness related issues, and ethical decision-making more than being hamstrung by procedures. It is, therefore, essential to understand the requirements of procedural fairness, but to balance it with our educational goals.

Legislative Intervention and Regulatory Requirements

As the founder of the then Association for Student Judicial Affairs (ASJA), now known as the Association of Student Conduct Administration (ASCA), Don Gehring warned many years ago that legislative intervention will continue to increase. He was so right! We can expect legislative and regulatory interventions to burden student conduct offices as a way of life – it will not go away. Many regulatory requirements necessitate reporting of data on any number of issues and must be provided by student conduct offices that are generally understaffed, particularly in the administrative areas. As regulations are being formulated it is wise to consider the potential impact and develop a plan for responding to future mandates, including considering necessary institutional resources to be allocated. Student conduct administrators should keep institutional leaders informed and educated about pending regulations that might affect student conduct programs and be prepared to present organizational and administrative proposals in order to properly respond.

Additionally, leadership of student affairs professional associations, particularly ASCA, should continue to make every effort to anticipate and respond to proposed legislation and regulatory requirements in an effort to balance goals of a proposal and the administrative impact on particularly small, understaffed college and university student conduct offices. Coordinated efforts with other professional associations have proven successful and will continue so in the future with effective leadership.

Parental Involvement

Should parents of our students be considered partners or the enemy? Often parents are viewed more of the latter than the former. Balancing the desire to promote students' adult development while at the same time responding to parents' desire to be overprotective has become a challenging juggling act. Gone are the days when parents or guardians dropped their student off at college with the expectation (or hope) of receiving a telephone call from the residence hall payphone once a week. Technology has created a virtual tether between parents/guardians and our students in ways that can be seen as both emotionally beneficial and potentially developmentally delaying independence. This is obviously the new reality, so how should we prepare?

In the absence of any form of parental expectations, we set ourselves for parents to dictate the terms. Institutions should consider adopting some form of relationship statement under which expectations are shared with parents—what parents/guardians can expect of the institution and what the institution can expect of parents/guardians. We should be clearer on the front end (upon admission) of the "role" parents/guardians play in the educational process, including privacy rights but also the developmental goal of helping young people become adults. It is not sufficient to merely say "We can't talk with you about your student because of FERPA/privacy rights."

It is helpful when considering the role of parents to put ourselves in that role. I recall several years ago a telephone conversation with a father of a student who was transported to the hospital for a psychiatric evaluation. This young woman had a history of suicidal threats of which her parents were aware. The father asked why he had not been informed of this transport, to which I responded in the usual way that "students are considered adults and therefore parents/guardians are not routinely notified." He then asked if I was a parent; I answered yes. After a discussion about our families he asked, "If your daughter were in this situation would you want to be notified?" My answer was yes. This caused me to initiate a discussion to evaluate whether parents should be informed under such circumstances. We now have a protocol that requires parents/guardians to be notified when their student is transported to the hospital for an emergency psychiatric evaluation. Over the past year since implementing this procedure there has not been one complaint from either students or parents/guardians, only compliments.

It may be time for us to reconsider our relationship with parents/guardians, not to overstep privacy laws but to better establish a "limited" partnership with parents/guardians in appreciation of the current generation of students and in consideration of their relationship with their parents/guardians.

Students of Concern

Behavior evaluation and threat assessment teams have grown not only in popularity but necessity. Over the past 15 years campuses have adopted various teams to evaluate concerning behavior and assess threat. It is difficult to measure degrees of success, but we do know anecdotally that evaluation or intervention teams have proven effective at addressing a population of students on campus who raise concern among other students, faculty, and staff.

Student conduct administrators play critical roles in either leading or serving as members of these teams. Often the types of concerning behavior are not necessarily disciplinary in nature, but require a careful evaluation through a student conduct lens. There is no reason to believe the case load associated with these students is going to abate anytime soon, and in fact we will see a continued increase as faculty, staff, and students report concerning behavior. Collaborative and cooperative teams will be essential in responding to these concerns and to determine if there is actionable conduct that warrants disciplinary action or more so, a nuanced approach based on the circumstances and possible underlying mental health issues. Working together with law enforcement to evaluate threats and to identify patterns of behavior that may be troublesome is essential.

As an extension of this topic, it has become important for student conduct officers to become more familiar with the identification of mental health signs and symptoms. More frequently, behavioral concerns that are referred to student conduct offices have an underlying mental health element. Being trained in mental health "first aid" could be a useful tool in promoting student success while addressing possible student conduct violations. If we are truly concerned about student success and well-being, disciplinary meetings can provide a unique opportunity to identify presenting issues and to support students.

Alcohol, Drugs, Sexual Assault, and Hazing

It seems the "big four" will continue to plague our campuses. Despite efforts across the country to address alcohol and drug use, hazing, and sexual assault there does not seem to be "model" programs to address any of them. While there are pockets of successful programs there seems to lack universal application or acceptance. A proliferation of online education tools offers some solace to institutional leaders that we are doing something about each of these problems, but overall impact is seems negligible on the number of cases.

During recent years institutions seem to have lost control over sexual assault adjudication through federal influence/intervention. No longer are sexual assault cases resolved through customary procedures and are now dictated by new procedures that involve special investigators hired to conduct inquiries that previously were conducted by student conduct administrator officers and/or hearing panels. It remains to be seen whether these procedures will sustain the current onslaught of legal challenges, but until a more effective alternative is developed that would meet both due process requirements and federal regulations, they are here to stay.

There should be concern that a similar fate may fall on our campuses if there continues to be tragedies related to alcohol, drugs, or hazing, particularly if due process requirements are not followed. The courts and legislators expect that student conduct administrators are competent at administering a fair and just disciplinary process. When we make unintentional mistakes in administering student disciplinary procedures, the door opens for others to question our ability to properly hear these cases. While I am not questioning the competence of student conduct colleagues, it is a warning that we must stay vigilant by carefully evaluating every case to ensure fundamental fairness and that we follow our proscribed processes.

These four issues present opportunities for collaborative preventive measures. Partnering with fraternity and sorority life staff to create an effective "premembership" education effort that incorporates elements of bystander intervention and empowering prospective members to walk away from activities that they find objectionable would be constructive. This certainly should be extended to other areas of the campus including athletics, club sports, clubs/organizations, honor societies, university bands, ROTC, and so on. Student conduct officers can play a lead role in initiating these efforts.

Our collaborative efforts with drug and alcohol prevention efforts on campus has produced positive results and should continue with particular attention to potentially impactful intervention programs. Joining with student activities staff to create "alternative" programming after dark on Thursdays through Saturday may be a productive effort. Through funding generated from the sale of alcohol in our football stadium and basketball arena, the University of Maryland creates "Terps After Dark," a six-week effort to create campus-wide programming during those critical first six weeks of the fall semester. While overall impact is still being measured, the sheer volume of students attending these events is impressive. Student conduct officers can be leaders in this kind of effort and at the very least contributing participants.

And finally, working with campus leaders to develop a more sustained and comprehensive approach to sexual assault education and prevention should be a high priority. Through the adjudication of sexual assault cases, student conduct officers have a unique perspective on our student's behavior and the factors affecting their decision-making. While requirements to complete online education programs provide some solace, we cannot assume such one-time interventions will solve the problem. Student conduct officers play a essential role in promoting prevention efforts.

Effectiveness and Efficiency

An administrative function that has grown in importance is assessment, particularly measures of both efficiency and effectiveness. As noted in chapter 8, assessment is critical to provide evidence of the work being performed—how well we do what we say we do. Student conduct administration on every campus is a vital function, but in order to enhance programs and services to better meet the changing climate, evidence and data is essential.

Student conduct offices now utilize sophisticated databases to manage many of the administrative functions and often interface with student data from the institution's student information systems. But collecting and retaining data is only as good as the analysis of the data. At many institutions data is collected, but there is typically insufficient staff to analyze the data. There should be attention to creating capacity to evaluate demographic data, look for trends, and employing predictive analytics that might help us to develop early interventions as a long-term goal.

How do we know we are effective? What actually is effective? Answering either question requires thoughtful goals for the student conduct process. I expect many of us can articulate lofty goals, but are they actually achievable and do they drive the process? Some colleagues employing principles of restorative justice have clearly stated goals to attempt to achieve, but for many there may not be articulated goals. In the ideal world with countless resources we could craft a longitudinal approach, following up with students over time. We rarely have the ability to perform such research, so assessment is usually performed immediately after a disciplinary intervention or shortly thereafter. Wouldn't it be great if we could perform an additional assessment six months to a year later, allowing for students to reflect? This may be possible with a carefully developed assessment plan, but it all begins with goals.

Another challenge we are faced with is providing evidence of impact. I have been an ardent defender of alternative or "educational" sanctions. As an educator, such tailored sanctions provide an opportunity to meet the developmental and disciplinary goals of each student. While imposing a fine might be efficient at punishment and deterrence, does it affect ethical judgment? To my knowledge, however, there has not been a study of the efficacy of alternative sanctions over punitive actions. I am not suggesting that we abandon alternative sanctions, but to first identify the goal to be achieved through the sanction and second to measure the impact. There is heavy human resource expenditure when using developmentally appropriate sanctions. We should be able to show some evidence that they actually have the intended effect.

Recognizing Who We Are

First and foremost, student conduct officers are student development educators; this is precisely why many of us entered this field. Increasingly, however, we spend more time managing processes and procedures that are sometime overly legalistic than working with students. The litigious nature of our society has pushed us to responding with increasing adversarial processes while the courts continue to push more legal requirements onto institutions. The professional pendulum needs to be pushed away from increasing legalism back toward the education and developmental focus. We do not need to hire more lawyers to administer student conduct programs on college campuses, but more student development educators as competent administrators. I am not suggesting getting rid of the lawyers—some of my best friends are lawyers (seriously). The priority, however, should be on the role of educator who has a firm understanding and confidence of fundamental rights of fairness in campus disciplinary proceedings. This requires keeping abreast with current case law and its applicability in our educational settings.

There must be greater recognition from institutional leaders and senior student affairs officers of the importance of the role student conduct administrators play on campus. Frequently in student affairs units, comparisons are made of the relative size of a budget and staff. Thus, often student conduct administrators are among the lowest paid in the division of student affairs, yet they carry some of the greatest institutional liability. There should be greater recognition of the education, training, and significant administrative responsibility for managing increasing complex rules and regulations both in recruiting talented staff and in retaining them. This is hard work! Student conduct administrators must educate and demonstrate to senior student affairs officers the degree of professional knowledge, experience, and skills that are necessary to do this work. This in turn should result in recognition of the vital role these administrators play and the importance of being compensated accordingly.

Likewise, staff holding these positions should be able to demonstrate a high degree of competence. There should be greater recognition of the skills and abilities sought to be a successful student conduct officer. ASCA could be instrumental in this endeavor by developing and promulgating a list of "core competencies" that could be used by hiring officials to "measure" levels of competence. This list could be rank ordered by levels of importance as determined by the profession association. Such competency lists could become the foundation of a certification process or at a minimum a professional "badging." In addition, ASCA could work with faculty in student affairs professional preparation programs to incorporate a law and policy course as a requirement for graduate work in this field, a minimum for being employed in the student conduct field.

The field of student conduct administration generally attracts young professionals who use the position as a stepping-stone to the next student affairs position rather than seasoned professionals making a career move. The field seems to have difficulty attracting professionals from other student affairs areas to move into student conduct. Resident life professionals are the most apt to have some of the necessary requisite background to make the change, but rarely from other functional areas. ASCA should consider the pipeline to better recruit good professionals, which might include an "identity" issue. Over the years when I have introduced myself as working in student conduct there is usually a groan: "Who would want to work in student conduct?!" Through working with masters' students in our professional preparation program, I have been successful at "recruiting" a number of graduate students to consider student conduct, some who have been quite successful and happy in this work.

Integrity, Character, and Ethics

This leads to ultimately what I assert are the goals of any student conduct office—to promote integrity, character, and ethics in the college students with whom we interact as well as the broader campus population. Whether it is through individual student contact, work with student hearing officers/board members, or through programmatic efforts across campus, the core of our work should incorporate these values. Fundamentally, it is what we do.

Student conduct administrators have the ability to impact integrity, character, and ethics in ways that many on campus do not. But this is largely focused on a small population of the campus—those who are referred for disciplinary violations. I would advocate for more time being spent on campus in the role of ethics educators rather than disciplinary officers. All too often colleagues lament the caseload as the reason they cannot spend more time in ethics education. We should evaluate the organization and staffing of our offices to create more time for this endeavor rather than less, and senior student affairs officers should be supportive.

Disciplinary discussions provide a platform to confront students about their lapse in ethics, but to also challenge them to consider their character. Do they want to be remembered as a cheater? A drug user? A thief? My dear friend and colleague Gary Pavela taught me to use a testimonial exercise with students to consider their character. Students are asked to write a testimonial that would be given at a retirement event attended by family, friends, and colleagues, answering the simple question, "What would you want people to say about you?" As one can imagine, when contemplating this question there is never the response "I made a lot of money and drive a big car." The types of phases include "a good friend," "caring and loving parent," "gave back to the community," "compassionate," "honest," "hardworking," and the list goes on. No one is perfect and we must recognize human fallibility. Underlying this indiscretion, no matter how small or large, there is character. It is at this moment that we have the opportunity to make an impact whether students realize it or not.

Role of Students in Student Conduct Administration

We have a unique opportunity to involve students in the administration of student conduct programs. Undergraduate and graduate students can play important roles as members of a student conduct panel or honor council. There may be a tendency to reduce or minimize their roles in lieu of full-time or graduate assistant staff. But students properly trained can and do play critical roles in the adjudication process. Students can do the following:

- Conduct "preliminary" meetings to introduce respondents to the disciplinary process, explaining the campus rules
- Serve on hearing panels as the majority sitting in judgment of their peers—often, our students are more harsh than faculty and staff in sanctioning
- Present cases of alleged misconduct to hearing panels as "advocates"
- Comprise appellate bodies
- Serve as members of an office/program educational team conducting workshops, presentations, and developing messaging and communication strategies

It is important to remind ourselves that these same 18–24-year-old traditional-aged students can and are empaneled to serve on jury trials, including the most serious criminal cases. Appointing them to serve in various roles not only creates a sense of community responsibility but also an avenue for leadership and ethical development of significant proportions. We should be developing more opportunities for students to be actively involved in the life of the student conduct office, not less. While it certainly takes time to prepare students for critical roles in student conduct administration, it is well worth the effort. Just ask any of our students who have served in such roles to reflect back on their experience and you will hear firsthand the incredible impact on them.

Professional Temperament

I was taught and trained as an educator and administrator. I am not a lawyer, although I have been accused of being one. It is through the lens of an educator that I view this work. Working in this field has allowed me to develop skills in fact-finding, decision-making, policy analysis, and, most important, judgment. These skills came through experience and trial and error. Yes, we all make mistakes. Looking back on my experiences there have been countless colleagues who provided professional wisdom. As a profession, we need to capitalize on colleagues who have developed a professional temperament and have wisdom to share with younger generations of professionals. Too often we move through the professional ranks and lose sight of our roots. But if we are to be truly generative as a profession, there should be greater opportunity for younger colleagues to engage with more "senior" professionals in the field.

Not everyone is cut out for this work, but it is important work. Future generations of student conduct administrators will be challenged by these issues and more. This work requires competence and confidence—competence at the core skills and abilities and the confidence to know what is right and to be willing to admit when you are wrong. At the core, promoting ethics, integrity, and character should drive our work. Without them, we resort to being bureaucratic functionaries rather than student development educators.

CONCLUSION

Challenges and Changes

James M. Lancaster and Diane M. Waryold

As we noted in our introduction, 12 years ago we coedited an edition of this book. It was based, in part, on our own prior edition as well as still earlier iterations by other editors and contributors. The book was then, and is now, designed as a guide to the practice of student conduct. The basics of this edition may appear similar to those of the earlier version, but the breadth and number of issues unanticipated 12 years ago is surprising. Though newer topics included here reflect those topical changes, the "established" law itself continues to evolve as well.

The late associate justice of the U.S. Supreme Court, Benjamin Cardozo (1922), wrote that "law never is, but is always about to be" (p. 80). So long as student conduct professionals are involved with the legal issues inherent in their work, they will need to understand not only the law at any single moment, but the law as it is interpreted, understood, and executed in relation to their practice. They will need to constantly consider the new, emerging topics we have included in this edition as well as those issues not yet on our horizon. Equally of concern, they will always need the understanding of self and the clarity of purpose so important to making good and fair use of the law, especially as it is influenced by new challenges in student behavior and in our society. Most importantly of all, they constantly will be in need of guidance, reflection, and meaning-making in order to serve their students, as well as their communities, institutions, and conscience. In the history of our profession, this has never been more important.

With this book, we hope you'll find that we have addressed these concerns and, in doing so, have helped to provide a source of thoughtful ideas about the state of practice in this field, no matter where you find yourself on your professional journey.

In 1992, Joe Kavanagh, a strategic planning consultant for the then Association for Student Judicial Affairs (the predecessor to the Association for Student Conduct Administration) characterized student conduct professionals as members of the "besieged clan" (D.M. Waryold, personal communication, July 30, 2019), frequently alone in understanding and defending their professional practices in student conduct work. This sometimes is still the case. In such times, it is good to remember the value of good colleagues. We invite readers to think of the many wise and thoughtful colleagues involved in this field. We hope you will come to see the authors of this edition of our book as wise and thoughtful individuals, gathering us around the communal fire of experience and knowledge, seeking to smooth the path of those with whom they share this journey. Whether you consider yourself as a member of a "besieged clan" or, more hopeful, as important members of this community of practice, we need one another in the ongoing exploration of wisdom in our practice.

As the editors of this updated version, we have sought to ensure that it will serve not only the needs of those newly entering the profession, but also of those continuing professionals who seek guidance or renewal, and of others who are simply interested in the "why and how" of student conduct administration. If there is a summary take-away for this edition, it is this: Students change, their conduct always presents challenges, and those who practice student conduct must constantly evolve to meet these ever-emerging needs.

New professionals, years ago, when first challenged with student conduct resolution, might have naively believed that what they were doing in this practice was unique to their institution, perhaps based on whim or local culture rather than anything more substantive. But today's practitioners can suffer no such delusions. Through discovering ASCA, the writings of scholars such as Peggy Barr, Don Gehring, Gary Pavela, and others, as well as the commitment and support of other long-standing professionals in the field, members of this profession have come to understand the "how and why" of what those who seek to excel in this work with students are trying to accomplish. The chapters in this book are designed to fulfill the same purpose of furthering the development of the profession and the professionals who administer student conduct on campuses.

As we noted, this profession, well based and more mature than in those earlier days, nevertheless is still evolving and changing, as we point out in chapter 1. While our authors have sought to be inclusive of these changes and trends, it is also true that the most important knowledge we offer in this book should be the realization that change is inevitable. Those who fail to recognize and respond to this reality will ultimately fail in this work. Thus, continual learning and adaptation must become an ingrained part of the personal and professional philosophy we offer in chapter 2.

But philosophy is critical, not only for best practice but also for self-pres-ervation, especially when a third party (your supervisor, a trustee or, even, a federal justice) asks, "Why do you do what you do in this work?" The time to consider that question is long before anyone chooses to pose it. That answer often is not simple. It involves combining that philosophy with knowledge of codes, law, and policy (see chapters 3 and 4) and principles of resolution (chapter 5), undergirded by our commitment to a sense of social justice and ethics (chapters 6 and 7). The synthesis we hope readers will see among these topics will be critical, not only in justifying our work to others, but also in clarifying our approach to the many topical issues our authors have addressed in the remainder of this book, in chapters 8 through 15.

Recognizing that most of these topics are in flux means that some foun-dational bedrock of professional standards and personal beliefs must be avail-able to cling to when the rising waters of controversy, dispute, and anger threaten to drive us to accept "easy" answers for complex challenges. The earlier chapters of his book are designed to provide some of the needed philo-sophic and structural bases for the discussions that should arise from the later, topical chapters.

Our colleague, Gary Pavela, always a wise counselor to our field, cites the advice given to him from then federal court of appeals justice Alfred P. Murrah, reminding us to hear cases before deciding them (G. Pavela, personal communication, October 1, 2019). We further encourage you to reflect on two questions as you hear cases: what matters here and what am I trying to accomplish? The answers to these questions should be easily discerned by students engaged in your processes and by any third parties who might be called to observe the manner in which you apply your own professional philosophy and practice to the issues, policies, and procedures we discuss throughout this book. The synthesis of these many parts should inform every day of your practice, regardless of how serious or trivial a student's situation may seem.

As this book goes to press, our society is riven with divisions as difficult as most readers will have witnessed in their lifetimes. College administrators, and especially those working in student conduct administration, may doubt that they can do anything to mend the tears in our social fabric through this work they have chosen. They may feel that their efforts in this work really do not matter in attempting to resolve some of these larger differences. The reality is very different: If you are involved in changing one or two lives at a time while bringing resolution to their conflicts, you may reasonably hope for that life, so changed, to make a difference in the future of the community.

We are fortunate to have the opportunity for initiating such change in every day of our work.

We hope you will be prompted to read, to reflect, to discuss, and to apply the ideas expressed in this book with colleagues, students, and others who might join you around that earlier-referenced "communal fire." The late Alan Turing (2014) has been said to have noted, "Sometimes it is the people no one can imagine anything of who do the things no one can imagine."

We encourage you to imagine and to believe that in your work you can do such things.

References

Cardozo, B. N. (1922). *The nature of the judicial process*. Hartford, CT: Yale University

Turing, A. (2014). *As portrayed in "The imitation game."* New York, NY: Weinstein.

CONTRIBUTORS

Jonathan M. Adams, a native Alabamian, currently serves as the director of student conduct and outreach at The University of Alabama at Birmingham. In his current role, he coordinates the university's student conduct processes and nonclinical case management system. With over 12 years of experience in higher education and student affairs, he has worked with policies and practices related to student conduct, behavior intervention, threat assessment, sexual misconduct, organizational misconduct, academic integrity, freedom of expression, and residence life. Prior to joining UAB, he served as the residence community director and conduct coordinator at Southern Methodist University in Dallas, Texas; the assistant director of student conduct and safety outreach at the University of North Carolina (UNC) at Charlotte; the associate director of student conduct at Appalachian State University in Boone, North Carolina; and the associate dean of students and director of student conduct and academic integrity at UNC Charlotte. During his professional career, he has held leadership positions in several professional associations, including NASPA, ASCA, and ACPA, and currently serves as an ASCA representative to the Council for the Advancement of Standards in Higher Education (CAS) Council of Representatives. He is also certified through the NASPA Student Affairs Law and Policy certification, has completed the National Incident Management System certification, and has attended the Donald D. Gehring Academy for Student Conduct Administrators on multiple occasions. He earned a Bachelor of Arts in political science (2005) and a Master of Arts in higher education administration (2007) from The University of Alabama.

Reyna M. Anaya is the dean of students at the Community College of Aurora (CCA) and is proud to serve and work at the most racially and ethnically diverse college in Colorado. Prior to her time at CCA, Reyna served as the assistant director of community standards and conflict resolution at the University of Northern Colorado (UNC) from 2013 to 2018. As a conduct administrator, Reyna served on the Association for Student Conduct Administration (ASCA) Diversity and Inclusion Task Force and was selected as a 2018 faculty fellow and 2019 faculty member for the ASCA Donald D. Gehring Academy for Student Conduct Administration. Reyna received her doctorate in the higher education and student affairs leadership in 2019 and Master of Arts in educational leadership and policy studies in 2009 from

UNC. Reyna also is a past attendee of the Social Justice Training Institute (2016) and a published scholar, with works focused on intersectionality in graduate school for graduate student mothers of color and self-care in higher education. Last and most importantly, Reyna is the mom of three to Aiyana, Mateo, and Antonio.

Patience L. Bartunek is the director for student conduct at the University of Mount Union where she has served since 2016. In this role, Patience oversees the student conduct process for the institution and works closely with the Title IX coordinator to facilitate that process. Since coming to the university, Patience has been tasked with updating and developing student conduct policies and practices as well as revamping the student conduct board and its training. Patience also has responsibility for advising gender equity matters and working with the diversity council in the areas of programming and advocacy. Prior to her time at the University of Mount Union, Patience served as the director of student conduct at Arkansas State University for 10 years. Patience received her Master of Education degree in college personnel services from the University of South Carolina and a Bachelor of Arts in English from Allegheny College. Patience has served as a faculty fellow for the 2017 ASCA Donald D. Gehring Academy and as a faculty member in the Mary Beth Mackin Foundations of Professional Practice Track for the 2018 ASCA Donald D. Gehring Academy.

Jeffrey A. Bates serves as an assistant director for student conduct at The University of Alabama at Birmingham. He received a bachelor's degree in early childhood and special education from Lebanon Valley College and a master's degree in college student development from Appalachian State University, where he worked with both residential education and student conduct. He has previously held positions in student conduct and residence life at Tulane University and the University of South Carolina. He is an active member of the Association for Student Conduct Administration (ASCA), having served on the conference committee and as a presidential graduate intern, and was recognized in 2018 with the Graduate Student of the Year award. In his daily work, he is committed to encouraging moral and ethical development in order to foster an environment that holistically supports the growth and success of all students.

Lee E. Bird served as the vice president for student affairs at Oklahoma State University, Stillwater for 18 years and led numerous functional areas, including the student union, campus life, university counseling, health services, career services, dining, residential life, student conduct education and administration, and the Department of Wellness. Dr. Bird continues to serve as an adjunct professor in OSU's Student Development graduate program. She received her doctorate from the University of Arizona in 1991. She has worked in some aspect of student affairs for 41 years. Dr. Bird serves as the president of the National Board of Directors for the Association of Student Judicial Affairs (now ASCA) and coauthored *The First Amendment on Campus: A Handbook for College and University Administrators* (2006), published by NASPA. In addition, she has authored and coauthored numerous book chapters on responding to emergencies and the First Amendment. Dr. Bird received both the Donald D. Gehring award and the Parker D. Young award for her work with the Association for Student Conduct Administration. She served on the University of Vermont's board of advisers for the Legal Issues in Higher Education conference for over a decade. Dr. Bird consults and speaks regularly on topics including student conduct, campus threat assessment, crisis management, and the First Amendment rights of students. Bird previously served as the vice president of the Colorado Chapter of the Association of Threat Assessment Professionals. She is a member of Phi Beta Delta Honor Society for International Scholars in recognition of her work in Chinese higher education. Bird served as the chair of the OSU behavioral consultation team and the Students of Concern committee from their inception until her retirement. Dr. Bird is a FEMA community emergency response team (CERT) and incident command instructor trainer. Since her retirement in 2019, Bird completed training as an EMT and is a nationally registered EMT and active volunteer with the American Red Cross and other emergency response agencies.

Patience D. Bryant is the director for student conduct and ethical development at California State University, Long Beach, where she oversaw the creation and implementation of the university's first restorative justice program, WAVE (Welcoming Accountable Voices and Education), and serves as the university's chief judicial officer. Dr. Bryant holds a doctorate in conflict analysis and resolution from Nova Southeastern University and previously worked at the University of Mississippi and Texas A&M University, Commerce where she led the introduction of restorative justice to their traditional student conduct processes. During the summer of 2018, Dr. Bryant was featured as a contributing author in the ACUHO-I/ASCA collaborative book *Conduct and Community: Residence Life Practitioners Guide*. Dr. Bryant serves as a faculty member for the ASCA Donald D. Gehring Academy and as the director of education for the ASCA board of directors.

Catherine L. Cocks has been a student affairs professional for over 30 years. She is currently a higher education consultant and an associate with D. Stafford & Associates, focusing on student conduct, threat assessment, and Title IX. Cathy was the director of community standards for the University of Connecticut for 14 years. She oversaw and managed the student conduct process and chaired the student care team, the university's student threat assessment team. Prior to that, she held several positions within residential life at the University of Connecticut and Roger Williams University. She is a faculty member for the Association for Student Conduct Administration's (ASCA) Donald D. Gehring Academy, teaching on subjects such as ethics, governance, threat assessment, and higher education trends. She was an affiliated faculty member for many years in the University of Connecticut's Higher Education and Student Affairs Master's program, teaching The Law, Ethics, and Decision-Making in Student Affairs.

Cathy was the president of the ASCA from 2018 to 2019. Other involvement in ASCA has included serving as a circuit representative, cochair of the Public Policy and Legislative Issues committee, and member of the ASCA Expectations of Members Task Force. Cathy was a member of the writing team for *CAS Standards' Cross-Functional Framework for Identifying and Responding to Behavioral Concerns*. She has served in a variety of leadership roles in NASPA Region I. She was the 2015 recipient of ASCA's Donald D. Gehring award. She is a past recipient of the NASPA Region I Mid-Level Student Affairs Professional award and the NASPA Region I Continuous Service award. She earned her master's degree in higher education administration from the University of Connecticut and her bachelor's degree in communications/media from Fitchburg State University.

Regina D. Curran currently serves the Title IX program officer for American University. Regina began her career in higher education during law school by serving as a graduate assistant to the Office of Student Conduct and Community Standards at Roger Williams University. Since that time Regina has worked in student conduct, conflict resolution services, and Title IX at Coastal Carolina University; St. Mary's College of Maryland; Towson University; University of Maryland, College Park; and American University. Regina received her law degree from Roger Williams University in Bristol, Rhode Island, and a bachelor's degree in sociology from Texas A&M University in College Station, Texas. She is a certified mediator and has trained students and professionals to mediate campus conflicts. Regina has been an active member with the Association for Student Conduct Administration throughout her career, serving in several leadership roles including conference committee roles and director of diversity and inclusion on the board of directors. Currently, she is an affiliated instructor with the Clery Center. Regina also provides training on topics including preventing and responding to sexual harassment in the workplace, assertive communication in the workplace, student conduct practice through a critical lens, and collaboration between law enforcement and campus administrators.

Derrick D. Dixon is the assistant director for conflict resolution and student conduct for the University of Mississippi where he has served since 2013. In this role, Dr. Dixon oversees the student conduct/conflict resolution process for the Department of Student Housing. Since coming to the university, Dr. Dixon has been tasked with updating and developing student conduct practices as well as implementing conflict resolution programs both campus wide and within student housing. He has also gained extensive experience utilizing conflict resolution practices including but not limited to conflict coaching, mediation, restorative justice and other methods of alternative dispute resolution. Outside of the University of Mississippi, Dr. Dixon is actively involved with the Association of Student Conduct Administration. During the summer of 2018, Dr. Dixon was featured as a contributing author in the *Conduct and Community: Residence Life Practitioners Guide*. The chapter coauthored by Dr. Dixon primarily focused on crafting and revising conduct processes. Additionally, Dr. Dixon served as a faculty member for the Restorative Justice Track at the 2018 ASCA Donald D. Gehring Academy and as the track coordinator for the Advanced Restorative Justice track at the 2019 Donald D. Gehring Academy. These experiences have also led to Dr. Dixon serving as a regional and national consultant for various institutions.

Brent E. Ericson is currently serving as the assistant dean of students and director of student conduct at George Mason University in Fairfax, Virginia. He has worked in higher education and student affairs for nearly 20 years and has expertise in student conduct, academic integrity, sexual misconduct, learning outcomes assessment, strategic planning, residence life, threat assessment and behavioral intervention, and mediation, and he has advised on legislation at both the state and federal levels. Brent earned his bachelor's degree from Augustana College (Illinois) and his Master of Science degree from Indiana University, and a doctorate from Boston College, where his research focused on college students and social media. Outside of work, Brent is a budding home chef and enjoys hiking in the Virginia countryside with his family.

Tricia Bertram Gallant has over 24 years of experience in higher education, including 16 years in the field of academic integrity. As the director of the

Academic Integrity Office (AIO) at the University of California, San Diego, Tricia has managed over 8,000 academic integrity violation allegations and enabled over 3,500 students to leverage the cheating moment as a teachable moment. As a volunteer, Tricia has served the International Center for Academic Integrity (ICAI) since 2002, including as a graduate student and general member of the board of directors, member and chair of the advisory council, and cochair of the Transition committee. In her capacity with ICAI, Tricia co-led the creation of regional consortiums, led the Academic Integrity Rating Systems (AIRS) project, participated in the development of the Trusted Seal program, led the development of the Academic Integrity Reader and the Contract Cheating Advocacy project, and is current cochair of the board's content committee. Tricia is the inaugural winner of ICAI's Tricia Bertram Gallant award for outstanding service, awarded in 2018. In addition to her practical work in the field, Tricia has authored, coauthored, or edited numerous articles, book chapters, book sections, and books on academic integrity. She is author of *Academic Integrity in the Twenty-First Century: A Teaching and Learning Imperative* (2008), coauthor of *Cheating in School: What We Know and What We Can Do* (2009), editor of *Creating the Ethical Academy: A Systems Approach to Understanding Misconduct and Empowering Change in Higher Education* (2011), and section editor and author for the *Handbook for Academic Integrity* (2015). Tricia has used her experiences and knowledge to help faculty, students, and administrators around the world to develop academic integrity systems, build cultures of integrity, manage academic integrity processes and offices, revamp online and face-to-face classrooms to reduce cheating and enhance integrity, and teach students about academic integrity, professional ethics, and ethical decision-making.

Michael R. Gillilan has been Ball State University's (Muncie, Indiana) director of student conduct since 2010. Prior to arriving at Ball State, Mike was the associate vice president for student affairs and dean of students at St. Cloud State University in Minnesota. Mike was inspired to a career in student affairs while a resident assistant at the University of Missouri, where he earned bachelor's degrees in education and English. He completed a master's program in student affairs at Western Kentucky University while working as a residence hall director. Mike completed his doctorate in higher education administration at Bowling Green State University (Bowling Green, Ohio). While a graduate student, Mike trained as a volunteer rape hotline counselor in Bowling Green, Kentucky. That experience led to a career-long (33 years) involvement in sexual assault prevention and sexual misconduct complaint resolution. For instance, he led Quinnipiac University's role in the 1987 Rape Awareness project along with several other universities in southwest Connecticut, and he chaired his first sexual misconduct hearing in 1991. At Ball State, Mike coordinated sexual assault investigation and adjudication procedures until a new Title IX office was created in 2012. His office now adjudicates sexual misconduct complaints after investigations are completed by the Title IX office. Mike's other responsibilities include review of applicants who disclose felonies, behavioral intervention, and Clery Act compliance.

Mike has served ASCA by reviewing conference program proposals and participating on the Dissertation of the Year award committee. He was a faculty member for the 2016 Sexual Misconduct Institute in Kansas City and the Advanced Sexual Misconduct Track at the 2018 Gehring Academy.

Brian M. Glick currently serves as associate director for student conduct at Northern Illinois University, located in DeKalb, Illinois, where he investigates and adjudicates alleged violations of the student code of conduct. He also supervises conduct operations for the office. Previously, he served in residence life positions at Southeast Missouri State University and Elmhurst College. Dr. Glick's doctoral research established that the practice of student conduct is a profession, as defined by published criteria. Glick earned a doctorate in education from Northern Illinois University, a Master of Science degree in college student personnel administration from University of Central Arkansas, and a Bachelor of Arts degree in communication from Kansas State University.

Kristen A. Harrell currently serves as an associate director in the Office of the Dean of Student Life at Texas A&M University in College Station. Dr. Harrell's responsibilities include supervision of the Student Conduct Office, GLBT Resource Center, and Women's Resource Center. Dr. Harrell holds a Bachelor of Science degree in psychology from the University of Washington, a Master of Science degree in student affairs in higher education from Colorado State University, and a Doctor of Philosophy in higher education administration from Texas A&M University. Dr. Harrell's dissertation was titled *Nonverbal Indicators of Sexual Consent in College Students* and was awarded the Dissertation of the Year award by ASCA in 2019. During Dr. Harrell's 20 years as a student affairs professional, she has worked in residence life, conduct, and alcohol and other drug prevention. Dr. Harrell has supervised numerous functional areas including an interpersonal violence prevention unit as well as an office that responds to student crisis. On the Texas A&M University campus, Dr. Harrell chairs the Sexual Assault Survivors Services committee composed of university and community stakeholders.

As a part of this committee, Dr. Harrell led the curriculum development of a workshop designed to train students, faculty, and staff on how to have trauma-informed conversations with individuals who disclosed traumatic experiences. Dr. Harrell, in collaboration with others who participated in the curriculum development, presented on this workshop at the NASPA Strategies Conference. Dr. Harrell has served as a chair and on committees for ASCA. In 2018 she was the coordinator and a faculty member for the Advanced Sexual Misconduct Track at the Gehring Academy in Indianapolis, Indiana. Dr. Harrell has authored and consulted on code revisions, including sexual misconduct codes, and has an outstanding record of speaking at conferences and webinars on sexual misconduct issues and hazing as an interpersonal violence issue.

Christopher T. Haug currently serves as vice president for student affairs at Neumann University, located in Aston, Pennsylvania, where he provides executive leadership for a comprehensive range of services, policies, and procedures related to student affairs programming, planning, and strategically related functions for the institution. Previously, he served in student affairs positions at the University of Portland, University of Notre Dame, Winthrop University, and Ball State University where he had responsibility for a wide range of student conduct administrative functions. A recipient of the 2019 ASCA Dissertation of the Year award, Dr. Haug's doctoral research established that moral distress is present among student conduct administrators in higher education. Dr. Haug earned a doctorate in education from University of Portland, a Master of Arts in student affairs administration from Ball State University, and a Bachelor of Science in education from University of Wisconsin-Whitewater.

Ryan C. Holmes is associate vice president for student affairs and dean of students at the University of Miami (Florida). He completed a Bachelor of Music Education degree from Loyola University, New Orleans, Louisiana, a Master of Arts degree in counseling and personnel services from the University of Maryland, College Park, and a second Master of Arts degree in bilingual/bicultural studies from La Salle University in 2008. Holmes completed his Doctor of Education in educational leadership and administration at the University of Texas at El Paso (UTEP) in 2014. Prior to joining the University of Miami, Dr. Holmes worked at UTEP as assistant dean of students, associate dean of students/director of student conduct and conflict resolution, and assistant vice president for student support in succession. Dr. Holmes has 17 years of experience in the field of student affairs, with 15 years of experience in student conduct. He is a past president of the Association for Student Conduct Administration (ASCA), has served ASCA as a past conference chair, and has served as foundation chair for the Raymond H. Goldstone ASCA Foundation Board. Dr. Holmes also served as a past track coordinator for the conflict resolution, mediation, and restorative justice tracks for the ASCA Donald D. Gehring Academy for Student Conduct Administration and was a past faculty member in the Gehring Academy's conflict resolution, mediation, restorative justice, and training institute tracks as well. Dr. Holmes served the American College Personnel Association (ACPA) as vice chair of outreach for the Commission of Social Justice Educators and was a contributing member of the ACPA Ethics Consortium committee. Dr. Holmes currently serves the National Association of Student Personnel Administrators (NASPA) as a committee member on both the NASPA AVP Steering committee and the 2020 NASPA AVP Symposium Planning committee. Dr. Holmes has given various talks and presentations dealing with social justice, bias, conflict resolution, and entitlement. He also contributed to *Reframing Campus Conflict: Student Conduct Practice Through a Social Justice Lens* (2009), *More Stories of Inspiration: 51 Uplifting Tales of Courage, Humor, Healing, and Learning in Student Affairs* (2009), *The State of Student Conduct: Current Forces and Future Challenges: Revisited* (2013), and coedited *Conduct and Community: A Residence Life and Practitioners Guide* as endorsed by both the Association of College and University Housing Officers, International (ACUHO-I) and the Association for Student Conduct Administration (ASCA) in 2018.

Seann S. Kalagher is the chief compliance officer and Title IX coordinator at Manhattanville College in Purchase, New York, where he oversees federal, state, and local compliance issues for the college, develops and interprets college policies, and serves as a member of the college cabinet. He also serves as an adjunct faculty member in Manhattanville's educational leadership doctoral program. Prior to Manhattanville, he worked for nearly nine years at Quinnipiac University in Hamden, Connecticut, serving as associate dean of students. At Quinnipiac, he oversaw the student conduct system, served as deputy Title IX coordinator, and worked with other student affairs initiatives. Seann also worked in the Student Conduct and Community Standards office at Roger Williams University in Bristol, Rhode Island. He has given presentations and conducted research on areas such as higher education legal issues, the Clery Act, campus crime, Title IX, organizational due process, cyber cheating, drug law and policy, and student conduct officer training. Seann is an active member of ASCA and NASPA and currently serves as the president of ASCA. He has served on the ASCA board of directors in various roles for over four years and has served as the chairperson for the 2014 ASCA National Conference and cochair of the ASCA Public Policy and Legislative Issues committee. In addition to his ASCA service, he served as the NASPA Region I representative to the NASPA Public Policy Division from 2014–2018. He also engages in consulting work related to student conduct and regulatory compliance. Seann earned a Bachelor of Arts degree from George Mason University, a Master of Science in education degree from Old Dominion University, and a Juris Doctor degree from Cornell University. While at Cornell, he served as executive editor of the *Cornell Journal of Law and Public Policy* and as a student officer in the Cornell Legal Aid Clinic. He is a member of the Massachusetts bar.

William L. Kibler has over 40 years of experience in higher education and currently serves as the president of Sul Ross State University. He previously served for a decade as the vice president for student affairs and was professor of counselor education at Mississippi State University. Dr. Kibler has served in a variety of other professional roles in student affairs administration, including 24 years at Texas A&M University and three years at the University of Florida. He earned a Bachelor of Arts degree in economics from the University of Florida; a Master of Education and a specialist in education degree in counselor education, also from the University of Florida; and a Doctor of Philosophy degree in educational administration from Texas A&M University. Dr. Kibler developed expertise in the areas of academic integrity, student rights and responsibilities, campus emergency management and response, and student conduct administration. He coauthored a book on academic integrity, *Academic Integrity and Student Development: Legal Issues and Policy Perspectives*, and coauthored and edited a book on student conduct, *The Administration of Campus Discipline: Student, Organizational and Community Issues*. He also edited the 10-year anniversary publication of the Association for Student Judicial Affairs, *The State of Campus Judicial Affairs: Current Forces and Future Challenges*. He has written several published book chapters and articles in the areas of academic integrity, student conduct, and student affairs administration. Dr. Kibler received the D. Parker Young award from the Association for Student Judicial Affairs recognizing outstanding scholarly and research contributions in the areas of higher education law and judicial affairs. He also received the Donald McCabe award from the International Center for Academic Integrity recognizing sustained work in research, teaching, or writing contributing to the understanding and promotion of academic integrity in society. He has consulted with several leading universities on student conduct policies, legal issues, academic integrity, and campus emergency management and response. Dr. Kibler has been actively involved in a number of professional associations throughout his career. He was a founding member and served as president of the Association for Student Judicial Affairs. He was also a founding member and served as president of the Center for Academic Integrity. He served in a number of leadership roles, including national conference chair of the National Association for Student Personnel Administrators. Dr. Kibler was an associate editor of the *College Student Affairs Journal* and on the editorial board of the *NASPA Journal*.

James M. Lancaster is currently a tenured professor of human development and psychological counseling at Appalachian State University where he teaches in the Student Affairs Administration program. He holds a doctorate in administration of higher education from the University of North Carolina at Greensboro. Prior to taking this position, he was associate vice chancellor for student affairs at the University of North Carolina at Greensboro and director of the offices of Student Conduct and of Academic Integrity. He has over 44 years of experience in student development practice, including student conduct advising and administration and in teaching in higher education. He is a past president of the Center for Academic Integrity. He is a past board member of the Association for Student Conduct Administration and a former director and faculty member of the Donald D. Gehring Student Judicial Affairs Institute of the Association for Student Conduct Administration. He has served on the editorial boards of the *Journal of College Student Development* and NASPA's *Journal of Student Affairs Research and Practice*. Dr. Lancaster has written and spoken widely on integrity and legal/developmental/ethical concerns in practice. He is the coeditor of a published monograph on new directions in student services titled *Beyond Law and Policy: Reaffirming the Role of Student Affairs,* editor of the book *Exercising Power With Wisdom: Bridging Legal and Ethical Practice With Intention,* and coeditor with Dr. Diane Waryold of *Student Conduct Practice: The Complete Guide for Student Affairs Professionals.*

Kara E. Latopolski is currently the senior associate director for undergraduate academic integrity at Virginia Tech. She has more than 10 years of experience as a university administrator at public universities, serving in the position of assistant dean of students for student conduct at Purdue University, West Lafayette, as well as holding positions at Purdue University, Northwest and the University of Georgia. Ms. Latopolski is a doctoral candidate in the Educational Administration, Leadership in Higher Education program at Indiana State University in Terre Haute, Indiana, and anticipates graduating in May 2020. She holds a master's degree in education from Mansfield University of Pennsylvania. She has presented at state, regional, and national conferences on topics related to student conduct and academic integrity. She is an active member of the Association of Student Conduct Administration and served as the state coordinator for Indiana in 2018–2019.

James A. Lorello is associate dean of students and director of student conduct and academic integrity at the University of North Carolina (UNC), Charlotte. In this role he provides overall leadership and direction to the office of Student Conduct and Academic Integrity and serves as chief conduct officer for the university. Before coming to the UNC Charlotte, Dr. Lorello was at Appalachian State University, where he served as associate director of student conduct and was an adjunct faculty member in the Student Affairs graduate program. Previously he worked in housing and residence life at both Appalachian State University and Georgetown University. Dr. Lorello received a Bachelor of Arts degree from the University of South Florida in religious studies, a Master of Arts degree from Appalachian State University in college student development, and a Doctor of Education degree from UNC Greensboro in educational leadership and cultural foundations. He has served as a cochair of the Men and Masculinities Knowledge community of the National Association of Student Personnel Administrators (NASPA) and is actively involved in both NASPA and ASCA. Dr. Lorello's main research interests have been with college men's development and meaning-making for college students.

John Wesley Lowery is department chair, graduate coordinator, and professor in the Student Affairs in Higher Education Department at Indiana University of Pennsylvania. Dr. Lowery previously served on the faculty at Oklahoma State University and the University of South Carolina. In addition to teaching, he coordinated graduate preparation programs at both those universities. He earned his doctorate at Bowling Green State University in higher education administration. He previously held administrative positions at Adrian College and Washington University in St. Louis. John holds a master's degree in student personnel services from the University of South Carolina and a bachelor's degree from the University of Virginia in religious studies. He is a frequent speaker and author on topics related to student affairs and higher education, particularly legislative issues and student conduct, on which he is widely regarding as a leading expert. John is actively involved in numerous professional associations including ACPA, ASCA, and NASPA. He has been involved in ASCA through his career and played a variety of leadership roles including chair of the Resolutions and Legislative Advisory committees; director at large, board of directors; board member, Raymond H. Goldstone ASCA Foundation; faculty and training institute coordinator, Donald D. Gehring Academy for Student Conduct Administration; and ASCA representative to the Council for the Advancement of Standards in Higher Education. Since 1992, John has made more than 100 presentations at ASCA events including the ASCA annual conference, regional ASCA conferences, ASCA webinars, and the Gehring Academy. Over his career, John has been honored by several professional organizations. In 2014, John was recognized as an ACPA Diamond Honoree for outstanding and sustained contributions to higher education and to student affairs. He has twice received the Tracy R. Teele Memorial award from ACPA's Commission for Student Conduct and Legal Issues for "outstanding contributions to the area of judicial affairs and legal issues" in 2005 and 2014. At the 2007 Association for Student Judicial Affairs conference, he received the D. Parker Young award for "outstanding ongoing scholarly research contributions to the fields of higher education and student judicial affairs." In 2007, he was also recognized by the Higher Education Administration doctoral program at Bowling Green State University as the alumnus of year in "recognition of outstanding contributions to the profession through teaching, research, and service."

Fran'Cee Brown-McClure is vice president for student affairs and dean of students at Union College. She has oversight of community standards, student activities, residence life, the health center, the counseling center, disability services, and Greek life. She has been in the field of student affairs for 15 years. Prior to joining the Union College administration, Dr. Brown-McClure worked at Spelman College, Stanford University, and The University of Texas at Austin. During her career she has served as an administrator in both public and private universities as well as large and small colleges and universities. In addition, she has had experience working at predominantly White institutions as well as historically Black institutions. Dr. Brown-McClure received a Doctor of Philosophy from The University of Texas at Austin in educational administration in 2015, a Master of Social Work from Boston University in 2006, and Bachelor of Science in psychology from Jackson State University in 2004. Leadership and community engagement are critical components of what helps her to thrive. She has served as foundations track coordinator for the Gehring Academy. She has participated in the Senior Leadership Academy sponsored by the Council of Independent Colleges and is a member of the 2018 Class of LEAD Atlanta. Dr. Brown-McClure is a sought-after speaker and facilitator. She frequently speaks to students and administrators about topics such as leadership in Greek life and emotionally intelligent leadership. She has presented nationally on motherhood and management, Black girl magic, cross-generational working relationships, and the importance of cross-racial friendships. The most important role that Dr. Brown-McClure holds is that of a mom. She is the mother of a 10-year old daughter. She tries every day to give to students what she was given in college and what she hopes future leaders will give to the future generations of students.

Saundra "Saunie" K. Schuster is a partner with TNG: the NCHERM Group. She is a recognized expert in preventive and civil rights law for education, notably in the fields of harassment, discrimination and sexual misconduct and violence, ADA, and disability issues. She has extensive experience and expertise in, and routinely advises clients on, the First Amendment and campus access issues, risk management and liability, behavior intervention and threat assessment, student discipline and campus conduct, intellectual property, and employment issues. She has provided extensive consultation to and training for the U.S. Justice Department, Office of Violence Against Women, the White House Task Force on Sexual Assault, and the Futures Without Violence organization. Her higher education legal experience includes serving as the general counsel for Sinclair Community College; as senior assistant attorney general for the State of Ohio, representing 53 public colleges and universities; and as the associate general counsel for the University of Toledo. In addition to her legal work in higher education, she has over 25 years of experience in college administration and teaching, including serving as the associate dean of students at The Ohio State University, director of the Office of Learning Assistance at Miami University, and assistant dean at Western College. She also served as a faculty member at The Ohio State University, Miami University, and Columbus State Community College. Ms. Schuster is an author and editor of many publications, including coauthor of *The First Amendment: A Guide for College Administrators* and contributing author to *Campus Conduct Practice* and *The Book on BIT: Forming and Operating Effective Behavioral Intervention Teams of College Campuses,* and many published articles and whitepapers. She is a founding member and former president of the Association for Student Conduct Administration (ASCA, formerly ASJA) and a cofounder and advisory board member of the Association of Title IX Administrators (ATIXA). She is a past president and current board member of NABITA (the National Behavioral Intervention Team Association). She is currently a member of the board of trustees for the Columbus College of Art and Design, where she serves as board secretary and chairperson of the Student and Academic Affairs committee. She holds master's degrees in counseling and higher education administration from Miami University and completed her coursework for her doctorate in organizational development at The Ohio State University. She was awarded her juris doctorate from the Moritz College of Law at The Ohio State University. She is admitted to practice law in the State of Ohio, U.S. District Court for the Southern District of Ohio, and the U.S. Court of Appeals for the Sixth Circuit.

Kathleen A. Shupenko currently serves as an associate director for the Office of Student Conduct at Pennsylvania State University. She earned her master's degree in education from Pennsylvania State University in 2005 and has spent the subsequent 14 years working within the Pennsylvania State University system. She has been instrumental in developing the university's student organizational conduct process, which is applicable to all Penn State commonwealth campuses system wide. Since helping to establish the university's new organizational conduct model in 2017, she has led the investigative team for the respective misconduct process within the Office of Student Conduct. She's adjudicated numerous organizational, student leadership, and individual conduct cases related to organizational conduct violations. In 2018 and 2019, Kathleen served as a faculty member in the Organizational Misconduct Track for the ASCA Donald D. Gehring Academy.

Matthew T. Stimpson is director of assessment in the College of Engineering at North Carolina State University and has worked in higher education for more than 15 years. Dr. Stimpson started his career in student conduct before transitioning into the assessment field. He has presented and published on the topics of access, assessment, and retention and held editorial positions for ASCA and the Council on Law in Higher Education. He has served on the faculty at the Gehring Academy in teaching assessment and served as track coordinator. In addition, he cofounded eduOutcomes, a consulting group focused on student conduct assessment and campus climate surveys. He earned a Bachelor of Arts degree and a Master of Education degree from the University of North Carolina at Greensboro and a doctorate degree from Virginia Tech.

Jane A. Tuttle is the associate vice provost for student affairs at the University of Kansas. In this senior leadership role, she has responsibility for the Student Conduct and Community Standards Office, the Student Involvement and Leadership Center, sorority and fraternity life, the Sexual Assault Prevention and Education Center, Student Money Management

Services, and the Student Affairs Assessment and Strategic Initiatives Office. She coordinates the Parent Services Department for the university. For over 20 years she was the campus Clery Act coordinator. While living in Bowling Green, Kentucky, she taught a graduate class on research methodology at Western Kentucky University. She has over 30 years of student affairs experience. Dr. Tuttle has served as treasurer for the board of directors of the Association for Student Conduct Administration and as board secretary for the Raymond Goldstone Foundation for ASCA, chaired several ASCA committees, and has been a faculty member for the ASCA Gehring Academy. Additionally, she was awarded the Distinguished Service from ASCA in 2016. She has been the NASPA IV-West Regional Representative on the NASPA Campus Safety and Violence Prevention Knowledge Community. She received her bachelor's degree in social studies education from Ball State University. Her master's degree in college student personnel is from Buffalo State College. She earned her doctorate in higher education administration from the University of Kansas.

Diane M. Waryold is a professor and program director in the Student Affairs Administration graduate preparation program within the Department of Human Development and Psychological Counseling at Appalachian State University. Prior to her current position, Waryold served as executive director of the Center for Academic Integrity and program administrator for the Kenan Institute for Ethics at Duke University. She was an accomplished student affairs administrator for 20 plus years before moving into the professoriate role. She is a founding and charter member of the Association for Student Judicial Affairs (ASJA) and served as president in 1995. Dr. Waryold has presented, published, and consulted on campus student conduct, sexual misconduct, campus safety and campus policing, and academic integrity throughout the country. She received a Bachelor of Science in education from the State University College of Cortland, New York, a Master of Education from the University of Florida, and a Doctor of Education in educational leadership from Florida State University. Outside of her university work, Waryold volunteers with disaster services for the American Red Cross.

Mackenzie E. Wilfong earned her Bachelor of Arts from the University of Oklahoma where she graduated Phi Beta Kappa and her juris doctorate from Southern Methodist University's Dedman School of Law. Following law school, she practiced litigation at a national law firm in Kansas City where she specialized in education and employment law, practicing in both Kansas and Missouri. After leaving private practice, she joined the United States

Department of Education, Office for Civil Rights as a federal enforcement attorney investigating allegations of harassment and discrimination in educational institutions in a five-state region including Oklahoma. Most recently, she was associate general counsel for the board of regents of the Oklahoma State University and Agricultural and Mechanical Colleges, representing nine colleges and universities across Oklahoma. Currently, she is the general counsel for Tulsa Community College, where she serves on the executive team and provides legal counsel to the college's four campuses in Tulsa County. She is also a board member of the Oklahoma Center for Community and Justice.

John D. Zacker is assistant vice president for student affairs at the University of Maryland, College Park overseeing the departments of Stamp Student Union and Center for Campus Life, Fraternity and Sorority Life, and Campus Recreation Services, and overseeing the university golf course. Much of John's career has been spent in student conduct administration, most recently as director of Maryland's Office of Student Conduct. Among his ongoing responsibilities are coordinating the behavior evaluation and threat assessment team (BETA team), assessment and student learning outcomes, hazing prevention, child abuse and neglect procedures, and sexual assault prevention and awareness. He also holds a faculty appointment with the College of Education, Student Affairs Concentration. Dr. Zacker has spent 31 years at the university. Prior to coming to Maryland, he served as director of resident life at Occidental College in Los Angeles, California. He earned a Bachelor of Science degree from Plymouth State College, a Master of Education degree from the University of Vermont, and a doctor degree from the University of Maryland. He has been actively involved in professional associations, particularly the Association for Student Conduct Administration, serving on the board of directors for three years before being elected its president; was appointed to the faculty of the Gehring Academy for Student Conduct Administration, completing two years as director of the academy; and was recognized for distinguished service to the association in 1997. He represented ASCA on the board of directors for the Council for the Advancement of Standards in Higher Education (CAS) for five years. He has published chapters in student conduct administration books on the topics of evaluation/assessment, technology issues, and foundational principles in student conduct. He is a frequent consultant on issues of student conduct administration and presents regularly at national association and regional meetings, most recently on the topics of ethical development, assessment/learning outcomes, and academic integrity/honor codes.

Eugene L. Zdziarski II is vice president for student affairs at DePaul University. With over 30 years of experience in student affairs and higher education, he provides overall leadership and direction to a comprehensive set of programs and services at the largest Catholic university in the United States. Throughout his career, he has been involved in, administered, or overseen the student conduct process at large public universities as well as private liberal arts colleges. At Texas A&M University, he was involved in the development and became the first director of the Student Conflict Resolution Center, which combined student conduct administration, student legal services, and mediation services into one campus dispute resolution center. Dr. Zdziarski received his Bachelor of Science degree from Oklahoma State University, his Master of Science degree from the University of Tennessee at Knoxville, and his doctor degree from Texas A&M University. Professionally, he has served in a variety of regional and national leadership roles in NASPA, Student Affairs Administrators in Higher Education. In addition, he has served as a member of the board of directors and as the central office manager for the Association for Student Judicial Affairs (ASJA), now known as the Association for Student Conduct Administration (ASCA). Dr. Zdziarski regularly makes professional presentations at national, regional, and state meetings on topics including crisis management, dispute resolution, and legal issues in higher education. He has also authored two books and several articles and book chapters on similar topics and has served as an expert witness and consultant to a variety of colleges and universities.

INDEX

Abbott, Greg, 186
abuse
  by law enforcement, 108
  against women, 106, 176–77
academic integrity, xii, 243–52
  conduct processes and, 38
access, 119
  to records, 76–77
accountability
  assessment and, 3
  Giacomini on, 163
  institutions and, 165
accreditation, 140
accusers, 74
ACE. *See* American Council on
  Education
ACPA. *See* American College Personnel
  Association
action, 104, 134, 163
  conversations and, 175
  ethics and, 19
  interim action, 50
  violations and, 49
adaptations, 11, 55
adjudication, 115, 163
  Schrage and Giacomini on, 160
  view of, 159
administrative hearing, 87–88
ADR. *See* alternative dispute resolution
advisors, 45
  conduct processes and, 46–47
  involvement of, 97–98
advocacy, 17–18
  for rights, 24
  sexual misconduct and, 172, 186
  students and, 31
affirmative consent framework, 180–81

African Americans, 102, 210
age, 133, 176
Alabama State College, 102
alcohol, 262–63
  consumption of, 129–30, 145–46
  drugs and, 182
  violations and, 127
allegations
  resolution and, 84
  violations and, 51
alternative dispute resolution (ADR),
  85
  forums and, 94–97
alternatives, 134
  to address bias incidents, 159–63
American College Personnel Association
  (ACPA), 11
  The Student Learning Imperative by,
  139
American Council on Education
  (ACE), 8
Annual Security Report, 73, 74
  consent and, 173
  DDV and, 176
  statistics and, 75
anti-Semitism, 106
appeal, 52
  rights to, 66
appeal administrators, 45
appellate board, 90
application, 4
  conduct codes and, 43
  of conflict resolution models, 113–15
articles, 158
  data and, 145
ASCA. *See* Association for Student
  Conduct Administration

ASJA. *See* Association for Student
    Judicial Affairs
assessment, xii
    accountability and, 3
    assessment plans, 141–43
    skills relation to, 140–49
    student conduct and, 138–50
    timing of, 142–43
Association for Student Conduct
    Administration (ASCA), 2, 107
    Conduct and Community publication
        by, 140
    conference of, 28
    practices and, 183–84
Association for Student Judicial Affairs
    (ASJA), ix–x
    founding of, 2
    Gehring and, 12
athletes, 206
attorneys, 46
    right to, 63–64
    role of, 47
authority, 42, 117
autonomy, 135
awareness
    of identities, 128
    threat assessment and, 219–20

BAC. *See* blood alcohol content
Banta, T. W., 144
behavior, xii, 30, 42
    awareness of, 219
    case studies and, 256
    expectation and, 44
    as incongruent, 181
    institution and, 23, 54, 129
    misbehavior, x, 52, 127
    non-compliant behavior, ix
    students and, 88
behavioral interventions, xii, 215–21
belonging
    messaging and, 116
    student organizations and, 240
benchmarking process, 39–40

articles and, 158
benefits, 32
    of conversations, 49
    from rules, 103
    Title IX and, 69, 170
bias, 27, 62
    courts and, 63
    data collection and, 128
    humans and, 111
    incidents on campus, 153–65
    motivation and, 74
    reporting and, 108
Black/African Americans, 102, 210
blood alcohol content (BAC), 182
Bloom's taxonomy, 144, 145
brave spaces, 112–13
Bring it to the Table program, 191, 210
Brinkmann, S., 130
Brown-McClure, Fran'Cee, 3
*Brown v. Entertainment Merchants
    Association*, 201
Burke, Tarana, 106

California, 201
    Leonard Law in, 195
Campt, D., 161
campus, 10
    advocacy and, 17
    bias incidents on, 153–65
    climate on, 156, 191
    conduct processes and, 32
    as microcosm, 1
    organizations on, 89–90
    safety on, 15
campus bias response teams, 156–59
campus community, xii, 96, 116
    engagement and, 31–32
    harm to, 164
    need and, 159
    student conduct board and, 91
    students in, 25
Cardozo, Benjamin, 269
CAS. *See* Council for the Advancement
    of Standards

case studies, 32–33
    clarity in rules, 255–56
    resistance to reporting, 255
Chaplinsky v. New Hampshire, 200–201
character, 266
checklists, 178–79
Chemerinsky, E., 192, 200
children, 8
    parents and, 245
    socialization and, 103
circumstances, 55–56
Civil Rights Era, 8–9
Civil Rights Restoration Act (1987),
    170
clergy, 6
Clery, Jeanne, 72
Clery Act, 53, 64, 172
    passage of, 72–75
Cloud v. Boston University, 65
Cocks, Catherine, 3
code construction
    elements of, 42–48
    language and, 53–56
collaboration, 217–18
colleges and universities, xi–xii
    demographics of, 138
    employees of, 170
    microaggressions at, 156
    society and, 1
The College Student and the Courts
    (Gehring and Young), x
Colonial America, 6–7
committees, 76
    development of, 158
commonality, 36
communication, 164
    nonverbal communication, 181
community policing, 118
compassion
    compassion fatigue, 19, 185, 239
    support and, 130
competency, 15, 140
complainants, 179
compliance

components of, 220
continuum, 25–26
    non-compliant behavior, ix
conciliation, 94–95
conduct administration, 45
    as terminology, 12
Conduct and Community (ASCA), 140
conduct codes, 71, 129
    advisors and, 98
    application and, 43
    courts and, 30–31
    crafting and revision of, 36–56
    expectations and, 74
conduct processes, 23–26, 107–8
    academic integrity and, 38
    advisors and, 46–47
    campus and, 32
    multipartiality and, 117
    oppression and, 118
    revisions and, 37
    social justice and, 109–15
    stages of, 48–53
conferences, ix, 12
    education conferences, 86
    Harris-Perry at, 28
conflict coaching, 114, 161–62
conflict resolution models, 159
    application of, 113–15
connection
    practitioners and, 129
    students and, 86
consent, 176
    annual security reports and, 173
    sexual misconduct and, 180–81
consistency, 26–27, 216
constituents, 149
    of process, 41–42
Constitution, U. S., 68
    First Amendment, 155, 191–212
    policies and, 196
    Sixth Amendment of, 89
    voting and, 105
content, 197, 202
context

current context, 139–40
    of interpersonal violence, 181
    for language, 173
conversations, 10, 161
    action and, 175
    benefits of, 49
Council for the Advancement of
    Standards (CAS), 14, 139
    review process by, 150
counsel, 45–46
courts, 60
    bias and, 63
    code management and, 30–31
    differences from, 18
    government and, 37
    private institutions and, 67–69
    retaliation and, 178
    speech and, 201
    student rights and, 9
    students and, 62
    Western District of Missouri, 23
Coveney, C. E., 178
creeping legalism, 67
Crime Awareness and Campus Security
    Act. *See* Clery Act
crimes, 74
    hate crimes, 155
criminal justice system, 9
criteria, for professions, 13–16
cultural/institutional socialization, 103
culture, 29–30
    of awareness and reporting, 220
    cultural training, 14
    institution and, 153–54
Curran, Regina, 3
curriculum, 147

Darley, J. G., 13
data, 141
    analyzation of, 148–49
    articles and, 145
    data collection, 128
    data management, 263
dating

date rape, 169, 175
    domestic violence and, 176–77
dating and domestic violence (DDV),
    176–77
*Davis v. Monroe County Board of
    Education*, 174
DDV. *See* dating and domestic violence
debate, 207
    dialogue and, 110
    speech and, 211
decision-making, 116
    domain approach to, 131–33
    ethics and, 126–36
    sanctions and, 51–52
defamation, 205–7
democracy, 191
demographics, 138
    data and, 263
Department of Education, U. S., 76,
    172
designated limited public forum, 198
designated public forum, 197–98
dialogue, 153, 161
    debate and, 110
    democracy and, 191
    dialogue pathway, 114
    facilitated dialogue, 114, 162
Dillman, D. A., 148
disabilities, students with, 37, 55, 106
disconnection, 118
    on sanctions, 255–56
discretion, 13, 49
    judgment and, 15
    SCA and, 132
discrimination, 196
    marginalization and, 108
    Title IX and, 178
discussion, 161
    regulations on, 197
diversity, 37
    students and, 138
*Dixon v. Alabama State Board of
    Education* (1961), 9, 18
    due process and, 30

rights and, 58–59
documentation
    documents and, 71
    of sanctions, 6
Doe v. Baum, 186
domain, 144
    approach to decision-making,
        131–33
domestic violence, 64, 73
    dating and, 176–77
doubt, 48
Drug-Free Schools and Communities
    Act, 77–78
drugs, 262–63
    alcohol and, 182
Duel SCO Model, 88–89
due process, 28
    concept of, 9
    Dixon v. Alabama and, 30
    equity and, 179
    after hearing, 65–66
    before hearing, 61–62
    during hearing, 62–65
    Pavela on, 227
    at private institutions, 67–69
    at public universities, 59–61

Early Federalist Era, 7
economics, 139
education, 161
    education conferences, 86
    morality and, 133
    sanctions and, 233–38
    society and, 2
Education Amendments
    Higher Education Amendments Act
        (1998), 76
    Title IX of, 10, 45, 69–72, 170–73,
        178
effectiveness, 263–64
efficiency, 263–64
Elonis v. United States, 202
emotional distress, 177
employees, 170

enforcements, 103
engagement, 29
    campus community and, 31–32
    parameters for, 112
    partnerships and, 228
enrollment, 7
    after World War II, 8
environment
    differences and, 153–54
    hostile environments, 170, 174, 204
    practitioners and, 28–29
equity, 117
    due process and, 179
Esteban v. Central Missouri, 60
ethics, 13
    action and, 19
    decision-making and, 126–36
    integrity and character, 266
    Kidder on, 26
    society and, 16
evaluation, 179
    self-evaluation, 34
events, 44
evidence, 48, 150
    standards of, 180
exhaustion, 19
expectation
    behavior and, 44
    conduct codes and, 74
    of institutions, 36
    of *in loco parentis*, 6
experiences, 20, 30, 115
    learning experiences, 141–42
    meaning-making and, 131
    of students, 27, 33
    of women, 176–77
explicit messaging, 27–28
expression, 197, 199
    restrictions on, 198
    student expression, 118

Facebook, 207
facilitation
    facilitated dialogue, 114, 162

by SCA, 87–88
  training and, 115, 162
facts, 134
faculty
  free speech and, 193
  information and, 17
  lawsuits by, 206
  resistance to reporting by, 255
  staff and, 164
fairness, 46, 89
  philosophy and, 26–28
faithfulness, 135
families, 8
Family Educational Rights and Privacy
    Act (FERPA), 75–77, 107
  organizations and, 229
Federal Register publication, 70
FERPA. *See* Family Educational Rights
    and Privacy Act
fighting words, 200–201
FIRE. *See* Foundation for Individual
    Rights in Education
First Amendment, 155, 191–212
First Amendment Center website, 194
first socialization, 103
flexible language, 55–56
forums, 50
  ADR and, 94–97
  resolution types and, 84–99
  types of, 197–99
Foundation for Individual Rights in
    Education (FIRE), 194
framework
  affirmative consent, 180–81
  ethical decision-making in, 133–35
Free Speech in the College Community
    (O'Neil), 193
French v. Bashful, 64
frequency distributions, 148–49

Gabrilowitz v. Newman, 63
Gallant, Tricia Bertram, 4
gay rights movement, 105
Gehring, Donald D., x, 67

ASJA and, 12
  warning from, 259
gender
  language and, 183
  segregation and, 7
  sexual harassment and, 174
Giacomini, N. G., 113
  on accountability, 163
  on adjudication, 160
  on campus climate, 156
GI Bill. *See* Servicemen's Readjustment
    Act of 1944
Gillman, Howard, 192
goals, 18, 28
  of brave spaces, 112
  mediation and, 95
  principles and, 264
  of resolution, 84–85
  social justice and, 108–9
Goldstein, A., 140
Goldwater Institute, 195
Gott v. Berea College (1913), 8
  in loco parentis and, 30
government
  courts and, 37
  funding from, 170
  regulation of student conduct, 58–59
Gray, Fred, 58
Great Depression, 7
Greek conduct board, 89
group consciousness, 16
guardians. *See* parents/guardians
guidelines
  for policy development, 195–99
  for sanctions, 53

Hall, Kermit, 194
Hall, Maximilian, 207–8
*The Handbook for Campus Crime
    Reporting* (2016), 72–73
harassment, 54
  case law and, 170
  mediation and, 95
  racial harassment, 204–5

sexual harassment, 172, 174–75
harm, 135
    campus community and, 164
Harris-Perry, Melissa, 28
Harvard College, 6
hate crimes, 155
    response to, 208–9
Hate Crimes Prevention Act, 105
hate speech, 200
hazing, 262–63
    antihazing laws, 229–30
Healy v. James, 223–24
hearing panels, 51, 181, 184
    administrative hearing, 87–88
    due process after, 65–66
    due process before, 61–62
    due process during, 62–65
    members of, 45
help, 130, 245
higher education, 5. *See also* colleges
        and universities
    landscape of, 20
history
    institutions and, 36
    socialization and, 102
    of student discipline, 2, 5–10
    United States and, 104–7, 119
Holmes v. Poskanzer, 64

Iconis, R., 177
ideals
    marketplace of ideas as, 193, 195
    values and, 136
identities, 1, 31
    awareness of, 128
    bias incidents and, 154
    considerations of, 182–83
    messaging and, 101
    privilege and, 104
ideology, 104
implicit messaging, 27–28
impressions, 116
incapacitation, 176
    from alcohol and drugs, 182

incitement, 203–4
inclusivity, 154
    inclusive/culturally responsive
        practices, 113
    inclusive language, 55
inequity, 109, 119
inferential statistics, 149
influence, 6
    outcomes and, 146
    on practitioners, 31
    on student conduct process, 109
informal resolution, 85–86
information, 38
    communication of, 44
    disclosure of, 15
    faculty and, 17
    listening and, 113
    methods of gathering, 241–42
    neutrality of, 116
    new information, 52
    standard of information, 47–48
    stories and, 131
    trauma-informed processes and, 181
injustice, 109
in loco parentis
    expectation of, 6
    Gott v. Berea College and, 30
institutional/cultural socialization, 103
institutions, 33
    accountability and, 165
    behavior and, 23, 54, 129
    culture and, 153–54
    history and, 36
    institutional knowledge, 38–39
    liability and, 70, 265
    promises of, 66–67
    protection and, 73
    requirements of, 41
    responsibility and, 227
    student conduct within, 24–25
    type of, 39–41
    VAWA and, 180
integrity, 266
intentionality, 112

Internet, 202
interpersonal violence, 173, 175–76
    context of, 181
intersectionality, 110–11
intervention
    behavioral interventions, xii,
        215–21
    regulation requirements and
        legislation, 259–60
interview
    preparation for, 232
    for student conduct board, 92–93
intimidation, 202
investigations, 50
    during and after, 233
    investigation model, 184
involvement
    of advisors, 97–98
    of parents, 260–61
    of parties, 96
issues, 126
    response to, xi

Jackson, Candice, 70
Jefferson, Thomas, ix
judicial affairs, 54
jurisdiction, 44
justice, 135. *See also* restorative justice;
        social justice
    criminal justice system, 9
    injustice, 109
    transformative justice, 96–97

Kalagher, Seann, 3
Kavanagh, Joe, 269
Keefe v. Adams, 207
Kidder, Rushworth, 26
Kitchener, K., 135
Knight Foundation, 192
knowledge
    institutional knowledge, 38–39
    specialized and systemized, 14
Knowledge Networks, 176–77
Koestner, Katie, 169

Lake, Peter F., 25
language, 133
    code construction and, 53–56
    context for, 173
    gender and, 183
    policies and, 43
    victim protection and, 202
Latopolski, Kara, 4
law enforcement, 40
    abuse by, 108
    reporting and, 49
laws, 195
    antihazing laws, 229–30
    lawsuits and, 66, 76–77
    nondiscrimination laws, 196
    policies and mandates, 58–78
    student conduct and federal,
        69–78
lawsuits, 133, 195
    defamation in, 206
leadership, 20
learning, 10
    bias, 155
    factors in, 138
    learning experiences, 141–42
    responsibility and, 109–10
legal system, 9
    student conduct system and, 107
legislation, 38, 173
    advocacy and, 17–18
    attorneys and, 47
    intervention and regulation
        requirements, 259–60
Lehigh University, 72
Leonard Law, 195
LePeau, L. A., 157
Levi, A. J., 147
liability, 238
    institutions and, 265
    limited liability, 70
Liberty University, 206
listening, 118
    information and, 113
Livingood, J., 155

Lowery, John Wesley, x, 24
    on terminology, 68–69

Magolda, Baxter, 126
mandates, 58–78
marginalization, 104
    discrimination and, 108
    unequal access and, 119
marketplace of ideas, 193, 195
McCluskey, Lauren, 177
McDermott, C., 157
meaning-making, 269
    shaming and, 157
    student conduct and, 130–31
mean values, 148–49
measures, 146–48
    direct measures, 142
mediation, 95, 162
    mediation pathway, 114
membership, 16
    alternate members, 91
    board recruitment and selection of,
        92–93
    of hearing panels, 45
memorandum of understanding
    (MOU), 40
men, 106
mental health, of students, 1
messaging, 27–28
    belonging and, 116
    identities and, 101
microaggressions, 103
    bias incidents and, 156
microinsults, 156
Milk, Harvey, 105
misbehavior, x, 52, 127
misconduct, 71
    student organizations and, 223
    University of Wisconsin and, 60
model codes, 38
moral distress, 19
morality, 132
    education and, 133
Moral Student Conduct, 98

Morrill Act (1862), 7
Moss, M., 158
MOU. *See* memorandum of
    understanding
Ms. Magazine, 169
Mueller v. Oregon (1908), 105
multipartiality, 111–12
    understanding of, 117
Murrah, Alfred P., 271

NASCAP project, 145
Nash v. Auburn, 63
NASPA. *See* National Association of
    Student Personnel Administrators
Nassar, Larry, 106, 186
National Association of Student
    Personnel Administrators
    (NASPA), 11
    publications by, 139
naturalization, 104
needs, 20, 270
    campus communities and, 159
    indispensable social need, 14
    interim action and, 50
    student conduct boards and, 90
New York, 68
New York Times, 200
New York Times v. Sullivan, 205
no conflict management pathway, 114
nonconfrontation, 86
non-consent framework, 180
nonpublic forum, 199
norms, 103
notice, 50–51
Notice of Proposed Rulemaking
    (NPRM), 70, 72

Oberlin College, 7
objectivity, 92
    objective tests, 147
obscenity, 201–2
observers, 46
Office for Civil Rights (OCR), 70, 170
    "Dear Colleague" letter by, 172, 204

preponderance of evidence and, 180
racial harassment, 204
sexual harassment and, 174
training and, 71
Office for Victims of Crime, 185
O'Neil, Robert M., 193
operational outcomes, 146
opportunities, 143
response to, 154
oppression
conduct process and, 118
privilege and, 101–2
organizations, 11, 33
on campus, 89–90
FERPA and, 229
organizing bodies and, 157
rogue organizations, 237–38
treatment of, 4
Osteen v. Henley, 63
outcomes, 141
development of, 143–46
path to, 15
speculation of, 18
types of, 142, 146

Palomba, C. A., 144
parameters
definitions and, 43–48
for engagement, 112
parents/guardians
engagement and, 32
help from, 245
involvement of, 260–61
participation, 92
of advisors, 47
parties, 45
equity for, 179
involvement of, 96
restorative justice for, 163
safe space for, 99
partnerships, 118, 218
internal and external, 228–29
with students, 136
Pavela, Gary, x, 227, 271

preamble by, 2
peers
board composition and, 90–91
peer institutions, 39–40
PEN America, 192, 208
performance, 147, 185
of duty, 15
personal domain, 132
personal pronouns, 113
perspective, xi
Peters, T. M., 185
Pew Research Center, 106
philosophy, 8, 270–71
fairness and, 26–28
introduction and, 84–85
of student conduct, 23–34
Piazza, Timothy, 229
policies, 18
constitutionality of, 196
guidelines for development of, 195–99
language and, 43
mandates and laws, 58–78
no platform policy, 192
policy development, 178–79, 225–27
practices and, 198, 221
requirements and, 41
politics
advocacy and, 17–18
rhetoric and, 191
Pope, R. L., 153
population, 106
assessment and, 141, 144
diversity of, 37
relationships and, 118
of United States, 1
pornography, 201
positionality statement, 127
student conduct and, 128
possession, 54
post-traumatic stress disorder (PTSD), 185
practices, 4, 34

ASCA and, 183–84
current, 5
implications for, 115–18
multipartiality as, 111–12
policies and, 198, 221
records and, 87
of restorative justice, 10, 114–15
social justice and, 101–19
practitioners, 17
challenges to, 20
connection and, 129
environment and, 28–29
influence on, 31
professional development for, 117
responsibility as, 165
understanding as, 126
preponderance, 48
principles, 140, 193
consideration of, 135
goals and, 264
survey construction and, 148
values and, 134
private institutions, 193
courts and, 67–69
distinction between public and,
194–95
due process at, 67–69
privilege
identities and, 104
oppression and, 101–2
procedure
manuals for, 93
procedural error and, 52
proceduralism and, 67, 258–59
professional associations, 11–12
professional temperament, 267–68
programs, 191
programmatic outcomes, 142, 143
program reviews, 150
training programs, 93–94
promises, of institutions, 66–67
property, 196
conduct and, 225
protection

free speech and, 193
institutions and, 73
language and victim, 202
PTSD. *See* post-traumatic stress
disorder
publications, 70, 139
Conduct and Community (ASCA) as,
140
public institutions
distinction between private and,
194–95
due process at, 59–61

Q&A on Campus Sexual Misconduct
(Jackson, 2017), 72

racial harassment, 204–5
rape, 173
date rape, 169, 175
Raymond H. Goldstone Foundation,
16
recognition, 264–65
of problem, 133–34
student organizations and, 224
Reconstruction (Post Civil War), 7
records, 76
practices and, 87
record retention, 53
Reframing Campus Conflict (Schrage and
Giacomini), 113
regulations, 76
on discussion, 197
government and student conduct,
58–59
regulatory guidance, 25–26
sexual misconduct and, 173
relationships, 118
campus community and, 164
parents/guardians and, 261
reporting, 40
bias in, 108
culture of awareness and, 220
resistance to, 255
submission and, 49

representatives, 158
requirements, 41, 68
  Annual Security Report, 73–74
  board membership, 92
  legislation intervention and
    regulation, 259–60
  VAWA and, 75
research
  continuation of, 18
  on inequity, 109
  qualitative research, 127
resolution, 3, 50
  application of conflict resolution
    models, 113–15
  resolution options models, 160
  sexual misconduct and, 184
  types and forums of, 84–99
resources, 97, 150
  SCA as, 86
  for threat assessment, 216
responsibility, 6, 24
  guilt and, 54
  institutions and, 227
  learning and, 109–10
  practitioners and, 165
restorative justice, 95–96
  goals and, 264
  parties and, 163
  practices of, 10, 114–15
results, 104
  usage of, 149–50
retaliation, 177–78
reviews
  program reviews, 150
  reporting and, 49
  standardization and, 42
Revised Sexual Harassment Guidance
    (2001), 71
rights, 9, 24
  to appeal, 66
  to attorneys, 63–64
  Dixon v. Alabama and, 58–59
  for women, 105
Rolling Stone magazine, 206

Rollock, N., 156
rubrics, 147
rules, 186
  benefits from, 103
  clarity in, 255–56
  vagueness of, 60

Saddlemire, John, 25
safety, 33
  brave spaces and, 112–13
  campus, 15
  law enforcement and, 40
  technology usage and, 99
sanctions
  decision and, 51–52
  disconnection on, 255–56
  documentation of, 6
  guidelines for, 53
  options for, 39
  violation and, 131
SCA. *See* student conduct administrator
Schirch, L., 161
scholars, 17, 270
  Black feminist, 110–11
Schrage, J. M., 113
  on adjudication, 160
  on campus climate, 156
sciences, 7
scientific principles, 14
scrutiny, 196
self
  self-authorship, 126
  self-care, 239–40
  self-evaluation, 34
  sense of self, 127–28
  understanding of self, 269
sense of self, 127–28
Servicemen's Readjustment Act of 1944
    (GI Bill), 8
sexual misconduct, 106, 169–87
  consent and, 180–81
  sexual assault, 65, 183, 262–63
  sexual exploitation, 176
  sexual harassment, 172, 174–75

sexual violence and, 45, 175
shaming, 157
shuttle diplomacy, 162–63
shuttle negotiation, 115
Sixth Amendment, 89
skills, 14
    assessment relation to, 140–49
Slogin v. Kauffman, 60
social conventional domain, 132
socialization, 101–4
    children and, 103
social justice, 3
    conduct processes and, 109–15
    student conduct practices and,
        101–19
social media, 98
    posts on, 209
society, 29
    colleges and universities and, 1
    education and, 2
    ethics and, 16
    obligations to, 13
    socialization and, 101
the Spectrum Approach, 160
speech. *See also* First Amendment
    free speech, 192, 193, 198
    power of, 211
    speech codes, 205
    threats and, 202–3
    unprotected speech categories,
        199–207
staff
    capacity and, 238–39
    faculty and, 164
    review by, 49
    threats to, 19
stakeholders, 41, 149
    list of, 141
stalking, 177
Stallman, S., 27
standardization, of reviews, 42
standards
    professional standards, 207
    standard of evidence, 180

standard of information, 47–48
standard of proof, 66
standards of conduct, 77
statistics, 38
    Annual Security Report and, 75
    DDV and, 176
    inferential statistics, 149
Stevens, D. D., 147
Stimpson, M., 146
    on assessment, 140
Stoner, Ed, x, 12, 24
    on terminology, 68–69
stories, 131
    choices and, 134–35
student affairs administration, field of,
    xi
    criteria and, 13–16
student conduct
    assessment and, 138–50
    Civil Rights Era and, 8–9
    divisions and, 40–41
    federal laws and, 69–78
    future of, 11
    impact of, xi
    institutions and, 24–25
    meaning-making and, 130–31
    philosophy of, 23–34
    positionality statement and, 54, 128
    property and, 225
    student organizations and, 223–40
student conduct, profession of
    establishment of, 12–16
    evolution of, 5–20
    understanding of, 17–18
student conduct administration
    profession, 266–67
    history of student discipline and,
        5–10
student conduct administrator (SCA),
    84–85, 148
    discretion and, 132
    facilitation by, 87–88
    as resource, 86
    restorative justice and, 96

student conduct board, 89–94
  board composition, 90–92
  board training, 93–94
  campus community and, 91
  interview process for, 92–93
student conduct professionals, 220–21
student conduct systems, 107
student discipline, 23
  history of, 2
student expression, 118
student learning outcomes, 142
  elements of, 144
student misconduct
  interim action and, 50
  resolution and, 84
  in United States, 6
student organizations, 223–40
student personnel movement, 7–8
student rights, 9
students
  accountability for, 163
  advocacy and, 31
  application to, 43
  behavior and, 88
  in campus community, 25
  connection and, 86
  courts and, 62
  with disabilities, 37, 55, 106
  diversity and, 138
  experiences of, 27, 33
  gains for, 144
  holistic view of, 87
  partnerships with, 136
  sexual harassment and, 174
  students of concern, 261–62
  understanding of, 39, 132
  in United Kingdom, 192
support, 41, 185
  compassion and, 130
  threat assessment and, 218–19
surveys, 147–48
suspension, 129–30
  student organizations and, 237
syllabus, 256

system efficacy, 146
system input and output, 146

technology, 155
  impact if, xi
  usage of, 98–99
terminology, 68–69
  conduct administration as, 12
  free speech zones and, 198
  sexual misconduct and, 175–76
tests, 147
Thompson, M. C., 160
Thorndike, E. L., 111
Thorne, A., 163, 164
threat assessment, 215–21
threats, xii
  to profession, 5
  speech and, 202–3
  to staff, 19
Time magazine, 169
timing, 171
  of assessment, 142–43
  conflict resolution and, 160
  timeline, of process, 42
Title IX, 10, 45, 69–72, 170–73
  discrimination and, 178
traditional public forum, 197
training, 183–84
  board training, 93–94
  cultural training, 14
  facilitation and, 115, 162
  OCR and, 71
transformative justice, 96–97
transparency, 119, 230, 251
trauma
  secondary trauma, 185
  trauma-informed processes, 181
Turing, Alan, 272

understanding, 34
  intersectionality, 111
  of multipartiality, 117
  practitioners and, 126
  of self, 269

of student conduct profession, 17–18
students and, 39, 132
values and, 128
uniqueness, 36
United Kingdom, 192
United States
history and, 104–7, 119
population of, 1
resolution forums in, 85–94
student misconduct in, 6
universities. *See* colleges and
universities
University of Georgia, 9
University of Maryland, 263
University of Michigan, 200
University of Mississippi, 158
University of Missouri, 157
University of Virginia, ix
University of Wisconsin, 60

vagueness, 60
speech codes, 205
values, 30
ideals and, 136
principles and, 134
statement of mission and, 165
understanding and, 128
value system, 102
VAWA. *See* Violence Against Women
Act
victims, 202
notification to, 73
video games, 201
violations

actions and, 49
alcohol and, 127
allegations and, 51
sanctions and, 131
Violence Against Women Act (VAWA),
73, 172
institutions and, 180
reauthorization of, 75
Virginia Tech, 215–16
Virginia v. Black, 202
voice, 95
voting, 105
Vozzola, E., 132

Watt, S. K., 153
Wessler, S., 158
Winkour, Julie, 191
witnesses, 64
women, 7, 169
abuse against, 106, 176–77
bias incidents and, 157
of color, 110
incapacitation and, 182
rights for, 105
Woodis v. Westark Community College,
60
workflow, 42
World War II, 8
Wrenn, C. G., 13

Yale University, 192
Young, D. Parker, x
Zacker, John, 4
Zittoun, T., 130

Also available from Stylus

Reframing Campus Conflict

Student Conduct Practice Through a Social Justice Lens

Edited by Jennifer Meyer Schrage and Nancy Geist Giacomini

Foreword by Edward N. Stoner

"This publication is endorsed by ASCA as a collaborative, collegial new lens through which to consider how social justice practices and student conduct administration can come together to inform best practices in conduct and conflict management on college and university campuses."—*Tamara J. King, 2009 President, Association for Student Conduct Administration*

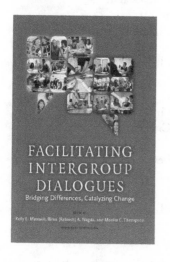

Facilitating Intergroup Dialogues

Bridging Differences, Catalyzing Change

Kelly E. Maxwell, Biren Ratnesh Nagda, and Monita C. Thompson

Foreword by Patricia Gurin

"This volume is a panoramic yet intimate examination of the value of intergroup dialogues and the training of the facilitators in many settings. It incorporates the best research and theory with anecdotal and eloquent accounts from participants, both faculty members and students. From survey research and personal experience, the authors explore the habits of mind and interpersonal skills needed to facilitate intergroup dialogue successfully in the cause of both education and justice. A must-read."—**Nancy Cantor**, *Chancellor of Syracuse University*

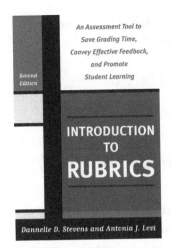

Introduction to Rubrics

Second Edition

An Assessment Tool to Save Grading Time, Convey Effective Feedback, and Promote Student Learning

Dannelle D. Stevens and Antonia J. Levi

Foreword by Barbara E. Walvoord

"Anyone struggling with the new landscape of direct assessment of student learning demanded by accreditors and employers will find this new and expanded edition of *Introduction to Rubrics* to be exactly what they need. Based upon their extensive experience, and drawing on a wide variety of examples of rubric use by faculty across institutions and disciplines, the authors clearly and insightfully present the value of rubrics, the process of developing rubrics and using them, and their usefulness for faculty, and for improving student learning. A must-read for anyone seriously interested in student learning enhancement."—**Terrel Rhodes**, *Vice President for the Office of Quality, Curriculum and Assessment - Association of American Colleges and Universities*

Using Focus Groups to Listen, Learn, and Lead

Mona J.E. Danner, J. Worth Pickering, and Tisha M. Paredes

Foreword by Jillian Kinzie

"I know personally that the results obtained from well-designed and well-executed focus groups can provide information that campus administrators need to make programmatic and strategic decisions. The authors used focus groups to help me learn more about the culture, values, and critical issues facing the campus when I became provost and vice president for academic affairs at Old Dominion University. This book is the next best thing to having them at your institution."—**Augustine O. Agho**, *Provost and Vice President for Academic Affairs, Old Dominion University*

Why Aren't We There Yet?

Taking Personal Responsibility for Creating an Inclusive Campus

Edited by Jan Arminio, Vasti Torres, and Raechele L. Pope

"This collection of seven essays on diversity in American higher education examines practical policies of inclusion and explores the ways in which overly simplified efforts at assimilation have failed to deliver meaningful results in the creation of campus experiences that address the needs of diverse student populations. Topics discussed include personal and professional development and self-awareness, relationship building, the historical context of diversity efforts, institutional culture, practical action versus policy, a diversity of solutions for a diversity of problems, and student affairs, values and inclusion. The contributors are academics in education and administrators in student affairs at U.S. universities."—*Book News Inc.*

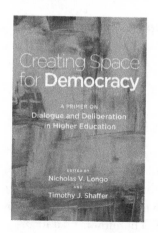

Creating Space for Democracy

A Primer on Dialogue and Deliberation in Higher Education

Edited by Nicholas V. Longo and Timothy J. Shaffer

"If democracy is in trouble, higher education is in trouble, so it is encouraging to see the cast of scholars who are mounting a response. This book is a vital contribution to the emerging field of deliberative pedagogy . . . . It is particularly encouraging to see new themes like the role of professionals in our democracy. Well done!"— *David Mathews, Kettering Foundation*

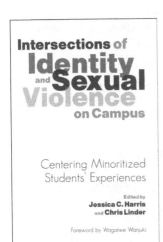

Intersection of Identity and Sexual Violence on Campus

Centering Minoritized Students' Experiences

Edited by Nicholas V. Longo and Timothy J. Shaffer

"I am amazed and humbled by the opportunity to introduce the contents of this book. It may sound like hyperbole when I say, 'It changed my life,' but I honestly cannot think of a better way to describe its impact on my beliefs on organizing to eradicate sexual violence—on campuses and off. This book outlines what I've needed as a survivor during my times as a student and activist; this book should be mandatory reading for every individual who works with the issue of campus gender-based violence. Journalists, activists, and administrators alike stand to gain the knowledge needed to spur the transformative work of a power-conscious, history-informed, and intersectional understanding of the dynamics of sexual violence."— *Wagatwe Wanjuki, feminist writer and activist*

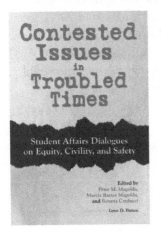

Contested Issues in Troubled Times

Student Affairs Dialogues on Equity, Civility, and Safety

Edited by Peter M. Magolda, Marcia B. Baxter Magolda, and Rozana Carducci

Foreword by Lori Patton Davis

"*Contested Issues in Troubled Times* offers fresh perspectives on the role of student affairs educators and practitioners in engaging in the difficult but crucial work of promoting inclusive environments on college campuses. Importantly, it does so in a way that does not hide—and indeed celebrates—the diversity of viewpoints shared among colleagues. This book will undoubtedly serve as a valuable springboard for rich discussions in the classroom and in the student affairs profession."—*Linda J. Sax, Professor of Higher Education and Organizational Change, Graduate School of Education & Information Studies, University of California Los Angeles*

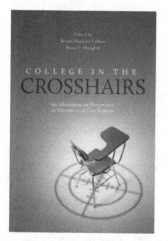

College in the Crosshairs

An Administrative Perspective on Prevention of Gun Violence

Edited by Brandi Hephner LaBanc and Brian O. Hemphill

Foreword by Kevin Kruger and Cindi Love

"*College in the Crosshairs* provides a truly interdisciplinary analysis of phenomena that were once thought of as primarily police responsibilities. As you read this book, prepare to enter the world of the frontlines gun violence, campus safety and wellness through the candid voices of the individuals who manage critical operational issues 24/7, 365. The book is not only edifying for those wish to learn more about weapons issues but also an indispensable resource for experts in the field. Most of all, the book is deeply inspirational, reminding us that the most powerful weapons against violence are the weapons of peace—education, science, compassion, forgiveness, and courage."—*Peter F. Lake, Professor of Law, Charles A. Dana Chair, and Director of the Center for Excellence in Higher Education Law and Policy, Stetson University College of Law*

22883 Quicksilver Drive
Sterling, VA 20166-2019   Subscribe to our e-mail alerts: www.Styluspub.com